TREATISE
ON JUSTICE

TREATISE ON JUSTICE

Edgar Bodenheimer

PROFESSOR OF LAW

University of California, Davis

PHILOSOPHICAL LIBRARY, INC.

New York

To Brigitte

CONTENTS

CHAPTER I: THE CONCEPT OF JUSTICE

CHAPTER II: THE GOALS OF JUSTICE

CHAPTER III: POLITICAL AND SOCIAL JUSTICE

CHAPTER IV: ECONOMIC JUSTICE

CHAPTER V: PENAL JUSTICE

CHAPTER VI: INTERNATIONAL JUSTICE

TREATISE
ON JUSTICE

THE CONCEPT OF JUSTICE

Sec. 1. Justice as an Ethical Value.

Many, perhaps most, people throughout the world will at some time during the course of their lives become exposed to an action of others which is experienced by them as an affront to their sense of justice. It may be an act of a parent or educator which will evoke this response, or an unfairness committed against a relative or friend, or an official act or court judgment affecting their personal or property interests. In such cases, the feelings and emotions of the persons concerned are often deeply aroused, and this fact may warp the objectivity of their conviction that they themselves or someone close to them, have been subjected to unjust treatment. Where immediate self-interest is at stake, the use of reason in appraising an action felt to be unfair is by no means impossible or improbable. But the danger that the person's judgment is influenced by irrational and emotional factors is always present in such situations.

It also happens quite frequently that people are called upon to weigh the justice or injustice of an action in a context more removed from direct personal concern. A legislator may have to decide whether to vote for or against a proposed piece of legislation. A judge, in a case where the positive law leaves him some amount of choice or discretion, may have to determine whether considerations of justice turn the scales in favor of one or the other party to a lawsuit. A legal scholar may wish to pass judgment on the fairness of a law enacted in ancient Rome, medieval England, or contemporary America. A layman or lawyer may strongly react to an event taking place in a far-away country which involves the inhuman or discriminatory treatment of human beings.

In the second class of cases, the chances for objective and

1

detached evaluation are greater than in the first group of situations described above. Emotional reactions may enter into the picture (for example, where cruelties have been committed in a foreign land), but they can usually be kept under control by the rational faculty. In the area of legislative and judicial activity, they should be suppressed altogether or at least be reduced to an unavoidable minimum. Sometimes, a judgment that an act is just or unjust originates in a flash of intuitive insight, but this does not exclude the possibility of subsequent rational substantiation.[1]

Regardless of whether the response is rational or affective, the experiences connected with the problem of justice are of a nonsensory character. They are not perceptions of data given by the five senses, that is, they do not involve the use of sight, hearing, touch, taste, or smell. They are phenomena of an intellectual, intuitive, or emotive nature, but they are nevertheless real and describable. A reaction or judgment in a matter concerning justice or injustice is something which takes place in the realm of *values*, that is, in a mental empire distinct from the domain of physical occurrences. More specifically, justice may be identified as a value of an ethical signification, as distinguished from an aesthetic or economic value, since it is concerned with the norms of right conduct which people should observe toward each other in society.

Turning our attention first to the nature of values in general, it must be observed at the outset that philosophers have never been able to agree on a definition or phenomenological description of the concept of value. Purely subjectivistic and relativistic interpretations have alternated with theories asserting that values are absolute, objective essences existing independently of valuing subjects, and various attempts have been made to find some middle ground between these opposing views. In the words of John Dewey, "a survey of the current literature on the subject discloses that views on the subject range from the belief, at one extreme, that so-called 'values' are but emotional epithets or mere ejaculations, to the belief, at the other extreme, that a priori necessary standardized, rational values are the principles upon which art, science, and morals depend for their validity." [2] The difficulty of arriving at a satisfactory answer is enhanced by the abstract and intangible nature of the subject matter.

At one end of the philosophical spectrum stands the view

2

advanced by Ayer, Carnap, and other representatives of modern logical positivism, according to which judgments of value are not grounded on knowledge, but are mere articulations of feelings, sentiments, and emotions. Their validity is declared to be incapable of verification, and they are considered pseudo-propositions which lie outside of the domain of scientific appraisal.[3] With respect to the value of justice in particular, Kelsen has asserted that justice is an irrational ideal, representing the emotive reactions of individuals or groups to the norms of the positive law, and as such is not a legitimate subject of philosophical cognition.[4]

According to the theory of the American philosopher Ralph Barton Perry, a thing is valuable when it is the object of an interest. In other words, whatever is an object of an interest is *ipso facto* valuable.[5] This conception of value is broader than that of logical positivism since, in addition to irrational desires and emotive responses, it includes in its ambit the objects of rational volition. It is, in fact, extremely broad, since "any object, whatever it be, acquires value when any interest, whatever it be, is taken in it." [6] Thus, when a person takes an interest in crime, slums, narcotics addiction, obscene literature, or illness, even though his interest may be directed toward fighting these evils, the target of his interest becomes automatically a value.

Moving away from purely psychological notions of value, the Austrian philosopher Victor Kraft and the American thinker Samuel Hart, following in the footsteps of Aristotle, have described values as general concepts which isolate and identify those elements and qualities which are common to the various classes of valuable objects. Thus, beauty, justice, truth are abstractions which denote the generic components of beautiful things, just acts, and true propositions.[7]

This approach was criticized by the German philosopher Max Scheler on the ground that it was impossible to discern the common qualities of valuable things, such as "good" or "beautiful" things, by logical-rational methods. According to his theory, which was accepted and fully elaborated by his contemporary Nicolai Hartmann, values are non-spatial, non-temporal entities existing in a realm of ideal being with its own order and laws; they can be experienced only by acts of intuitive perception.[8] In this view, which bears much affinity to the Platonic philosophy of ideas, values are ideal essences which are severed from any relation to an evaluating subject and therefore

3

independent of individual acts of perception or judgment. They are objective a priori structures, not derived from experience, and valid under all conditions.[9]

This controversy concerning the nature of values raises many questions with respect to the particular value under investigation in this study, the value of justice. Is justice merely the object of irrational desire or emotional preference, impervious to rational and objective analysis? Or is it merely the referent for some types of interest of a person or group? Or is it a definable generic notion which identifies the characteristic qualities of just persons or acts? Or should justice be considered an immutable, self-existent essence or ideal entity which must be perceived or discovered by human beings through intuitive processes rather than by means of intellectual, reflective analysis?

Any conclusions that might be reached concerning the nature of justice and its formal and material ingredients are apt to throw a certain amount of light on the character of values in general. The question will be raised at the end of this study as to what kinds of insights an analysis of the concept of justice might be able to yield in reference to this difficult and controversial problem.[10]

Sec. 2. The Scope of the Concept of Justice.

Kelsen has said that "we may define at will those terms which we wish to use as tools in our intellectual work."[1] He has qualified this statement, however, by declaring that "any attempt to define a concept must take for its starting-point the common usage of the word."[2]

Without broaching the question at this point whether the freedom of the scholar to define his conceptual tools is more narrowly restricted than Kelsen assumes,[3] one must certainly agree with him that the common usage of words should be taken into account in framing a scientific vocabulary. This would appear to be highly desirable because the scholar should avoid living in an ivory tower insulated from contact with his community. He ought to remain in active connection with it and keep open as many avenues of understanding as possible. One means that can be used in furtherance of this aim is the eschewing of an unnecessarily esoteric apparatus of communication between the scholar and the non-academic world, and the use

4

of commonly understood terms wherever this will facilitate rapport without inhibiting accuracy and preciseness of exposition. Quite frequently, of course, the technical semantic apparatus of science will have to deviate from the common signification of terms, and it will become necessary to introduce concepts whose meaning is not evident to the layman, or to the expert in other fields. In such instances, however, every attempt should be made, in communications destined for the community at large, to explain the meaning of scientific terms in an intelligible manner.

When we embark upon the endeavor to clarify the common usage of the term "justice," we shall soon discover that the range of this concept is very wide. It refers to a great multitude of acts—past, present, and potential—which are done by nations, rulers, government officials, administrative bodies, judges, public institutions, private associations, and even individuals. Since it is easier to indicate the contours of justice, in a preliminary and tentative way, by a consideration of instances where an absence of justice is felt to exist than by a description of its positive attributes,[4] we shall proceed to outline the scope of the concept by the use of this negative method.

From the Roman era to modern times—with the exception of a brief period during the nineteenth and early twentieth centuries when the notion of justice became temporarily atrophied by positivistic thinking—nations and their governments have often been accused of waging "unjust wars" for purposes of self-aggrandizement.[5] Autocratic rulers have been chided for unjustly depriving persons of life or liberty for slight or spurious causes. Governments have been charged with depriving persons or groups of opportunities to work and earn a living, or with perpetrating injustices upon foreigners through instigation of mob violence, disregard of their safety, or confiscation of their property. Legislatures on innumerable occasions have been criticized for passing unjust laws, for example, laws inequitably distributing tax burdens, or laws unduly favoring special interest groups, or enactments discriminating against racial or religious minorities.

Legislative bodies and courts have been castigated for imposing cruel punishments for slight offenses. A clear case of injustice is, of course, to convict an innocent person. Judges have in many other instances been blamed for rendering unjust decisions, even in situations where they had formally complied with the letter of the law.[6] An administrative agency may be guilty of an unjust act if, within an area of discretion, it denies a well-substantiated claim for purely political reasons or willingly lends its ear to the peddlers of influence. Public institutions, such as universities, have sometimes been censured for the unjust dismissal of staff members who had openly espoused unpopular causes. School teachers have had to defend themselves against charges of injustice in the grading of examination papers.

A private association was held by an English court of law to have offended against "principles of natural justice" for starting proceedings against a member for expulsion without giving him a chance to be heard,[7] and there is no doubt that many members of corporations, labor unions, and other private organizations have had occasion to complain of unjust treatment by the organization or its officers. Employers have often been criticized for failing to pay a "fair" or "just" wage to their employees, trading firms for charging an unduly high price for their products. Within the circle of the family, partiality and favoritism shown by the parents to one of their children have often produced strong resentments on the part of the other children.[8] The term "injustice" is even employed with respect to the relationships between two individuals. If A has falsely accused B of dishonesty, injuring him perhaps in his employment or reputation, it is often said in common parlance that he has done an injustice to B. Misrepresenting the value of a commodity in a sales transaction will deprive the purchaser of a fair and just equivalent for what he is paying to the seller. An individual also acts unjustly if, without a convincing reason, he disappoints expectations which, by his words or actions, he has raised in another person.

Is it possible to find any common denominator underlying these examples of acts and measures against which the indictment of injustice has been leveled? Or are these illustrations of such a diversified, heterogeneous character that they are incapable of being brought within the firm bounds of a unifying definition or description? If this were true, it would not mean that the terms "just" and "unjust" would have to be rejected as pseudo-concepts.[9] What is just or unjust might still be susceptible of direct apperception, through reason or intuition, in an individualized situation.

It would seem, however, that a general determination of the meaning of justice, however broad and imprecise it may be, is not beyond the bounds of possibility. In all of the examples given above, the actions of governments, groups, or individuals were challenged or condemned on the ground that these actions deprived some persons of something to which they were entitled, or that they withheld something from them to which they had a claim. In the example of the unjust war, a nation was deprived of its right to a peaceful and undisturbed existence within the community of nations. The oppressive ruler was charged with having disregarded the right of the people to bodily integrity and safety of person. When a legislature passes an inequitable tax law, it may curtail the means of subsistence of the disfavored groups or infringe unduly on their property rights. The dismissal of a university professor for uttering unpopular opinions is or may be in violation of what is considered his freedom of teaching. Unjust and discriminatory grading practices are deemed inconsistent with the right of students to be dealt with fairly in accordance with the merits of their work. In the expulsion case, a member of an association was thought to be deprived of his membership rights without an opportunity to be heard in his defense. The father who openly prefers one of his children violates the—usually deep-seated—feeling of the other children that they are entitled to non-discriminating treatment by their parents. An excessive sentence may be said to violate a person's right to punishment proportional to the severity of his offense. The man who accuses himself of having made an unjust charge against another person realizes that he has impugned the honor and reputation of an individual.

It cannot be emphasized too strongly that the "rights," "claims," and "entitlements" that were allegedly infringed upon or disregarded in the foregoing situations need not have any anchorage in the positive law of the state or community in which the charge of unjust treatment was raised. In some of the above examples, the claim or entitlement unjustly withheld was one which in the opinion of the critic *should* have been recognized by the law or by those entrusted with its administration. In others of the mentioned instances, the question of whether or not the neglected right was founded on the positive law was left open as being irrelevant to the determination of the justice of the action. Furthermore, considerations or sentiments of justice were also found to be operative in the sphere of relations which in some of their aspects are untouched by the law, for example, family relations or the raising and prejudicial disappointment of expectations.

7

While the essence of justice is respect for the justified claims of others,[10] it is necessary to realize that tasks of great multiformity and complexity must be discharged in order to reach the goals of a just order of society. The concept of justice has many dimensions: among its numerous facets are avoidance of injury, fulfillment of obligations, granting opportunities for the satisfaction of basic material and nonmaterial needs, concern for freedom, equality, and security, fairness of compensation in contract and tort, proportionality of reward and punishment. Furthermore, justice must take into account not only the claims of particular individuals and groups, but also the effect which satisfaction of these claims would have upon society as a whole. For that which is beneficial to one segment of the population may be detrimental to another segment or adversely affect the total social equilibrium. For this reason the fulfillment of justice is not a set of dispositions running unilaterally from those in authority to those who make their claims and demands for just treatment. It also requires the cooperation and understanding of the latter, and the discharge of functions and duties by them in the interest of the social whole.[11]

The problem of justice is closely related to the problem of a healthy order of society. It is concerned with the healthfulness of the parts as well as with the sound condition of the whole. These two aspects of justice are, of course, inseparable. If the needs and aspirations of the individuals composing society are reasonably taken care of by the system of justice, and if reciprocal concern for the health of the social body exists among the members of society, there is a good chance that a harmonious and flourishing society will be the result. It needs hardly to be mentioned that a fully satisfactory group order will rarely be achieved in an imperfect world burdened with limitations of resources which stem not only from inadequacies in the system of production but also from deficiencies in the intelligence and moral character of human beings.

A conception of justice narrower in scope than the one suggested here has been advanced by some philosophers and legal thinkers. The English jurist H. L. A. Hart, for example, has proposed to restrict the scope of justice to the postulate of equal treatment of equals. "The general principle latent in . . . diverse applications of the idea of justice is that individuals are entitled in respect of each other to a certain relative position of equality or inequality." [12] Thus, according to Hart, when we protest against a law in the name of justice, we criticize it on the ground that it discriminates between persons who are entitled to equal treatment, or draws distinctions between situations which are, in all relevant respects, alike.

There can be no doubt that the idea of justice is closely related to the notion of equality, and that infractions of the equal-treatment principle constitute the most conspicuous instances of a denial of justice.[13] Nothing is more certain to cause widespread indignation than a form of discrimination which offends against generally recognized standards of equality and fairness. Thus, if two offenders who have committed exactly the same type of dereliction receive widely discrepant punishments, this will be distasteful to the popular sense of justice, unless a reasonable explanation for the differentiating treatment can be offered.

Problems of justice are also bound to arise where the measuring rods used by dominant groups in society stand in irreconcilable opposition to those of disfavored minorities. Social disturbances and political revolutions have often been caused by the discriminatory or oppressive treatment of the lower classes in society. In our own era, the issue of racial justice has attained an overarching importance in the domestic politics of a number of nations and has also cast its shadow into the domain of international relations.

Granting the immense impact which the equal-treatment principle has upon the solution of pressing problems of justice, is Professor Hart correct when he suggests that the concept of justice exhausts its significance in the postulate of nondiscrimination? He asserts, for example, that

> a man guilty of gross cruelty to his child would often be judged to have done something morally *wrong, bad,* or even *wicked* or to have disregarded his moral *obligation* or duty to his child. But it would be strange to criticize his conduct as *unjust.*[14]

It may be asked, however, whether it offends against the natural linguistic use of the term justice to state that beating a child cruelly for no reason visits an unjust treatment upon the child, although no element of discrimination is present. The observation was made earlier in this discussion that persons who without justification have done harm to a fellowman often consider

9

themselves, or are considered by others, guilty of an injustice. The German philosopher Schopenhauer saw the very essence of justice in the *neminem laedere* principle, i.e. in the avoidance of acts which cause pain, suffering, or injury to others, and John Stuart Mill defined the sentiment of justice as "the animal desire to repel or retaliate for a hurt or damage to oneself or to those with whom one sympathizes." [15]

The notion of justice may be expanded even further. A political order which denies elementary rights to all citizens or subjects may be censured as an unjust system without doing violence to semantic usage. If a law is passed authorizing confinement for lifetime to a concentration camp of anyone criticizing any public official, would it be improper to argue that such a law perpetrates an injustice upon the citizens, even though it is equally applicable to all who fulfill the requirements of the statute? If libel and slander laws were repealed so that the honor and reputation of every citizen would be at the mercy of defamers, would it be unjustifiable to brand such a law as unjust? If a denial of rights considered essential to civilized living is viewed as a proper occasion for raising the issue of justice—and this proposition appears to hold true for the civilized countries of the world today—, a limitation of the concept of justice to discriminatory actions is subject to serious objections.

Sec. 3. Justice and Legality.

It is axiomatic in a societal order founded on the principle of legality that those who exercise political power in any form must act under the authority of a general law which defines, allocates, and circumscribes the power in question. Impersonal norms rather than the "charisma" [1] or the assertedly inspired intuition of a political leader control the discharge of governmental functions in such a commonwealth. Especially the application of coercive sanctions against individuals is deemed legitimate only when it is authorized by some norm of law which has been duly promulgated and is presumed to be known to the addressees of the law.

A good description of legality as a pervasive political ordering principle has been given by the sociologist Philip Selznick. These are his words:

10

The essential element in legality, or the rule of law, is the governance of official power by rational principles of civic order. Official action, even at the highest levels of authority, is enmeshed in and restrained by a web of accepted general rules. Where this ideal exists, no power is immune from criticism nor completely free to follow its own bent, however well intentioned it may be. Legality imposes an objective environment of constraint, of tests to be met, of standards to be observed, and, not less important, of ideals to be fulfilled.[2]

In this passage, Selznick appears to identify the principle of legality with the notion of the "rule of law." This identification might be open to objection on the ground that the rule of law does not exhaust its significance in the institutionalization of legality, but in addition requires for its realization a modicum of substantive rationality in law and the recognition of at least some minimum standards of due process.[3] The principle of legality, on the other hand, is neutral toward the contentual structure of the positive law; it only demands that executive and administrative acts must be legitimized by, and keep within the confines of, general laws or legal rules.[4] But, although legality and the rule of law are not synonymous, there can be no doubt that the principle of legality forms an important constituent in bringing about and maintaining the rule of law.

The term "legality" is often used in a somewhat narrower sense. In that sense it serves as a criterion of the legal validity of particular governmental actions (including perhaps judicial acts), even though the social order in question is not permeated by the principle of legality in its more comprehensive significa- tion. For example, under a political system in which certain categories of governmental commands may be issued without authorization by a general law, a concrete command may be lacking in legality because it did not originate from the organ entrusted with the administration of the subject matter to which the command pertains. To take another example, an administra- tive regulation or judicial sentence may be declared illegal because it is not consonant with a law placing restrictions on the discretion of administrators or judges in a particular area of the law. A statute may be devoid of legality if it is repugnant to a constitutional norm of superior validity. The terms "legality"

11

and "illegality" are also often applied to private actions and transactions. Thus, a contract may be illegal if it conflicts with the statutory or common law of the jurisdiction in question, and we also speak of the illegality of tortious and criminal acts.

In recent times, the subject of legality has become a prominent focus of discussion in the Soviet Union and the countries of the Soviet orbit. Government officials, judges, and citizens are exhorted to adhere to "socialist legality," which is defined as a guaranty that "all organs of the soviet state, official personages, and citizens strictly and unswervingly observe the legislation enacted by Soviet authority." [5] It is emphasized that "only adherence to socialist legality can assure a situation in which regulation by legal norms is actually implemented in life and social relationships and truly regulated in accordance with these norms, and the goals posed in the process of lawmaking are thereby attained." [6] The drive for enforcement of socialist legality was apparently spurred by the existence of widespread lawlessness and disregard of superior commands by lower officials in the post-revolutionary decades, a condition subsequently and for easily understandable reasons attributed to the activities of saboteurs.[7] The legality emphasized in this campaign obviously involves the narrower denotation of the term, since it is a call for compliance with the law rather than a plea for subjecting all executive and administrative acts to previously announced normative prescriptions.

We must now turn to the question as to whether any relationship exists between justice on the one hand and legality, in the two senses explained above, on the other. Are these concepts synonymous or at least overlapping in part?

It might be argued convincingly that without the effectuation and implementation of legality in the broad sense, i.e. government by law rather than fiat, justice cannot flourish in society.[8] This argument would have to rest chiefly on the assumption that a purely administrative state, in which all official actions are *ad hoc* measures induced solely by considerations of practical expediency in the light of a concrete situation, would be an unjust form of government, because it deprives the citizens of the freedom to plan their lives on the basis of previously announced official permissions and prohibitions and introduces an unbearable amount of frustrating unpredictability into the social order. There is certainly a danger that the administrative state might convert men into puppets pulled or tossed around by officially-manipulated wires. That such a condition, if it became general or widespread, would create a sense of insecurity, arbitrariness, and injustice among the citizens can hardly be doubted. The law state, although it cannot altogether eliminate the incidence or even necessity of *ad hoc* governmental action, will be able to reduce the hazards connected with it substantially by the promulgation of general directions setting limits to administrative discretion. The risk of arbitrariness can be cut back further by providing judicial relief in cases where the bounds of administrative legality have been exceeded by an official organ.

Although in this way a relationship can be construed between the notion of justice and the principle of legality conceived as a general axiom of governmental organization, it can nevertheless not be said that the two ideas are wholly or largely coterminous. First of all, blueprints for an ideally just social order have been advanced by influential thinkers, such as Plato, which are not predicated on a preference for government by law, but proceed from the assumption that government by free, unfettered intelligence, addressing itself to the solution of concrete issues of social policy in an individualized setting, is possible and desirable, provided that superior personalities competent to discharge this task are selected.[9] In more recent times, Frederick Engels has called for a replacement of government of persons through state power and law by "the administration of things and the direction of the processes of production." [10] Regardless of whether or not such proposals are feasible or desirable, the fact that they have been suggested as solutions of the problem of justice shows that it is improper to use legality and justice as synonymous terms.

More important perhaps is the consideration that neutrality toward values other than orderly government, which is characteristic of legality in the sense here discussed, militates against its identification with justice. As was pointed out earlier, adoption of the principle of legality does not ensure a beneficial or enlightened content of the laws controlling administration, or their popular acceptance. The law state thus can be an unjust state, although this danger—especially when the laws are made by representatives answerable to the popular will—may be less acute than in the case of the administrative state.

Legality in its second meaning denotes, as we have seen, compliance of an official or private action with a controlling statute or rule of law, or conformity of an inferior norm with a norm of superior validity. Is it possible or desirable to identify justice with legality in this sense?

Such an identification has been advocated by some influential representatives of the positivist school of jurisprudence. John Austin, for example, has said: "By the epithet *just*, we mean that a given object, to which we apply the epithet, accords with a given law to which we refer it as to a test. . . . By the epithet *unjust*, we mean that the given object conforms not to the given law." [11] Hans Kelsen has expressed the opinion that justice, in any scientifically meaningful sense, must be adjudged a quality that relates not to the content of a positive order, but to its application. " 'Justice' means the maintenance of a positive order by conscientious application of it." [12] This sentiment was echoed by Alf Ross, who declared that "the idea of justice resolves itself into the demand that a decision should be the result of the application of a general rule. Justice is the correct application of a law, as opposed to arbitrariness." [13]

Thus, if a law provides that it is a criminal offense to supply any kind of education to the members of the colored race, a judicial decision is just according to this theory if it sends a man to prison for teaching the elements of mathematics to a Negro. If a statute decrees that confessions shall be obtained from persons accused of crime, whenever necessary, through the use of torture, a magistrate who gives the order to put the arrestee to the rack commits a just act. It is not even necessary to think up extreme examples of objectionable laws in order to demonstrate the inadequacy and artificiality of the view which identifies justice and legality in the sense here indicated. This theory is utterly at variance with the meanings and ideas which mankind from the early days of civilization has associated with the term justice. People have never been willing to equate positive law with just law. They have over and over again criticized existing laws on the ground that they were unjust and unacceptable and have often been successful in persuading their legislators to change or repeal such laws. Political and social revolutions have been staged in the name of a higher justice. The entire history of the law, including the rise of equity jurisprudence as an antidote to the strict, formal law of the state, and the struggle for progress and law reform, would be incomprehensible and meaningless if justice and status quo legality were synonyms. The view which asserts their identity flies in the face of the historical record and is totally at odds with social-psychological reality.

14

Professor Granfield rightly emphasizes that "a divorce between legal thinking and the actual conditions of life is fatal to a sound jurisprudence." [14] The view which identifies legality and justice must therefore be vigorously combated. It is quite surprising that a theory which rests on such a weak foundation was able to attract a rather wide following in Western jurisprudential thought during the last one-hundred years.

The correct view concerning the meaning of justice has been well stated by Professor Jenkins:

> If we were to ask that mythical creature, the man in the street, for a quick, unprepared definition of "justice," the answer we would almost surely get would be roughly this: "justice is what the law ought to be". . . For both common sense and sophisticated thought, the most elemental meaning embedded in the concept of justice is that of the perfect accomplishment of the tasks of the law. [15]

Jenkins rightly observes that it is this conception of justice that has served as the point of departure for most reflections on the nature of justice throughout recorded history. [16] According to this view, justice is an ideal of good and beneficial law which may or may not be realized by the positive law of the time and place. There is nothing utopian or esoteric about this conception, because it is perfectly possible and often true that large portions of the positive law of a society, or some particular branches thereof, are fully or at least substantially in harmony with the prevailing notions of justice. Thus, although justice and legality are not coextensive, it does not follow, as Del Vecchio has pointed out correctly, that they are necessarily contradictory. In his view, the respect for legality should in itself, within limits, be regarded as one of the requirements of justice. [17]

One of the additional indicia pointing to the separation of justice and legality is the fact that it is contrary to linguistic usage to call every man who obeys the laws a "just" man. [18] A man who in a totalitarian state turns over to the public authorities a person persecuted by the secret police for his race or religion and seeking refuge in his home may be called "law-abiding," but few people might be willing to call him just. When the Fugitive Slave Act was passed, Ralph Waldo Emerson, who was by no means a radical thinker, wrote in his diary: "I will not obey it, by God." Obviously he felt that justice would be served better in this case by not observing the law than by complying with it.[19] When someone earns the commendation "he always acts in a fair and just manner," reference is usually made to the intrinsic character of his acts, and not merely to the fact that he has remained within the boundaries of the positive law.

The same considerations hold true for the evaluation of the work of a judge. It can certainly not be denied that a judicial decision which is in conformity with the law may be reacted to by informed observers or the community at large as just. But the reason why it is felt to be just is not simply because the judge has observed the letter of the law, but because the law itself, as applied by the judge, is deemed to be conducive to a satisfactory disposition of the case. It may also easily occur that a judicial decision strictly in accordance with the law will evoke the opposite response, either because the law relevant to the decision has been widely condemned as a bad law, or because the law in its concrete effect upon the particular fact situation produces an unfair result. It might also be noted that the term "just decision" is often applied to a pronouncement which was not governed by any strict and determinate rules of law, but flowed from the exercise of discretion by the judge himself, as for instance a sentence in a criminal case or a judicial decree induced by broad principles of equity.

If the sense of justice is not derived from the positive law but often exerts itself in opposition to it, where do we find the roots of the standards which in the opinion of an individual, a group, or perhaps the majority of the people the positive law should conform to?

The Calvinist theologian Emil Brunner has offered the explanation that the feeling for justice goes back to an "underived, primal order of things established by no human lawgiver." [20] There is a certain mystery surrounding the true foundations of the sentiment of justice, but the mystery may simply be due to the complexity of its origins and evolution. It is probably rooted in the psychological structure of human beings, in their subjective sense of personality as well as in their empathic, other-regarding impulses. It is also shaped by factors of historical development, modeled by education and training, conditioned by personal and collective experiences, and made articulate by rational reflection and analysis. It thus constitutes an intricate web consisting of multifarious strands and tissues.

16

Situations may arise when the sentiments or postulates of justice come into irreconcilable clash with the positive mandates of the law. How should conflicts of this character be resolved? Should the position be taken that the norms of the positive law must be observed and enforced under all conceivable circumstances? Or may private persons or officials charged with the administration or application of the law in some extraordinary situations refuse to comply with a law considered utterly repugnant to deeply-anchored feelings of justice?

Different answers have been given to this question in the course of history. The question is not so much one which relates to the meaning and requirements of justice but involves principally the recognition or nonrecognition of boundaries to the effective force of the positive law. It will not be discussed as a general problem in this volume, but reference will be made to it in connection with the treatment of some particular issues of justice.[21]

Sec. 4. *Justice and Morality.*

Morality is concerned with the question as to what is good and bad, right and wrong, in the conduct of human beings. It is characteristic of a moral judgment that it contains an approval or disapproval of actions in the light of certain normative standards. Since the problems of justice also involve an evaluation of human conduct, and of legal prescriptions pertaining to such conduct, in terms of approval and disapproval, the drawing of a line of demarcation between morality and justice becomes necessary.

The view that justice and morality are inextricably connected and perhaps largely coextensive in scope was taken by Aristotle, who defined justice, in its broadest sense, as "perfect Virtue, though with a qualification, namely that it is displayed toward others." [1] A modern advocate of this ethical approach toward justice was Felix Cohen, who formulated his thesis in the following words:

> When we say, for instance, that a given law is bad, that one judicial decision is better than another, that the American constitution ought to be revised, or that laws ought to be obeyed, we are passing judgments whose

truth or falsity cannot be established without a consideration of ethics. That portion of jurisprudence which is not
concerned merely with the positive nature of law or with
its technical relation to assumed ends is, accordingly, a
part of the domain of ethics.[2]

Although Cohen, as this statement shows, is well aware that
there are problems of valuation in the law which relate only to
its technical utility or the effectiveness of its processes, he holds
that the most important issues of justice, since they deal with
the rightness or wrongness of human conduct, lie within the
field of morality.[3]

The relation between morality and justice is indeed an intimate one. Although, as will be shown later, there are norms of
morality which do not at the same time constitute norms of
justice, broad areas exist in which morality and justice overlap.
One general difference that might be stated at the outset lies
in the fact that the obligations of justice are felt to be of a
peculiarly strong force, so that every effort, including use of
compulsion, will be made to insure compliance with their mandates. This distinction was brought out well in the following
observation by Adam Smith:

> We feel ourselves under a stricter obligation to act
> according to justice than agreeably to friendship, charity,
> or generosity; . . . the practice of the last-mentioned virtues
> seems to be left in some measure to our own choice,
> but . . . somehow or other, we feel ourselves to be in a
> peculiar manner tied, bound, and obliged to the observ-
> ance of justice.[4]

Attempts have been made by philosophers and jurists to
deny that justice and morality are closely bound together and
often coextensive, and to make out a case for their clean-cut
separation. The roots of most of these attempts must be traced
to the Kantian philosophy. Kant was firmly convinced that
"nothing can possibly be conceived in the world, or even out of
it, which can be called good without qualification, except a
good will." [5] From this premise Kant deduced that a good will
is the *summum bonum*, i.e. the highest good, and that morality
is the science of the proper motivation of the will. This view
imparted to morality a subjective tinge, at least in the sense that

18

the existence or nonexistence of morality was not linked by Kant to the external consequences of an action or its effect upon other persons, but was associated by him exclusively with the inner attitude of a person toward his acts. In the words of Karl Mannheim, Kant placed "all the moral emphasis not upon objective and overt behavior and its visible consequences, but upon the intention of the doer." [6] Mannheim adds the observation that this subjectivist approach to ethics is "historically nothing more than an elaboration of the Protestant idea that conscience is the essential thing in action." [7]

Justice and law, on the other hand, were in Kant's opinion concerned with the external relations of men and things. "Whatever is juridically in accordance with External Laws is said to be Just . . . ; and whatever is not juridically in accordance with External Laws, is said to be Unjust." [8] According to this view, morality on the one hand, and justice and law on the other, deal with different subject matters, since morality is interested in purely internal phenomena, while justice and law look toward proper modes of regulating external social relations.

This view of Kant cannot be accepted.[9] Although the attitude or disposition accompanying the doing of an act may have an important bearing on the evaluation of the act from a moral point of view, the significance of morality does not exhaust itself in the requirement of good intentions. There is little value in calling a person moral who is of a kindly mind and harbors the best of intentions, but who because of awkwardness or gross unskilfulness achieves in his actions the opposite of what he intends to do and thereby causes harm and suffering rather than good. The case against placing an exaggerated weight on states of mind was well put by Samuel Hart:

> Man's being cannot be separated from his acting, which may leave the total situation better or worse, may increase the amount of happiness or misery of other sentient people. It is not generosity as a state of mind or will which is moral, but a generosity which eventuates in doing things conducive to man's quest for an enduring satisfaction. Neither do we acclaim kindness as a character trait without its consequences in reality, but rather kindness which increases the good things in life.[10]

Morality requires more than a benevolent will. It also

19

demands some foresight of at least the immediate consequences of one's action and a careful appraisal of the probable impact of such consequences upon other persons. Furthermore, awareness of the dangers attendant upon miscarriage of intent and a constant readiness to avert them also form part of the morality of a course of action. If, in spite of careful and responsible planning, the action goes wrong because of unforeseeable or unavoidable circumstances, no moral blame should of course be visited upon the agent in that event.

Conversely, it may occur that a person invested with power over others will display the greatest considerateness and friendliness toward them and do everything within his ability to further their aspirations and interests, but that the chief motive governing his actions is the drive for power and the desire to maintain his hold over other men. It would seem to exhibit a rigoristic attitude in matters of ethics to call such a man "immoral" because of his motives, if his actions produce thoroughly beneficial consequences; it may be argued, however, that the self-regarding nature of his motivation detracts from the morality of his acts.[11]

The necessity for introducing objective elements into judgments of moral worth stems from a proper realization of the essential goals of morality. Throughout history, men have set up ethical systems, not for the purpose of appraising subjective states of mind, but with the aim of creating tolerable conditions in social relations. Human beings have to live together, get along with each other, and solve many problems common to them. The tenets of morality are designed to help them curb those physiological and emotional tendencies which interfere with their living together harmoniously in society. Among these tendencies must be counted excessive selfishness, the use of a dual standard of proper conduct for oneself and one's fellow-men, grossly deceptive practices, overt aggressiveness in its various manifestations. It is the goal of morality to substitute peaceful behavior for violence, good faith for fraud and overreaching, considerateness for malice, cooperation for the dog-eat-dog attitude. In this way, morality teaches us to "moderate our impulses and adjust our demands so as to reconcile them as far as possible with those of our fellows." [12]

These goals of morality are by no means confined to the orbit of Christian civilization. The Golden Rule, which enjoins people to act toward others as they would have others act toward themselves, and which epitomizes the ends of social morality as sketched above, was proclaimed in similar words as the Alpha and Omega of morals in the Apocrypha, the New Testament, the Analects of Confucius, the Indian Mahabharata and the Buddhist Dhammapada.[13] Thomas Hobbes pronounced the rule to be a "law of nature"[14]; John Stuart Mill adopted it as the supreme ideal of utilitarian morality,[15] and Immanuel Kant, in a more abstract and less suggestive formulation, gave it expression in his Categorical Imperative.[16] When John Locke was once asked by a friend to write a treatise on ethics that would match his famous works on epistemology and government, he replied that as long as the Golden Rule was available, it was not of primary importance to write a speculative treatise on ethics.[17] The American sociologist Robert Maciver has argued that the Golden Rule "is the only rule that stands by itself in the light of its own reason, the only rule that can stand by itself in the naked, warring universe, in the face of the contending values of men and groups."[18] It is, of course, theoretically possible to found a system of ethics on principles other than the Golden Rule, but, as will be shown later, there is every likelihood that such a system will be self-defeating and unable to maintain itself for long.[19]

If it is the purpose of morality to prevent or impede practices which an individual would thoroughly resent if they were directed against himself, and thereby to reconcile and adjust the desires and actions of the members of a community, must we not conclude that the ends of justice are essentially the same? Is it not the function of justice to ensure that each person is protected in his rights and receives what is due to him, so that social frictions and disruptive forms of discord are reduced? The subsequent discussion of the goals of justice should make it clear that this is a true statement of some of the most fundamental objectives of a just order.[20] But this does not mean that the fields of morality and justice are wholly identical. There are broad areas in which the two concepts overlap, but there are others in which morality poses relevant problems while justice is not directly involved.

Some of the injunctions set forth in the Ten Commandments are typical examples of normative prescriptions which have moral as well as legal significance. "Thou shalt not kill," "Thou shalt not steal," "Thou shalt not bear false witness against thy neighbor" are imperatives whose infringement subjects the violator to moral censure; because the forbidden acts are at the same time considered unjust and unlawful, their commission will also result in the invocation of legal sanctions. All or most of the other common crimes, such as robbery, rape, assault, arson, defamation, likewise fall within the dual classification of being immoral as well as unjust and illegal. Some tortious actions which may or may not form part of the law of crimes, like fraud or other sharp practices, are considered unethical as well as contrary to justice.

In a generalizing way, it might be said that those actions which are repugnant to the most elementary and indispensable requirements of human social intercourse are deemed unjust and immoral at the same time. If they are viewed as unjust, there is a likelihood that they will be proscribed by the positive law of the community and be made subject to coercive legal sanctions. We have already seen, however, that a gap may exist between that which is considered unjust and that which has been declared illegal by the positive law. Prior to the adoption of the Nineteenth Amendment, for example, the conviction became widespread that it was unjust to deny the voting franchise to women. After a period of intense political debate, the demand for correction of this injustice eventuated in the passage of an amendment granting equal suffrage to men and women. There can be no doubt that one of the most important aspects of justice consists in the tendency to convert its postulates—at least insofar as they relate to the life of the community as a whole and thus have a bearing on the achievement of the common good—into enforceable rules of positive law.

This tendency does not exist—or at least does not exist nearly to the same extent—with respect to those rules of morality which transcend the domain of justice. We may distinguish here between two fields of morality which remain, entirely or largely, outside the sphere of justice: the field of strictly personal morality on the one hand and those demands of social morality on the other which are generally not considered proper objects of legal regulation.

Lon Fuller has spoken of the "morality of aspiration," which is designed to prompt an individual to attain the fullest realization of all his powers and talents.[21] A human being inspired by the morality of aspiration will attempt to live in the highest center of his energies and constantly work for his self-perfection. Such a drive for excellence and self-perfection involves primarily the position which an individual takes toward himself and therefore lies in the first place in the domain of individual morality. However, society is not disinterested in individual self-improvement, since the efficiency, productivity, and cultural level of a social group is greatly enhanced if all members of the group make a sustained effort to develop their capabilities to the fullest. Because of the utilitarian value of individual aspiration, it would not be entirely out of place to pose the question as to whether self-perfection should perhaps be made a legal duty enforceable by sanctions.

Thus far, civilized society, whether it operates on individualist or socialist principles, appears to have given a negative answer to this question. One obvious reason for rejecting the legal road in making the morality of aspiration effective is the impossibility of policing the whole citizenry for the purpose of detecting whether or not everyone's efforts at self-perfection are pursued with sufficient energy and perseverance. Not only would this entail an official appraisal of the maximum capabilities of each individual, but it would also necessitate a continuous surveillance of everybody's activities in order to make sure that he does not relent in his endeavors to reach his highest potential. The problem need only be posed in this fashion to demonstrate the utter impracticability of its solution through the use of legal machinery. Furthermore, in societies that place great value on the freedom of the individual, a scheme of legal regulation of this type would be held to offend against the principles of personal autonomy and self-determination. This does not mean, however, that all attempts to promote human self-improvement through the instrumentality of the law must be repudiated from the outset. A law forcing young people to go to school for a certain number of years is in part directed toward this objective, and some societies would not frown upon laws making physical fitness programs compulsory. But such isolated enactments with limited objectives are a far cry from legislative schemes designed to implement and enforce a general duty of self-perfection. In the words of Fuller, "there is no way by which the law can compel a man to live up to the excellences of which he is capable." [22]

There are other facets of personal morality which the law cannot or will not invade. An individual may consider it his moral duty to be honest with himself, discern his inadequacies, admit and correct his mistakes, and "know himself" in the

Socratic sense of perpetual self-criticism. But who would think of transforming such moral commitments into legal imperatives?

In the domain of social morality, too, there are values and virtues which do not lend themselves to legal control. Charity, generosity, and neighborly love are good examples. Their very recognition as moral values depends on their being dispensed freely and spontaneously, without pressure or coercion. If a law would provide that every beggar on the street must be given at least 50 cents by every passer-by, this would to the extent of the statutory minimum remove almsgiving from the sphere of charity and generosity and place it in the domain of legal obligation. Such a law could hardly be justified as a legal reinforcement of a moral duty, since it would in many instances lead to such abuses of the chance to obtain something for nothing that its total effect would be the promotion of immorality. Also, the moral value of generosity on the part of wealthy persons who choose to dedicate large parts of their fortune to humanitarian causes would be blunted rather than fortified if the law, in addition to general taxation, would make it a duty to set aside portions of large fortunes for such purposes.

Similar observations can be made with respect to the relationship between justice and love. "Love thy neighbor like thyself" is a postulate which, like the maxims of justice, is concerned with the behavior of men toward their fellow men. But it is not a postulate which could be converted into an enforceable right; and it would be even less feasible to set up the command of the Sermon of the Mount to love your enemies and do good to those who hate you as a duty protected by law. Love is anchored in the sentient part of man's nature, it cannot be demanded as a matter of right, it is subjective and largely irrational, and it is often totally unrelated to the accomplishments and deserts of the person who receives it. Justice, on the other hand, requires a rational evaluation of claims and counterclaims, it is in many respects closely related to merit and demerit, and its standards are or should be objective. Leo Tolstoy believed that it would be possible to replace the regime of law based on justice by a kingdom of Christian morality founded on universal love.[23] But it might be asked whether a sentiment as unpredictable and nonrational as love, and one which lends itself so little to social control and direction, could be successfully adopted as the chief ordering principle of social life. This might perhaps be possible if all or most men would become deeply imbued with, and be guided in all their steps, by a religion which, like

Christianity, elevates love of one's fellowmen to the rank of the supreme moral duty. Our past experiences with average human nature cannot, however, engender a sanguine optimism with respect to this possibility.

The conclusion at which we must arrive as a result of the foregoing considerations is that justice occupies a broad segment of the moral universe, but that justice and morality are not coextensive.[24] The scope of justice is narrower than that of morality. Justice seeks to secure the creation of a network of rights and obligations apt to minimize friction and open struggle between the members of a social group and to satisfy all of their important needs. Superimposed upon the system of justice is a sphere of higher morality intent upon promoting a "righteousness which fulfills and exceeds that minimum of respect for other persons which justice requires."[25] The postulates of this righteousness are not made obligatory upon human beings by the use of the legal machinery of the state; although their violation may bring forth hostile or at least adverse community reactions, these reactions are different in character and strength from those visited normally upon offenders against the system of justice.[26] It is likely that no social system can dispense with some tenets of higher morality which go beyond the requirements of justice. For the inner freedom and spontaneous impulses of human beings call for the preservation of a sphere in which the uncommanded expression of sympathy and regard for other human beings is possible and encouraged.

Sec. 5. *Justice and Utility.*

The principle of utility was defined by John Stuart Mill in the following terms:

> The creed which accepts as the foundation of morals "utility" or the "greatest happiness principle" holds that actions are right in proportion as they tend to promote happiness; wrong as they tend to produce the reverse of happiness. By happiness is intended pleasure and the absence of pain; by unhappiness, pain and the privation of pleasure.[1]

Mill went on to say that the utilitarian theory of life was grounded on the belief that pleasure and freedom from pain were the only things desirable as ends, and that all things were desirable either for the pleasure inherent in them or as means for the promotion of pleasure and the prevention of pain.[2] He also made it clear that he wished to use the word "pleasure" in a broad sense which would include the pleasures of the intellect, the imagination, and the moral sentiments.[3]

John Stuart Mill had been preceded by Jeremy Bentham in the philosophical endeavor to elevate utility to the rank of the highest ethical goal.[4] The notion of utility, according to Bentham, was also entitled to be made the ruling principle of law and legislation. "The diffusion of Pleasures and the avoidance of Pains are the only ends which a legislator should have in view." [5] A good legal system was for Bentham one which secured the greatest amount of pleasure for the greatest number of people.

The necessity for discussing the relationship between utility and justice arises from the fact that other authors have regarded justice rather than utility as the guiding rationale for lawmaking. Thus it becomes necessary to pose two questions: Are the objectives of justice and utility the same, or at least similar to each other? Or are we dealing here with two conceptions of entirely different content?

Both Bentham and Mill addressed themselves to these questions, but answered them differently. Speaking of the votaries of religion, who in his opinion did not pay sufficient attention to the principle of utility, Bentham remarked:

> Sometimes, in order to better conceal the cheat (from their own eyes doubtless as well as from others) they set up a phantom of their own, which they call Justice: whose dictates are to modify (which being explained, means to oppose) the dictates of benevolence. But justice, in the only sense in which it has a meaning, is an imaginary personage, feigned for the convenience of discourse, whose dictates are the dictates of utility, applied to certain particular cases. Justice, then, is nothing more than an imaginary instrument, employed to forward on certain occasions, and by certain means, the purposes of benevolence.[6]

According to this view, justice is a fictitious and somewhat misleading notion which has been used by some authors to obfuscate the truth of the principle of utility. Bentham seems to intimate that it might be well to excise the concept altogether from a discussion of social problems.

Mill viewed the idea of justice with friendlier eyes. One entire chapter in his book on *Utilitarianism* is devoted to an exposition of the connections that exist between the notions of justice and utility.[7] Mill points out that it is considered unjust to deprive anyone of his personal liberty, his property, or any other thing that belongs to him or *ought* to belong to him by law. Furthermore, justice demands that each person should obtain that which he deserves. Justice also enjoins persons to keep their commitments, to satisfy the reasonable expectations of others raised by their own conduct, and to avoid partiality. Finally, the idea of justice requires the equal treatment of equal situations, although in Mill's opinion this ingredient of justice, more than any of its other elements, is interpreted differently by different persons and always conforms in its variations to their individual notion of utility.[8]

Mill expressed the opinion that the *origins* of the sentiment of justice could not be traced to the principle of utility but are to be found in "the impulse of self-defense and the feeling of sympathy." [9] It is natural for us to resent and repel any harm done or attempted against ourselves. We also experience the impulse of retaliation when others with whose grievance we sympathize have suffered an injury. At last, our antagonism to the infliction of harm becomes generalized in the feeling of justice so as to include society at large.[10] From this *origin* of the notion of justice Mill distinguished the *standard* of justice which should be applied in the framing of laws. The standard he advocated was social utility, and he believed that justice comprised that part of social utility which was concerned with the essentials of human wellbeing. "Justice is a name for certain moral requirements which, regarded collectively, stand higher in the scale of social utility, and are therefore of more paramount obligation, than any others." [11]

One can well agree with Mill that justice refers to that area of social conduct which is of particular importance for the effective and harmonious operation of the social system, and that the norms of conduct postulated by justice deserve to be invested with an obligatory force of particular strength.[12] But the further question remains whether the standard of utility advocated by Mill is or is not the most satisfactory one that can be employed in the solution of the problems of justice. The criterion proposed by him and Bentham was, as we have seen, whether or not a particular legal measure served to increase pleasure and decrease pain; and it was his own as well as Bentham's view that that which enhanced the pleasure and happiness of an individual was generally (though not necessarily) apt to promote the happiness of the social body as a whole.

The doctrine of hedonism underlying the teachings of Bentham and Mill is based on the premise that pleasure alone is good as an end.[13] Inasmuch as both of these authors were anxious to build their philosophy of utilitarianism on a strictly empirical basis, they believed to have found convincing proof for the correctness of their doctrine in an empirical fact which they assumed to be true: namely, that people actually strive for pleasure as the only desirable thing, and that other objects of desire, such as knowledge, virtue, and beauty, merely serve as means for the enhancement of pleasure and happiness.[14] There is thus a psychological as well as an ethical element comprised in the doctrine of hedonism. It assumes that each person seeks his own happiness in terms of the maximization of pleasure, and that the support of this desire should be rendered the supreme goal of all social effort. Both the descriptive and axiological components of this view offer much ground for doubt and criticism.

Psychological studies made in the present century have shown that the basic assumption of the hedonists, pronounced as a universal truth, does not stand unbiased scrutiny. Man is a goal-seeking being, and the goals he pursues are manifold and highly diversified, including many objectives other than pleasure. Producing great works of art, literature, architecture, and engineering often involves much toil and renunciation of comfort. Organizing or taking part in an expedition for the discovery of unknown lands exposes the participants to many hardships and dangers, including the possible loss of life. The same applies to travel in outer space. Mountaineers undertaking difficult ascents often have to overcome obstacles of an extremely arduous nature. It might perhaps be contended that such ventures are embarked on for the sake of the ultimate pleasure of having accomplished one's objectives. But it seems quite obvious that a person who takes upon himself a task which involves jeopardy of life or limb does so, not for the sake of pleasure, but for the sake of the task itself which he considers worth the possible renouncement

28

of all future pleasures. Also, a great composer who toils through the night to produce a symphony may consciously and willingly face serious disappointments in the future when the public will perhaps be unready to accept his unorthodox composition. A realistic psychology will acknowledge that it is primarily the urge to create, and not the anticipation of future pleasure, that keeps this man going in spite of all impediments and possible setbacks.

Among others, the great psychologist Erich Fromm has demonstrated that pleasure is not a primary motive of action, but merely a potential companion of productive activities.[15] He has also pointed out that the subjective experience of satisfaction, according to the findings of psychoanalysis, is not a valid criterion of true happiness.[16] Kurt Goldstein considers the full actualization of one's energies and potentialities as the chief urge of the healthy individual, and holds that the hedonistic theory originates in the abnormal isolation of one attribute of human nature.[17] Samuel Hart says:

> Man is an acting being. Pleasantness and unpleasant-ness are epiphenomena and not motives of psychic func-tions. There is no other reason for acting, discharging of energies, than growth and expansion. We do not act because of pleasure, rather because we act, we experience pleasure and displeasure. Hedonism converts these con-tingent, emotional occurrences, which are results or effects, into causes. It fails entirely to describe and explain our volitions.[18]

Turning from the psychological foundations of the hedonistic doctrine to its ethical postulates, the weaknesses of the doctrine become even more manifest. The pleasure principle, in its intrinsic character and also because it lends itself easily to misinterpretation,[19] may present a serious obstacle to worthwhile human effort and social improvement.

One serious danger stemming from exclusive concentration on the pleasure-pain dichotomy becomes clear when we examine the soundness of Bentham's "felicific calculus" as a guide to wisdom in living. This was his admonition:

> Sum up all the values of all the *pleasures* on the one side, and those of all the pains on the other. The balance,

if it be on the side of pleasure, will give the good tendency of the act upon the whole, with respect to the interests of that *individual* person; if on the side of pain, the *bad* tendency of it upon the whole.[20]

If this calculus is used by men as the chief test in making decisions, it will often prevent highly beneficial and desirable actions. If Christopher Columbus had accepted this criterion as a basis for determining whether or not to embark on the venture which led to the discovery of America, he would probably have abandoned the project. One might also surmise that Sir Edward Hillary would on that basis have decided against making the ascent of Mount Everest, since the risk of encountering agonizing difficulties was very great and the success of the undertaking (in terms of the pleasure later to be derived from it) very much in doubt. The American astronauts of the 1960's could hardly have reached an intelligent decision in favor of making their space trips upon the calculation whether or not the satisfactions to be expected from the trip were going to outbalance the serious discomforts, anxieties, and hazards that might be in store for them. It is in fact doubtful whether anything truly worthwhile would ever have been accomplished on this planet if men had chosen Bentham as the mentor of their activities. Pain and suffering are integral parts of the human experience and have been willingly shouldered by many men without the use of the Benthamite balance sheet.[21] In the words of Moritz Schlick:

> Again and again we hear that if one strives for greatness he must renounce happiness. 'The fate of the great men of history has not been happy,' says Hegel. If it is true that the highest in life cannot exist without sorrow and pain, then, so it seems, pleasure is not simply the valuable, but must give up its rank as the standard of value to something altogether different.[22]

It also bears emphasis that, when man's striving becomes directed exclusively at the seeking of pleasure, the result will often be frustration accompanied by neurotic symptoms, rather than satisfaction and joy. As Nicolai Hartmann has pointed out, hunting for happiness usually diminishes the possibility of its achievement.[23] Happiness inures to man as a gift and cannot

30

be forced from life by a direct assault aimed at its acquisition. "It pursues him jealously so long as he, diverted from it, is pursuing other values. But it escapes from him the moment he snatches at it. It flees beyond his reach if he passionately pursues it." [24] Max Scheler added the observation that conscious dedication to pleasure may be evidence of deep inner discontent and malaise. Where man is dissatisfied with himself because he has not lived a meaningful life in the proper center of his energies, he seeks pleasure for the purpose of covering up his inner emptiness; but when man is unhappy in the central and crucial sphere of his life, the pleasure he strives after will usually elude him. [25] In Scheler's view, the various forms of practical hedonism are in most instances symptoms of failure to realize the higher values of life.

It is interesting to note that John Stuart Mill himself became aware of the deficiencies of a hedonistic philosophy after he had gone through an intellectual crisis in his life. He wrote in his autobiography:

> I never, indeed, wavered in the conviction that happiness is the test of all rules of conduct, and the end of life. But I now thought that this end was only to be attained by not making it the direct end. Those only are happy (I thought) who have their minds fixed on some object other than their own happiness; on the happiness of others, on the improvement of mankind, even on some art or pursuit, followed not as a means, but as itself an ideal end. Aiming thus at something else, they find happiness by the way. [26]

The foregoing rejection of a hedonistic philosophy as an ultimate gauge of law and legislation should not be taken as a suggestion that lawmakers ought to be unconcerned about human happiness. The true happiness of the human race must be the lodestar for all those who are engaged in building the good society. But the readiness to bear hardships and make sacrifices for the sake of attaining the higher goals of life might be a necessary condition for the realization of genuine contentment and psychic harmony. In the words of Fromm:

> Happiness is often considered the logical opposite of grief or pain. Physical or mental suffering is part of

31

human existence and to experience them is unavoidable. To spare oneself from grief at all cost can be achieved only at the price of total detachment, which excludes the ability to experience happiness. The opposite of happiness thus is not grief or pain but depression which results from inner sterility and unproductiveness.[27]

Those who wish to come to the rescue of hedonism might perhaps argue that it is the hard way, leading us upward by a rough road, that gives us true pleasure. The martyr, they might say, thus derives pleasurable experiences from his suffering and agony. But this type of argument is not very satisfactory and convincing. It means, in the words of Lon Fuller, "to expand the notion of pleasure to the point where it becomes, like utility in economics, an empty container for every kind of human want or striving." [28]

What ultimate conclusions regarding the relation between justice and utility can we distill from these considerations? The tenor of the preceding remarks has been that a concept of utility which rests on a universalist form of hedonism cannot be deemed useful for the accomplishment of the aims of justice because, empirically, it is not founded on a sound psychology and, axiologically, society is not well served by a universal pursuit of pleasure. We found that many of the most worthwhile undertakings of mankind were not prompted by the pleasure motive and, if they had been, probably would not have been undertaken. It was also emphasized that no inference should be drawn from this critique of traditional utilitarianism that the effectuation of true human happiness was not among the most worthy aims of social organization. An affirmative discussion of these aims will be found in another part of this book.[29]

If the term "utility" is not defined in orthodox utilitarian terms, but is taken in its broad sense of denoting measures useful to the accomplishment of social and legal objectives, no contrast arises between utility and justice. Depending on the scope that is assigned to the concept of utility, the two terms may actually become coextensive, so that the choice between them turns into a matter of semantic preference. The choice has been made in this book in favor of the term "justice," first, in the interest of preserving an old and venerable tradition which has fixed upon justice rather than utility as the ideal of guidance for legal systems, and, secondly, because we shall become confronted with ethical aspects of justice which are controlled by considerations other than mere pragmatic utility.

Sec. 6. *Justice as a Rational Ideal.*

The Italian jurist Piero Calamandrei has told us that the word "reason" in the early Italian language was synonymous with justice. To "render reason" meant to do justice, and in some northern Italian cities the court house is still called today *Palazzo della ragione* (Palace of Reason).[1]

A view diametrically opposed to this early Italian identification of justice and reason was put forward in modern times by Hans Kelsen. Justice is to Kelsen not an instrument of reason but, on the contrary, a totally irrational ideal.[2] He argues that the norms which are used as standards of justice vary from individual to individual, and from group to group, and are often mutually irreconcilable.[3] The liberal regards freedom as the ideal of justice, while the socialist sees this ideal in equality. Many writers in antiquity declared slavery to be just; today this institution is held by most people to be unjust, but men in future times might revert to the position of the Greeks and Romans. In primitive times, blood revenge based on collective responsibility was generally considered a just form of atoning for crimes; but today the opposite idea prevails in most countries, namely, that only individual responsibility is just. As to systems of procedure, ordeal and battle were at one time deemed to constitute fair and reasonable modes of trial, while today some nations favor adversary types of procedure and others inquisitorial ones.

Before the merits of this argument are discussed, it should be observed as a preliminary matter that the advocacy of different conceptions of justice by different men and at different times does not, in the absence of additional philosophical assumptions, furnish proof for the proposition that the content of justice is unascertainable by reason. The possibility remains that some people have clung to erroneous and untenable views of justice, while others have seen the problem in its correct light. To use a parallel from a related area, the fact that some judges have misinterpreted and distorted the positive law of their state or community cannot be adduced as evidence that no rational decision based on the positive rules of law is possible because divergences have occurred in the judicial interpretation of norms. In this last

33

instance, Kelsen himself would probably admit the possibility of a rational process of decision. For it is his belief that "positive law is known, or more correctly is revealed, to reason." [4]

The further assumption Kelsen is making when he excises pronouncements on justice from the field of rational discourse is based on his conviction that all value judgments lack absolute validity and cannot for this reason be declared right or wrong. Such value judgments express feelings and emotional reactions rather than rational and objective propositions.[5] They are therefore relative to the person or group making the judgment. If this is true, it obviously becomes impossible to characterize any particular opinion on what is just and unjust as correct or incorrect, valid or invalid.

Before the issue raised by Kelsen can be discussed intelligently, it becomes necessary to clarify the key terms relevant to the discussion. What do we mean by the terms "reason" and "rational judgment"? What are the elements that distinguish a rational act from an irrational one? Many works on legal philosophy simply presuppose that the meaning of these fundamental notions is either known or obvious. But in reality the concepts of reason and unreason, rationality and irrationality, are complex terms which have several significations and are therefore in need of elucidation.

Generally speaking, reason might be described as a faculty which enables men, within certain limits, to comprehend external reality, to cope with the conditions of their existence, to modify or improve these conditions, to choose goals and pursue them by the selection of means adequate to their realization. The absence of reason and rational design severely restricts the chance of achieving these objectives or renders their successful pursuit altogether impossible.

Without delving into the epistemological question as to whether or not human beings are able to apprehend and understand the outer world "as it really is," it seems clear that men today possess a fairly broad (although certainly incomplete) picture of nature as it surrounds and affects them. This statement appears to hold true regardless of whether nature as an object of human perception is regarded as a "phenomenon" (appearance) or as a thing-in-itself which reveals itself to us in its true structure and constitutive elements.

What is the function of reason in this process of discovering the secrets of nature? Some philosophers and scientists have as-

34

serted that we gain knowledge of nature solely by observation and sensory experiences, and not by the use of our rational faculty. But the weaknesses of this view are obvious. Scientists constantly draw inferences from their measurements, observations, and experiments, and the drawing of inferences and conclusions from observed data is clearly a function of reason. Facts do not explain themselves; interpretations and theorems are often needed to fit them together into a coherent pattern. The theorems may have to be verified by subsequent experiments, but without the formulation of a rational hypothesis which connects and synthesizes the empirical data the natural scientist, especially when he does research in an unexplored field, will often be lost on his way.[6] In the words of Morris Cohen:

> Observation unillumined by theoretic reason is sterile. Indeed, without a well-reasoned anticipation or hypothesis of what we expect to find there is no definite object to look for, and no test as to what is relevant to our search. Wisdom does not come to those who gape at nature with an empty head.[7]

Thus, every creative scientist must invoke assumptions and frame concepts which are not supplied by sensory experience as such. Even speculation cannot always be excluded from the researcher's field of operation, as Einstein observed. These were his conclusions:

> Every theory is speculative. When the basic concepts of a theory are comparatively "close to experience" (e.g., the concepts of force, pressure, mass), its speculative character is not so easily discernible. If, however, a theory is such as to require the application of complicated logical processes in order to reach conclusions from the premises that can be confronted with observation, everybody becomes conscious of the speculative nature of the theory.[8]

The concepts necessary to explain the facts and phenomena of human social life likewise cannot be gained from empirical observation alone. Reason is needed to apprehend the relations between the objects of our observation and to form generalizations useful in predicting the behavior of men. The psychiatrist Kurt Goldstein has shown that the ability to make abstractions

35

and draw general conclusions from experience is one of the most characteristic features of the rational mind, and that this capacity is lacking in persons afflicted with serious mental deficiencies.[9] Such abstractions and generalizations distilled from observation through the use of reason enable men to adjust their conduct to the anticipated reactions of others and are thus significant instrumentalities in bringing about an ordered and peaceful social life.

We shall turn now to the second element in the general determination of reason proposed above. Human beings employ reason not only in order to gain an understanding of their natural and social surroundings. They make use of this faculty also for the purpose of coping with the practical problems of their existence. Reason plays an important part especially in organizing and adjusting our relations with our fellowmen. In contrast to the irrational man who is apt to be carried away by his unanalyzed impulses and unconscious drives in disregard of the feelings and sensibilities of those with whom he comes into contact, the reasonable man is able to project himself into the personality of others and to anticipate their response to his actions. This capacity to abstract from our own selves, to put ourselves into the position of others, and to adapt our needs and interests to those with whom we become closely associated, is very distinctly an attribute of the rational part of our nature. When we analyze our relations with others in a detached fashion, we must necessarily come to the conclusion that certain controls on our impulses are needed in order to avoid actions that are offensive to our neighbors and likely to provoke retaliation. In the light of this necessity, the Golden Rule presents itself as the very prototype of a rational axiom of conduct. It is this capacity to reflect impartially upon the requirements and inevitable conditions of social coexistence that makes it possible for men to frame generalized ethical systems and codes of law.

One of the most significant facets of this capacity is the power to predict reciprocity in evil. "If I do this to him, he will get square with me." This furnishes a strong incentive for replacing the rule of passion by the rule of reason. Rational contemplation realizes the undesirability and especially the insecurity of a condition in which self-centered impulse alone governs the actions of men. Where non-rational behavior prevails, all means including violence are used to carry out the fleeting volitions of the moment. Where rationality is dominant, there is a strong tendency to prefer the method of persuasion to the method of force and to substitute peaceful processes for violence and repression wherever possible. A peaceable settlement of controversies usually requires that those who are trying to find a satisfactory solution must exercise considerable impartiality and neutrality in order to do justice to those involved in the dispute. Since these qualities will be found more easily in a third person not directly affected by the controversy than in the parties thereto, a judgment or arbitrament by an impartial agent would appear to be a particularly rational method of dealing with this problem.

A third function of reason has received the special attention of Alfred North Whitehead. It involves the use of this faculty for the purpose of changing and improving social conditions. In the opinion of Whitehead, "Reason is the practical embodiment of the urge to transform mere existence into the good existence, and to transform the good existence into the better existence." [10] If men were not endowed with reason, a mere static survival on a primitive level might be their inescapable fate. Reason can serve as an agency of innovation, a progressive power which "civilizes the brute force of anarchic appetition." [11] While Whitehead does not deny the theoretical and speculative constituents of reason, it is the practical use of this faculty in devising means for the improvement of the human condition that has above all caught his imagination. "Reason," he says, "is the organ of emphasis upon novelty." [12]

Whitehead has also shown the close connection which exists between rationality and teleology.[13] This brings us to a fourth and very significant ingredient in the concept of reason. Reason provides the judgments which are needed and used in the effectuation of human purposes.

First of all, reason in this sense is or may be helpful in the very act of framing purposes. If a person should decide to devote his life to the promotion of international understanding through the publication of books and delivery of lectures, such a decision will normally not be reached primarily on the basis of unconscious urge or emotional impulse, although these factors may have played some part in bringing it to fruition. It will usually be reached upon a careful and judicious consideration of the reasons which make such a course of action worthwhile and attractive. The person in question may have concluded that the threat of war was the greatest danger confronting mankind in our age, and that all political action programs aimed at economic growth or social reform were secondary in importance as compared with the urgent need to promote a conciliatory attitude in international affairs. He presumably also considered the obstacles standing in the way of realizing the objective and convinced himself that they could be surmounted. Furthermore, he decided that he was capable of embarking upon this venture because of his proven capacity to write and speak eloquently.

Quite obviously a decision reached in this manner is a rational decision. It is characteristic for such a decision that an intelligible ground or reason can be given in its favor and that it was reached after a thorough consideration of all factors speaking for and against the proposed action. Furthermore, if external evidence is available to support contradictory conclusions, an effort must be made to determine the weight of such evidence.[14]

Reason also performs an important function in the selection of the means employed in the pursuit of chosen or given ends. If a person in his attempt to reach a goal uses means and methods which in the light of the best available knowledge are totally inadequate to accomplish it, he acts in an irrational manner. This relationship between means and ends has often been viewed by American courts as the touchstone in administering the "rational basis test," which is often employed to determine the constitutionality of legislative acts under the due process clause of the Constitution. If the beliefs of the legislators responsible for the passage of a statute designed to accomplish certain social or economic objectives were "so irrational that none of these objects would result from the passage of the act," then the court may strike down the enactment as an arbitrary exercise of power.[15]

Returning to our earlier example, if the man who is firmly resolved to work for international reconciliation prepares for his chosen vocation by studying foreign languages, taking extensive work in international relations and international law, and seeking to become associated with an institution or organization which is sympathetic to his aims and will support his activities, it will be concluded that he has rationally selected the means helpful to him in attaining his goal.

An attempt to summarize the main functions of reason was made by the English sociologist Morris Ginsberg. The relevant passage reads as follows:

I conclude then that the function of reason in conduct is to clarify and define the ends of endeavour and to relate them to one another, to disclose the nature of the forces, internal and external, necessary for their realization, to insist on the widest consideration of all the claims that are relevant and the greatest impartiality in dealing with them, and, in cases of conflict whether within the individual or between individuals, to avoid the use of repression or force and to seek rather to evoke willing acceptance. Desires or preferences so informed or guided would be rational desires or preferences.[16]

This statement is restricted to the practical functions of reason and does not include the theoretical aspects of this faculty, as sketched above. Furthermore, it does not make reference to the uses of reason in changing and improving social conditions, as emphasized by Whitehead. But the passage aptly points up in nutshell form some of the most significant facets of the rational attitude.

Can we define justice as a rational ideal in the light of the foregoing analysis of the faculty of reason? As far as the theoretical side of reason is concerned, there is no doubt that it can be employed as a vehicle for probing into the multifarious phenomena which are connected with the workings of the sense of justice in society. For example, reason aids us in analyzing the psychological findings relative to the human sentiment of justice and to draw conclusions from the collected data as to the origins of this sentiment and the directions in which it manifests itself in the social process. The cognitive branch of reason is also useful in sifting and collating the historical facts concerning the responses of people to problems of law and justice in different places, times, and civilizations, and to arrive at certain generalized conclusions with respect to the universal or contingent, typical or untypical character of these responses. In this way, the framing of a theory of justice which rests on a historical, psychological, and sociological foundation and attempts to weave the multifarious strands into a coherent interpretative scheme becomes a possibility in social science.

When we turn to the second function of reason, that of coping with the practical problems of life, especially those involving our relations with our fellowmen, we shall discover that issues of justice are deeply enmeshed with these problems. The fair and just treatment of other persons, although it may in many instances also be dictated by benevolent sentiments, is in its essence a command of reason. We use our rational faculty to devise ways and means to make life in society tolerable and worthwhile, and although the norms of social intercourse may with the passage of time become customary and nonreflective, their origin and anchorage in rational considerations does not thereby become unhinged. When the father does not show undue favor to some of his children, when the employer deals fairly with his employees, when the government refrains from discriminating against certain classes and groups in society, this means the observance of justice pursuant to standards of reason. Many of the postulates of justice, and especially the maxim not to injure and mistreat others, are immediate derivations from the Golden Rule which, as we have seen, is the prototype of a rational axiom and almost universally recognized as a necessary condition of social relations. Because of the endowment of rationality which we possess, we are able to realize and foresee that the harm done to others may also be done to our own persons, if the conduct in question is sanctioned as unobjectionable.

Human reason, as we have seen, is also instrumental in devising means and schemes for changing the social environment and bringing about improvements in societal conditions. In this sphere we become directly confronted with the dynamic components of justice. Many innovations in the political, economic, and social order were brought about, in an evolutionary or revolutionary way, under the battlecry of justice. The demands for political and social reform are usually traceable to rational causes, although emotional factors may also play a part in their emergence. In the words of Morris Cohen: "The worship of reason was a potent influence in minimizing or abolishing agelong abuses like slavery, serfdom, and persecution for witchcraft and heresy." [17] When women asked for the right of suffrage, they advanced reasons for their claims which large numbers of people regarded as well-nigh irrefutable: for example, that women were receiving a basic education on a par with that of men and were therefore in an equal position to evaluate political issues; that biological science had discovered no innate intellectual inferiority of the female sex; and that the effects of political choice fell upon women the same as upon men, so that they should have a voice in bringing about or obviating these effects. When the plebeians in Rome demanded that they be made eligible for public office, they supported these demands not only by political pressure (which played an important part in their strategy), but also by convincing assertions of equal qualification which the ruling patricians found it hard to resist and which in the end helped to bring about a legal compromise solution in which the ruling class cooperated. In our own day, the battle for racial equality has its rational basis in the accumulation of proof to the effect that no inherent differences of native endowment exist among the races of men.

The fourth use of reason discussed above relates to the selection of the goals of individual and social life and the implementation of these goals through appropriate means designed for accomplishing them. This raises, first of all, the question as to whether or not a rational determination of the goals of justice is possible. The second chapter of this book deals with this question in some detail, and judgment on the proper answer should be reserved until an appraisal of the relevant considerations has been made. It might be observed at the outset, however, that if an individual is able to make a choice of the goals of his life in the light of deliberations that can withstand rational scrutiny, as suggested earlier in this section, there do not appear to exist any intrinsic obstacles to rational goal-setting by the members of a social group or those who represent them. In many historical instances, such goal-setting has been motivated by rational ideals, especially by the hope of instituting a social order in which people can live together peacefully and with a degree of cooperation which yields mutual benefits to the members of the group, and a strengthening of this ideal has been sought with the advance of civilization.

After the goals of social life and organization have become established in a societal unit, either by choice or by habit, the further question arises as to whether in the area of administration of justice the means selected for the effectuation of these goals are or can be rationally determined. For broad sectors of a system of justice this question can be answered in the affirmative, generally as well as in relation to particular problems.

The method of justice *in general* bears the hallmarks of rationality because it operates through the application of reasoned, articulated judgment and peaceful adjustment of differences rather than through the use of force. Of course, the

41

employment of force is not excluded against those who cannot be influenced or moved by argument or entreaty. But this is in itself a rationally determined resort to force as an *ultima ratio* where all vehicles of persuasion have failed.

When we turn to the methods used in accomplishing specific objectives of the legal system, the problem becomes more intricate. In the early period of many legal systems, for example, the ordeal was used as a method of trial and considered a fair method of settling litigation. Today, this device is almost universally condemned as arbitrary and irrational. This development would seem to lend weight to Kelsen's charge that, on an overall historical basis, no necessary or even probable connection between rationality and justice can be discerned. But this charge has only a superficial plausibility. At the time when the ordeal was used, it was generally felt that it represented an entirely reasonable way of deciding the guilt or innocence of a person. The accused was put in peril, being forced, for example, to carry a hot piece of iron or to swallow a large morsel of food. If he succumbed to the peril, this was considered a sign that he was guilty. The sign was deemed to come from God, and it was firmly assumed that God would actively intervene in a judicial proceeding by revealing the party who should be punished or pointing out the innocent party by his use of unmistakable and reliable signals. Where such a belief in supernatural intervention exists, the tests used in invoking the intervention cannot be said to be lacking in rationality. If God will not let justice falter, all that is required is an appeal to his powers which will call forth the token that points to the truth. To use another example, when heretics were burned at the stake during the days of the Inquisition, it was firmly believed that this procedure would save their souls from the worse fate of eternal damnation.

The objection which we level at such practices today is directed primarily at the basic assumptions on which they were predicated. In this respect, the rationality or non-rationality of a legal institution or mode of procedure is always clouded by some measure of uncertainty. We believe that our present system of criminal procedure, in which the truth is supposed to be brought to light in a legal combat between the prosecutor and the defendant, is rational because we are sure that it leads to the correct result in most cases. If this assumption should ever be shattered or put in serious doubt, other means of trial procedure in criminal cases would probably be resorted to. The illustration is used to show that our convictions as to the rationality of a legal device or institution depend to a considerable extent on the state of our knowledge and on the means available for verifying the adequacy of this device or institution. What may have been deemed a rational vehicle for obtaining justice at one time may have to be rejected later as irrational as we gain new insights into the relations between the means used and the ends to be obtained. But we should not necessarily condemn a legal technique or legal institution utilized in an earlier time as irrational if in the light of the sum of knowledge and aggregate of ultimate beliefs obtaining at that time, good and convincing reasons could be given in justification of these techniques and institutions.[18] The rationality of the ultimate beliefs, of course, is another matter which is not at issue at the present stage of the argument.

It is not contended here that problems of justice are always solved in a rational manner, with the qualification that our determinations as to what is rational may be subject to change and evolution. Emotions, prejudices, and pure sentiments can never be wholly excluded from the administration of human affairs. It is argued, however, that rational considerations have played a tremendously large part in the framing and development of legal institutions, and that the purposes to be attained by a just ordering of the human social life are of an essentially rational character. These purposes will be analyzed in some detail in the following chapter.

CHAPTER II

THE GOALS OF JUSTICE

Sec. 7. *Social Goals as Objects of Cognition.*

The first chapter of this book dealt with a question which was primarily analytical in character. This discussion focused on the content and boundaries of the concept of justice, and an attempt was also made to delimit this concept from other notions exhibiting some affinity with it. The main orientation of the present chapter, on the other hand, is synthetic and teleological. Its purpose is to consider specific social goals and policy objectives which may be relevant to the attainment or maintenance of a just order of society. Since a treatment of this question cannot avoid the necessity of making some normative choices between conflicting social goal values, the method of pure description will in many places have to give way to arguments of an evaluative cast.

Such an endeavor will inevitably provoke an assertion on the part of many social scientists that the subject matter indicated by the title of this chapter is not a legitimate theme of scientific inquiry. In the opinion of scholars who are of this persuasion, the goals of social life or social organization cannot be discerned by a process of cognition or rational judgment. They must be chosen by an act of will, or be grasped through faith or intuition; it is also possible that they might have evolved by way of a slow, almost unconscious historical growth and are simply accepted by the community and reflected in its institutions and mores. These goals cannot, according to this view, be "proven" by science in the sense that they can be shown to be true or false, right or wrong, desirable or undesirable. The main thesis of this creed of "scientific value relativism" has been well stated by Arnold Brecht, one of its most distinguished and articulate protagonists:

44

[Scientific] method does not enable us to state, in *absolute terms*, whether the purpose pursued by us or by others is good or bad, right or wrong, just or unjust, nor which of several conflicting purposes is more valuable than the other. It only enables us to answer these questions in relative terms, with reference to some purpose that is actually being pursued, or which the scientist in some "working hypothesis" assumes ought to be pursued, or with reference to ideas that are actually held or might be held. In particular, Scientific Method cannot state in absolute terms which of several conflicting ultimate purposes is better than others except in relation to some presupposed goal or idea. In short, it does not enable the scientist to render an unconditional scientific value judgment, and especially not a moral one. It cannot set the goal.[1]

Brecht insists, therefore, that references to ultimate goals or purposes of human life must be debarred as evidence from scientific discussion, except to the extent that science might aid in clarifying the implications and consequences of the value judgments relating to such matters.[2] In developing this position, Brecht was influenced by the epistemological ideas of the German sociologist Max Weber. Weber was strongly convinced that social science is able to discover what human beings *can* do and how their volition is determined, but incapable of teaching what human beings *ought to do*. Philosophical notions as to the proper way of organizing human societies, he maintained, can never be the product of advancing empirical knowledge, but are adopted by human beings as strictly personal commitments, according to their conscience and individual view of the world.[3] "It can never be the task of an empirical science to provide binding norms and ideals from which directives for immediate practical activity can be derived."[4] To judge the validity of values and ideals was to him a matter of faith, not of science; "everybody must decide," he said, "what shall be God *for him* and what the devil."[5]

Weber believed, on the other hand, that science was able to elucidate the meaning and implications of social ideals, and the consequences to which their adoption and implementation would lead. Furthermore, the determination of the appropriateness of means chosen for the achievement of given ends was deemed by him accessible to scientific analysis. In this way, he stated, "we can indirectly criticize the setting of the end itself as practically meaningful (on the basis of the existing historical situation) or as meaningless with reference to existing conditions." [6] Differently expressed, scientific investigation of a social goal may lead to the conclusion that under the conditions of the time and place no adequate means for its attainment are available, and it will thereby prove the goal to be a practical impossibility.

If normative evaluation must be considered outside the province of science, on whom devolves the task of setting social, political, and spiritual goals for the human cooperative venture? In the opinion of Weber, this task is reserved to the saviors and prophets; [7] but Weber was aware that, since such inspired men are not always present when they are most urgently needed, it is often performed by demagogues. [8]

The chief reason for denying scientific character to normative statements must be sought in the difficulties inherent in the verification of such statements. In the words of Morris Ginsberg, "ideals cannot be 'verified' in the sense of being shown to correspond to fact, since they do not claim to formulate what is but what, through our action, ought to be." [9] In the field of the natural sciences, the hypotheses formed with respect to natural occurrences or physical laws can often be corroborated by direct proof which gives us confirmation of their existence and operation by means of sense data. Thus, the law that metals expand when heated may be tested and proved by measurements whose accuracy can be established beyond a reasonable doubt. Where this is not possible, as in the microcosmic world of ultimate particles, indirect proof of their structure and behavior can sometimes be obtained through experiments in the macrocosmic sphere which may lead to compelling inferences supported at least in part by sense perception. But even in the natural sciences a margin of error must be allowed in many instances with respect to the processes of verification, and it is well established today that areas of uncertainty and doubt remain in existence as to some of the most fundamental phenomena in nature. [10]

In the realm of descriptive sociology and social science, too, reliable confirmation of scientific statements and propositions can often be secured. Thus, the sociological law that voters in rural areas tend to be more conservative in their political outlook than voters in urban districts can be corroborated by an analysis

46

of the actual ballots cast in an election. Statements as to wage differentials in various regions of a country can be supported by trustworthy statistics.

When we move from the world of factual reality into that of normative ideality, we encounter considerably greater difficulties in the path of verification and proof. Moral ideals and social goals reside in the realm of the human spirit, a sphere which is different in structure from that of material reality. One of the most essential differences lies in the incorporeal character of many of its emanations and manifestations, which renders exact measurements, adduction of physical evidence, and reliance on sensory data impossible. How can we prove, for example, whether Montesquieu's principle of separation of powers is a "true" postulate for the building of political systems? How can we verify a statement to the effect that it is a goal of justice to promote the freedom and equality of human beings? In what way can the proposition that it is immoral to steal and commit fraud be corroborated by compelling evidence? One possible way of verifying normative assertions is to demonstrate that the majority of people believe these assertions to be valid. But this type of validation, as will be shown later, might with some degree of legitimacy be rejected on the ground that proof of majority opinion is not synonymous with proof of the truth.

It cannot be denied, on the other hand, that people are deeply concerned with the question as the whether their moral judgments and ideals are "true," "correct," or "valid." Large numbers of persons are disinclined to think that moral and ideological convictions, because they have no physical substratum, are devoid of reality and constitute mere flights of fancy of individuals without an objective basis. The ideals and goals devised by the human spirit are powerful forces in the life of human beings and human groups. Nicolai Hartmann has shown convincingly that one must abandon the positivist prejudice which assigns existence only to tangible and material substances. He points out that the products of the spirit in their non-material forms, such as ideals, world views, and value patterns, have a definite reality of their own.[11] Individual men have before them mental pictures of what they wish to become or to accomplish, and their personal ideals directly influence their actions and conduct. Human groups and political societies impress the stamp of the social goals which they pursue upon

47

the fabric of their institutions and are often guided by them in their activities and policies.

If the realm of the spirit forms an important part of the reality of human existence, it thereby becomes a legitimate object of scientific investigation. For it is the task of science to explore human nature and human life in all of their aspects and forms of expression. But this insight does not provide us with an immediate solution to the puzzling problem posed in this section. Perhaps the proposition that science may undertake a descriptive analysis of human spiritual activity would today command widespread acceptance. But does science still keep within its proper bounds if it proceeds beyond the precincts of factual and phenomenal investigation and enters into the domain of normative valuation? Can science give assistance and advice to the men of practical affairs on the problem whether certain political ideals or social goals are better than others and whether an exclusive or paramount importance should be assigned to some of them?

The prevailing opinion of our day would strongly tend to answer these questions in the negative. It would hold that science may inquire into the factuality of normative ideas and their impact on human behavior, but that it is barred from determining their validity and rank.

Vigorous challenges to the ruling contemporary view have been flung by the American philosopher F. S. C. Northrop and the Danish jurist Frederick Vinding Kruse. Northrop takes the position that certain normative statements relating to ethical issues are cognitive in a genuine sense rather than merely emotive or hortatory. In his opinion, the "ought" toward which the political, social, and legal order of a society should orient itself can to some extent be determined by empirically testable theories of natural man.[12] An adequate philosophical anthropology, he argues, can point the way toward reaching objective criteria for adjudging the social order or living law of a given society to be "good" or "bad" or in need of specifiable reform.[13] Thus, an ethics derived from a philosophy of nature, and especially human nature, can supply certain moral and legal norms universally valid for all men. "Ethics is merely true (that is, empirically verified) natural philosophy applied to human conduct and relations. When the empirically verified philosophy of the true for natural man is pursued with respect to what man must do to fulfill what it indicates the full and true nature of natural

48

man to be, then the philosophy of the true for nature and natural man becomes the idea or measure of the good for culture, cultural man and the humanities." [14]

Vinding Kruse, like Northrop, was convinced that it was possible to establish valid principles of morality and justice on a scientific basis. In all human communities throughout the ages, he wrote, the elementary command not to harm your fellowmen has been in force as a general principle. The reason why men in all spheres of life have arrived at this fundamental commandment is that its observation saves men from suffering, creates peace and security for the individual, and therefore constitutes an indispensable prerequisite for all constructive human achievement.[15] Assuming that men wish to create harmonious and workable social organizations in which they can live healthy and productive lives in full use of their powers and skills, certain ethical norms conducive to bringing about this condition can be shown to be scientifically correct.[16] If these norms are not recognized, social life will break down and men will revert to the level of beasts of prey.

Vinding Kruse has proposed that the ethics of the future should not, like religious and traditional morality, be taught in an imperative fashion. It should take on a hypothetical form and say to men: If you want to avoid harmful effects in social life, you must conduct yourselves in such and such a way.[17] But he makes it clear that this ethics, in spite of the hypothetical form of its presentation, is an ethics not only of means but also of ends: its true objective is to promote the good society, the psychic sanity, and the rightly understood happiness and inner satisfaction of human beings.[18]

In evaluating such proposals for a scientific treatment of normative problems, one must keep in mind the chief difficulty confronting those who are engaged in such a task: the difficulty, namely, that stems from any attempt to establish the validity of ultimate goals for the human cooperative endeavor by convincing evidence. As Vinding Kruse himself puts the question: "Why should we strive for the satisfaction and progress of the community?," and not for opposite ends? [19] On an even more elementary level, the question might be formulated thus: Why should we prefer life to non-life, constructive social organization to disorganization and chaos? If someone asserts that so much misery and suffering exists on this earth that it would be better to prevent men from perpetuating their kind or, as a proper "final solution," to bring humanity to extinction by the violent means so readily available in the present age, what answer can be given to him? Can such a view be disproved by showing that the large majority of men are not in sympathy with it?

The last-mentioned argument certainly cannot be rejected out of hand. If most men prefer life to death (at least in ordinary circumstances), if they wish to conduct their lives in a well-ordered society rather than wage a daily struggle for mere physical survival under conditions of destructiveness and anarchy, if they desire to marry and work productively, practice their skills, and enjoy the manifold beauties of life, this indicates a wide sharing of fundamental values which cannot be ignored in considering whether a generally valid system of ethics can be devised.

On the other hand, the fact that men desire certain things does not furnish irrefutable proof that they *ought* to desire them. Let us assume, for example, that in a certain epoch of history all that men would aim at was the satisfaction of sensual pleasure. Would such a universal striving *eo ipso* render invalid the activity of men who, opposed to this philosophy of life, would teach that its effects were self-defeating and not conducive to the fulfillment of man's true and complete nature? There is certainly much that can be said in favor of the proposition that a scientific ethics, if it is possible at all, cannot solely rest on consensus.

We move a step closer to the solution of the problem, however, if we ask ourselves whether a consensus with respect to certain fundamental ethical propositions may not have its roots in certain characteristic traits of human beings which no reasonable man would wish to change or abolish. The will to live is an attribute or propensity of human beings which may be frustrated or overcome under certain circumstances, but which normally exists in great strength and is the ultimate source of most of the actions and events which occur on this planet. Even wars are waged for (well or ill conceived) purposes of self-preservation or growth, and not for the end of self-annihilation. Religions, such as Buddhism, which have sought to impose substantial restraints on the life-will, have done so for the therapeutic objective of reducing suffering, and not in order to induce mass suicide, prevent births, or shorten the life span of the individual. Buddhism (excepting perhaps a small class of ascetic monks) admonishes its adherents to go out into the world, get married, raise a family, and lead a life of service to one's fellowmen.[20]

It might still be objected that the prevalence and strength of the life instinct furnishes no evidence in favor of an objective ethics founded on its recognition. The existence of the instinct, it might be contended, does not prove that life is a positive good; the unborn might be better off than those who will have to experience the vicissitudes, sorrows, disappointments, and frustrations of life. No one, the pessimistic philosopher will declare, will ever be able to show by means of rational, scientifically acceptable evidence that life is better than non-life.

No argument can be advanced against such contentions which has the certainty and infallibility of mathematical proof. Since nobody who feels called upon to answer the pessimistic thesis has had the experience of non-existence, he will be hard put to demonstrate convincingly that existence is the preferable mode of being. All he might be able to state is that life, despite the sufferings, frustrations, and anxieties which it brings in its train, harbors enough moments of satisfaction and joy for most people to make it a worthwhile venture; that although it is possible (although not likely) that in primitive times or under unfavorable conditions people may have experienced life as an unbearable burden, we know today that an advanced technology combined with a humanitarian social philosophy can insure a fair amount of happiness for all or most people; that as a general rule (subject to exceptions) men wish to live out and even prolong their lives rather than to cut them short; that most rational men and teachers of wisdom have approved the life-affirming impulses of the human race; and that, since a great deal can be done by civilized men to make life a rich, worthwhile, and rewarding experience, the statement that life should be continued rather than destroyed on this earth cannot be met by truly convincing counter-arguments and therefore bears the prima facie indicia of validity.

We have deliberately avoided the use of the word "truth" in attempting to render plausible the thesis that, as a general proposition, life not only is, but ought to be, preferred to non-life, and have instead spoken of the "validity" of the proposition. Although the terms "true" and "false" lend themselves to broad as well as narrow linguistic usage, there may be good reasons for applying these terms exclusively or chiefly to the verification of factual statements. In the Kantian sense, "truth" means the concordance of a cognitive insight with the object of

51

cognition.[21] With respect to normative propositions, as has been stated before, such concordance is difficult to establish because their object is an "ought" (that is, something mental and non-tangible) rather than an "is." There is undoubtedly a wide difference between a statement to the effect that "snow is white" and one which says that "life on this earth ought to be continued" or "indiscriminate killing is evil." In the first case, there exists congruity of the statement with the facts of ontological reality, and we have proposed to restrict the use of the term "true," at least in the main, to such instances.[22] For propositions denoting an "ought," a reality corresponding to the statement is missing. They refer to values, which are non-material configurations, and (enhancing the element of ideality) they point not to values which have found an actual realization, but to valuable aims which, in the opinion of the person making the statement, *should* be pursued and attained. Such value judgments cannot be verified by showing that they conform to the facts but, if at all, can be validated only by offering rational and plausible arguments, based to the greatest possible extent on empirical data, which are so convincing and so superior to potential counter-arguments that reasonable men are prone to accept them and act upon them.[23] Value judgments substantiated in this fashion may be claimed to be "valid" or "right," while the opposite judgments may be asserted to be "invalid" or "wrong."

It stands to reason that in many instances the validity or rightness of normative statements is by no means obvious or incontestable, but remains the subject of doubt and debate. In this respect judgments about values do not differ materially from statements about facts, for example statements about the structure of the final particles of nature. A natural scientist can often do no more than to assert the probable truth of a factual statement in this area, and others may vigorously dispute his claims. The natural sciences and the social disciplines are similar in that many of the most elementary data and phenomena with which they are concerned cannot be verified with absolute certainty, but remain in the sphere of hypotheses endowed with probable validity only. If human science would be restricted to propositions and axioms which can be corroborated by proof of a mathematically exact and irrebuttable character, its scope would shrink to rather small dimensions.

It is necessary to add that, notwithstanding the foregoing

observations, the truth or falsity of factual propositions often enters decisively into the process of validating normative axioms. A value judgment based on an erroneous finding or analysis of facts will usually be subject to justified challenge and criticism.[24] For example, a law or social norm creating or perpetuating racial discrimination which is based on the assumption of inferiority of the disfavored race opens itself up to legitimate objection if biological science is unable to establish the existence of innate qualitative differences between the races. A policy espousing war on the ground that the inherent pugnacity of human beings makes this outlet for aggressive conduct necessary becomes highly questionable if psychology by convincing evidence refutes the theory that the destructive impulses of men are primary and ineradicable.[25]

There exists, thus, a close connection between normative valuation and truth.[26] A further example of their interdependence was mentioned earlier, when it was pointed out that certain legal institutions, such as the ordeal or trial by battle, which are deemed wholly irrational by us, lose some of the earmarks of unreasonableness with the realization that their adoption was due to firmly held factual beliefs which made them seem adequate vehicles of adjudication to the men of their times.[27] It is therefore an indispensable prerequisite for a fair appraisal of social goals and ideals to probe thoroughly into the elements of fact which underlie the confidence of men in their validity. "The deeper our knowledge of the facts, the greater the chance of increased insight into the nature of values." [28]

The intermixture of factual and normative components in the processes of evaluation has an important bearing on the question as to who should be accorded competence for setting up the tables of political and social values governing the life of a society. Should leadership in goal-setting be delegated, exclusively or primarily, to the prophets and the politicians, as Max Weber seemed to think? The positivist philosophy is strongly inclined to hold that scholars, thinkers, social scientists, and academic persons in general should be barred from entering the domain of normative valuation in their professional (as distinguished from their private) activities. This philosophy assumes that it is the business of academic institutions to transmit scientific truth, and that science is concerned with the discovery and rational analysis of knowledge, while valuations merely express subjective feelings and emotional preferences. This presupposi-

53

tion leads to the consequence that those who are competent to discover and investigate the sociological, psychological, biological, and other empirical data which underlie and condition the various modes of exercising social control, may have no part in drawing the normative conclusions which may often be derived pragmatically from an analysis of the pertinent factual materials. The prophets and political leaders are frequently not as well equipped for this task as the thinkers and scholars who use rational and judicious methods in making proposals for change and reform based on scientific findings. Furthermore, the prophets do not always appear on the scene when their services are needed, and if they do appear, they sometimes turn out to be demagogues who may lead a nation to disaster.

If, as it has been argued here, problems of morality and justice are amenable to rational analysis and judgment, then this sphere of the normative "ought" need not be considered prohibited territory for the thinker, scholar, and academic teacher. He may enter the gates to the realm of values, provided he is aware that he is treading on difficult and often treacherous ground. He must therefore take special precautions to remain dispassionate, detached, and broadminded when he occupies himself with normative questions. He should always predicate his conclusions on a solid basis of facts, weigh his evidence against countervailing evidence, and attempt scrupulously to divorce subjective opinion from what he considers to be objectively demonstrable propositions. He must also realize that whatever conclusions he reaches in this field can be no more than tentative in character, subject at all times to reconsideration and revision in the light of new findings and insights. Dogmatism and intolerance are particularly dangerous in dealing with social ideals and collective goals, since emotional responses are apt to occur with particular strength in this area of human values.

It must also be realized that the results to be obtained from inquiries into normative issues are often apt to be less reliable than those achieved in many branches of the descriptive sciences. The kingdom of values is extremely rich, highly intricate in its structure, and not easily surveyable.[29] The law of causality is less operative, and teleological factors play a more conspicuous role in this realm than in the world of material reality. There are often wide opportunities for choices between alternative solutions, and it is harder to prove that a certain kind of choice should be made than that a material phenomenon is due to certain determinate causes.

The question reduces itself perhaps in the last analysis to the degree of proof and the quality of the evidence which is considered acceptable for the substantiation of a normative conclusion. Since a conclusion of this type is usually verifiable only by rational argument supported by empirical facts, and not by direct observation or sense perception, much could be said in favor of using the term "social philosophy" rather than "social science" in relation to normative inquiries, and to consider the theory of justice, with which this book is concerned, as a part of social philosophy rather than social science.

This does not mean that in this discipline we can permit the thinker to roam around at will and abandon himself freely to his speculations, fancies, and intuitions. As pointed out before, we must insist on the highest degree of rational proof which he is capable of offering in support of the validity of his ideas and theories. But the quantum of proof which we are willing to accept from him may have to be somewhat less exacting than what we would require, in most instances, in the descriptive sciences.

Social philosophy, including the philosophy of morality and law, then stands somewhere in between the world of science and the domain of religion, although in most of its fields of activity it will probably be closer to the former than the latter. In science, we should demand certainty of proof wherever possible, although probability of truth must frequently suffice. In philosophy, the probable validity of a conclusion is perhaps the highest degree of proof capable of attainment, but a strong possibility of correctness buttressed by an impressive array of well-developed reasons will sometimes pass muster before the critical judgment. In religion, faith and belief, bolstered perhaps by arguments showing the possibility of the truth of a religious conviction, are frequently the only vehicles of validation available to us.[30]

According to the view here proposed, there can be no reason for barring the social philosopher from the halls of academic learning and from the community of scholars. The sphere of scholarship and learning embraces everything that rational thinking can reach, grasp, and absorb. When Plato, Aristotle, Kant, and Hegel taught in the academic institutions of their time, numerous students received the greatest inspiration of their lives from listening to their disquisitions.[31] Many radical positivists would today consider such men as purveyors of nonsense, because in elaborating ambitious theories of the cosmos, philosophies of history, and blueprints for social orders they went beyond the realm of that which can be physically observed and tested. But this antipathy to broad-gauged philosophical inquiry merely shows the pedantic aridity and narrow dogmatism of the positivist approach. Nothing can be more important and at least potentially beneficial to mankind than to permit constructive minds to turn their thoughts to the great problems of human values and the building of the good society.

It was the aim of this discussion to indicate and, in a preliminary way, justify the methodological premises on which this treatise is based. The concrete attempts to use this approach in dealing with various problems of justice will be found in the ensuing parts of this volume, and the reader is asked to reserve his judgment on the feasibility and fruitfulness of the method until he has familiarized himself with its application to particular questions.

Sec. 8. *Respect for Life.*

It was pointed out in the preceding section that the will to live, which normally exists in great strength in human beings, constitutes an ontological fact which, in general opinion as well as in reason, supports and validates some of the most fundamental axioms of morality and law. Especially those normative postulates which, with variations in details, have found reflection in all or most social and legal orders, usually owe their recognition in the last analysis to the human propensity to prefer life to death. Life and bodily integrity are among the chief values protected by basic moral commands and the provisions of criminal laws. The law of torts likewise provides sanctions against assaults upon life and invasions of physical health committed by men against other men. A system of law which, on the intragroup level, would permit or reward indiscriminate killing and wanton acts of aggression would certainly be regarded as unjust by the members of the social unit. We are confronted here with an objective element in the concept of justice which derives its well-nigh universal force from certain typical attributes of human nature and may therefore be designated as a postulate

56

of natural law.[1] Any generalized theory of ethical relativity breaks down at this point, because no legal system which regulates the relations of members of an organized society penalizes respect for life and puts a premium on destructiveness.[2]

The moral notions of "good" and "bad" are also, in their most widely accepted meaning, centered on the difference between the constructive, life-affirming instincts and the destructive, life-negating impulses. Shakespeare suggests in his *Othello* that the essence of evil, as symbolized in the figure of Iago, is action based on the belief that life was created but to feed death. Albert Schweitzer has said: "It is good to maintain and encourage life; it is bad to destroy life or to obstruct it." [3] A transvaluation of values which would identify "good" with maximum ruin and harm wrought upon the human race and "evil" with reverence for life and furtherance of life-enhancing aims would be repudiated by the overwhelming majority of men unless, perhaps, the conditions of life on this planet should reach such a degree of deterioration that the life-will, which has hitherto dominated human individual and social activity, should become transformed into its opposite.

It may therefore be stated as a general axiom that a just order of human relations must be founded on respect for life. It cannot be emphasized too strongly, however, that this statement should not be construed to imply that life is an absolute, invariant value, and that preservation of life is required by justice under any and all circumstances. There are special conditions under which the principles of justice may permit or sanction a sacrifice of life for the sake of other values.

The most persistent and difficult problem of justice relating to the sanctity and protection of life is posed by the phenomenon of war. From the beginnings of history to the present day, the killing of large masses of human beings has been viewed as justifiable or even praiseworthy if it occurs as a result of collective fighting between different political units. The members of tribes, city states, and nations have been encouraged or commanded to engage in large-scale slaughter in order to defend their own society against aggression or threats to its existence (actual as well as pretended), or to enlarge its living space, or to avenge an insult to its honor. Whatever the cause of war may be in a particular instance, warfare almost inevitably results in the extermination of human beings who were not responsible for its initiation and perhaps unsympathetic to the purposes for which it is waged. In other words, the conduct of war always entails the killing of innocent persons. The idea of collective responsibility, i.e., responsibility of all members of a political unit for the decisions of their governing authorities regardless of their personal position toward these decisions, dominates the waging of war, although this idea has been largely abandoned in the internal affairs of civilized nations in favor of the notion of individual responsibility. That this state of affairs presents problems of justice of a most incisive character should not be denied by anyone. Because of the magnitude and greatly enlarged dimensions of the problem in the present-day world, it will be treated separately and in some detail in the chapter on "International Justice." [4]

The principle of respect for life also suffers a curtailment or diminution when a political unit recognizes and enforces capital punishment as a sanction of its criminal law. For many centuries, the use of the death penalty, not only as a mode of punishment for the gravest crimes (such as murder and treason) but also for a number of other derelictions widely varying in seriousness, was hardly discussed or questioned. An almost indiscriminate use of capital punishment was made in eighteenth century England.[5] But the human sense of justice tends to rebel against a serious disproportionality between crime and punishment, notwithstanding the possible utilitarian value of radical policies of deterrence. English juries, during the period of excessively wide employment of capital punishment, were reluctant to convict when lesser crimes had been committed.[6] The realization that this form of punishment may defeat its own purposes was one of the factors instrumental in engendering the modern debate on the utility of the death penalty.

The position here advocated is that respect for life is entitled to the strongest possible presumptive recognition as a supreme value of the social order. Only the most weighty arguments in behalf of its disregard in particular situations should be deemed adequate to dispel the force of the presumption in favor of the sanctity of life. If it could be shown, for example, that the death penalty is clearly superior to other criminal sanctions in deterring persons from committing serious crimes, especially homicide, then a legitimate purpose would be served by its application. Particular strength would be imparted to the argument in favor of its use if it can safely be assumed that the execution of one criminal would save many, or at least some, persons from becoming the victims of murderous assaults. It is certainly not irrational to hold under these circumstances that a sacrifice of one life may be resorted to as a means for salvaging several other lives.

The argument tends to lose its persuasive force, however, if it can be demonstrated that measures of less extreme severity would produce the same beneficial result. All reasons in favor of capital punishment which are based on its deterrent effect suffer a diminution of their intrinsic validity if other penalties not involving disregard of the principle of respect for life, such as life imprisonment, afford society an equivalent degree of (limited) protection against the commission of homicides. But here again rebuttals and counter-rebuttals of this train of reasoning are possible. It has been said, for example, that a quick and relatively painless form of execution is a more humanitarian form of punishment than incarceration for lifetime, provided that the life sentence is carried out in earnest. This view can probably be defended, but it is exposed to the replication that, even if this be true, the finality of the death sentence in the face of a possible miscarriage of justice is such a powerful objection to its use that the force of all countervailing considerations is thereby seriously impaired.

An entirely different line of approach is chosen if it is contended that, regardless of the equivalence of the death penalty and other criminal sanctions from the point of view of their potential deterrent effect, the human sense of justice demands the imposition of death in the face of crimes of a particularly heinous character. Such an argument has seemed to carry particular weight in the case of war criminals who, deliberately and chiefly for the gratification of their lust for power, have decreed the extermination of whole peoples or races. Large numbers of reasonable persons felt after World War II that the mass murders of innocent people committed by the Nazi leaders could be atoned for, if at all, only by death. There is also wide support for the view that certain mercenary crimes of a particularly repulsive nature, such as the kidnapping of children for purposes of gain, call for the death penalty, more so perhaps than certain forms of murder motivated by passion or strong emotion.

It is not easy to make a choice on rational grounds between these various conflicting positions.[7] A good deal of statistical material has been gathered in recent times which tends to show that the abolition of the death penalty, and its substitution by life imprisonment, would not result in any appreciable increase in the number of homicides.[8] Many of these statistics are based on the short-term experiences of American states which eliminated capital punishment for some period of time and then reintroduced it. The statistics seem to indicate that the death penalty exercises no appreciable influence on the rate of capital crimes. Whether or not all causative factors that might have a bearing on the figures and fluctuations of homicide death rates were taken into account in these computations cannot easily be determined. A prima facie case of serious doubt as to whether the death penalty is a more effective deterrent than other forms of punishment has, however, been made out.

These statistics do not, on the other hand, dispose of the problem whether the human sense of justice is so constituted that it is not content with lesser forms of punishment where the enormity of the crime is felt to be great. Opinion polls on a worldwide basis would be of interest in casting light on this question, but they would be of value only if those who are polled had previously been acquainted with the manifold ramifications of the problem and the various positions taken on the chief controversial issués. Furthermore, such polls would not be accepted as conclusive by everybody since many experts, especially those of a strongly deterministic persuasion, would claim that the responses to them were predicated on unscientific and irrational attitudes. Others would take the position that there was nothing irrational about the human demand for proportionality between crime and punishment, and that it was a logical concomitant of an enlightened sense of justice.[9]

In the face of the present state of our psychological and sociological knowledge, it does not seem possible to arrive at an objectively valid conclusion regarding the justice or injustice of capital punishment. The last word on the issue has not as yet been said, and we cannot be entirely sure that it will ever be spoken with persuasive force. As long as this is the case, each political unit or nation must solve the problem as best as it can according to its own experiences and prevailing moral convictions.[10] It might be suggested, however, that capital punishment, especially because of its finality and irrevocability, should be employed very sparingly and cautiously in countries where it is retained, and that its imposition, where authorized by statute, should not be mandatory but always within the discretion of the sentencing judge.

Another interesting problem concerning the protection of human life as a supreme value of the legal order is presented in the case of euthanasia. Is it permissible from the point of view of justice to sanction the taking of human life by a physician where this is done to relieve a person afflicted with an incurable and fatal disease from unbearable pain, provided the consent of the patient is obtained?

An affirmative answer to this question can be defended on strong rational grounds, provided that adequate safeguards against an abuse of the right of mercy-killing are set up by the law. The principle of sanctity of life is not really sacrificed in such cases if it is insisted that the illness ended by euthanasia must be fatal beyond a reasonable doubt, and that no other way of relieving insufferable pain except the merciful extinction of life is possible. In the case of animals, such acts of a Good Samaritan have always been viewed as proper and commendable.

The point might, of course, be made that some illnesses believed by the doctor to lead to certain death may take an unexpected turn for the better, and that the discovery of a cure might intervene to render the doctor's prediction invalid. Here a reasonable amount of discretion would have to be left to the medical practitioner if euthanasia is legalized. If the chances of recovery, according to the best knowledge of the medical profession, are minimal to an extreme degree, and if the possibility that a new and effective remedy will become available before the illness ends in death appears altogether remote, the doctor's judgment, if exercised in good faith, would have to be respected and upheld. Consent of the patient should be made mandatory in all cases; and the problem of formalizing such consent in some appropriate way may deserve serious consideration. Furthermore, the administration of euthanasia would have to be reserved to a licensed physician; to permit relatives to put an end to the suffering of an incurably sick person would raise grave dangers of abuse.

It might be replied that the danger of abuse remains substantial even if euthanasia is entrusted exclusively to medical practitioners, and if consent of the patient is required. The doctor may have been persuaded or bribed by a relative intent upon bringing the patient's life to an end for purposes other than relieving agony, and the latter's consent may have been fabricated. This argument does not hold ground because desirable solutions to legal problems should not be obviated on the

61

theory that the chosen solution might open the door to unconscionable practices. Every right can be misused and perverted; almost every statutory permission or prohibition can result in absurd or thoroughly unreasonable applications thereof. If strong policy grounds exist in favor of recognizing certain rights or powers, the conjuring up of possible evil consequences that might ensue from their exercise in exceptional cases should not be considered a legitimate objection. The case of abuse should be dealt with separately and specifically by the law.[11]

Furthermore, the danger of reprehensible acts performed under the guise of mercy-killing also exists under the present-day Anglo-American law which adjudges the deliberate, premature termination of life, even with the consent of a dying patient, to be an act of murder. As Glanville Williams points out, the doctor, without incurring fear of prosecution under the present law, may give pain-relieving drugs whose quantities may have to be increased over a period of time, even though he knows that the cumulative effect of these drugs will accelerate the death of the patient.[12] If this is done, not in good faith, but for corrupt motives, it will not be possible in most instances to prove the unlawful intent, so that the doctor will for all practical purposes be immune from criminal liability. Even where a deliberately administered overdose of drugs was the cause of death, it is usually very difficult to establish this as a fact. The physician's fear of conviction will be reduced further by the knowledge that juries are quite prone to acquit in cases of mercy-killing.[13]

Where religious objections against euthanasia are strong and widespread in a community, legalization of the practice by the legislature will ordinarily not be possible. But if religious scruples are limited to certain sectarian groups, there would appear to be no reason to impose their convictions upon the community at large. As Glanville Williams rightly observes, "the prohibition imposed by a religious belief should not be applied by law to those who do not share the belief, where this is not required for the worldly welfare of society generally." [14]

The position which the legal order should take toward suicide and attempted suicide presents a somewhat more difficult problem. Unlike euthanasia, suicide in most cases involves the taking of life which is not destined to expire in any event. The English common law, contrary to the Roman law and the European continental legal orders, regarded suicide as illegal and the attempt to commit it as punishable, and a number of American jurisdictions have followed suit.[15]

The criminality of suicide has been defended on the basis of a religious conviction that "life, even one's own life, is not man's own possession but a trust from a power beyond himself." [16] On a secular basis, it has been contended that a person committing suicide often shrinks from obligations and responsibilities which he has assumed toward other persons, such as his spouse, children, and other dependents. In order to shorten a life which has become a burden to him, he inflicts harm and suffering upon others. The underlying thought is that man in this life is placed on a post which he must not quit of his own accord. It is also felt by some that attempts to commit suicide constitute acts of cowardice, and that it is sometimes legitimate (as, for example, in war) to punish cowardly acts.

The religious justification of punishment is not dealt with here, since it is believed that religious convictions (which are usually not shared by everybody) should not be made the basis of a law of the state unless they are supported by rational considerations pertaining to the general welfare of society. The assertion that the person committing suicide is evading his duties toward others may in some situations furnish sufficient ground to condemn a particular suicide on moral principles, but it would not seem acceptable as a basis for imposing penal sanctions. Few people commit or attempt suicide lightheartedly or precipitately. It is usually resorted to as an *ultima ratio* when the person in question has reached such a depth of despair and depression that the capacity to recover the normal life-will has been seriously impaired or altogether destroyed. There always exist serious doubts in such circumstances whether a person making an unsuccessful attempt will be able to regain sufficient psychological and moral strength to be helpful to others and adequately discharge his duties toward them in the future. The experience that abortive endeavors to take one's life are often repeated bears eloquent testimony to this fact.

The argument that suicide should be discouraged by legal sanctions because its commission inflicts pain and suffering on relatives and friends is likewise not compelling. The continuation of a life blasted by misfortune and frustration may cause equally strong grief to others, and the possibility can never be discounted that those close to the person abandoning his life were not altogether free from blame.

One of the strongest reasons that can be advanced against the punishment of attempted suicide is the inhumane character of such a measure. At a time when the subject of an unsuccessful suicide attempt needs all his energies and will power to regain his balance, the law visits humiliation and disgrace upon him, so that the likelihood of a further attempt is increased. No rehabilitative effect can possibly be expected from the punishment. The consideration that others will be discouraged from resorting to this extreme step also does not carry much weight. The person who tries to take his life is usually convinced that he will succeed—otherwise he would not make the attempt—and the threat of punishment in case of failure will only make him doubly determined to carry the act through to its intended conclusion. The mere desire to be law-abiding would rarely offset or overbalance the determination to end a life not considered worth living.

Further arguments against the criminality of suicide are that the act is sometimes committed for entirely unselfish and occasionally for heroic reasons,[17] and that there are also situations when society itself was at fault by not affording a person the opportunities that would have made his life meaningful, or by neglecting to show him that minimum degree of consideration for his efforts or accomplishments to which every human being is entitled. Thus, when the ledger of arguments on both sides of the controversy is made up, the reasons (apart from religious beliefs) which speak in favor of a legalization of suicide appear to carry a lop-sided preponderance.[18]

A peculiar instance of voluntary abandonment of life which does not occur very frequently in our day is the refusal, on strictly religious grounds, to consent to medical measures by which such life could have been saved. The problem was dramatically presented in the case of *Application of the President and Directors of Georgetown College*.[19] The Georgetown University Hospital had applied for a judicial writ to authorize administration of a blood transfusion to a patient who refused to consent to it on religious grounds, although the transfusion was necessary to save her life.[20] The writ was granted by the Court of Appeals for the District of Columbia. The Court pointed out that this was not a case of preventing the commission of suicide since the patient did not want to die, but merely felt unable to authorize the transfusion because of religious scruples. The Court declared that the judicial authorization to perform the act preserved for her the life she wanted without the need to sacrifice her religious beliefs. The judge who signed the order emphasized, however, that the compelling reason for his action was the fact that life hung in the balance. "I determined to act on the side of life."

This decision may well be applauded on the basis of the general approach here advocated. Respect for life is presumptively to be considered a supreme principle of the legal order, which may be departed from for the strongest reasons only. Where a person who wishes to live feels prevented from preserving his life because of religious convictions which even the large majority of devout believers would deem far-fetched and even foolish, the law may intervene to save the person from the consequences of carrying out such convictions.

Situations may also arise where the policy of safe-guarding life may come into conflict with the protection of other secular goods such as, for instance, property values. Since the possession of life is the foundation for the enjoyment of all other earthly goods, human beings will in the overwhelming majority of cases assign to life a higher rank than to property. But this value judgment has sometimes been questioned in situations where the property involved consisted of an extremely precious treasure of art whose destruction would inflict an irreparable loss on mankind. Suppose, for example, that a burning house contains a small child as well as Raphael's Sistine Madonna, and only one of these two can be rescued. Some commentators on the question have taken the position that in that event preference should be given to the Madonna. The same question was raised in connection with the shelling and obliteration of the sixth-century monastery on Mount Cassino in Italy, a great monument of civilization, by the American Army during World War II, an action which was justified by the military commander on the ground that it was necessary to save the lives of American soldiers.[21] Even if one assigns a very high priority in the scale of values to the trans-personal objects of culture, especially those possessing an unusual degree of excellence, strong reasons exist for maintaining that the desire to prevent the loss of one or some of them (and their number is quite large) does not justify the sacrifice of even one single human life. No extended discussion of the problem is offered here since it is rarely presented in reality in a setting in which a crucial decision becomes inevitable.[22]

The foregoing disquisition has taken as its point of departure the thesis that the human will to live, although it is a primary and elementary fact which everywhere underlies and guides the normative control of human affairs, is not an absolute good requiring unconditional protection under all circumstances. History supplies us with a great deal of empirical evidence to the effect that life is not necessarily regarded by men as the *summum bonum*. The story of mankind is replete with instances where men have deliberately given up their lives, not only in order to save the lives of others, especially loved ones, but also for the sake of political, religious, or ethical causes in which they strongly believed. The history of heroism and martyrdom tellingly confirms the truth that life-abnegation may become a strong force among men whose life-will as such is unimpaired, but who consider it necessary to sacrifice themselves in order to further values which they hold higher than the impulse of self-preservation. But it should be emphasized that self-abnegation in such cases is usually motivated by the desire to help mankind advance to new and higher forms of individual or collective life. Such acts therefore do not, in the last analysis, contradict the basic postulate of ethics and justice that existence, as a general rule, is to be preferred to nonexistence.[23]

Sec. 9. The Building of Civilizations.

The conclusions thus far obtained in this chapter may be reduced to the propositions that the large majority of men prefer life to non-life, that even acts of life-abnegation were frequently in history designed to serve the broader purposes of human collective life, and that a rational ethic can and should accept life-affirmation as a fundamental axiom underlying normative social control through morality and law. In advocating this position it is not suggested, however, that the *quality* of life to be lived by human beings is an irrelevant factor in developing an axiological basis for laws and social arrangements. In connection with the problems of euthanasia and suicide the view was taken in the preceding section that not every individual life is worth living and therefore in need of legal protection against voluntary abandonment under all conceivable circumstances. On a social level, likewise, the recognition of life-affirmation as a supreme principle of normative regulation becomes meaningful only if the quality of life in society is not such that it is experienced by the members of a social group as a dreadful burden to be mercifully relieved by death. Where unmitigated misery and degradation prevail without hope of alleviation, it becomes difficult if not impossible to maintain and justify a philosophy of life-affirmance. The emergence in earlier periods of history of pessimistic, other-worldly religions, characterized by an attempt to subdue the life-will, may have had its origin primarily in the existence of social conditions which were felt to be wretched and hopeless by large numbers of human beings.

If this is true, there is much reason for adopting the Aristotelian position that the aim of social organization is not life as such, but "the good life." [1] The mere maintenance of life on a vegetative level, enabling men to survive barely on an uncertain day-by-day basis but not affording them even a minimum of physical and social well-being, means the reduction of life below the animal level and is repugnant to man's nature and potentialities. From the earliest times, therefore, men have striven to overcome conditions in which nothing but plain survival was secured to them, and to gain sufficient control over nature and their environment to be able to build a worthwhile life. One of the most illuminating testimonials to man's desire to accomplish more than the satisfaction of the most elementary physical needs is the anthropological discovery that even under the most primitive conditions men have produced some forms of art to embellish their lives. It is as natural for men collectively to use their powers and capabilities in a joint effort to expand the horizons of human existence as it is for man individually to develop his gifts in order to grow and enhance his life. Here lies the true road to individual and collective happiness.

When men are attempting to gain mastery over nature, to improve living conditions and human relations, and to foster the life of the mind, they are said to be engaged in the task of civilization-building. This is the most significant activity of the human race, and individuals as well as collectivities have almost universally been judged by the contributions they have made to this great enterprise.[2] The reason why the building of civilizations is the natural destiny of men and has occupied their best energies is that the secret of life lies in expansion, in enlargement and diversification of the various forms in which human dynamic power can express itself. It has been noted that the faces of men condemned to static condition and inactivity are often sad, sullen, and lifeless. We may touch here the hidden springs not only of human, but also of animal life. Animals, too, appear to be happiest when they can exercise their energies in a manner most congenial to their nature.

What do we mean by the term "civilization"? A thorough analysis of the concept was made by Albert Schweitzer. He defined it as "progress, material and spiritual progress, on the part of individuals as well as of the masses." [3] According to him, civilization is twofold in its nature: it realizes itself "in the supremacy of reason, first, over the forces of nature and, secondly, over the dispositions of men." [4] Thus, civilization in his view has a material and an ethical side. On its material side, it is struggle against the harshness of nature for the purpose of improving the outer conditions of human existence. Men seek to fight hunger by increasing the food supply and regulating its distribution, to overcome the discomforts created by climate and weather by building suitable shelters, to gain access to natural resources and the beauties of nature by devising means of transportation and communication. Progress in this area is judged by the extent to which the forces of nature have been harnessed and utilized, men's basic physiological needs have been satisfied, and the means of production have been developed and perfected.

But Schweitzer rightly emphasizes that material progress is not sufficient to guarantee the well-being of the human race. If men are able to control the forces of nature but unable to control their own brutal and destructive impulses, the conditions for the flourishing of civilization have not been secured. The struggle against nature may have been won, but the struggle of men against men will continue and perhaps become even more relentless and devastating than under primitive conditions. To attain the good life in society, material progress must therefore be matched by ethical advancement. Men must learn to tame their aggressive instincts, to refrain from harming each other, to compose their differences by rational methods, and to afford each other mutual help in the pursuit of their common aims. [5]

Schweitzer argues that the ethical component of cultural growth is even more important than the material one. These are his words:

> The supremacy which we secure by reason over external nature represents not unqualified progress, but a

progress which brings with its advantages also disadvantages which may work in the direction of barbarism. The reason why the economic circumstances of our time endanger our civilization is to be sought for partly in the fact that we have pressed into our service natural forces which can be embodied in machines. But with that there must be such a supremacy of reason over the dispositions of men that they, and the nations which they form, will not use against one another the power which the control of these forces gives them, and thus plunge one another into a struggle for existence which is far more terrible than between men in a state of nature. . . . The true sense for reality is that insight which tells us that only through ethical ideas about things can we arrive at a normal relation to reality.[6]

In other words, technical advance creates instrumentalities which men may use in the service of mass destruction. Only ethical progress can insure the survival of the human race and the good life.

To the material and ethical sides of civilization must be added a third one, which may be called the cultural side. A high civilization is unthinkable without the unfolding of productive activities in fields such as philosophy, literature, architecture, art, and music. In these cultural pursuits, true immortality can be achieved by individuals as well as collectivities. The works of great thinkers, poets, novelists, composers, painters, and sculptors have been continuous sources of deep enjoyment for millions of human beings throughout the world. The same is true for the great collective monuments of mankind which embody the cooperative efforts of many productive minds and hands, such as the temples of antiquity, the cathedrals of the Middle Ages, and those cities and towns which the judgment of mankind has appraised as beautiful. Without the works of culture and the achievements of the human spirit, human life would be impoverished and monotonous.[7]

The concept of civilization provides a unifying focus for the determination of the chief goals of individual and social effort. The perfection both of the individual and of society lie in the direction which leads to the building and improvement of human civilized life.[8] No individual can attain his full stature and realize his potentialities without being of some service to his fellowmen in connection with the performance of this common task.[9] A healthy human being tries to enhance his existence by reaching out beyond the confines of his own self. A young man who seeks to perfect himself by one-sidedly cultivating his ego, making it the sole object of his concern, and ignoring the world around him will almost certainly experience frustration and failure. Even if his ideal is a purely religious one of finding a proper relation to his God, he will hardly regard his chosen life task as accomplished unless, by his mode of living or through teaching, he will have set an example to others.

"Man's whole life is a struggle to gain true existence, an effort to achieve substantiality so that he may not have lived in vain and vanish like a shadow." [10] A man who at the close of his life will come to the conclusion that he has made no use of his capabilities and no effort, in a broad or narrow circle, to be helpful to human beings around him or to promote a cause deemed meritorious by him, will depart with the bitter feeling that he has wasted his existence. This enlarged ideal of self-fulfillment was given beautiful expression by Albert Schweitzer:

> The essence of the will-to-live is its determination to actualize itself to the fullest extent. It carries within itself the tendency to attain the highest possible perfection. In the flowering tree, in the wondrous shapes of the jellyfish, in the blade of grass, in the crystal: everywhere it strives to reach the perfection which is in it as a potentiality. In everything that exists, there is at work an imaginative force determined by ideals. In us beings who can move about freely and are capable of deliberate, purposive activity, the urge for perfection is given in such a way that we aim at raising to the highest material and spiritual value our own persons and every existing thing which is open to our influence.[11]

The contributions which an individual, depending on his abilities and talents, can make for the promotion of the common good are of a widely varying character. Some of them will be regarded as relatively small and their effects as temporary, others as major achievements of lasting worth. A broadminded view of human affairs must acknowledge, however, that even menial work of the lowliest character can be an indispensable building stone in the creation of social orders and civilizations, and that it is unfitting for a man to look down with aristocratic disdain on the activities of a common workingman. Civilization is a pyramid which must rest on a broad foundation. The performance of many small-scale tasks is necessary to fulfill the needs of day-to-day living. Without the routine work of farmhands, unskilled laborers, sales clerks, and others performing more or less mechanical functions, the higher and more refined pursuits would hang in midair. Man has to be fed, clothed, and housed before he can turn to the lofty expanses of the spirit. A tremendous technical apparatus, requiring the cooperation of many human beings performing the most varied chores, is necessary to sustain a highly developed civilization.

It is therefore essential to foster in all human beings the conviction of the dignity and value of their work, whatever it may consist of, as long as it contributes in a constructive way to the accomplishments of the aims of human social organization. The mental sanity of a human being is dependent upon his feeling that what he is doing is worthwhile and meaningful.

Thus far we have spoken about the duty of participation in social processes which the individual owes to society for the promotion of the chief goal of human effort, the building of civilizations. There is a reverse duty on the part of society to create the conditions under which the individual can develop his potentialities and practice his aptitudes, so that he can be of service to his country or humanity in general. There must be social institutions which enable men to learn, acquire skills, and prepare themselves for their future vocations, and there must be opportunities for work and self-actualization. No individual or small group is, under the conditions of our time, able to set up the intricate network of services, facilities, and institutions necessary to render civilized life in an overpopulated world possible. A common effort of large-scale dimensions is indispensable for the creation of conditions under which civilization can thrive. Thus the individual is dependent upon society for the attainment of his aims, while society needs the creative contributions of individuals for its proper functioning. The individual can complete his destiny only if he does not lose sight of the common interest and the concerns of his fellowmen, whereas society can perfect itself only if it is sensitive to the existential needs and the personal aspirations of the individuals composing it.

But while the interests of the individual and the collective whole coincide as far as the general goals of civilized life are

71

concerned, it would be a grievous mistake to assume that the individual can have no interests contrary to those of his society. Such an assumption has sometimes been made in totalitarian states and its consequences are, in the long run, likely to be disastrous. Wisdom and reason is not always to be found on the side of society. An individual with unusual gifts of insight and foresight may, in his thinking and doing, be several steps ahead of the collective knowledge and ethics of his age. Dissenters from socially approved standards, although they may have been ostracized because of their non-conformist beliefs, will sometimes be admired by later generations as trailblazers of a new and higher form of social organization or morality. As Samuel Hart has said: "To accept customary moral standards as final is to forsake ethical reflection. The most dogmatic supporter of customary morality must admit that customs and mores may become obsolete." [12] The ethical or religious convictions of a great individual, although originally in conflict with those of his society, may ultimately emerge victorious and reshape the social and moral fabric of society with beneficial effects. Thus an individual may sometimes perform a higher service to society by becoming a vigorous critic of its institutions than by giving support to the collective objectives of his nation or time.

At this point it appears appropriate to mention and discuss an influential theory which views the concept of civilization in a less affirmative and optimistic light than was done in the preceding argument. Sigmund Freud, in the later years of his life, advanced the thesis that the development of civilization, with its stress on the higher mental activities of men, brings in its train a substantial repression and curbing of powerful instinctual urges, especially those of a sexual character. These cultural privations, according to Freud, weaken the vital energies of men and, in the long run, tend to produce an antagonism of men and—especially—of women against the supposed blessings of civilization.[13]

Furthermore, Freud said, civilization necessitates the suppression of the aggressive, destructive impulses which in his opinion constitute primary and irrepressible components of human nature. "Men clearly do not find it easy," he stated, "to do without satisfaction of this tendency to aggression that is in them; when deprived of satisfaction of it they are ill at ease." [14] By imposing many restraints on sexuality and aggressiveness, civilization makes it hard for men to adjust to it and feel happy in it. Primitive man was better off in this respect, for he knew no such curbs on his instincts.[15]

Perhaps the best answers to this deeply pessimistic view of civilization were presented by Max Scheler and Erich Fromm. Scheler attacked the position of Freud according to which the higher, cultural activities of men were not an expression of original, natural human powers but merely deflected manifestations of repressed libido. Civilization, he said, is not a huge apparatus for the suppression of "normal" instincts and their conversion into unnatural, sublimated forms of energy. From the dawn of history, unspoiled and healthy men endowed with vigorous instincts have undertaken the work of civilization-building and have willingly assumed restrictions on the unfettered reign of impulse necessitated by it. This proved to him that the activities of the human spirit were just as "natural" to men as the gratification of their physical needs. "In our view, all levels of mental life, from sensual apprehension up to the highest acts of the spirit, are derived from an independent fund of mental energy, which is in no way borrowed from the instinctive energy of libido." [16]

According to Freud, Scheler said, the suppression or inhibition of libidinous urges forms the chief cause of neurotic disturbances. Must we then conclude that civilization is nothing but a huge collective neurosis resulting in human unhappiness and frustration? Or if repression, as Freud also seemed to assume, may lead to sublimation rather than neurosis, under what circumstances is the one or the other result obtained? Freud's work, said Scheler, throws no light on this question.[17]

Fromm likewise criticized the one-sided assumption of Freud that sexual libido was the basic energy lying at the root of all human action. "Powerful as the sexual drive and all its derivations are, they are by no means the most powerful forces within man and their frustration is not the cause of mental disturbance. The most powerful forces motivating man's behavior stem from the condition of his existence, the 'human situation.' " [18] Fromm could find no evidence supporting Freud's belief that civilized man was bound to be neurotic or unhappy because of limitations on his sexual freedom. In support of his position it might be mentioned that in our day many of the inhibitions of the sexual drive which characterized the Victorian age and the Vienna in which Freud lived have been substantially reduced, and man's sexual freedom has become larger. But the incidence of neurosis and mental illness has increased rather than diminished in the course of this development.

Fromm also challenged Freud's theory of a primary, biologically rooted impulse of destruction. This is his answer to Freud:

> Destructiveness is a secondary potentiality, rooted in the very existence of man, and having the same intensity and power as any passion can have. But—and this is the essential point of my argument—it is only the *alternative* to creativeness. Creation and destruction, love and hate, are not two instincts which exist independently. They are both answers to the same need for transcendence, and the will to destroy must rise when the will to create cannot be satisfied.[19]

He showed that the rate of destructiveness, as manifested in certain criminal or pathological acts, fluctuates enormously in different countries and under different social conditions, while Freud assumed a constancy of the destructive impulse.[20]

While the criticism of Scheler and Fromm appears to be well-taken and essentially convincing, it can probably not be denied that the psychological and mental refinement which is the concomitant of an evolving civilization, as well as the softness and comfort accompanying the growth of civilized living, may cause some threat to man's vitality and robust healthfulness. It is well known, for example, that individuals of the greatest intellectual genius, or their immediate descendants, often produce offspring with weakened physiological or mental powers. The spirit, if cultivated one-sidedly at the expense of the vital forces, gnaws at life and may cause an erosion of biological vigor.[21]

Thus Freud was probably correct in pointing out that nations attaining great heights of cultural development and refinement have to pay a price for these accomplishments. It would seem, however, that the adverse consequences are limited to the classes which are the carriers and chief exponents of high cultural achievement. Furthermore, there is reason to believe that the danger can be mitigated by a frank recognition of the fact that exclusive emphasis on intellectual effort may jeopardize the physiological health of a civilized society, and that body and spirit require equal attention and care. There are many ways in which society and the individuals composing it can control the conditions under which sound minds can dwell in healthy bodies. To the extent that vital decline is an unavoidable consequence of a highly developed civilization, we should be willing to pay the price gladly. After going uphill, we usually have to make a descent, and we would not think of stopping the growth of individual life because of our knowledge that after reaching its peak it was bound to turn downward. If the collective life is subject to similar laws of growth and decay, we have to accept these laws if we find ourselves unable to change them.

If the creation of a rich and flourishing civilization is the chief goal of human social life, the institutions and instrumentalities of social organization must be placed in the service of this goal. This includes the institution of law, which is the chief vehicle by which the postulates of justice are to be realized. The law cannot, of course, promote the aims of civilized life in all of its multifarious forms of expression. It cannot be directly instrumental in helping men to improve technology, formulate the ethical principles governing social relations, and produce great works of art and music. It also cannot teach individuals how to improve and perfect their personalities and become useful members of society. But the institution of law, if guided by sound principles of justice, can secure the basic conditions of human coexistence which are indispensable or beneficial to the growth and maintenance of civilized life. Some of the requisites which seem to be particularly important in achieving the objectives of social control through law will be discussed in the remaining sections of this chapter.

Sec. 10. The Concern for Equality.

If normative legal philosophy recognizes the building of civilizations, which has been the chief constructive enterprise of the human race, as the supreme goal of social effort, the question arises as to what general policies of social organization the legal order must promote in order to assist in the accomplishment of this goal. What are the value patterns that have to be established and fostered in order to release and activate the energies of men in the service of material and cultural progress? How much freedom should be granted to men, what degree of equality and security is salutary for them, what kind of a political and

75

economic order is most conducive to the achievement of the dominant objective? Is it possible to give any general valid answers to these questions, or must the answer to them depend on contingent factors and the particular conditions and characteristics of a given society at a particular period of its development?

One of the most crucial and controversial problems that has arisen in the minds of those who believe in material, ethical, and cultural progress as the foremost goals of human social endeavor is the determination of the role which human equality should play in the pursuit of this aim. Some thinkers have voiced the opinion that the development of a high civilization is possible only in a non-egalitarian, aristocratic form of society, and that the promotion of social equality will necessarily result in a reign of mediocrity destructive of cultural values. This doctrine was preached in an extreme form by Friedrich Nietzsche and, since his ideas have strongly influenced the minds of many men in Europe and America, they shall be presented here as the prototype of an anti-egalitarian philosophy of civilization. The presentation of his views is rendered difficult by the fact that Nietzsche offered his philosophy in the form of disjointed aphorisms rather than in systematic fashion, and that many discrepancies and inconsistencies can be found in his statements. Nevertheless, the final form which his philosophy assumed in the period of "transvaluation of values" (which preceded his mental breakdown) shows a fairly coherent pattern at least as to the most essential aspects of his thinking.

Nietzsche followed the traditions of German idealism in assigning an extremely high priority to the pursuits of the human spirit; the production of creative geniuses was to him the chief task of mankind. He especially admired Greek civilization and the culture of the Renaissance for their rich harvest of superior artistic achievements. As a decided amoralist, however, he was much more concerned with the aesthetic manifestations of culture—such as musical compositions, works of architecture, literary productions—, and with psychological and philosophical criticisms of the prevailing moral and social value system, than with the ethical side of civilization which was later emphasized by Schweitzer.[1] Nietzsche was convinced that the prevalence of ethical valuations was always a sign of a low culture.[2] He was thoroughly opposed to the Judeo-Christian system of morality which he wished to see replaced by a set of value patterns which in many respects reversed the traditional notions of good and evil held high in our civilization and in most others.

Nietzsche also thought that a great civilization could thrive only under conditions which were somewhat disorderly from a political point of view. "Culture and the state," he said, "are antagonists: A culture-state is merely a modern idea." [3] He believed that large wilderness areas in political life, such as were characteristic for the Renaissance period, were beneficial to cultural growth because they permitted great and independent personalities to achieve their creative purposes without too much interference from the organs of government. Modern democracy, inspired by liberal or social welfare ideals and dedicated to the achievement of the greatest happiness of the greatest number, he considered "the historical form of the decay of the State." [4] The purpose of the state was to enable the higher individuals to fulfill their destiny, not to permit the majority to lead happy and contented lives.[5]

Nietzsche was vehemently antagonistic to the idea of political and social equality, which is generally considered a desirable objective in modern democratic states. "The doctrine of equality! But there is no more deadly poison than this; for it *seems* to proceed from the very lips of justice, whereas it draws the curtain down on all justice." [6] The concept that "all men are equal before God" does an extraordinary amount of harm, he contended, and no greater lie could be uttered than the assertion that men are entitled to equality of treatment.[7] He went so far as to proclaim that it was necessary for the higher individuals to declare war upon the masses,[8] and that in treating the majority of men, those in power may legitimately resort to falsehood and injustice.[9] He also expressed the view that men "ought to learn anew about cruelty. . . . Almost everything that we call 'higher culture' is based upon the spiritualizing and intensifying of *cruelty*." [10]

Nietzsche was convinced that every true culture must necessarily rest upon slavery and exploitation. Exploitation, he said, "does not belong to a depraved, or imperfect and primitive society; it belongs to the *nature* of the living being as a primary organic function." [11] Greek civilization was great and productive because it was fed and sustained by large armies of slaves. "Slavery and the division of labor: the higher type alone possible through the *subjection* of the lower to a function." [12] Even among the free citizens, their division into castes possessing an unequal legal status was to Nietzsche an indispensable condition for a healthy ordering of society.[13] Nietzsche thus agreed with Plato that political organization must rest upon a class basis; but while Plato believed that the rulers of the state should promote a just order and the good of all, Nietzsche considered the aim of the state exhausted in the creation of proper conditions for the growth of a culture-producing elite.[14]

Strong echoes of Nietzsche's elitist philosophy are found in Adolf Hitler's book "Mein Kampf," which formed the political bible of the German Nazi movement. In even stronger terms than Nietzsche (whom he admired though he sometimes misunderstood him), Hitler denounced democracy as a "universal plague." [15] Nature is aristocratic in structure, and every outstanding deed in this world has been a protest of genius against the inertia of the masses.[16] He preached a doctrine of power for the sake of power, and the suppression or elimination of the weak by the strong, within each nation as well as in the struggle between nations.[17] The refinements of Nietzsche's philosophy of culture were foreign to his thought, but there can be no doubt that his disdain of the masses and glorification of ruthlessness finds support in the anti-Christian immoralism of the late Nietzsche, even though the latter probably would have repudiated the particular Hitlerian form of the rule of the "blonde beast." [18]

Since equality was rejected absolutely and uncompromisingly as a political organizing principle by a philosopher as influential as Nietzsche, and by some political leaders inspired by his ideas,[19] the question must be discussed whether it is true that human equality serves no valuable purpose in the building of a healthy social order. If a high state of civilization can be attained only by sacrificing human equality and brotherhood, if the advanced forms of cultural life depend on the submission of the weak to the domination of the strong, if democratic types of social organization lead to the disintegration of civilized endeavor,—then many people will be seriously in doubt whether it is morally permissible to destroy the dignity and happiness of large masses of human beings for the sake of a culturally abundant life. They might conclude that it would be preferable to abandon the goal of a high civilization in order to allow for a decent treatment of human beings under democratic and humanitarian ideals.

If the above-described alternative of decision were a genuine one, it would pose a frightful dilemma to social philosophers and statesmen. It is submitted, however, that the predicament portrayed by Nietzsche is merely an imaginary one, and that we have no reason to believe that humanitarianism and civilization are mutually exclusive sets of values. Nietzsche has not furnished us with any convincing proof to the effect that slavery and exploitation are indispensable conditions of a high cultural life. It is true that Greek society during the period of the most profuse burgeoning of the Hellenic spirit had its economic basis in slavery, a system of production which tends to exploit human labor power to the utmost. It can also be granted to Nietzsche that there might have existed a causal relation between the practice of slavery and the amazing flowering of culture in ancient Greece, because the performance by slaves of the tremendous amount of heavy manual work required to operate a pre-industrial economy released the energies of the free citizens for the higher cultural tasks. The inference that might be drawn from the Greek experience—although it is not an absolutely compelling inference—is that in lowly developed systems of production human machines are necessary to secure the material bases of social life, and that the use of such human machines enables the upper classes to devote themselves to the realm of the spirit.[20] This assumption, if it is correct, does not, however, force us to conclude that civilization can under no circumstances and under no conceivable system of economic organization flourish in the absence of exploitation of labor.

Compared with the ancient system of slavery, the subsequent history of Europe shows a decrease in the oppressive exploitation of labor. It would be absurd to contend, however, that this development was accompanied by a corresponding erosion of cultural vitality. The Middle Ages produced an imposing civilization, although slavery was eliminated in favor of a system of serfdom which recognized the personality of the serf and gave him certain enforceable rights against his lord. The European bloom of civilization in the eighteenth and nineteenth centuries surpassed Greek culture in richness and diversity, but at that time the freedom and mobility of labor had been recognized in most countries of Europe. Although the laborer was often exploited by having to work long hours at low wages, the system was a far cry from the chattel slavery of antiquity in which the power of the master over the slave was well-nigh unlimited.

Many advances in the elimination or reduction of unfair or

oppressive labor practices were made in more recent times. Nietzsche would have us believe that a social order in which every worker and employee was paid a fair wage for his work and protected by other measures of social welfare policy, would be unable to produce great works of science, literature, art, and music. He owes us the evidence for this contention. The fact that there has been a certain cultural lag in the last few decades as compared with the productivity of the past two centuries merely confirms the historical experience that the development of culture is subject to upward and downward trends. There are no data tending to show that this lag has any causal connection with the benevolent social and economic policies pursued by the advanced countries today.

A rational theory of justice cannot discern any convincing reasons for maintaining a division of mankind into masters and slaves, or exploiters and exploitees. Nietzsche believed that such a division was dictated by inexorable laws of nature whose non-observance would lead to social disintegration. He was also convinced that it was natural and necessary to subject both groups to different kinds of morality. To the masters practically everything was allowed,[21] while the main duty of the herd was submission and obedience. The answer must be that it is utterly irrational to permit a small number of self-appointed "masters" to claim rights for themselves which they are determined to deny to the large majority of men.[22] The Nietzschean masters assert that they have the right to rule and oppress, but that the bulk of mankind only has the duty to submit to rule and oppression. This is diametrically opposed to the Golden Rule, which we have found to constitute a supreme principle of rational morality.[23] Inasmuch as there exist no discernible physical signs or workable psychological tests by which the "master" type can be segregated from the "slave" type, the assignment to one or the other group will be left to the more or less arbitrary fiat of the dominant classes. Since the decision involves subjection to different moralities and ways of life, it would have to be made in an early period of a person's life. At that time, the potentialities of a person are more or less unknown; it is most unlikely that government officials could devise practicable ways or means for detecting whether someone was born a master or a helot, and most people do not fit either description.

Since Nietzsche does not advocate a hereditary aristocracy but an aristocracy of capacity for the exercise of power, the process of selection into a favored or disfavored class becomes unavoidable under his system. It can easily be seen that the system involves insuperable difficulties of administration, and that it would also carry with it an abundance of favoritism and faulty exercise of judgment. It is also obvious that the system is tainted with an intrinsic immorality. What type of convincing argument can be contrived to prove that a few people have a right to unfettered freedom and happiness, while the majority of men have no such rights? Men, by their nature, have a strong desire not to be dominated arbitrarily by others, and this natural urge has furnished one of the main springs for the creation of legal systems curbing the rights of the powerful. Nietzsche's thesis would be tenable only if there existed no other basis for organizing society effectively than total domination by a few and extreme inegalitarianism. Modern history has shown that civilized social orders can be built in which all are given a chance to lead worthwhile and satisfying lives without being subject to the arbitrary power of autocratic rulers.

Apart from the irrationality and immorality of Nietzsche's superaristocratic scheme, it would also be utterly impossible to impose such an order upon the peoples of the twentieth-century world. A stirring for freedom and equality is noticeable in large areas of the world. The underprivileged nations wish to rise to the level of the more fortunate ones. The underprivileged groups within each nation demand a larger share of the total national product and a broadening of opportunities. This emancipatory struggle of nations, races, and classes could not be reversed or stopped by a reimposition of ancient forms of exploitation and class domination. Such attempts would produce uprisings, revolutions, and wars of liberation, and only an insane mind could welcome such a prospect in an atomic age. The fate of the Third Reich, planned for one-thousand years, reaching a life span of twelve, and ending in chaos and dismemberment, should serve as a warning to those for whom the anti-humanitarian ideas of Nietzsche might carry any degree of persuasiveness.

In contrast to Nietzsche another German philosopher, Immanuel Kant, insisted that an individual must never treat other individuals merely as means for the attainment of his aims, but always at the same time as ends in themselves.[24] This postulate is not an obstacle to cultural growth, as Nietzsche believed, but a necessary concomitant of an advancing civilization. The postulate is grounded in the psychological structure of human beings, who experience themselves as persons pursuing their own aims rather than things serving the purposes of others. Each human being, by his natural inclination, seeks respect for his independent personality, his feelings and claims from others; he cannot deny such respect to his fellowmen without defeating his own demands on them. It might be remarked in this connection that the slaveholders of antiquity were often intelligent and enlightened enough to treat their slaves as human beings and thus to ensure their loyalty and cooperation.[25] In certain periods of Roman history when mistreatment of slaves on the large agricultural estates became widespread, slave uprisings and slave wars ensued which disrupted the economic life and the political order.[26]

The treatment of human beings as ends rather than means is an important ingredient of the equality postulate. If the Kantian principle is accepted and carried out, human beings are treated equally at least to the extent that their basic dignity as persons capable of self-determination is recognized.[27] Such a policy does not embody an arbitrary preference but takes into account the nature of normal human beings who desire to mold their own lives rather than function as the inert tools of others.

But the requirement of equality postulated by justice goes far beyond the repudiation of chattel slavery and ruthless exploitation of labor. It extends to another prerequisite for the achievement of happiness, namely, that opportunities for the actualization of their energies and capacities be afforded to men. This is a corollary of the notion that mankind can find its self-fulfillment only in the building of civilizations, an endeavor which releases and utilizes all the latent potentialities of the human race. Hence "institutions which guarantee to men the opportunity of becoming the best of which they are capable are the supreme political good." [28]

It is not sufficient, of course, to grant the right of self-actualization in merely formal, abstract terms. A society which has torn down the barriers of caste and class but which does not open up sufficient avenues for the activation of human productive power and talent, although it would be in a position to do so, is derelict in its duties toward its members. A social order in which many important tasks remain unfulfilled but where a substantial volume of human energy lies fallow because of failure to create working opportunities for all offers a depressing sight. If private effort is unable to provide the widest chances for productive activities, the public power must step in to fill the gap. Human nature and the true calling of human beings are seriously frustrated if men capable of doing useful work are condemned to inactivity. If there are some persons who enjoy this condition, they are the exception rather than the rule; it is safe to state that a prolonged period of unemployment, even if accompanied by compensation payments, will have a deeply depressing and demoralizing effect on the large majority of men. It might be added that the duty of society to secure, by private, public, or combined effort, the broadest possible opportunities for all of its members applies to the material as well as cultural sectors of civilization.

Although men should have sufficient equality to enable everybody to reach the place for which he is best fitted, such equality should not make impossible a certain natural hierarchy of ability and leadership. As Tawney observes, "the fact that, quite apart from differences of environment and opportunity, individuals differ widely in their natural endowments, and in their capacity to develop them by education, is not open to question." [29] Because of these profound differences of individuals in capacity and character, those who excel in intellectual and moral qualities should not be prevented from exercising a certain leadership over others who are less favorably endowed. Thus, while there should not be any preestablished stratification of men into classes or castes, certain relations of authority will develop in practically all societies by natural processes which have their roots in the inequality of personal ability.

The equality principle thus conveys no right to us to assert that everybody is as good as everybody else. Its essential meaning in relation to the equalizing of opportunity is that those in power, because they are not omniscient, cannot be trusted with the task of assigning people to their proper place in society,[30] and that the primary obligation to find a suitable position in the social order devolves upon each individual personally. Society will, of course, exercise certain controls (through examination requirements, standards of qualification, etc.) over vocational choice to insure that persons unfit for certain types of work will not cause harm to society.

Two types of equality have thus far been found to be demanded by the postulates of justice. The first was the equal right of all to be treated as persons rather than things, the second was the granting of equal opportunities to all to reach the position in society commensurate with their abilities. A truly just order should also realize a third kind of equality, which may be called the equality of condition on the lower level. As a general rule, human beings are entitled to the minimum income necessary to lead an existence worthy of a human being. The wages they receive should be sufficient to give adequate sustenance to them and their families, the housing available to them should meet some basic standards of size, safety, and sanitation, the clothing they are able to afford should be suitable in protecting them against the vicissitudes of climate. They are also entitled to the amount of recreation necessary to maintain health and to an elementary education. This rock bottom level of human existence can be rationally justified by the consideration that all men are equal with respect to their most essential needs, and that the most elementary commands of humanitarianism require a standard of living above the absolute minimum of subsistence.[31] As Galbraith points out, "to secure to each family a minimum standard, as a normal function of the society, would help insure that the misfortunes of parents, deserved or otherwise, were not visited on their children. It would help insure that poverty was not self-perpetuating." [32]

Justice further requires the equal treatment of equal persons in identical or essentially similar circumstances.[33] This axiom has its ontological roots in the universal experience that human beings (including children) react strongly against discriminations which they feel to be arbitrary and capricious. People in equal circumstances resent being treated differently "unless a reasonable ground can be given for so treating them." [34] The recognition of this ineradicable trait of human beings, which is a concomitant of the rational side of their nature, is one of the central constituents of the notion of justice. If a legal classification or differentiation does not rest upon a reasonable basis but is purely arbitrary, a cardinal command of justice is infringed.

It cannot be denied, however, that the yardsticks governing the equal and unequal treatment of persons and groups have greatly fluctuated in different epochs of history and in different nations. Women have often been excluded from participation in higher education and from the exercise of political rights on the ground that their physical and mental characteristics made them essentially unequal from men. Certain races have been subjected to discriminatory treatment on the theory that they were biologically and intellectually inferior to the dominant race. Voting rights have frequently been reserved to those possessing a certain amount of property. Eligibility for high political office has sometimes been conditional on membership in a certain church. Do these examples prove that the concept of equality is wholly relative to the political and social ideas of a certain time and place, and that no generally valid statements can be made regarding the justice or injustice of legally sanctioned inequalities? [35]

It contributes much to the clarification of this question if one realizes that views concerning essential equality and inequality depend, like so many other problems of justice,[36] on the validity of certain factual assumptions underlying the treatment of persons and groups by the law. If women are excluded from participation in higher education and public life because it is firmly believed that they are not the intellectual peers of men and unable, for example, to approach scientific, political, and legal problems in a rational and detached manner, the injustice of the discrimination becomes apparent when the factual premises allegedly supporting the unequal treatment are proved to be without foundation. We know today that women are capable of outstanding attainments in the spheres of medicine, science, education, law, government, and others. For this reason legal disabilities based on the factor of sex have gradually been removed in the legal systems of the advanced countries of the world. Discriminations based on the alleged inferiority of certain races likewise stand and fall with the truth or untruth of the factual presuppositions.[37]

We are dealing here with a domain of the law in which the link between the "is" and the "ought" is a particularly strong one. What should be treated equally by the law depends to a large degree on what is equal *in fact*. The discovery that a finding of inequality made in the past was contrary to scientific truth will engender strong demands that the inequality be eliminated in the legal system.

We are confronted here, not with emotional predispositions, but with an objective measuring rod for the determination of the justice or injustice of a legal classification. It is simply not true in a great many instances that the question as to what should receive equal or unequal treatment is purely one of subjective judgment or irrational preference, as the logical positivists would have us believe. To mention some additional and obvious examples of where the subjective theory falls to the ground: By what train of reasoning could anyone support the position that red-haired persons should be denied voting rights, or that left-handed individuals should not be eligible for public office?

A fifth connection between the notion of justice and the principle of equality exists in the domain of law enforcement. Once a rule of law has been established by legislative enactment or judicial recognition, it should in principle be applied indiscriminately and without respect of persons to all coming within the purview of the rule. Thus, if A is convicted under a law forbidding speeding by automobile drivers, but B, because he is a politically influential personality, is not prosecuted for an identical offense, a clear injustice has been committed. The reason for this conclusion must again be sought in the incompatibility of justice and arbitrariness.

To the Danish jurist Alf Ross, the demand for nondiscriminatory enforcement of the positive law constitutes the only concrete meaning that can possibly be assigned to the notion of justice.[38] This is an unduly narrow delimitation of the concept, and it holds its ground not even within the confines allowed to it by Ross. Ross formulates his basic position as follows: "That a decision is unjust means that it has not been made according to law and is either based on an error (unjust in the objective sense), or is due to a conscious deviation from the law (unjust in the subjective sense)."[39] But can the general and equal application of a law be of any significant value if the law itself is utterly unjust? Let us assume that a public prosecutor, who is charged with the enforcement of a law imposing severe penalties on persons furnishing education to the members of a certain racial group, adopts a policy of reducing prosecutions under the law to an unavoidable minimum, thus deliberately sparing many persons who were guilty of violating it. Or suppose a law is passed decreeing the mandatory death penalty for any criticism of government officials, and a judge thoroughly convinced of the injustice of the law acquits a violator on the pretense of disbelieving a witness. Is it obvious that an injustice has been committed in these two cases because the principle of equal application of the law was disregarded by a law-administering authority?[40] This principle, because it is essentially formal in character, comports with the requirements of justice only in cases in which the law to be applied is not itself subject to severe condemnation on the ground of material injustice. Where honest differences of opinion exist with respect to the fairness of a law, the principle of even-handed enforcement applies, of course, with full force.

It has sometimes been stated that the demand for equal treatment of equal situations finds its counterpart in the postulate that unequal situations must be treated unequally.[41] In this broad formulation, the statement does not stand up to close scrutiny. If, for example, the fines decreed for violation of an antitrust law happen to be more or less identical with the penalties imposed for breach of certain customs regulations, this does not necessarily signify a disregard of justice, although the two infractions are "unequal" in character. If the measure of damages awarded for breaches of certain types of contracts equals that permitted in some tort situations, an objection based on considerations of justice may fail to carry persuasive force.[42]

There is, however, a substantial element of truth contained in the unequal-treatment axiom. This truth becomes apparent when under the pertinent standards of evaluation a highly material difference can be shown to exist between two situations, and where a neglect to give recognition to this difference results in arbitrariness or disproportionality in the legislative or judicial treatment of the problem. If, for example, the same punishment is provided for a severe crime and a light misdemeanor, the sense of justice of a civilized community will normally take offense at such a result. The same is true when the amount of compensation recoverable for a permanent disability caused by an industrial accident is equal to that obtainable for a battery which causes inconsequential physical damage only.

The postulate of unequal treatment also becomes material when an obvious injustice is produced by the equal application of a general rule to two situations which are dissimilar but apparently fall both within the scope of the rule. The occurrence of such problems stems from the fact, noted already by Aristotle, that "law is always a general statement, yet there are cases which it is not possible to cover in a general statement." [43] In such cases, it may become necessary to rectify the defect by a differentiating treatment on the assumption that the lawmaker himself would have provided for it had he been cognizant of the problem.

Most legal systems have created vehicles for the dispensation of an individualized justice in situations where the application of a generalized yardstick would accomplish harm rather than good.[44] A legal order striving for justice must accommodate both the need for normative generality, insuring the equal treatment of equal situations, and for an individualized equity, insuring the fair handling of unusual cases not lending themselves to disposition according to general patterns. When the one or the other approach is to be adopted cannot be determined by a universal formula but must be decided in the context of specific problems of the legal order.[45]

Sec. 11. *The Promotion of Freedom.*

The most widely accepted meaning of the term "freedom" and its synonym "liberty" is John Stuart Mill's definition: "Liberty consists in doing what one desires." [1] This definition comprises both the negative and positive components of freedom. Implicit in it is the recognition that a man is not free if he is restrained from carrying out his wishes, but it also conveys the notion that a free man is in a position to pursue positive goals and desired objectives.

Mill's view of freedom, although it seems to comport with commonsense and general experience, poses certain difficulties upon closer examination and therefore has not remained unchallenged.[2] It has been argued that the freedom to carry out one's wishes may under some circumstances lead to the loss or destruction of freedom and should therefore not be considered the most essential element in a definition of the concept. The following statement by the British biologist Haldane is typical of this approach:

> Freedom is something more than being able to do what one desires so far as the laws of nature permit. The drug addict with unlimited supplies of his drug is at least relatively unfree. His actions are controlled by a single motive, and lead to madness and death.[3]

In a similar vein it might be asserted that an alcoholic unhindered in the gratification of his desire to drink will become a slave of his habit and thus cease to be a free man.

In the light of such considerations, some philosophers have maintained that freedom is not the power of doing what one pleases, but the capacity and determination of doing what one ought to do. Thus Kant remarks that the possession of moral restraint alone makes man truly free, because it enables him to keep his irrational impulses under control.[4] The same position was taken even more strongly by Hegel. "If we hear it said," he declared, "that the definition of freedom is ability to do what we please, such an idea can only be taken to reveal an utter immaturity of thought." [5] To him, freedom was "liberation from dependence on mere natural impulse" and rational action in conformity with the objective ethical order, motivated by a sense of duty.[6]

Another avenue of approach was chosen by some authors of a deterministic persuasion, who arrived at the conclusion that freedom meant no more than the recognition of natural necessity. Engels, for example, was convinced that knowledge of the laws governing physical and social phenomena, and action in accordance with these laws, constituted the essence of human freedom.[7] As long as we do not understand the inexorable forces working in nature and society, they seem to us blind and often destructive. But once we comprehend the manner of their operation, we can subject them to our will and use them intelligently for the attainment of our ends.[8] The same position was more rceently taken by Haldane.[9]

It is submitted that Mill's commonsense definition of freedom is preferable to the two other approaches outlined above. Kant and Hegel were perhaps right in emphasizing that in the long run only the man able to control his irrational impulses will remain truly free. It would nonetheless seem desirable to make a distinction between free and rational action. Freedom to act irrationally is still freedom, even if the irrational man by abandoning himself to his cravings will in the end become chained to his passions.[10] By the same token, an economic system based on the laissez-faire principle should be called free even though, if permitted to operate without any checks and controls, it might usher in an era of monopolistic domination and economic unfreedom.

The view which identifies freedom with knowledge of natural necessity obviously sets very narrow limits to the boundaries of human liberty and will be defended chiefly by those who adhere to a rigid theory of determinism with respect to physical processes and human affairs. Although some of the protagonists of this view believe that with advancing knowledge of the laws of nature men will become increasingly free to use them for their benefit,[11] this enlargement of the scope of freedom is relegated to a future improved state of mankind and is to that extent speculative. Those who hold that man's creative powers, even at the present stage of human development, go beyond the faculty of intelligent adaptation to some inevitable laws of natural and social evolution will be strongly inclined to take a broader view of freedom.

There is much reason to believe, in opposition to the views of the social determinists, that freedom is greater in the world of the human spirit than in the realm of matter. The more material an object is, the more "law-bound" it will tend to be.[12] The human mind is to some extent free to disengage itself from the shackles of mechanical causality and to blueprint worlds of high purpose and ideal objectives. In these potentialities of the human mind to bring forth ideas for the betterment of human affairs lies one of the most salutary features of freedom.[13] Ideas are not merely mental mirrors of events taking place in social and economic reality, but often precede social changes and are instrumental in bringing them about.[14]

Idealism has overshot its mark, however, by posing the thesis of a more or less unlimited capacity of the human spirit to mold the world according to the wishes and dreams of men. The transformation of ideas into practical realities will often be impossible or unsuccessful if social conditions are not ripe for their materialization. The constellation of interests and other real factors in the social order must be propitious to the reception of ideas or ideologies in order to make their conversion into social institutions feasible. Social change therefore takes place only when normative thought directed at its accomplishment is sown in a soil which is favorable to its germination and fructification. The proper attitude to be adopted by social innovators under these circumstances is one that might be described as "idealistic realism." Where far-reaching reforms are initiated in disregard of actual conditions and probable human reactions, the social reformer, like Don Quixote, will often accomplish the opposite of what he set out to do.

Even though for purposes of practical action it is necessary to check ideal postulates against the hard facts of life, the unfettered roaming of the human mind in search of better solutions of human problems should by all means be encouraged. There can be no doubt that the emancipation of thought which began in the sixteenth century was beneficial to the development of civilization, not only in the Occident, but throughout the world.

Freedom of research resulted in a new picture of the physical world and in many discoveries resulting in technological progress. There was a resurgence of the arts which greatly enriched mankind's treasure of literature, music, painting, and sculpture. Many different philosophies and theories of social action were put forth by eminent thinkers, and out of the ferment of discussion and ideological controversy emerged many valuable experiments in organizing human society and human relations.

Freedom of thinking beneficial to social experimentation and progress is not, however, the only aspect of freedom which is relevant in dealing with the problems of justice. The urge for freedom manifests itself in many domains of human activity and must be counted among the most elementary constituents of human nature. The child as well as the adult person strongly resents confinements of his movements, and restraints on freedom have in most eras of history been considered effective measures of pedagogical and penal policy. Children and adults object to obstructions placed in the path of carrying out their desires and intentions, unless they can be convinced of the necessity or utility of such restrictions. Thus liberty is highly valued by human beings. The greatest reward that could be accorded to the slaves of antiquity was emancipation by their master, which meant the acquisition of freedom.

Human beings experience joy in being able to use their bodily and mental powers for purposes pursued by them and to reap the benefits accruing from the exercise of these powers. They also have a strong and legitimate desire to acquire property which, according to Hegel, forms the external sphere of their freedom.[15] They wish to possess a home corresponding to their needs, to own books which they appreciate, to surround themselves, if possible, with some objects of art congenial to their tastes. They wish to be free to enter into contracts and other transactions which further their interests and help to satisfy their needs. They also wish to travel, to explore, to be free to communicate with others.

The human craving for freedom is so manifest and so strong that an American philosopher, Henry Aiken, views as unnecessary and futile any attempts to justify, on utilitarian or idealistic grounds, the enthronement of freedom as a principal value of political and social organization. These are his arguments:

Liberty is not a moral good only because it may conduce to the general happiness, nor even because, by an extension of the original meaning of that idea, it may form a part of the happiness of most men. Such a defense is wholly problematic and leads those who employ it into unreal distinctions and imponderable appraisals. The moral foundation of liberty, I contend, is nothing other than the right to be at liberty itself. In short, the fountain-head of freedom, if I may employ the phrase, is not utility but simply and solely the principle that every person has a right to be at liberty. This principle requires the indulgence of no other principle whatever . . . In the language of Kant, the principle of liberty is categorically imperative.[16]

The core of truth contained in this passage is that, since the exercise of freedom is so greatly cherished by men and has led to so many constructive results, it is perfectly meaningful to speak of a "natural right" of human beings to be free. As Aiken himself indicates, however, his statement is subject to the qualification that the right to freedom cannot be unlimited, and that human freedom is always circumscribed and subject to restraints.[17] Since man possesses powers for both good and evil, not all exercises of freedom are valuable.[18] In this respect, freedom may be compared with equality, which likewise constitutes a relative rather than absolute value; a social order resorting to extreme and rigid forms of egalitarianism is likely to suppress or discourage outstanding achievement and may thus fail to promote the cause of civilization.

There are various classes of actions and situations requiring restrictions on human freedom. The first category consists of voluntary acts which are considered contrary to good public order and the purposes of organized social existence. Some men would welcome the freedom to take the life of others whom they hate or fear; but society will always deny to its members the freedom to kill. Some people would like to appropriate or use the property of others, but such invasions of property rights are rendered criminal or at least tortious in practically all societies. People are also not at liberty to kidnap the children of others for the purpose of extorting a ransom. Many people have on certain occasions the desire to attack the reputation of other persons, but defamation of character going beyond certain limits is proscribed by the laws of all civilized countries. There can be no freedom to produce worthless drugs endangering the lives of those who use them. A considerable number of men have polygamous inclinations and would welcome the opportunity of contracting marriages with more than one woman; but in the large majority of the present social orders polygamy is considered a depreciation of the role of women and is outlawed and punished for this and perhaps other reasons (such as equalization of opportunity for marriage in a world in which the discrepancy in the number of men and women is relatively small).

The actions and practices thus far discussed are generally viewed as undesirable or reprehensible *per se*. There are others which are not in their nature deemed antisocial or *contra bonos mores,* but which are prohibited or regulated because they tend to interfere with the freedom, curtail the equality, or reduce the opportunity of other persons or groups in society. A law which compels certain manufacturing companies to install smoke-control devices in their factories constitutes a restraint on the power of manufacturers to run their business as they see fit, but it may enhance the freedom of property owners in the vicinity of the plant to enjoy their homes free from noxious or annoying emissions. A statute or judicial decision prohibiting restaurant owners from discriminating against Negroes limits the liberty of such owners to serve whom they please, but it widens the freedom of Negroes to patronize eating places of their own choice and also takes a step toward granting them equality of status with white people. A fair employment law barring employers from refusing employment to anyone on grounds of race, sex, or religion is an interference with the freedom of one particular group, while at the same time it tends to broaden the chances of other groups to find remunerative work. A compulsory education law operates as a restraint on the freedom of both parents and children but enlarges the opportunities of children in later life, especially their freedom of vocational choice.

In the light of these examples, the widely-held view that every law is a limitation on liberty, and that liberty exists only in the interstices of the law, must be regarded as untenable.[19] The exercise of one liberty may be inconsistent with, or adverse to, the exercise of some other liberty. Many laws, therefore, are designed to portion out or balance various liberties, or to restrain the liberty of some persons in order to increase that of other persons. There are also laws which reduce liberty for the purpose of promoting other values of the social order, such as security or equality of opportunity.[20] A man may be theoretically at liberty to work in his chosen calling, but if no work is available, or if he is the victim of discrimination, his right is of merely academic value to him. Thus laws which, though limiting certain manifestations of liberty, aim at augmenting the sum total of liberty by implementing it through a broadening of possibilities for self-realization comport, according to the theory here proposed, with the requirements of justice. As Tillich observes, "freedom is dependent not only on political forms but also on a social structure in which the self-fulfilling creativity or the creative happiness of everyone is guaranteed in order that complete fulfillment of man and society may be achieved." [21]

The German legal philosopher Coing has advanced the thesis that in situations where freedom comes into conflict with other values, such as equality or social justice, and a decision between the two conflicting principles becomes necessary, the decision should be made in favor of freedom.[22] Stated in this abstract and apodictical manner, the proposition appears to be unduly dogmatic. As we have seen, there are many different forms and manifestations of freedom, and freedom in its broadest and perhaps most significant sense includes the equal opportunity for self-actualization and participation in social effort, which is one of the supreme postulates of social justice.[23] Where conflicts arise between freedom and other values protected by the legal order, the general question that must be asked in resolving the conflict is the following: What particular solution of the problem would contribute most effectively to the establishment of a state of affairs where maximum opportunities are afforded to all members of society to use their productive capacities (manual or mental) in helping to build a civilization which aims at material achievement, cultural richness, and ethical progress? [24]

The final conclusion to be derived from these reflections must be that an interplay of freedom and restraint is a necessary aspect of a just and civilized social order.[25] Unlimited freedom to do what one pleases would result in anarchy and chaos. Constraint as an exclusive political organizing principle would destroy the initiative and creative power without which civilization cannot flourish. An effective social order will combine and reconcile liberty and restraint in such a way that everyone can use his liberty fully and constructively in contributing to the common good according to his best lights and talents, while nobody can misuse it for the purpose of harming others or blocking their road to achievement. The following words of Thomas Mann appear to be apposite in this connection:

> Reason tells that pure individualism and absolute freedom are just as humanly impossible and contrary to culture as their liberty-destroying opposite. There would be no hope for humanity if it had a choice only between anarchy and that extreme socialization which destroys personality.[26]

Sec. 12. *The Need for Order and Security.*

Order is in general a life-sustaining force, while disorder and anarchy are bound to have disintegrating and destructive effects. Physical life is preserved through an orderly balance between growth and decay of cell tissue, and the unchecked, anarchical proliferation of such tissue produces cancer and the destruction of the body.[1] Anarchy in social life engenders strife and disorganization and, if it develops into a chronic and prolonged condition, leads to the dissolution of the social body. A just order of society is impossible if lawlessness becomes widespread; observance of the law is therefore, as a general rule, an indispensable condition of the reign of justice. It cannot be denied, however, that in the case of obsolete or utterly unhealthy political and economic systems, a temporary prevalence of disorder or revolutionary turmoil may sometimes be the only expedient for securing necessary change. Such situations do not occur very frequently in history and must be regarded as exceptions which confirm the rule.

The creation of a just and civilized legal system does not only require that a proper measure of freedom, equality, and opportunity be granted to the members of society, but also that orderly procedures and suitable institutions be available for the realization and implementation of these rights. The recognition of basic human rights by the legal order raises certain expectations in the minds of the intended beneficiaries which would be grievously disappointed if such recognition had a purely theoretical significance. Men's right to life and bodily integrity remains largely on paper if they cannot walk the streets of their cities safely, and if crimes of violence are widespread and ineffectively combated by the public authorities. The right to freedom of speech is a merely academic prerogative if individuals who seek to make use of it are not adequately protected against those who, out of political or ideological fanaticism, strive to nullify it for their adversaries.[2] Freedom of transaction is of little value unless security of transacting business is guaranteed through proper procedures for the enforcement of contracts. The right to equality of opportunity becomes meaningless if discrimination is practiced on a large scale, and no attempt is made to eliminate or reduce it by whatever means are considered practicable and effective. The equal treatment of equal situations demanded by justice is impossible without an orderly body of standards of equality guiding adjudication.

Thus order and security form indispensable adjuncts of justice. There exists, in the words of Pound, "a social interest in the general security." [3] Jhering likewise insisted that law and justice should be directed toward *securing* the conditions of social life.[4] Bodily integrity, liberty, acquisitions, and transacactions must be made safe against unlawful courses of conduct which threaten their inviolability. It has also been pointed out convincingly that the protection of the body, of property, of personal freedom of action is a precondition for the realization of those higher values, especially spiritual and cultural values, which are not as a rule directly affected by the arrangements of the law. These higher values cannot flourish where life, possessions, and the right to create are not adequately safeguarded by the law, so that man's energies are consumed in a struggle for self-protection.[5]

It can therefore be stated that vigorous law enforcement is an important requisite of justice. Anarchy, spotty execution of legal commands, existence of large areas of disorganization in the political and social order are generally incompatible with the attainment of justice in society. A different situation exists only where a particular positive legal order is thoroughly permeated with gross injustice. In that case, an effective enforcement of this order cannot claim to be of great value to those who suffer from the prevalence of unjust conditions and institutions. Such an order usually cannot maintain itself for long periods of time and is likely to give way to a social system better adapted to the needs and interests of the people.

In an age in which nuclear war has become a reality, internal security against aggression and violence is no longer sufficient to guarantee a just order of civilized life. Human rights become meaningless, and justice a chimera, when the world is threatened with destruction on an unprecedented scale. External security to safeguard peace among nations therefore becomes a precondition for the achievement of justice in any societal order today.[6]

So far the discussion has centered around the problem of securing the effective implementation of certain rights and liberties which previously had been identified as fundamental postulates of justice. But "security" is also used in another sense which up to this point has received little attention in this treatise. It is maintained by many that a just legal order must provide security to men and women against certain hazards, risks, and contingencies that are inevitably or frequently connected with human life. The most important of these are old age, illness, accidents, and unemployment. Alleviating the hardships incident to these contingencies is the task of a system of "social security," and this area of the law has in the last hundred years assumed great significance and undergone considerable expansion.

The protagonists of social security take the position that a modicum of economic security should be given to people under circumstances in which their normal earning capacity is impaired or altogether absent, and that this is a simple command of decency and humanitarian sentiment. The antagonists of social security assert that it is not the function of government to provide paternalistically for the needs of the people. Sustenance in periods of old age, unemployment, disability, or sickness, they say, should be financed out of personal savings or, to the extent possible, be secured by means of private insurance. The argument is also made by some that social welfare legislation destroys self-reliance, promotes shiftlessness, and thereby weakens society.

In discussing the merits of these conflicting contentions, the various categories of social insurance must be considered separately. The need for old-age insurance was brought about by a change in the social and economic configuration of the advanced countries of the world. In the period of agricultural civilization, there was always room for the old people on the farm; there existed a wing in the house to shelter them, and there was ordinarily some household work for them to do for which they did not have to be compensated in money. These conditions made old people an economic asset to the younger generation and helped to preserve their morale and self-respect.

Today most families no longer live in houses where one can build on a room or wing to shelter aging parents, uncles, or aunts. The younger people often do not have the space to take aging relatives into their homes. If they do, they sometimes act with reluctance, and friction and ill-will may be engendered by the feeling of the parents that they are unwanted and useless. This is a psychologically undesirable condition. Old people, especially when they were self-reliant during their active lives, dislike and resent becoming dependent, and often they cannot give anything in return. A modest old-age pension will do much to raise their sense of dignity and independence, and it will also in many cases alleviate a serious financial problem of the younger generation, which otherwise would have to use a considerable part of its income to support the parents and perhaps other relatives. Notice must also be taken of the fact that old people, because of rapid medical progress in this century, form a substantial and growing percentage of the population.

The argument that social security destroys self-reliance and promotes shiftlessness has little merit in its application to old-age insurance. In periods of unemployment, not much encouragement is given to old people who desire to work, while in times of abundant work opportunities such people will normally be attracted to employment by pay rates likely to exceed old-age benefits. The contention that, in order to encourage thrift, sustenance in old age should be provided by personal savings does not hold much ground, because the earnings from employment made by the average person are hardly ever sufficient to carry him through a prolonged period of old age. It is also pertinent to observe that the beneficiaries of old-age insurance, under the system in force in the United States and most other countries, are not recipients of a dole, but are required to make contributions of their own to the system through taxes or other payments.

Industrial accident insurance (workmen's compensation) seeks to protect working people against the severe hazards connected with the operation of industrial plants in a technological age. It grants protection to the worker regardless of whether or not he was negligent in incurring the accident. The social policy underlying this type of insurance rests on the experience that the injured worker is usually unable to bear the burden of permanent or temporary disability, and that an enlightened community, since it cannot let the victim starve in the street, must provide financial and medical benefits for him.[7] This form of social insurance has become practically noncontroversial in the modern world, except as to specific problems of implementation, and it is usually the first type of social legislation introduced in countries entering the ranks of the industrial nations.

Many countries today have public programs of health insurance, either for all members of society or at least for the lower income groups, but in the United States this form of insurance is available only on a small scale. It cannot be denied that because of its limited scope in this country, a large volume of illness is unattended or inadequately attended.[8] Many people are without the means necessary for the purchase of medical services. Private insurance is too expensive for the lower income groups, and the coverage of private policies is often quite restrictive. Many convincing arguments can be advanced in favor of the adoption of a public health service. One consideration is the tremendous value that everybody attaches to the possession of good health, coupled with the fact that its preservation is in most instances the indispensable prerequisite for the performance of productive work and therefore of human happiness. From a social standpoint, it might be observed that widespread conditions of ill health are likely to produce a serious deterioration of human resources.

A further factor to be taken into account is that inability to bear the professional service costs of serious illness creates a paralyzing fear which may accompany a person, especially the head of a family, throughout a large part of his life. It would seem to be demanded by principles of humanitarian policy that this fear be mitigated or alleviated, especially since incapacity to pay the increasing cost of medical service is usually not due to personal inadequacy or fault. For these and other reasons, the large majority of the advanced countries provide today for some form of medical care financed by taxes or special contributions.

Unemployment insurance is designed to relieve the hazards of inability to find work, and its availability is generally conditioned on the presence of willingness to accept suitable work if offered. The desirability of this kind of social security is hardly being questioned in our day. The argument often advanced in earlier times that incapacity to find work is attributable to ineptitude or sloth no longer carries any weight in countries where unemployment can clearly be traced to general economic conditions.[9]

For the reasons sketched above, these and other measures of social security [10] have been widely adopted in the advanced and developing industrial nations of the world.[11] They are generally considered as conforming to the requirements of justice. No political party in these countries—including the United States—could succeed on a platform which would advocate abandonment of these measures of social welfare. The basic rights to social security are also recognized in the International Declaration of Human Rights, which was approved by forty-eight members of the United Nations and opposed by none.[12]

Sec. 13. *The Importance of Proportionality.*

The postulates of justice discussed in the preceding sections were for the most part related to the recognition and protection of certain basic rights, such as freedom, equality, opportunity for self-actualization, security against certain hazards of life, and security against invasion of the legally guaranteed sphere. It bears emphasis that this justice of human rights is a relative latecomer in the history of law and the state. We find no elaborated theory of the rights of men in the writings of Plato, Aristotle, Cicero, St. Thomas Aquinas, and other ancient and medieval thinkers. Although the need for protection of the human personality is implicitly recognized in some of the older philosophies of law, the express incorporation of freedom, equality, and other basic rights into the theory of justice did not take place until the emergence of individualistic doctrines of natural law in the seventeenth and eighteenth centuries.

For long stretches of time in the evolution of law, the conception of justice centered on ideas and notions other than human rights. Among the oldest of these notions were the twin concepts of reciprocity and retribution. Aristotle informs us that pursuant to the doctrine of the Pythagoreans justice consisted essentially in retaliation for injury done, and that the reciprocation to be inflicted in response to a damaging act was conceived by them in strictly mathematical terms.[1]

It is likely that the Pythagorean doctrine, the details of which are unknown to us, bore much resemblance to the "eye for eye, tooth for tooth" principle referred to in the Old Testament.[2] This axiom has often been denounced as the prototype of a barbaric conception of justice. But there is much reason to believe that it represented a step forward on the road to progress in the administration of the law. The most ancient procedure for the redress of wrongs, which can probably be found in all primitive societies, was the blood feud. When a member of a sib or clan was killed or injured by an outsider, the whole group went out to avenge the deed on the wrongdoer and his kin. In that case, the reprisals often turned out to be entirely out of proportion to the offense. Indiscriminate slaughter of innocent persons might be the requital for any act of violence. Thus, when the community started to regulate retaliation, its first concern was to forestall excessive forms of vengeance. "An eye for an eye" meant that the penalty should be assessed according to the gravity of the offense, "since otherwise there would be no object in stopping, once we have begun to do wrong; we would not run any greater risk by proceeding to extremities." [3]

Although the idea of exact retaliation was an improvement on the older forms of group vengeance, the evolving sense of human justice came to find much fault with it. Aristotle pointed out that "in many cases reciprocity is at variance with justice: for example, if an officer strikes a man, it is wrong for the man to strike him back; and if a man strikes an officer, it is not enough for the officer to strike him, but he ought to be punished as well." [4] Sometimes the principle of retribution in kind would run into insuperable obstacles of execution; the infliction of a light wound leading to death through infection was a wrong that could not easily be penalized by an equivalent retaliatory action.

When, in the subsequent stage of development, injured men and their kinsmen were persuaded to accept pecuniary compensation as redress for the wrong, the notion of *proportionate* reciprocity made its entrance into the law. When damages are paid in return for the commission of an unlawful act, an exact, mathematical equivalence of injury and compensation can almost never be accomplished. The same is true for transactions of exchange. The compensation paid for an article purchased or leased is usually not a precisely equal return; it is felt, however, that the *quid pro quo* should normally bear a due proportion to the value of the article or service. In consideration of this principle, the English Court of Chancery and many American equity courts granted specific performance of a contract only when the performance agreed to by the plaintiff in return for the defendant's promise was considered sufficient and fair under the circumstances.

To Aristotle, the notion of proportionality was of the essence of justice. "Justice," he said, "is . . . a sort of proportion." [5]

101

His insistence on proportionality in the administration of justice reflected itself in two forms, depending upon whether *distributive* or *corrective* justice was involved. Distributive justice according to Aristotle is concerned with the distribution by the State to the citizens of offices, honors, rights, and other benefits. These should be allotted pursuant to the yardstick of geometrical proportionality. Equal things should be given to equal persons, unequal things to unequal persons, according to the standard of worthiness and merit. "There will be the same equality between the shares as between the persons; for if the persons are not equal, they will not have equal shares." [6] Corrective justice, on the other hand, seeks to rectify wrongs committed by one member of society against another. Here the principle of arithmetical proportionality should prevail. A loss must be made good by restoring to the party who suffered it an approximate equivalent for what he was deprived of.[7]

In our own day, the view that justice means the maintenance of proportionality in dealings of exchange, in the rectification of wrongs, and perhaps in the allotment of rights and benefits has not disappeared from the legal-philosophical scene. Del Vecchio, for example, says: "Justice, in the most general sense, connotes a conformity, a congruence, a proportion of some kind." [8] In the words of Henri Bergson, "justice has always evoked ideas of equality, of proportion, of compensation. . . . Justice is represented as holding the scales." [9] The German jurist Bernhard Rehfeldt finds the main roots of justice in the related notions of reciprocity and retaliation.[10]

The idea of proportionality, although according to the theory here proposed it does not constitute the whole of justice, forms indeed an important ingredient of the concept. Some correlation between achievement and reward, between crime and punishment, between performance and counterperformance in mutual undertakings is demanded by the human sense of justice. Fair prices for goods, fair compensation for services form or should form part of the ethics of a responsible business community, and fraudulent representations which deprive a party to a transaction of an adequate equivalent for his own performance should be remediable.[11] Damages in tort actions should be adapted to the character, scope, and consequences of the wrongful act committed. A substantial disproportionality between the wrong and the compensation awarded for it by a court should always be ground for appeal.

In the law of crimes, the idea of retributive punishment has suffered a decline in the modern age. It cannot be denied, however, that meting out an extremely severe punishment for a slight offense, or imposing a nominal punishment for a grave dereliction, are actions which the average man still experiences as violations of the sense of justice.[12] Where prizes are allotted for excellence in performance, some proportionality between accomplishment and reward will always be expected. If the Nobel Prize would be evenly divided between two scientists, one of whom has made a monumental discovery after many years of intensive research, while the other has contributed to the advancement of science in a minor way and by standing largely on the shoulders of others, complaints of injustice in the distribution of the award would be justified. A teacher who rewards a mediocre examination performance with a high grade exposes himself to charges of bias and unfairness.

Can the two chief forms of justice identified at the beginning of this section be correlated or harmonized? Do any connections exist between the justice of human rights and the justice of reciprocity and proportionality? Bergson suggested that no substantial link between the two conceptions could be detected. The justice of proportionality was to him a "closed" notion of justice, pointing toward stability and expressing the "automatic equilibrium of a society fresh from the hands of nature." The justice of freedom and equality, on the other hand, he considered a dynamic, future-oriented form of justice which is "open to successive creations." [13]

It is undoubtedly true that the identification of justice with reciprocity and proportionality reflects a somewhat conservative, stationary attitude. This is the reason why this view tends to preponderate in primitive communities, which are always tradition-bound and slow to accept changes of custom and law. The examples offered earlier in this section seem to prove, however, that the notions of fair exchange and proportionality between wrongdoing and redress still have a valid role to play in the legal system of modern society.

Furthermore, the idea of proportionality is not foreign to that domain of justice which concerns itself with the recognition and enforcement of human rights. It is necessary in this realm to refrain from attaching an exaggerated weight to one particular value entitled to protection at the expense of other values whose safeguarding is likewise essential. Freedom, equality, security of life and possessions, and security against certain hazards of human existence must be harmonized in such a way as to bring about a maximum of individual self-realization within the framework of the common goals of humanity. Limitless freedom, especially in the economic field, may lead to unfair competition and other unscrupulous practices. Imposition of rigid equality may thwart or blunt the striving for excellence, self-perfection, and outstanding achievement. A one-sided emphasis on security may stifle self-reliance and venture. Thus, the various goals of justice must be correlated and adjusted to each other; a right proportion must be established between the degrees of freedom, equality and security promoted by the legal order.[14] This postulate creates a major link between the two forms of justice discussed in this chapter.

Sec. 14. *Necessity as a Limitation of Justice.*

According to the theory advanced in the preceding sections, the realization of justice in the social order requires that a reasonable amount of freedom and equality be granted to human beings, so that they can develop and use their powers and capabilities in the service of civilization. It was also demonstrated that these fundamental goals can normally be achieved only when the rights and opportunities to which men are entitled are secured to them by legal safeguards and orderly and effective enforcement procedures. Finally, it was pointed out that proportionality and fairness must prevail in a just order of society with respect to the assignment of rights and rewards, in the imposition of duties and burdens, and in meting out punishment. If we wish to summarize the chief aim of the administration of justice in a brief formula, we might say that justice must assist in the creation of a great and humane civilization by promoting certain values that are conducive to material and spiritual growth.

At this juncture of the discussion it becomes necessary to inject, at least temporarily, a note of pessimism. When we take a look backward into the history and evolution of legal systems for the purpose of appraising the legal realities of the past in the light of the criteria and goals of justice, disillusionment and despair may easily befall us. Throughout most of recorded history, human freedom remained in a highly precarious condition.

104

Slavery was practiced on a large scale and in many countries. When it was later replaced by serfdom, as in medieval Europe, the status of the serf was still characterized by a substantial degree of unfreedom, such as, for example, his inability to leave the estate to which he was attached as an appurtenance. Under some systems of law governing broad areas of the civilized world, women and children stood under the despotic power of the family head and in some instances, as under the Roman legal order, this dominion extended even to grown-up sons and unmarried adult daughters.

The realization of equality was likewise nonexistent or fragmentary in many countries and many periods of time. Rigid class divisions, accompanied by an unequal allotment of rights, were common in numerous historical societies known to us. Women were frequently excluded from participation in political life, denied access to the educational facilities, and subjected to other disabilities. Aliens were looked upon with suspicion and often denied the most elementary forms of protection. Discriminations on religious and, later, racial grounds were introduced into the legal arrangements of a number of nations. Excessively severe punishments were often decreed in retribution for relatively slight offenses.[1] Viewed from the vantage point of the theory of justice here propounded, the conclusion might easily be drawn that human history is largely a record of human injustice, and that even in our own day justice remains an unrealized ideal in many parts of the world. The question may also be asked whether a theory of justice which finds so little confirmation and support in historical reality serves any useful purpose whatsoever.

On closer scrutiny, however, the picture does not look as dark as first impressions would make it appear. We must not close our eyes to the fact that the human race has developed slowly and unevenly in the acquisition of knowledge, the gaining of productive skills necessary for civilized life, and the strengthening of the moral sense. By a prolonged and gradual process man has evolved from the stage of the caveman, who was unacquainted even with the most primitive tools for making his life comfortable, to modern man, who is in possession of a great amount of scientific and technological know-how, and who in the course of the centuries has also gained a modicum of experience in the art of living together with his fellowmen. There has also occurred during the growth of civilization a certain re-

105

finement of the moral sense, manifested among other things in the revulsion of civilized man against the savage cruelty of early warfare and punishment. Of course, it must be realized that the gains made in the process of human evolution are by no means irreversible and secure. Disturbing events in the twentieth century have taught us the lesson that there is no ground for smugness and complacency, that the veneer of civilization is a thin one, and that reverses into barbarism and bestiality are always within the bounds of possibility.

The slow and uneven development of man's control over nature, of his modes of producing goods, of his brain power and moral sensibilities, retarded further by temporary setbacks, must be counted among the chief reasons for the imperfections which have marred the realization of justice in the historically known societies. The factors which up to our own day have limited and impeded the effectuation of justice, and which are not traceable to an unwillingness or deliberate refusal to consider its claims, shall be denominated here by the term *necessity*. It might be observed at the outset of the discussion, however, that it is not always possible to determine in historical retrospection whether the existence of unjust conditions or laws in a given society must be attributed to confining factors stemming from necessity, or whether its cause lay in a conscious will to do injustice. It is not intended here to offer a "theodicy" of human development which attempts to explain historical events in terms of a cosmic teleology according to which everything that happens is rational as well as inevitable, and which tends to gloss over the fact that men and governments sometimes become guilty of the commission of deliberate and inexcusable wrongs.

The institution of slavery provides a good testing ground for the doctrine of necessity. Aristotle offered two possible justifications for the use of unfree human labor power. His first argument was that some persons are by nature free, others by nature slaves, and that for the latter the condition of slavery was both beneficial and just. He immediately added the caveat, however, that "it is easy to see that those who hold an opposite view are also in a way correct." [2] He alluded to the fact that most slaves in Greece were recruited from the ranks of prisoners of war, and that the reduction of such prisoners to the status of slavery might not be defensible if the cause of the war was unjust, or if a particular person was by nature equipped to be a free man. Aristotle may also have been aware that, even if it is true that some persons are servants by innate disposition, this does not entail the consequence that they must be treated as chattels devoid of any human rights.

The second argument advanced by Aristotle in favor of slavery is of much greater significance. He made the following observation:

> There is only one condition on which we can imagine managers not needing subordinates, and masters not needing slaves. This condition would be that each [inanimate] instrument could do its own work, . . . as if a shuttle should weave of itself, and a plectrum should do its own harp-playing.[3]

The thought that Aristotle is trying to convey in this passage is that in a technically developed civilization automation could take care of the mechanical work of production, so that men might be able to get along without human machines.

This argument raises the question whether slavery is indispensable under conditions where civilization has taken some significant forward strides but where technology is as yet weakly developed. Under such a system, a tremendous amount of time and effort is used up in the task of providing the most elementary necessities of life. A great deal of repetitive, monotonous, and exhausting work is necessary to keep the economic system in operation. It was found difficult in antiquity to induce free men to perform the low and menial functions in the production and distribution of goods. If slaves had not been available, free men would have been forced to undertake these tasks, but in that event (unless the time had been ripe for the invention of labor-saving devices) the higher pursuits of culture would have suffered. All or most free men would have had to engage in drudgery, such as making bricks with primitive, time-consuming means, tilling the fields, or acting as oarsmen in the operation of ships.

If, as suggested in this treatise, it is the chief goal of human cooperative effort to produce civilizations which offer a wide scope for the display of the manifold talents and capabilities of human beings, then the question becomes relevant whether the practice of slavery was a necessary condition for the high development of culture in Greece, Rome, and other ancient countries.

107

The question was answered in the affirmative by the legal philosopher Josef Kohler. Slavery was to him a necessary renunciation of justice for the sake of culture during the period of early growth of agricultural and industrial life.

Before the rise of technical, especially of industrial arts, slavery was the only means of obtaining a division of labor on a large scale in a uniform undertaking, for works of that kind require distinct subordination, monotonous and steady exertion, tasks which the workman dislikes, and absolute discipline and order, such as were impossible among free persons in those times. Even the oarsman in the rowing bank could scarcely be a free person; for everywhere that enterprises requiring mass labor were set on foot, slaves could not be dispensed with, since machines were wholly lacking.[4]

Technical arts must advance, Kohler said, humanity must make progress, and for long periods of time many human beings must sacrifice their freedom and comfort so that later generations may enjoy a more abundant life. The anthropologist Bronislaw Malinowski agreed with him on this point:

Slavery is an institution which is based on the principle of the fundamental denial of freedom and of human rights to the slave class. It had also its contributions to make towards human progress. Under conditions where large numbers of human beings were necessary for the performance of engineering tasks on a great scale, slave labor was an asset. The coercion of force can be the most effective short-cut in certain human activities. . . .

Perhaps the most positive function of slavery was the creation of a leisure group. The aimless, unwilling, and unpurposeful labor of some gave others more scope for the development of culture. However amoral this may sound, it is a fair description of facts.[5]

There were a number of philosophers and jurists in antiquity who thought that slavery was an unjust institution because man was by nature destined to be free. But if Aristotle, Kohler, and Malinowski were right in their conclusions, slavery was an inevitable byproduct of an evolving civilization and a stepping stone

108

toward higher forms of economic and cultural life. This would perhaps allow a judgment on ancient civilization which would hold that slavery was unjust, but that its practice was necessitated by conditions which rendered the institution an indispensable vehicle for the achievement of progress.

In reaching such a verdict we must be aware, however, of certain limitations of our capacity to evaluate the institutions of a remote past. In stating that slavery, though unjust, was necessary to prepare the ground for higher forms of civilization, we are making the assumption that no alternatives to this practice were available which would have permitted an equivalent degree of cultural accomplishment without depriving large numbers of human beings of their basic human rights. Such an assumption cannot be made with complete assurance. If slavery had been eliminated, men would perhaps have made a determined and successful effort to invent labor-saving devices suitable to take the place of unfree human labor. It might be true that the time was not as yet ripe for the development of technology, but who could categorically make such an assertion? All we can safely state is that slavery *might have been* a necessary way station on the road to progress, and that for this reason we should be reluctant to visit an outright condemnation on the social system of antiquity because it tolerated slavery.

Warfare is another institution which is unavoidably connected with the commission of grave injustices. Millions of innocent men, women, and children have been killed in wars throughout the centuries, including many persons who were not in sympathy with the war aims of their community. Yet here again the hypothesis that war has been a necessary instrumentality for the accomplishment of man's foremost task, the building of civilizations, carries a considerable measure of plausibility. War and conquest have often in history served to enlarge the ambit of a civilization by extending it to areas previously untouched by it. Moreover, the forcible creation of larger political, economic, and cultural units, allowing for a greater division of labor and the pooling of resources and productive powers to promote greater prosperity was of considerable benefit to mankind. Here again, a wholly pessimistic interpretation of history as a chronicle of slaughter and suffering caused by war and subjugation would appear to be onesided and unwarranted.

The legal and social status of women in the ancient Oriental

109

countries and in Greece was grossly inferior to that of men and might therefore invite a further verdict of injustice. For example, women were excluded from the educational facilities and, because of the resulting lack of acquaintance with the political and social problems of their time, from eligibility to public office and participation in public affairs.[6] It is possible and perhaps likely that this policy was prompted primarily by the fact that educational facilities were extremely limited, due to the low state of technology in the construction industries, dearth of qualified teachers, and absence of printed teaching materials. If it was necessary to restrict education to selected groups, it was not entirely unreasonable to close the doors of schools and academies to women, on the ground that most of them were needed at home and by their children. It is certain, of course, that many intellectually gifted women were thereby prevented from developing their talents and from contributing to the intellectual life of their society; we know that in Greece, for example, the unmarried females in need of making a living could do little else than sell their bodies. But it is quite possible that no way out of these difficulties could have been found at that time.

The creation or maintenance of racial discriminations has in some instances been brought about by a strong belief in the intrinsic inequality of the races, which at one time seemed to find some support in the literature on the subject and could not easily be tested as to its validity or invalidity. Although present-day biological science has found no proof whatsoever of innate differences in the intellectual or moral endowment of the various races, it is still true that the members of two races may not be "contemporaries" in the cultural sense. Because of historical factors or more or less accidental circumstances, one race at a particular point of time may have attained a more advanced stage of cultural evolution than another race. There are, for example, regions in Africa today where the people have been lagging behind on the road to culture, and where the conditions of existence are as yet on a primitive level. However, the gaps existing between these areas and the more developed countries in Africa and elsewhere are slowly but steadily diminishing.

Where contacts eventuate between higher and lower cultures, or where both become absorbed by the same political sovereignty, the impression of inborn superiority and inferiority may easily,

110

but falsely, arise. It should be pointed out in this connection that human intellectual capacity appears to increase as conditions of life become more complex and greater resourcefulness is needed to meet new challenges.[7] It seems to be well established today that the brains of early men were less developed and less powerful than those of men living in advanced civilizations. For the same reason the average intelligence of racial groups living under simple conditions presenting a limited range of challenges may be temporarily inferior to that of a group facing complex problems in a highly differentiated environment. As the more primitive group adopts the higher culture, or becomes absorbed by it, the intellectual handicap will gradually decrease and finally disappear. In the case of absorption, however, this will happen only if the absorbed group is given the opportunity to become integrated into the ways of life of the more advanced group.

Before such integration occurs, the original inequality in the cultural and mental level may produce the impression of congenital differences. The result may be that unjust discriminations are perpetrated simply because insufficient information and experience are available to view the problem in its proper light. This is an instance where the possibilities of accomplishing justice are hampered by shortcomings of knowledge which are perhaps unavoidable and which it will take time to remedy.

Situations may also arise where a government or the ethical leaders of a community are willing to carry a new vision of justice into effect but where a large part of the community is not, or not as yet, ready to accept a new order of things. In a democratic society, or even in a nondemocratic order in which the rulers reject forcible solutions, such resistance on the part of the population may easily defeat or stall the initiation of needed reforms. Even though the new program may be superior from the point of view of justice to the existing state of the law, popular inertia or rigid clinging to established custom may present an insuperable obstacle to legal and social change. An example is the refusal of the Swiss male population to grant the franchise to women by way of popular referendum, although no conceivable considerations of justice can vindicate this discrimination today in view of the active and responsible participation of women in business, education, and industry.

There is another sense in which it may be said that necessity sometimes places obstacles in the path of justice. The occurrence

111

of serious emergencies, such as war, civil strife, or natural catastrophe, may require the taking of expeditious measures which may be questionable from the vantage point of justice, or which may violate a law considered fair and reasonable under ordinary circumstances. "Necessity brings with it a dispensation," said St. Thomas Aquinas, "since necessity knows no law." [8]

The problem was squarely posed in World War II when the Japanese-Americans were evacuated from the West Coast of the United States and removed to relocation camps in the interior. The military authorities defended the measure by asserting that there existed a serious threat of Japanese invasion of the Pacific Coast, that the loyalty of the Nisei was under a cloud, and that there was no time to separate the reliable from the unreliable elements by a screening process. If these facts had been borne out by the record, the obvious injustice done to loyal Japanese Americans might have found its justification in pressing military necessity. The existence of a serious invasion threat at the time of the evacuation and the charge of widespread disloyalty among the members of the group were, however, questioned by a number of authorities after a thorough analysis of the facts and records.[9]

As was pointed out earlier, justice requires that reasonable laws be carried out diligently in the interest of order and legal security.[10] But it may happen that in extraordinary circumstances deviations from the law become necessary in order to save a nation or mankind from disaster. Survival values may be at stake which may have to take precedence over law observance. Norms are designed to apply in normal situations; where totally abnormal and unprecedented events occur, the established law, though unobjectionable from the point of view of justice, may cease to be the ultimate authority and may have to yield to inexorable necessity.[11] But since respect for the law is one of the major conditions of civilized life, it should be emphasized that only extreme reasons of emergency and self-preservation can justify a suspension of law and regular legal processes.

The problem is exemplified by the international crisis of October, 1962, when President Kennedy ordered a partial blockade of Cuba after the installation of Russian missile sites on the island. This action was not authorized by the Charter of the United Nations or by the principles of customary international law. It could be defended only on the ground that the Russian missiles posed an intolerable threat to the security of the United States, and that self-protective measures were called for under these circumstances. It might be suggested, however, that in the atomic age the defense of necessity should be used with utmost caution in the field of international politics, since the repercussions of an action contrary to law might be more fateful in their consequences than the original threat against which the action was directed.

It should also be emphasized that, unless a case of imperious necessity is made out, considerations of political expediency or social utility do not form a sufficient ground for setting aside the claims of justice in domestic and foreign affairs. The assertion of usefulness of a governmental action in terms of power, prestige, or other public advantage does not justify the suspension of the principles of justice because justice ranks higher in the scale of social values than expediency.

The superiority of justice stems, in the first place, from the fact that the solutions of justice are directed toward ethical objectives, while expediency may serve worthy purposes as well as unworthy ones.[12] A nation may find it "useful" to oppress its minorities, imprison its non-conformists, or plunder its neighbors.[13] Secondly, justice is more broad-gauged and embracive as a method of political and social problem-solving than expediency. When a certain course of action is viewed by the public authorities solely from the angle of political or social expediency, there is danger that the decision will be controlled by an appraisal of the immediate advantages to be derived from the action. The method of justice, on the other hand, will weigh the short-term effects of the action against its long-range impact on the citizens of the national or (in some instances) international community. Considerations of the common good are by no means foreign to the approach of justice, but in determining the requirements of the common good justice will not lose sight of the welfare and legitimate concerns of individuals. There exists, as shown before,[14] no necessary contradiction between utilitarian expediency and justice, but when a conflict arises between them, preference should—in the absence of highly abnormal and pressing circumstances—be given to justice.

Some conclusions of a general character might be derived from the observations made in this section. It has often been assumed that the variety of conflicting ideas about justice defeats the possibility of arriving at any general and objective criteria for the evaluation of the problem. This conclusion is based on the belief that these differences of opinion stem from more or less personal, arbitrary, and fortuitous sentiments and reactions. It has been suggested here that an alternative and more convincing explanation for the diversity of historical patterns of justice is available. Imperfections of knowledge, limitations of vision due to lack of experience, an undeveloped state of the productive facilities, and other inevitabilities, contingencies, and shortcomings have often hampered the realization of justice in society. The possibilities of effectuating a just order are dependent upon a certain degree of advance in sociological, technical, educational, and psychological science. When optimum conditions of productive and intellectual development prevail, it would probably be possible to obtain a broad consensus of opinion with respect to the chief requirements of a just social system. This is to be expected chiefly for the reason that, in spite of individual differences between men, there exists a common human nature, expressing itself in typical and uniform responses to many facets of life and the actions of other men, and thus providing a measuring rod for the appraisal of legal and social arrangements. There are signs that, as the nations of the world progress in social experience and knowledge of human nature, they will slowly converge upon similar and mutually consistent notions of justice, unless events in the international arena should plunge humanity down into a new era of barbarism and ignorance.

The observations on the nature and general postulates of justice which have been presented in the first two chapters will be followed by a consideration of more specific problems in the remaining parts of the book.

CHAPTER III

POLITICAL AND SOCIAL JUSTICE

Sec. 15. *The Functions of Government.*

The term "political justice," which appears in the title of this chapter, may be used in a broad or narrow sense. In its broad sense, the term applies to the contributions which the political system can make to the effectuation of justice in a societal order. How can the goals of justice be furthered by the political form in which governmental power is exercised? What limitations on these powers are necessary in the interest of the promotion of justice? What should be the structure of the political institutions which provide frameworks for the discharge of governmental functions? These are some of the chief questions with which political justice in its broader aspects is concerned.[1] In its narrower denotation the term refers to those legal arrangements and procedures by which the security of a particular political system is safeguarded against sedition, overthrow, or subversion. In other words, political justice in this more restricted sense sets itself the task of meeting the threat of assaults directed against the political order and the established form of government.[2] In the discussion which follows the term will be used in its broader meaning.

By juxtaposing political and social justice in the title of this chapter, the view is implicitly rejected that the political structure known as the state embodies social cooperative activity in its totality and must therefore be considered a metaphysical unity, or "invisible personality,"[3] which draws the individual parts into an organized whole. If this position is taken, the social principle loses its independence and becomes fully absorbed by the political principle. Although attempts have been made in totalitarian states to subject the whole range of the "social" to direct control by the state, these attempts have never been

115

entirely successful. It is likely that there will always be some autonomous activity of society which the state cannot completely integrate into its regulatory or planning scheme.[4]

The distinction between etatistic activity and the separate movements of societal groups, whether these are spontaneous or directed by non-governmental organizations, is reflected in the disciplinary boundaries between political science and sociology. It is possible, of course, that in a particular social order the sphere of autonomy possessed by society, and by organizations standing between the individual and the state, has been reduced to small proportions. In that event, sociology will become almost fully fused with political science. But such a condition is not likely to be permanent, and at some later stage of the development society is apt to regain some of its vitality and independent power and to reassert its strength against the forces striving for total control.

Social justice is that part of justice which is oriented toward the interests of the individuals and groups composing society and concerned with the safeguarding of their rights and opportunities. While political justice considers the forms and institutional devices utilized by state power in the accomplishment of its functions, social justice deals with the allocation of substantive rights and powers to the members of the body politic. It is not confined to normative arrangements which spring from the womb of society as "living law," but also includes constitutional and other norms which belong to the imperative area of the law. The dichotomy of political and social justice reflects the dialectical relationships and tensions existing between government and society and their partial reconciliation in a legal order which seeks to give to society and its component parts that which is due to them. The distinction between these two kinds of justice cannot always be sharply upheld since they are often intertwined, and they will be dealt with conjointly in some parts of this chapter.[5]

The first question to be discussed addresses itself to the functions of government and the nature and scope of the powers it needs to perform its tasks properly. This is clearly a question of political justice, in the sense previously indicated, and it is undoubtedly the foremost and most crucial problem in this area.

In the opinion of the Swiss Calvinist theologian Emil Brunner, "the essence of a state is not justice but power." [6] This does not mean that according to Brunner the realization of justice is not a proper objective of statecraft. On the contrary, Brunner maintains that a power structure which ignores the claims of justice cannot in the long run maintain itself. The thought he seeks to convey is that an evil, tyrannical, and unjust state is still a state, while a political entity which is powerless to carry out its functions ceases to be a state.[7]

Brunner is undoubtedly correct in holding that a political unit in which power is exercised in an arbitrary and despotic fashion does not thereby lose its character as a state. But this proposition would appear to be different from asserting that the essence of the state is not justice but power. The essence of a knife is to cut, but a knife whose edge has become blunted will still be called a knife. If we mean by essence the most significant property of a thing conceived in terms of its *functions,* the validity of Brunner's statement becomes questionable.[8]

The essence of a state cannot be power, because power is merely a means to an end; the essential nature of an institution should be determined in the light of its end, and not by reference to the means it uses to attain it. The state performs an important and valuable function in human social life; its activities are or should be directed toward some determinate goals other than the acquisition or perpetuation of power.

It is, on the other hand, perfectly proper to declare that the state requires power as a means for accomplishing its objectives. A state which is powerless to fight disorder, civil strife, and crime, to enforce the law, and to maintain its position in the international community becomes a caricature of a state. But this is not equivalent to asserting that the essence of the state is power. A state which would use the power secured by it to decimate its population, to prevent any constructive activity on the part of its citizens, to lay waste the fields, forests, and other natural resources, to foster destruction rather than attempt to build the good society would violate the fundamental law of its being.[9] Power can be beneficial as well as hostile to life. From the point of view of the promotion of values, power is a wholly neutral concept; it may be used for highly laudable or utterly reprehensible purposes. Governmental activity, on the other hand, is not neutral to value. It is accepted and sanctioned by human beings because its exercise, if rightly conceived in its objectives and kept within its proper confines, is a necessary and beneficial aspect of community life.

117

In seventeenth and eighteenth century thought, government was usually looked upon as the product of a social contract. It was assumed that men, in order to eliminate the inconveniences of a state of nature characterized by the absence of government, entered into a mutual pact by which they transferred certain powers to a ruler or ruling assembly. It was the function of the governmental organs to provide order in society and enable men to go after their various pursuits in tranquility. The purposes for which such powers were allegedly delegated to the governing authorities varied to some extent with the political philosophy of particular authors. To Hobbes, the purpose of government was chiefly the preservation of peace and order, to Locke the protection of liberty and property, to Rousseau the effectuation of the general will of the people. If government failed to fulfill its functions, or overstepped the bounds of its legitimate sphere of operation, its exercise of power became illegitimate and, under some circumstances, could be resisted by the subjects. Even Hobbes, who was strongly inclined to confer unlimited powers on the government, absolved the subjects from obedience if the public organs failed to carry out their principal duty, viz., the maintenance of internal peace and order.[10]

The social contract theory has often been assailed as an unhistorical construction and unverified hypothesis. Ernst Cassirer has shown, however, that this criticism is off the mark because the large majority of the social contract philosophers had no intention of depicting the occurrence of actual historical events. Their objective was to offer a validation for political rule, a justification for the exercise of governmental powers.

Only a few thinkers were so naive as to assume that the "origin" of the state, as explained in the theories of the social contract, gave us an insight into its beginnings. Obviously we cannot assign a definite moment of human history at which the state made its first appearance. But this lack of historical knowledge does not concern the theoreticians of the state-contract. Theirs is an analytical, not a historical, problem. They understand the term "origin" in a logical not in a chronological sense. What they are seeking for is not the beginning, but the "principle" of the state—its *raison d'être*.[11]

The valid ingredient in the social contract theory consists

in the recognition that states and governments are not ends in themselves but are designed to serve certain needs of human beings. "One can say in general," Del Vecchio points out, "that the contract doctrine represents an attempt to demonstrate the original value of the human personality vis-à-vis society and the state." [12] To the proponents of the doctrine, a human being was not merely an expendable pawn for the attainment of the power purposes of the state. He was an end in himself, and in conjunction with his fellowmen he had instituted governments to help bring about conditions beneficial to self-fulfillment and the enhancement of life. It is no less true today that government cannot exist for its own sake but must serve the interests of the people.[13]

It was once believed that the functions of government should be confined to the protection of life and property, and that that government was the best which governed least. The increasing complexity of modern life and the occurrence of serious economic crises, which could be met only by governmental intervention, have rendered this thesis untenable. Modern government has to solve many problems which private action is unable to cope with. Unemployment can often be eliminated or reduced only by public works programs. The preservation of natural resources, the initiation of protective measures such as flood and fire control, the establishment or enlargement of facilities for universal education, the safeguarding and improvement of public health constitute tasks which, along with many others, can in many instances only be discharged by the government. It is a doctrinaire approach, of benefit to no one, to declare that certain functions conducive to the increase of productive power, to esthetic improvement, or cultural growth should not be performed by government, if this means that they will not be performed at all.[14]

If it is the purpose of human social effort to create flourishing civilizations, providing the widest possible opportunities for the activation of human constructive powers and capabilities, the scope of governmental powers is circumscribed by this ultimate goal. Very frequently governmental activity serving this end will merely be supplementary to private effort. The beautification of cities cannot be accomplished by governmental measures alone, but if public parks and recreational facilities are needed and cannot otherwise be procured, government should step in to supply this need. If a good orchestra cannot maintain

119

itself from private sources, a governmental subsidy will promote the interests of culture and preserve the work opportunities of musicians. If private hospital facilities in a city are insufficient and incapable of being augmented, the building of public or publicly-aided hospitals becomes necessary. Sound fiscal policy may dictate limits to governmental activity, but a great deal can usually be accomplished if the objectives are clearly and intelligently defined.

In the preceding chapter, the attempt was made to show that the concept of justice must be appraised in the light of the overriding objective of civilization-building. This objective, it was stated, is furthered by granting men freedom for creative and constructive purposes, equality in the sense of broadest opportunities for self-realization, and security of life and possessions to make productive effort in the service of civilization possible. Substantial powers must be conceded to government to enable it to promote these goals of justice, but the nature of the objectives also imposes certain limitations on governmental action. Government must use care not to impede effort by doing for the people what they can do for and by themselves, thereby stifling the energies of men instead of liberating them. Never should governmental action lead to the oppression and degradation of human beings.[15] A political order will do well in delineating certain boundaries which may not be overstepped by the organs of public power, and to set up agencies charged with the task of supervising the proper observation of these limits.[16]

Sec. 16. The Forms of Government.

The next question to be discussed is whether there are certain forms of government which are better equipped than others to discharge the functions which the apparatus of the state is designed to fulfill. In approaching this question, those types of regime may at the outset be eliminated from consideration which merely feed the power hunger of the rulers and are of benefit to no one except themselves and perhaps a small clique serving their interests. A theory of justice which rejects oppression, arbitrariness, and exploitation as proper ends of governmental policy [1] need not pay much attention to forms of political rule which, in the words of Thrasymachus, promote only "the

120

advantage of the stronger."[2] It is presupposed as axiomatic in the following discussion that a system of government can derive its intrinsic legitimacy only from a bona fide endeavor to give full consideration to the interests of all members of the body politic.

It is often assumed as self-evident that a democratic order in which the right to exercise political power rests upon the consent of the governed represents the only form of government which is capable of guaranteeing the reign of justice in society. And there are, indeed, many features of democratic government which tend to support this claim of superiority. In democratically organized societies, the laws which regulate the affairs of the community are made by the elected representatives of the people. These representatives are chosen by the people with the understanding that they will promote the interests of all or most and protect the values of liberty and equality in the performance of their functions as legislators. If they become neglectful of their trust, they can be voted out of office and replaced by others more sensitive to their call of duty. The highest functionaries of the executive arm of the government are likewise made responsive to the popular will, either directly by being chosen by the populace or indirectly by being made subject to the approval and confidence of a democratically-selected assembly. It is expected that under this system a close link will at all times exist between the general will of the people and the policies pursued by the government.

In practice, however, this expectation is often likely to be disappointed. First of all, many democracies have had the experience that members of the legislative body, although they are supposed to function as the faithful representatives of their constituents, may become subservient to the interests of special groups to whose support they owe their election, or to whom they have become indebted in some other way. Secondly, even if the elected representatives are not directly connected with any such special groups, the pressures exercised by influential and effectively organized lobbies on the legislators are often so strong that the latter are unable to resist the thrust of these interests. It is a well-known fact that the broad masses of consumers usually receive less consideration in the legislative bodies than tightly organized groups representing industrial, commercial, or professional interests.

In addition to such defects in the representative character

121

of democratic assemblies, the democratic form of government exhibits other weaknesses. The manner in which candidates for legislative or executive posts are initially selected by political parties—which play a prominent role in all democracies—does not offer a guarantee that public offices will be held by the best qualified men. Quite frequently the candidates are picked on the basis of qualities which are not necessarily related to an effective discharge of their duties, as, for example, their expected popular appeal or their skill in conducting election campaigns. Their competence for the handling of difficult problems of statecraft often remains a secondary consideration.[3] Furthermore, after the selection of the candidates by the party organizations has been completed, the people are not always in a position to exercise their voting rights intelligently and in full possession of all facts. They are, especially in the case of new candidates for office, remitted to superficial external impressions and unable to appraise the true qualifications of the men or women whose names appear on the ballot.[4] And when the voters make their choice in consideration of a political party program rather than on the basis of personalities, a proposal in a party platform may appeal to their immediate, short-term interests, whereas in the light of the long-range concerns of the nation the proposed policy may be subject to weighty objections.

In spite of these defects of the democratic process, it can be argued strongly that the drawbacks of other forms of government are more serious and far-reaching. This is obvious in the case of hereditary monarchy, provided that the position of the monarch is not merely that of a head of state without substantial powers. It is pertinent at this point to quote the following observations by Vinding Kruse:

> It *did* happen that a genius like Frederick the Great or a man of great ability and initiative like Charles XI of Sweden was born to the throne. But it was also possible for the throne to be inherited by a mentally diseased person like Christian VII of Denmark, a man of poor mental gifts and weak character like Louis XVI of France, mediocrities like Charles II and James II of England, or incapable persons like Charles IV of Spain. And unfortunately the latter cases are bound to be more frequent, recent statistics on intelligence tests indicating how small a per-

122

centage of aggregate men is constituted by people with superior gifts (about 4 to 5 per cent).[5]

Where the position of the monarch or ruler is obtained through designation by his predecessor, as was the case during certain periods of the Roman Principate, the result may at times be beneficial. Some great Roman emperors, like Hadrian, Antoninus Pius, and Marcus Aurelius, owed their office to this mode of selection, and they performed great services for the Roman state and people. But the danger exists that the designation even by a capable ruler may be determined by emotional factors of family affections. Marcus Aurelius, for example, chose his son Commodus as his successor, who later became one of the most cruel despots in the history of the Roman Empire. The rule of self-perpetuating aristocracies is subject to criticisms similar to those that may be levelled against monarchy in its various forms.

In his discussion of the best form of government, Aristotle came to the conclusion that a moderate democracy based on the strength of the middle classes offered the best chance of success under ordinary circumstances. Such a democracy, he suggested, was likely to avoid the undesirable consequences of plutocracy as well as of mob rule.

It is therefore the greatest of blessings for a state that its members should possess a moderate and adequate property. Where some have great possessions, and others have nothing at all, the result is either an extreme democracy or an unmixed oligarchy; or it may even be—indirectly, and as a reaction against both these extremes—a tyranny.[6]

Aristotle was convinced, however, that under certain conditions the rule of one man, or a small group of men, was preferable to democratic government. This was the case when individuals of outstanding eminence and ability were available to solve pressing problems of statecraft:

If there is one person (or several persons, but yet not enough to form the full measure of a state) so pre-eminently superior in goodness that there can be no comparison between the goodness and political capacity which he shows (or several show, when there is more than one) and what is shown by the rest, such a person, or such persons, can no longer be treated as part of a state. Being so greatly superior to others in goodness and political capacity, they will suffer injustice if they are treated as worthy only of an equal share; for a person of this order may very well be like a god amongst men. . . . Such men will accordingly be the permanent kings in their states.[7]

Aristotle insisted that even in a government of superior men there must be a body of laws, and that laws must be sovereign in all cases except those which the law was unable to settle by a general pronouncement.[8]

In recent times, the Aristotelian view that democracy is only relatively, but not absolutely and under all circumstances, the best form of government was restated by Emil Brunner.

To forestall any misunderstanding, it must be said at once that democracy, given the necessary conditions, is doubtless the most just of all polities, because it gives every citizen a share in the responsibility for the exercise of a political power. That statement, however, of itself implies that democracy is not *in all circumstances* the best political order, the one which provides the best guarantee of justice. It does so only in definite circumstances which we Swiss particularly, having lived under democratic institutions longer than any nation on earth, are only too inclined to take for granted. There are circumstances in which democracy can be the worst of all political orders, namely when the people are not ripe for it, or when social conditions are so disorganized that only a strong central will, a "strong hand," is capable of curbing the anarchy latent or manifest in the body social.[9]

There is undoubtedly a solid kernel of truth in the view of Aristotle and Brunner, which modern experience tends to confirm. As a general rule, the best chance that justice will prevail in a commonwealth exists in a democracy, because more rapport is usually established between the governors and the governed under this form of government than in other systems. But the very fact that in a democracy those in control of the legislative and executive branches of government have their ears close to the ground and are inclined to listen to as many voices as make themselves heard, may at times prevent the taking of measures which are necessary for the promotion of the common good. Everyone who closely watches the legislative process in a democratic state comes to realize that meritorious legislative proposals are sometimes defeated or not acted on because some business, labor, or professional organization, whose particular interests may be adversely affected by it, has expressed opposition to it. The tendency not to alienate any group whose vote might influence the outcome of an election can easily result in a frustrating legislative inertia, and the same phenomenon may form an impeding element in executive and administrative policy. When such conditions persist in the face of special and unusual circumstances requiring prompt and decisive measures, and democratic government is unable to adjust itself to the situation, it is likely to fall and give way, at least temporarily, to autocratic forms of government. The same may occur when democratic freedom degenerates into license and lack of discipline, producing disrespect for law, general laxity, or even anarchy, and destroying the moral stamina of society.[10]

It is well attested by history that periods of vigorous social and legal reform have sometimes coincided in time and place with periods of nondemocratic government. The age of the Antonine emperors in Rome was not characterized by a great deal of democratic participation in the activities of government. But Antoninus Pius and Marcus Aurelius were, on the whole, men of vision and wisdom, and they accomplished many improvements in the social and legal structure of Rome. Gibbon went so far as to characterize the age of the Antonines as the happiest era in the history of mankind.[11] This was perhaps an exaggeration, but there is no doubt that the reign of peace and the humanitarian policies of the emperors compared favorably with the turmoil and civil strife which had prevailed during the last one hundred years of the Roman Republic. In more recent times, a number of reforms on which posterity has conferred its praise were accomplished by autocratic rulers such as Cromwell, Frederick the Great of Prussia, and Napoleon.

The Roman historian Polybius has argued that each form of government has its intrinsic advantages and inevitable drawbacks, and that for this reason it was likely that systems of government would always alternate with each other in a cyclical movement of political history.[12] To alleviate some of the defects of the pure systems and reduce the frequency and disrupting effects of periodic changes, Polybius advocated the adoption of mixed systems combining and synthetizing elements of monarchy, aristocracy, and democracy.[13] This mixed form was conceived by Polybius as "a system of checks and balances in which each of the three elements has an equal share in the political power, and in which the political powers are interlaced in such a way that none of the three elements can make use of its powers without constantly being checked by the other two." [14] Polybius believed that a constitution of this type would make a country strong and stable and at the same time guarantee the liberty of the citizens.

Polybius realized, however, that it was not easy to produce the ideal type of a mixed constitution, and he anticipated that some of the basic charters of government embodying his ideas would be destroyed through hidden faults in their construction.[15] The difficulties involved in establishing a truly balanced system of political rule are indeed considerable. When a strong and determined ruler or ruling group are at the helm of the state, it may easily happen that the democratic component of the constitutional order will be rendered nugatory. If, on the other hand, the monarch or aristocracy are weak, the system will become unbalanced in the opposite way. It might also be observed that, if the system of checks and balances designed to forestall a lopsided exercise of power by any one of the coordinate branches is carried too far, this situation may lead to a paralysis of governmental processes.

It is unlikely for these reasons that either a pure or mixed type of constitution will ever become a permanent possession of a nation, or of mankind as a whole. There will be alternations of political systems and fluctuations within each system for an indefinite future. What counts most decisively from the point of view of the theory of justice is not so much the form of government but the distribution and enforcement of rights, powers, and duties insofar as they affect the members of society, and the quality and wisdom of the policies pursued by the organs of authority.

Sec. 17. *The Public Interest.*

The argument was propounded in the second chapter that justice must aim at the creation and maintenance of a civilized society in which all human talents are fully utilized in order to achieve material progress, enable men to live harmoniously together in a community of mutual respect, and cultivate the arts and the life of the mind. If these are the goals of a good society, the conclusion is inescapable that it is in the public interest to pursue them with perseverance and vigor. It must be granted, on the other hand, that these goals are of an extremely broad and general character and require concretization and implementation by a great variety of ways and means. The question arises frequently in a specific and narrow context whether a certain policy, law, or other device proposed or adopted with a view to advancing the general purposes of social organization is or is not in the public interest.

As is to be expected, there exists no unanimity of opinion as to the criteria which are to be used in specific situations in order to determine the public interest. Leys and Perry found as the result of a comprehensive investigation that four basic approaches have been suggested for dealing with the problem. The first approach is purely formalistic and simply identifies the public interest with the aggregate of authorized governmental decisions and actions. The second proposed solution is thoroughly individualistic and equates the public good with the arithmetical sum total of private interests. The third approach is procedural and considers the public interest test fulfilled when fair methods of procedure are used in arriving at authoritative decisions. The fourth is normative, in that it proceeds from the conception of a public order which aims at the realization of certain goal values assumed to have objective validity.[1]

The formalistic approach to the public interest problem is highly unsatisfactory. In disposing of it, an earlier rejection by this author of the argument that the public interest coincides with the policy decisions of the public authorities shall be repeated here:

> It cannot be conceded that the public interest consists in whatever the public authorities by their fiat declare it to be. If the organs of government were always and

necessarily endowed with the will to accomplish as well as the capacity to discern the best interests of the community unfailingly and without deviation, then perhaps there would be room for an identification of the public interest with governmental decision-making. Every informed person is aware of the fact that, under the conditions of the actual world, this identification is without a rational basis. Government officials may misconceive the community interest, make serious and unquestionable mistakes in framing and executing public policies, and may lead the ship of state to ruin and disaster. They may also be motivated by selfish desires in exercising their responsibilities and interpret their functions purely in terms of personal advancement or aggrandizement of power. These facts are so well understood that no elaborate documentation or historical verification would appear to be necessary.[2]

It is also not tenable to assert a congruence of the public interest with the sum total of private interests. It was Bentham who put forth this equation in his social philosophy.[3] He was convinced that the pursuit by each individual of his private utilities would necessarily advance the general utility and result in the greatest happiness of the greatest number. Bertrand Russell has pointed out that this assumption rests on an erroneous psychology.[4] Individuals often engage in selfish actions which are detrimental rather than beneficial to the common good. Deceptive business practices motivated by hopes of easy gain, for example, may harm the public in many ways. To avert such harm, it was found necessary to pass laws against fraudulent issuance of securities, against adulteration of food products, against production of worthless or dangerous drugs, against unscrupulous practices in the competitive struggle. Such laws are generally deemed to be in the public interest, but they do not necessarily coincide with the aims of certain fly-by-night sectors of the business community. As long as individuals or groups will pursue self-regarding objectives which the community refuses to legitimize or accept, the common good must be conceived as an entity separate and distinct from the sum total of private interests.

A purely procedural interpretation of the common good is likewise subject to serious objections. A fair, democratic *method* of decision-making is not necessarily a guaranty for the promulgation of laws or policies which promote the general welfare. For example, the practice of holding hearings at which interested parties are given an opportunity to express their views on proposed legislation has not, as everyone knows, brought about unfailing excellence of legislation in the democratic states. The substantive content of a legislative enactment is always of greater significance than the procedure used in its adoption. It must also be realized that the participation of many voices in the preparation of legislation, although it is quite desirable from the point of view of procedural due process, will sometimes result in politically-motivated adjustments or compromises which detract from the chief purpose of a law, reduce its intelligibility, or impede its effective enforcement. Although it often does not hold true for the legislative process that "too many cooks spoil the broth," and although it is highly desirable to predicate legislation on a broad basis of consent, the danger of adulteration of a law by an attempted accommodation of multifarious conflicting interests will always loom in the background.

The only feasible method of determining the public interest is the elaboration of certain normative standards which may be of use in the appraisal of public policies.[5] Generally speaking, these standards cannot be different from the criteria which should govern the realization and administration of justice in a political society. The concept of the public interest is, however, somewhat broader than the notion of justice because it must also include measures that are dictated by inescapable necessity, although they may be questionable from the vantage point of justice.[6] Thus acts designed to insure the survival of a society under conditions of extreme emergency may be said to be in the public interest, although they may impose deprivations and sacrifices on persons and groups which considerations of justice as such could not sustain.

The position was taken in the second chapter that justice cannot be achieved by an exclusive deference to one particular value of social ordering, whether this value be freedom, equality, order, security, or fairness. A just society must promote a plurality of values and endeavor to harmonize or adjust them whenever they come into conflict. Since justice and the public interest coincide to a substantial extent, the accommodation and reconciliation of heterogeneous value patterns becomes a frequent postulate and need of sound public policy.[7] That rational

129

and objective criteria are available in resolving some value conflicts of this character shall be demonstrated by several examples.

Where a law penalizes group defamation, such as the written or spoken denunciation of a race, ethnic unit, or religious group as unworthy, criminal, or contemptible, such a law obviously contains a curtailment of freedom of expression. However, there are other values likewise within the contemplation of justice which a law of this kind would tend to protect. Above all, there is an interest in public order which may be seriously endangered by a prolonged campaign of hate and defamation directed at a racial, national, or religious minority. Since there will always be people susceptible of being influenced by such denunciations, outbreaks of violence aimed at the disparaged group may easily occur. These may pass beyond the bounds of isolated incidents and escalate into race riots or other serious disturbances. Antireligious propaganda, if it attains a certain degree of virulence, may create intolerable conditions of tension in communities in which the defamed group is represented in substantial numbers. Political propaganda launched against national minorities has often in history led to the massacring or even extermination of such groups.

But not only the interest in public order and internal peace are jeopardized by an unrestricted freedom to conduct campaigns of libel and vilification against unpopular groups. Such campaigns may also affect or destroy the equal opportunities of the members of such groups to participate in the political, economic, and social life of their community or state. Discrimination in employment, inability to obtain political office, social ostracism may be the consequences of a systematic dissemination of slanderous propaganda.

It would seem that in this instance the values endangered by group defamation rank higher in scale upon a rational analysis of the problem than freedom of expression. Although the value of truth, which is generally furthered by an unfettered right of discussion and dissemination of views, must naturally occupy a top position in the value hierarchy of the social order, there is no possibility that the horizons of truth may become enlarged by an indiscriminate hate propaganda directed at an entire racial, ethnic, or religious group. It could never be shown with any claim of truthfulness that all Negroes are criminals, that all Filipinos are a menace to humanity, or that all Catholics are unworthy members of a community. Such utterances, in the

130

words used by the United States Supreme Court in another con-text, are "utterly without redeeming social importance." [8]

It is assumed, of course, that the minorities protected by a group libel law have not engaged in activities inimical to the peace or security of the state, or in practices incompatible with the basic principles of public order recognized in the community to which they belong. If they have engaged in such activities, problems of a different order are presented. It is further assumed that the law in question is one which is directed at certain particularly vicious types of propaganda, and not one which abridges the freedom to criticize certain religious dogmas or to discuss the characteristics, positive as well as negative, of certain racial, ethnic, or religious groups. Furthermore, a law of this type would incur grave objections if it inhibits the freedom of scientific research concerning racial, ethnic, or religious problems in their biological, sociological, or ethical aspects. It may also be demanded that such a law must be limited to the curtailment of propaganda which has a tendency to incite to violence or disorder, cause serious mental harm to the members of the defamed group, or bar them from participation in community life.[9] Subject to such restrictions, the proposition would seem to be unassailable that freedom of speech should in this instance give way to other fundamental values which, for the reasons stated, are entitled to preferential consideration. The following statement by Walter Lippmann may be cited in support of this conclusion:

> But when the chaff of silliness, baseness, and deception is so voluminous that it submerges the kernels of truth, freedom of speech may produce such frivolity, or such mischief, that it cannot be preserved against the demand for a restoration of order or of decency. If there is a dividing line between liberty and license, it is where freedom of speech is no longer respected as a procedure of the truth and becomes the unrestricted right to exploit the ignorance, and to incite the passions, of the people.[10]

Accommodations between the rights of liberty and equality are also imperative, on public interest grounds, in the area of race relations in the United States. The principle of freedom of association and the prerogative of conducting one's business as one sees fit would at first sight seem to sanction a private

131

policy of excluding Negroes from restaurants, hotels, and stores. It cannot be gainsaid, on the other hand, that such a policy results in consequences which are seriously harmful to the colored race and deprive it of a substantial share of freedom and equality. A Negro may be unable to find any hotel accommodation or eating place in a city and may thus be prevented from traveling to this city for important purposes. If stores refuse to extend their facilities to Negroes, they may be deprived of an opportunity to buy food, clothing, and other goods, unless there exist equivalent facilities operated by members of their own race. The psychological damage inflicted on persons who are treated in this discriminatory fashion is incalculable. Furthermore, the long range effects of such a policy in terms of maintaining public order and preserving the political loyalty of the disfavored group must also be thrown into the scale.

Freedom is, of course, a value of supreme importance, but the freedom of innkeepers to exclude persons seeking room and board has always been deemed by the law as being limited by the public service element of this calling. It would seem perfectly fair to reason by analogy that restaurant and store owners also hold out their services to the general public and are therefore restricted in their freedom to exclude customers. Thus the argument of preserving freedom carries little persuasion in this situation. Neither is a policy of protecting irrational prejudices (which are often solely the product of environmental factors) entitled to serious consideration in a rational theory of justice. Where the arguments opposed to discrimination are as preponderant and weighty as in this instance, a conclusion in favor of a public policy of integration would appear to be objectively justified.

The further contention is sometimes made that discrimination, even if conceded to be an evil, should not be dealt with by the forcible imposition of prohibitory laws, but should be combatted by moral means, especially by encouraging a change in the attitudes of people. With respect to the particular problem under discussion here, the argument falls short of persuasive force. It happens often that the owner of a store or other facility is perfectly willing to serve colored customers but genuinely afraid that he might lose white patrons if he abandons his policy of discrimination while his competitor at the next street corner chooses to maintain it. In that event a law which ends competitive advantages derived from discriminatory prac-

132

tices may not only be fair to the disfavored racial group but may at the same time be necessary and desirable from the point of view of those who in the absence of such a law cannot afford to terminate discrimination because of justified fear of economic loss.

There are, of course, many instances in which the weighing of opposing interests or values does not, as in the case of group libel and racial discrimination, lead to a lopsided preponderance of arguments on one side of the balance sheet. The right to a fair trial, for example, may under certain circumstances come into conflict with the freedom of the press. As Judge Holtzoff has stated, "the dissemination in the press of an opinion of the defendant's guilt, the circulation of derogatory information that may arouse prejudice against the accused, or the publication of evidence, such as a confession alleged to have been made privately to law enforcement officers, if done prior to the hearing, may hamper and hinder a fair trial for the accused. Specifically, they may create difficulties in selecting a fair and impartial jury." [11] Statements not subject to crossexamination have in some cases been elicited from prospective witnesses by representatives of the press. The record of previous convictions of defendants in criminal cases has been published prior to trial in a number of instances. Persons accused of serious crimes have been interviewed on television, while in custody of the police and before being brought before a magistrate or commissioner, and have been asked whether or not they committed the crime of which they were suspected.[12]

In such situations a clash occurs between two liberties both of which are essential to the preservation of democratic values. There is a strong need for a vigilant eye of the public on the administration of justice. People should be able to observe what is going on in the court rooms, and the press is one of its eyes. Furthermore, there is a need for free criticism of the law, its development and application, the conduct of judges and lawyers. It is desirable that all channels of information be kept open.

But there is another side to the picture. The process of law must be due process. It is not for public opinion or the news media to decide law cases. As Justice Holmes observed in *Patterson v. Colorado*,[13] "the theory of our judicial system is that the conclusions to be reached in a case will be induced only by evidence and argument in open court and not by any outside influence, whether of private talk or public print." Trying to keep out evidence prejudicial to the defendant is of no avail if the press has an unlimited right to publish such evidence.[14] There is little use in attempting to keep the minds of jurors and judges free of bias and prejudice if the press can sway their thought processes by inflammatory comments.[15]

The public interest demands an accommodation of the two basic freedoms which protects each of them to the maximum degree consistent with the preservation of the other. There are various expedients by which this objective may be accomplished, and a solution might be found which would keep the necessity of imposing outright restrictions on the freedom of publishing to a minimum. The situation might be improved greatly, for example, if law enforcement officers were prohibited from divulging certain prejudicial types of information to the media of communication and authorizing interviews of defendants in their custody by representatives of the news-disseminating agencies.[16] It would probably also be necessary to forbid press, radio, and television statements that a witness will testify to particular facts, publication of the names and addresses of the jurors sitting in a case, and publication of matter which appeals to racial or religious bias.[17]

Difficult adjustments between individual rights and legitimate concerns of the public must be made in many areas of criminal procedure. Persons accused of crime must be given all the protection they need in order to be secure against unfair treatment and erroneous conviction. That this can be done without jeopardizing the effective enforcement of the criminal law is demonstrated by the experience of Great Britain and other countries. In the United States, the trend in the 1960's has been towards a strengthening of the procedural rights of criminal defendants, which was badly needed in many instances, but the necessity of protecting the safety of the public in the face of an ever-mounting crime rate has not always been sufficiently emphasized by the courts, including the United States Supreme Court. For example, in view of the serious difficulties encountered in securing criminal convictions on the sole basis of circumstantial evidence, it is desirable to encourage rather than discourage confessions obtained by fair means. There might be some question, in the light of this consideration, as to whether the tendency appearing in the decisions of the United States Supreme Court to invalidate confessions made in the absence of counsel during the early stages of the investigatory proceedings ought to be welcomed under prevailing conditions.[18] As Justice Jackson observed in *Watts v. Indiana*,[19]

> to subject one without counsel to questioning which may and is intended to convict him, is a real peril to individual freedom. To bring in a lawyer means a real peril to solution of the crime because, under our adversary system, he deems that his sole duty is to protect his client —guilty or innocent—and that in such a capacity he owes no duty whatever to help society solve its crime problem. Under this conception of criminal procedure, any lawyer worth his salt will tell the suspect in no uncertain terms to make no statement to police under any circumstances.

Because of the desirability, under the highly complex modern system of criminal law and procedure, to allow a broad scope for the right to counsel, the most satisfactory solution of the problem would seem to be a more liberal attitude toward the admission of confessions, whether obtained in the presence or absence of counsel, provided that fair means and no coercive tactics are used by the investigating authorities. One may also hope for a growing awareness on the part of all members of the bar that as officers of the court they owe duties to society as well as to their clients.[20]

Procurement of evidence through searches and seizures is another field where private rights must be reconciled with the requirements of the public welfare. Protection of the home against unreasonable police intrusion is a value of major importance, but a swift and effective detection and punishment of offenders is essential in order to safeguard the security of life, limb, and property. The present law of the United States and the several states has placed some unduly severe restrictions on the powers of the police pertaining to the production of evidence in criminal cases. For example, private documents and other chattels of the defendant which are wanted by the federal government only for their evidential value are not subject to seizure.[21] And the extremely strict interpretations of the constitutional requirement for demonstrating probable cause that a crime has been committed, which have been adopted by the courts for purposes of testing the legality of searches, seizures, and arrests, have in some cases proved great obstacles to an effective enforcement of the law.[22]

The examples which have been presented were designed to show that the public interest, depending upon the concrete problem to be solved, may call for the protection of the basic rights of individuals or groups or, conversely, for the restriction of such rights in view of the need for guaranteeing the rights and opportunities of other persons or groups.[23] It was also found that the public interest sometimes demands regulation or limitation of individual rights for the purpose of protecting the public order and safety; other restrictions may aim at the preservation of public health and morality.[24] The final goal to be served by measures enacted in the public interest, as was pointed out at the beginning of this section, is the achievement of justice in the social order, subject to occasional limitations imposed by conditions of emergency or compelling necessity.

Sec. 18. *Judicial Review.*

If the achievement of justice is held to be the principal aim of good government, much can be said in favor of setting up an organ within the political system to which the task of exercising a certain degree of surveillance over the lawmaking processes of the state is delegated. Even in a democratic commonwealth laws are sometimes enacted which fail to measure up to the requirements of justice, either because some special groups brought undue pressures to bear upon the legislature, or because this body passed a bill in haste without giving sufficient thought to its probable effects. There can be little doubt that the creation of institutionalized channels for the invalidation of thoroughly unjust laws is preferable to the sabotaging or evasion of enactments which large segments of the population consider unacceptable. Since the considerations which determine the validity of laws are peculiarly within the competence of the legal profession, the surveillance of the legislative processes with a view to preventing the perpetration of serious injustices ought to be entrusted to a body of trained judges.

The charge has sometimes been made that a judicial review of legislation results in the defeat of the popular will as expressed in the actions of the elected representatives of the people and is therefore an essentially undemocratic device.[1] If the term "democratic" is understood in the sense of an indisputable supremacy of the majority will, as was suggested in the political theory of Rousseau, judicial review must indeed be deemed incompatible with popular sovereignty. If, on the other hand, a constitution resting on popular support sets up legal restraints on the powers of legislative majorities, it may be validly argued that this constitution itself is the product of the people's will, through the exercise of which it has become the supreme law of the land. If this constitution, explicitly or implicitly, grants the judiciary the power to uphold its mandates against legislative attempts of infringement, the democratic principle appears to be vindicated under this theory.[2] Furthermore, since the effectiveness of political action in a democracy depends on the maintenance of certain liberties of expression and communication, while the ethical basis of democracy rests to a large extent on its claim to be the government of *all* the people, a strong argument can be made in favor of establishing a guardian for the preservation of fundamental democratic principles and minority rights.[3] It might also be observed that the institution of judicial review is not necessarily foreign to nondemocratic forms of government, as long as the governing authorities are intent upon protecting individual rights and preserving the rule of justice.

Where judicial review forms part of a political system, the principles and guarantees which the judiciary is called upon to shield from adverse legislative action are usually laid down in a written constitution. It often happens that some clauses embodied in such a constitution are so broad and elastically-worded that a wide margin of discretion with respect to their interpretation is left to the judiciary. Examples are the due process and equal protection clauses of the American Constitution and the "dignity of man" pronouncement in the West German Constitution of 1949.[4] Some courts are also willing to recognize non-positive principles of adjudication which are not explicitly mentioned in the constitutional document but are deemed to constitute basic premises of the political and social order endowed with legal force.[5]

It has often been argued that a judicial veto power on legislation, if it can be based on broad, amorphous concepts like "due process," "equal protection," "just compensation," etc., converts the judiciary into an organ of politics and opens up vast possibilities for the exercise of subjective and idiosyncratic judgment. Where the judges deal with the fundamental value presuppositions of the social order, it is said, highly personal reactions are unavoidable and cast a cloud on the idea of impartiality

137

which should be the lodestar of all judicial action. "There is no objectivity in constitutional law," Braden asserts, "because there are no absolutes. Every constitutional question involves a weighing of competing values." [6]

Conceding to Braden that the making of value choices is inevitable in exercising the power of judicial review, Wechsler reasons that it is nevertheless possible for a body of judges to agree on a set of objective, neutral principles which can serve as guidelines in the process of constitutional litigation. These are his words:

> I put it to you that the main constituent of the judicial process is precisely that it must be genuinely principled, resting with respect to every step that is involved in reaching judgment on analysis and reasons quite transcending the immediate result that is achieved. To be sure, the courts decide, or should decide, only the case they have before them. But must they not decide on grounds of adequate neutrality and generality, tested not only by the instant application but by others that the principles imply? [7]

Other writers have questioned not only the possibility, but also the desirability of objectivity and "neutrality" in determining constitutional questions whose solution cannot be derived directly from the constitutional text. In the opinion of Miller and Howell, for example, the quest for detachment in the area of judicial review of legislation is largely a futile one. In making choices among the competing values of the social order, these authors contend, the judges of the reviewing court are necessarily guided by normative preferences. Not only do the provisions of the constitution carry varying and often inconsistent meanings for individual judges, but they also have a different rank and importance to them. Furthermore, the argument continues, the judges can never be disinterested in the result which they achieve by their decision, as the doctrine of "neutral principles" seems to demand. There can be no escape from the fact that the reviewing court is an organ of power which enters the political battleground and consciously attempts to shape community values. [8] Addressing themselves specifically to the role of the United States Supreme Court, these two authors argue that "acting at least in part as a 'national conscience,' the Court should help articulate in broad principle the goals of American society." [9]

The problem debated by these authors has great significance for the theory of justice. Broad constitutional clauses requiring adherence to "due process of law," guaranteeing the "equal protection of the laws," or protecting the "dignity of man," embody certain basic postulates of justice and, if judicial review of legislation is available under the constitutional system in question, confer upon the judiciary a far-reaching power to uphold and enforce these postulates. If interpretations of vaguely-phrased constitutional mandates represent nothing more than the predilections and subjective reactions of a fortuitous and ever-shifting majority of judges, it is difficult to discern convincing reasons for imposing these haphazard products of judicial idiosyncrasy upon a community and its legislative organs as binding norms of supreme law. The popular response to such pronouncements would then depend solely upon whether a particular individual or group in society happens to share or not to share the value preferences of a temporary majority of judges in a given case. If these suppositions were correct, it would certainly become highly questionable whether such a subjectivistic dispensation of constitutional justice by a small group of men performs any truly useful and constructive function within the legal system.

In the actual administration of judicial review, however, the subjective element in constitutional adjudication, although it cannot be completely eliminated, is usually reduced in scope by a number of factors. Sometimes the nature and spirit of the constitution itself indicates the direction in which the selection between competing sets of values should proceed. The constitution, viewed as an integrated whole, is found to give preference to certain values of the social order at the expense of others. In other cases, prevailing opinions with respect to fundamental principles of social ordering may furnish some guidance to the judges in resolving constitutional problems. Presumptions and firmly entrenched patterns of constitutional interpretation may also set certain limits to the unrestrained roaming of judicial discretion. Sometimes, the priority to be given to a particular value or interest is obvious under the circumstances of the particular case.[10] In many instances, the controlling principle has been firmly established by a sequence of decisions and the court is unwilling, at least for a considerable period of time, to permit deviation from it. Thus it is true that "judges are not entirely at large in choosing among values." [11]

There will remain, however, substantial areas of judicial disagreement as to the principles of constitutional adjudication and the scope of their application, especially when hitherto undecided questions come before the court. Freedom of expression may come into clash with national security, freedom of the press with the right to a fair trial, the right of property with the need for public safety. A judge dedicated to a philosophy of undiluted individualism may differ in his attitude toward the balancing of private and public interests with a colleague who believes that individual liberty must be made subject to overriding considerations of common welfare. This is particularly true in periods of transition when no clearly discernible "objective spirit" of the times exists and the value patterns of the community are split and confused.[12] Furthermore, in an open society whose traditional climate of opinion favors philosophical and doctrinal diversity, it is often difficult to discover, in the face of conflicting currents and counter-currents, a predominance of trends of thought which could be helpful in filling the lacunae in the positive system of constitutional law.

Under such circumstances, a wise judiciary should try to avoid an excessive reliance on subjectivism and personal predilection. For the purpose of hammering out some consistent principles of constitutional policy likely to evoke a broad measure of general assent, each judge ought to make some sacrifice of his personal convictions, even if they are deep-seated, for the sake of reaching a common meeting ground with his brethren on the bench.[13] It may, of course, become necessary to revise, expand, or restrict the principles on which argreement was achieved when this is made imperative by the circumstances of a particular case. The judges can never be insensitive to the results which they obtain by the application of the standards devised by them, especially where the validity or invalidity of a piece of legislation is at issue.[14]

When decisions on the constitutionality of laws are reached on the basis of broad constitutional provisions designed to guarantee essential justice in the social order, and when there is no lopsided preponderance of arguments on one side of the controversy, disagreements among the judges should ordinarily be resolved in favor of the legislature, and the latter's choice of

140

values should be upheld. Only when the challenged enactment is palpably unfair or unreasonable in the light of the controlling standards of justice should the power of judicial censure be exercised. For the primary task of passing laws must rest with the legislature, and the courts ought to interfere with the legislative process only in cases in which a clear violation of a constitutional mandate has occurred.

CHAPTER IV

ECONOMIC JUSTICE

Sec. 19. *Laissez-faire.*

The problem of justice occupies a prominent role in the economic organization of a society. Every person is directly and decisively affected by the opportunities existing for remunerative work, the amounts of compensation paid in different occupations, the rates of taxation, and the scope of other financial burdens imposed upon him. The standard and style of living is determined primarily by economic factors. The way in which a society is organized economically therefore has a strong bearing on the justice or injustice of its institutions and arrangements.

The theory of economic justice which prevailed in Western Europe and the United States during the nineteenth century was the laissez-faire doctrine. This doctrine was for the first time enunciated in 1776 by Adam Smith in a cautious and somewhat qualified form. His formulation was as follows:

> Every man, as long as he does not violate the laws of justice, is left perfectly free to pursue his own interest his own way, and to bring both his industry and capital into competition with those of any other man, or order of men. The sovereign is completely discharged from a duty, in the attempting to perform which he must always be exposed to innumerable delusions, and for the proper performance of which no human wisdom or knowledge could ever be sufficient: the duty of superintending the industry of private people, and of directing it towards the employments most suitable to the interest of the society. According to the system of natural liberty, the sovereign has only three duties to attend to; three duties of great importance, indeed, but plain and intelligible to common understand-

142

ings: first, the duty of protecting the society from the violence and invasion of other independent societies; secondly, the duty of protecting, as far as possible, every member of the society from the injustice or oppression of every other member of it, or the duty of establishing an exact administration of justice; and, thirdly, the duty of erecting and maintaining certain public works and certain public institutions, which it can never be for the interest of any individual, or small number of individuals, to erect and maintain; because the profit could never repay the expense to any individual or small number of individuals, though it may frequently do much more than repay it to a great society.[1]

In this passage, Adam Smith declares his preference for an economic system based on the principle of free competition between private individuals. He absolves the state from the duty of "superintending the industry of private people" and admonishes the public authorities to refrain, as much as possible, from interfering with the spontaneous unfolding of the economic life. But he qualifies his thesis by entrusting to the state the duty of "erecting and maintaining certain public works and certain public institutions, which it can never be for the interest of any individual, or small number of individuals, to erect and maintain." Since Smith had previously stated that the defense of the commonwealth and the administration of justice were within the proper precincts of the sovereign power, it is clear that the public works and public institutions envisaged by him were not to be confined to these two domains of governmental activity.

In the next chapter of his work Smith explains that what he had in mind were public works and institutions set up "for facilitating the commerce of the society, and those for promoting the instruction of the people." [2] Thus the state, according to him, had the right to build and maintain roads, bridges, canals, harbors, and post offices.[3] Municipalities, he said, may operate lighting systems.[4] The government may to some extent regulate companies engaged in foreign trade, especially trade with remote and uncivilized countries.[5] The government may fix the rate of interest by law.[6] Furthermore, the state may maintain or superintend a system of public instruction and require examinations as a condition of admission to certain professions.[7] It is obvious,

143

then, that the duty of government to abstain from economic activity and regulation was upheld by Smith only as a general principle, not as an absolute command without exceptions.

The restraint which characterized the formulation of the laissez-faire doctrine by Adam Smith was abandoned by some English and American thinkers of the nineteenth century. In England the doctrine was advocated in an uncompromising and extreme form by Herbert Spencer. He sweepingly condemned governmental action beyond an indispensable minimum by the apothegm: "Officialism is stupid." [8] Private bodies, on the other hand, were without fail "enterprising and progressive." [9] Inasmuch as the institution of government was an evil, the scope of governmental activity was to be limited to the narrowest possible range. The function of government was to protect the citizens from crime, invasion of rights, and external aggression, but the state had no jurisdiction to embark upon any positive programs of public welfare. Spencer rejected any kind of public health measures, including the control of epidemics, he denounced public education, castigated state operation of the postal system, deplored poor laws, and wished to open up the legal and medical professions to anyone without proof of qualification. He also opposed governmental regulation of the currency and of labor conditions, and any form of public works.[10] Natural selection and survival of the fittest were to him the chief vehicles of progress, and he viewed any governmental interference with the beneficent operation of these laws of nature as a symptom of supreme folly.

In the United States, the most vigorous protagonist of a radical laissez-faire philosophy was William Graham Sumner of Yale University. Like Spencer, he sought to reduce state action to an unavoidable minimum. "At bottom there are two chief things with which government has to deal. They are the property of men and the honor of women. These it has to defend against crime." [11] If the state does not interfere in the economic life, the rewards of productive activity will go to those most deserving of them, and the fittest will survive. "Society," he said, "does not need any care or supervision." [12] Maximum freedom of individual action, especially in the economic sphere, was to him the only end worthy of being promoted by social policy; attempts to secure a greater social and economic equality he considered unnatural and ill-advised.[13] The weak and the poor deserve their fate because "they are the shiftless, the imprudent, the

144

impractical, and the inefficient, or they are the idle, the intemperate, the extravagant, and the vicious." [14] Schemes for improving the condition of the working classes were anathema to him. "A free man cannot take a favor. One who takes a favor or submits to patronage demeans himself. He falls under obligation." [15]

Public expenditures to combat vice were deemed beyond the jurisdiction of the state by Sumner. "If we let nature alone, she cures vice by the most frightful penalties. . . . A drunkard in the gutter is just where he ought to be. Nature is working away at him to get him out of the way." [16] Public outlays for the rehabilitation of criminals were likewise regarded as misplaced by Sumner.[17] Their reeducation could be accomplished only at the expense of the industrious members of society. All attempts to make the world over, he said, are foolish and condemned to failure.[18] "The truth is that the social order is fixed by laws of nature precisely analogous to those of the physical order." [19] Men should not by their actions mar the operation of these laws. Even alms-giving was disapproved by him as an interference with nature's design.[20]

The laissez-faire doctrine cannot be correctly understood without a realization that it is based on a certain view of man's nature and of the relation between his private pursuits and the wellbeing of society. Adam Smith stated the connection between private action and the common good as follows:

> It is thus that the private interests and passions of individuals naturally dispose them to turn their stock towards the employments which in ordinary cases are most advantageous to the society. . . . Without any intervention of law, therefore, the private interests and passions of men naturally lead them to divide and distribute the stock of every society, among all the different employments carried on in it, as nearly as possible in the proportion which is most agreeable to the interest of the whole society.[21]

Thus Smith was convinced that the self-interest of man, as manifested in his efforts to better his condition, was a psychological force which worked toward economic improvement on the broadest scale and the achievement of the general welfare. Underlying this conviction was his strong belief that an "invisible hand," using man's selfish desires as a vehicle of progress, was guiding mankind toward a state of affairs, which, even though its accomplishment was no part of the intention of any single individual, was productive of social harmony and beneficial to all classes of society.

The produce of the soil maintains at all times nearly that number of inhabitants which it is capable of maintaining. The rich only select from the heap what is most precious and agreeable. They consume little more than the poor, and in spite of their natural selfishness and rapacity, though they mean only their own convenience, though the sole end which they propose from the labours of all the thousands whom they employ be the gratification of their own vain and insatiable desires, they divide with the poor the produce of all their improvements. They are led by an invisible hand to make nearly the same distribution of the necessaries of life which would have been made had the earth been divided into equal portions among all its inhabitants; and thus, without intending it, without knowing it, advance the interest of the society, and afford means to the multiplication of the species. When Providence divided the earth among a few lordly masters, it neither forgot nor abandoned those who seemed to have been left out in the partition. These last too enjoy their share of all that it produces. In what constitutes the real happiness of human life, they are in no respect inferior to those who would seem so much above them. In ease of body and peace of mind, all the different ranks of life are nearly upon a level, and the beggar who suns himself by the side of the highway possesses that security which kings are fighting for.[22]

Spencer shared many of the sentiments of Adam Smith. He, too, was certain that man, if left undisturbed by government, would pursue his own ends in a way that would conduce to the good of all. As time went on, he argued, man's adaptation to his environment would become more perfect and the cooperative side of his nature would be strengthened. "Evil perpetually tends to disappear." [23] Progress, in his opinion, was not an accident but a necessity.[24] Eventually a stage of development would be reached by mankind in which the state would wither away, or, in his own words, "in which the individual is everything, and the state nothing." [25]

Such were the convictions of the chief protagonists of laissez-faire. Subsequent experiences acquired in the practical operation of laissez-faire principles in the economic order have demonstrated, however, that some of the psychological and social-philosophical foundations of the doctrine were ill-conceived and faulty. We know today that allowing full play for economic self-assertion does not necessarily produce a congruence and harmony between private and public welfare.[26] It was found that the uncontrolled exertion of the drive for economic gain engendered many practices which were detrimental to the wellbeing of the people. Unfettered competition often resulted in the payment of substandard wages, with a consequent diminution of the purchasing power of wage earners. This was one of the factors responsible for the occurrence of severe economic crises during the laissez-faire era. The desire to realize maximum profits by reducing overhead costs led in many instances to a neglect of plant safety, a condition which caused a large number of industrial accidents. Instances of exploitation of the labor power of men, women, and children in factories and "sweat-shops" did not remain isolated occurrences. Unsanitary conditions in the meat-packing industry and others imperiled the health of the people. A considerable amount of adulterated food was produced, and many worthless or harmful drugs appeared on the market. Investors of securities were often injured by fraudulent prospectuses on which they relied, or by other deceptive practices. Railroads adopted discriminatory rate policies which favored some shippers while making the transportation of goods by others prohibitive in cost. A squandering of natural resources took place on an alarming scale.[27]

Even though only a minority of producers and businessmen abused their economic liberties, the impact of the abuses which occurred was substantial enough to force down the moral level of economic life. Conscientious businessmen who had to compete with unscrupulous rivals, in order to insure their own survival in the economic struggle, often had to adjust their policies and tactics to those pursued by undesirable elements in the trade. It was discovered that those who remained above the water were not always the fittest, i.e. those who gave the best and most efficient service to the public; not infrequently the winners in the competitive race were those who played the game most ruthlessly and without any inhibitions.

Furthermore, laissez-faire by the natural operation of its intrinsic laws produced a contradiction which, if allowed to develop without hindrance, would lead to its inevitable demise. Early in the history of free enterprise in the Western World it became manifest that the ideal of all-out competition did not necessarily comport with the desires and interests of the business community. In order to avoid the rigors and hazards of the competitive system, entrepreneurs, bankers, and industrialists moved toward consolidations and mergers. Since a monopoly or semimonopoly in a certain branch of business or trade provides a greater degree of security and considerably more guarantee of success than the rough-and-tumble of unrestrained economic warfare, competitors often laid down the battle ax and combined to fix prices, regulate output, or divide the market. To William Graham Sumner, such combinations and consolidations of capital seemed indispensable, and he could visualize no dangers arising from large aggregations of wealth.[28] But it became soon apparent that the freedom which laissez-faire ostensibly sought to promote would in the long run be turned into a state of affairs where small businessmen were pressed against the wall and dependence on monopoly power became the prevailing feature of the economic system. Moreover, the laissez-faire system produced alternate booms and busts, including some severe depressions, harmful to rich and poor alike, which were entirely beyond the control of private entrepreneurs engaged in big or small business.

Another drawback of an economic system founded on laissez-faire principles consists in the inevitable creation of an imbalance between private and public expenditures.[29] Government under this system is relegated to the functions of a constable and military guardian because of the belief that the best government is the one which governs least, and its income is therefore sought to be severely limited. This produces the result that the government becomes unable to discharge certain tasks which private individuals or private organizations cannot successfully perform because, in the words of Adam Smith, "the profit could never repay the expense to any individual or small number of individuals, though it may frequently do much more than repay it to a great society." [30]

Under the complex and crowded conditions of twentieth-century industrial civilization, many kinds of public services have become well-nigh indispensable. To avoid traffic congestion and a high rate of automobile accidents, there must be an ample supply of highways. The police forces must be adequately staffed and—in order to get competent men—attractively paid for their hazardous work. If the facilities of private hospitals are insufficient to meet the needs of the population, publicly-aided hospitals must be provided. Recreational programs for children must be established to take them off the streets and reduce juvenile delinquency. There must be an adequate supply of well-trained probation officers to supervise children who have become delinquent. The courts must have a sufficient number of judges to make an expeditious administration of justice possible. The cities should be kept clean and slum areas, breeding crime, disease, and discontent, should be eliminated. To attract good men and women to the all-important teaching profession, the salaries of teachers in public institutions should be raised to a higher level than is presently attained in many states and local communities. When unemployment raises its ugly head, public work programs and facilities for the vocational retraining of jobless workers become an urgent need. Natural resources must be conserved, because their spoliation and depletion impedes the work of civilization-building.

Advocacy of such programs and policies is not merely a matter of personal predilection or political party allegiance. If the services mentioned above, and various others which have not been discussed, are not provided by government, the entire society, or large parts of it, will suffer grief or loss. All classes of society are affected by a high incidence of crime and juvenile delinquency. Millions of people will undergo severe privations when the rate of unemployment reaches substantial dimensions. Sumner was quite wrong when he attributed the fate of the poor to shiftlessness and sloth. In a large army of unemployed people, only an insignificant minority will consist of idlers; it is a well-known fact that the large majority of jobless persons will suffer gravely from lack of work and will make every effort to secure new employment. Hardly anybody will agree today with Adam Smith when he said: "In ease of body and peace of mind, all the different ranks of life are nearly upon a level, and the beggar who suns himself by the side of the highway possesses that security which kings are fighting for".[31]

The depletion of natural resources, such as water, forests, oil, etc., will adversely affect industrial activity and the conveniences of living unless adequate substitutes can be developed. Lack of education will lower the performance of society on all levels, because a great deal of knowledge, information, and mental training are needed to cope successfully with the complexities of modern life.

We can thus concur with Galbraith that "failure to keep public services in minimal relation to private production and use of goods is a cause of social disorder or impairs economic performance".[32] Galbraith, for the purposes of illustrating his thesis, graphically describes the conditions which a family taking a pleasure trip in an automobile may face because of an imbalance between private and public outlays:

> The family which takes its mauve and cerise, air-conditioned, power-steered, and power-braked automobile out for a tour passes through cities that are badly paved, made hideous by litter, blighted buildings, billboards, and posts for wires that should long since have been put underground. They pass into a countryside that has been rendered largely invisible by commercial art . . . They picnic on exquisitely packaged food from a portable ice-box by a polluted stream and go on to spend the night at a park which is a menace to public health and morals.[33]

There was a time when many economists and social scientists thought that laissez-faire, in spite of its imperfections, was in accord with natural law as it operated in the social sphere and constituted therefore a necessary form of economic and social life. The conviction was widespread that human interference with the forces of nature, through legislation or other artificial means, was foolish and could produce nothing but mischief. As mentioned earlier, it was above all Sumner who denounced all attempts to "make the world over" as "absurd" efforts. "The greatest folly of which a man can be capable", he said, is "to sit down with a slate and pencil to plan out a new social world".[34]

We know today that deliberate policies designed to control economic forces and better the condition of man are by no means futile and condemned to failure. It is possible to promote the common interests of the people by legislation and administrative action. Public health, public safety, security against grievous hazards, and the general welfare and prosperity can be furthered through intelligent and efficacious governmental effort. The laws which were passed by many countries after the demise of laissez-faire, such as industrial safety regulations, workmen's compensation laws, public works projects, minimum wage and maximum hours laws, child labor laws, pure food and drug laws, slum clearance projects, measures for the conservation of natural resources, and laws against monopoly and unfair competition have become lasting acquisitions of the legal system in many countries, and no political party can be successful today which proposes to repeal the major achievements made in the field of social legislation.[35]

The theologian Emil Brunner, a man of conservative leanings, characterized a pure laissez-faire system as an example of a "highly unjust economic order".[36] The fact that the system could prevail nowhere in the Western World because of the disadvantages, abuses, and avoidable hardships connected with it would seem to bear out the validity of his charge. A progressively-minded industrialist like Henry Ford agreed with the critics of laissez-faire that economic exploitation and injustice were not, as some authors had contended, to be accepted as ineradicable byproducts of economic activity. He said:

This much we must believe as a starting point:
. . . That it is possible for labour, production, distribution, and reward to be so organized as to make certain that those who contribute shall receive shares determined by an exact justice.
That regardless of the frailties of human nature, our economic system can be so adjusted that selfishness, although perhaps not abolished, can be robbed of power to work serious economic injustice.[37]

Governmental controls, if wisely contrived and applied, can stimulate creative energies, open up new avenues of enterprise, widen the opportunities for employment, combat predatory practices, and thus ameliorate the general conditions of life. Such a controlled or supervised system of economics can bring about the results which benefit all or most members of society. An unparalleled prosperity was achieved in the Western World after World War II under conditions in which the powers of government were used to improve the performance of the private econ-

151

omy. The growth of production was more rapid in many countries under a regulated system of economics than during the days of rugged individualism and laissez-faire. Per capita incomes were increased and the instabilities of the business cycle mitigated. The judgment which Brunner expressed is therefore not merely the product of an irrational feeling.[38] It is a judgment which can be verified by historical experience. The laissez-faire system was abandoned throughout the civilized world because it produced inequalities, hardships, and injustices which, in an objectively meaningful sense, could not pass muster before the forum of rational scrutiny.

Sec. 20. Compensation for Work.

The passage quoted in the preceding section from Henry Ford's "Life and Work" expressed the view that it was possible to organize production in such a manner as to make certain that "those who contribute shall receive shares determined by an exact justice".[1] This belief was by no means concurred in by the classical economists. Ricardo, for example, was convinced that wages would always tend downward toward that minimum which was necessary to keep a worker and his family alive.[2] Even though Ricardo conceded that, under favorable conditions, the actual wages paid to laborers might exceed the "natural" wage rate for prolonged periods of time, he thought that *in the long run* the "iron law of wages" formulated by him would prove its validity.[3] His train of reasoning is summarized by Rothschild as follows:

It was assumed that every increase in wages above the subsistence minimum would at once induce workers to have larger families. The consequent increase in the supply of labour would then bring wages back to the old level. On the other hand, a wage level that fell below the subsistence minimum would mean starvation, increased infantile morality, postponed marriages, all resulting in a reduced supply of labour which would ultimately lead to an increase in wages. Long-run supply of labour thus being assumed to possess perfect elasticity, it was not necessary to analyze the demand for labour in any detail. As it was thought that, no matter what the

152

demand conditions were, supply would adjust itself until wages equalled the subsistence level, it was clear that changes in demand could have no permanent influence on the wage level.[4]

The wage theory held by Ricardo and other classical economists was adopted by Karl Marx and came to form one of the chief dogmatic springboards from which he launched his attack against the capitalistic system. Like Ricardo, Marx proceeded from the assumption that the average price of wage labor in an unregulated economy is the amount that is absolutely requisite to keep the laborer and his family alive and maintain his working ability. He then argued that the value which the laborer creates by his work is always higher than the compensation which he receives in the form of wages. The excess of the value of the commodity over the amount of the wages is retained by the employer in the form of a profit; this difference was called *surplus value* by Marx. Capitalistic profits were to him essentially the proceeds of unpaid labor, resulting from the fact that the workman is deprived of part of the fruits of his efforts.[5] One of the chief program points of the socialist movement founded by Marx was the demand that surplus value be eliminated through a radical change of the economic system.[6]

The general validity of the Ricardo-Marxian theory of wages for capitalistic economies was subsequently disproved by economic developments in the most advanced capitalistic countries. The rise of labor unions and the constant increase in their bargaining power led to a gradual improvement of wage levels in many branches of the economy. These improvements were caused by deliberate policies, often backed by force, which were adopted by the unions for the purpose of bettering the condition of the workers. While the classical economists and Marx had assumed that wage levels are determined solely by impersonal, mechanical forces operative in the market, the actual development proved the efficacy of purpose-directed human effort, although the unions had to adjust the pursuit of their aims to certain objective conditions existing within the social system and could not altogether ignore the laws of supply and demand.[7] The role which unions have played in the shaping of labor conditions demonstrates that the structure of wage rates is not determined exclusively by economic factors. The relative power and bargaining strength of capital and organized labor are con-

153

tributing causes in fashioning the financial position of workers. Governmental interference with the laws of the market place, by the enactment of minimum wage laws and other measures, may also have a decisive influence on such developments.[8]

What bearing do the foregoing considerations have on the problem of economic justice? It would seem that a social philosophy which sees in the worker merely an instrument of production which has to be kept alive because it otherwise does not perform its functions for the employer cannot be justified from the vantage point of justice. As was pointed out earlier, justice, in view of the structure of the human personality as a purposive being striving for self-fulfillment, demands that human beings be treated as ends in themselves and not solely as means for the attainment of the aims of others.[9] Moreover, the Golden Rule, which constitutes the chief axiom of rational thinking in the ethical field,[10] is violated when one group claims an excessively large share of the national income for itself, while it is unwilling to grant more than a minimum of bare subsistence to another group. It is of interest to note in this connection that those classical economists who believed in the subsistence theory of wages did not dispute the validity of these observations. What they were convinced of was that mankind was confronted with certain iron laws of economic necessity which human deliberate action could not set aside or change. The subsequent economic history has shown that this assumption was incorrect.

Some socialist theoreticians sought to replace the orthodox approach of Ricardo by a theory of compensation which would grant the worker the right to the whole produce of his labor, thus eliminating the "surplus value" inuring to the entrepreneur in the form of profits. It is worth noting that this socialist demand, after an initial period of experimentation, was rejected in the Soviet Union on the ground that it was unworkable. In 1943, a group of leading economists issued a declaration which reflected the official governmental position and dealt with the problem in the following way:

> The matter has been often presented as though the surplus product does not exist under socialism, which is of course quite wrong. In point of fact, surplus labor (labor over and above what is necessary for the immediate personal needs of the workers) must always exist, under any system of society . . .

154

A certain part of the product of social labor must be systematically devoted to purposes of accumulation, even under socialism. . . . Furthermore, a certain part of the surplus product goes to cover the current needs of the society as a whole. It is sufficient to recall the significance for the country of the expenditures for strengthening the armed forces of the U.S.S.R. A certain portion of the surplus labor goes toward realization of such rights of Soviet citizens as the right to education (the maintenance of schools, universities and libraries), the right to rest (sanatoria and rest homes), the right to security during sickness and old age (hospitals, pharmacies and homes). Thus, in socialist society, the surplus product is at the disposal of society as a whole, for the satisfaction of all social needs and demands.[11]

Other socialist countries have followed suit. The workers in socialist economies do not receive the full value of the produce of their labor. There remains a "surplus product" (i.e., the creation of value over and above what is necessary for the personal needs of the workers),[12] which is used for the improvement of capital equipment, for education and cultural purposes, and to provide the means for national defense. It must also be noted that the salaries paid to the managers of industry are substantially higher than the wages paid to the ordinary workers, so that a part of the value created by the workers is diverted for the purpose of compensating the managers for work considered to be of superior quality, difficulty, and importance.

The notion of profit has also been reintroduced in the economic system of socialist countries. Plants are encouraged to reduce costs, so that their income will exceed expenses. It is considered axiomatic that "each economic enterprise should be profitable in the sense that the monetary value of its operations should exceed that of its expenditures, and second, that each enterprise must be financially responsible for its obligations." [13] The excess of income over expenses is used, among other things, to pay bonuses to managerial personnel, provide certain benefits for the labor force, and hire additional workers.

There is, however, an ultimate ideal of socialist reconstruction, retained as part of communist ideology, which varies considerably from the practice followed today in free-enterprise as well as socialist economies. This ideal received the following formulation by the pen of Karl Marx: "From each according to his ability, to each according to his needs." [14] Since this postulate is usually contrasted in socialist literature with the principle that people should be compensated in proportion to the quantity and quality of their work, it can only mean that in a fully developed communist society any equivalence between performance and reward is to be abandoned. Every person is expected to contribute to the common good to the best of his ability, and at the same time he has the right to obtain satisfaction of his needs. Since this principle has been propagated by communists as a supreme tenet of future economic justice, its meaning, implications, and merits deserve some consideration.

The first problem that is posed by this principle is whether a person who does not make a productive contribution to the social whole which is commensurate with his capabilities and talents will receive any compensation at all, or perhaps only such compensation as comports with his actual performance. Kelsen has pointed out that Marx gives no answer to this question.[15] His probable answer can, however, be deduced from the general vision of the perfect communist society which can be gleaned from his writings and those of Frederick Engels. Both men believed that in the communist order of the future selfishness, indifference, and sloth would disappear from the social scene. Men would become so thoroughly socialized that their cooperativeness and eagerness to produce would become a matter of firmly entrenched habit. Social consciousness and responsibility would have won the day, and no man would therefore do less than place his talents and abilities fully in the service of the community.

The second question that must be answered in an appraisal of the Marxian social ideal is whether the needs of the individual, which form the standard of remuneration, are to be assessed by each person according to his subjective desires, or whether there is to be some organ of society which will determine and rank the needs of persons authoritatively according to some official criteria.[16] If the second alternative reflects the Marxian view, then the scope of the communist ideal would be rather modest and limited. All that a communist government might then be able to achieve would be the establishment of an economic system in which nobody is deprived of the essentials of life and is reasonably well fed, clothed, and housed; a fair amount of rest and some security against the vicissitudes of life

156

might also be guaranteed under such a system. The gratification of the more fastidious desires and the more refined tastes would lie beyond the aims of social organization. Such a program would tend to bring society below the standard of living which has already been achieved by some non-communist societies. It is likely that Marx struck out for more ambitious objectives in drawing up a blueprint for the society of the future.[17]

If the goal of communism is the maximum satisfaction of the actual and highly individualized wants of the members of society, some serious difficulties stand in the way of its attainment. If, as seems to be the aim, these needs are to be met without taking into consideration the volume and quality of the individual's productive contribution, it may happen that a person performing a marginal service for society will obtain gratification of highly expensive demands. There will be no reward for superior achievement, since even the most unproductive and the most untalented member of society will succeed in having all of his wants fully satisfied.

It has sometimes been argued that no injustice would be committed by the adoption of such a system of distribution because the capabilities of a person are innate in him from birth, and those who receive an inadequate endowment of talent cannot be blamed for this deficiency. The argument is of questionable validity, since it takes a great deal of effort and perseverance to actualize and perfect an inborn capacity. But even if the contention should be meritorious, it would not dispose of the problem satisfactorily. The experiences of many generations of men have demonstrated that the prize of substantial reward provides a potent incentive for work of superior quality.[18] If everybody in society who is engaged in some kind of activity can expect the gratification of his fondest wishes, the stimulus for excellence is likely to become blunted or extinguished, at least for the majority of men. It is true, of course, that there are persons who make a maximum effort but are unable to accomplish much because of inferior native endowment. If such men receive a compensation commensurate with their work, no basic principle of justice appears to be infringed as long as their essential needs are taken into account in fixing their remuneration.

An adherent of Marxism might assert that the incentive of special reward for special merit will not be needed in the society of the future, because in this society men will be mature

157

enough to give their best without external inducements. This answer cannot be refuted with incontrovertible arguments, since there is always the possibility that human nature will improve with the progress of civilization. All that can be said is that the experience of the past and present, including the experience gained thus far by socialist experimentation,[19] renders such expectation speculative to an extreme degree.

There is a further reason why some reservation and restraint with regard to the Marxian social optimism might be advisable. The realization of the communist ideal of justice would require a volume of material affluence and abundance far in excess of anything that has been accomplished to this day in the most advanced industrial countries. Here again, the possibility of such an achievement cannot be disproved; but the registration of doubts can hardly be construed as an act of bad faith, or as a lack of realistic assessment of human potentialities.

From the point of view of the individual himself, a system of distribution which would satisfy all his wants could hardly be considered unjust. If it is kept in mind, however, that schemes designed to achieve the good society cannot ignore the bearing which adoption of a certain policy would have upon the well-being of the whole community, it may be doubted whether the materialization of the communist ideal would be productive of genuine justice. This might perhaps be the case if the strongly ingrained feeling that superior achievement deserves special reward could be extirpated from the consciousness of mankind. There may be grave doubt whether this would be possible or even desirable. As long as most men need external spurs to achievement, the possibility of realizing the Marxian vision of justice is apt to founder on the rock of harsh reality.

We reach the conclusion that distributive justice in the economic area can best be accomplished by a system of compensation which takes into account the quantity and quality of the work performed. It is true, however, as Perelman points out, that "it is very difficult to determine the just wage and the just price, seeing how disturbing are the effects of the law of supply and demand." [20] The difficulty exists even in socialist countries, to the extent that they preserve freedom of occupational choice and may thus be compelled to attract people to the less desirable kinds of work by tempting rates of remuneration.[21]

In spite of these obstacles, an attempt should be made to fix wages and salaries on the basis of criteria which assign weight to the skill needed to perform the work, the quality of the product, the time spent in completing it, and perhaps also the length of training necessary for obtaining vocational competence. One of the guiding notions of wage policy should be the realization that there exist creative or highly difficult types of work which require rarely available degrees of ability, and that in order to increase incentives for developing and cultivating talents of this unusual character compensation for such work should be made as attractive as possible. For example, achievements in the fields of social planning and economic leadership, legal control, education, the arts and sciences should be rewarded generously. A high and constructive intellect and a great artistic talent are relatively infrequent occurrences. Strong organizing and directive abilities are likewise rare.[22] Hence the most substantial emoluments should be reserved for those who are the architects of material and spiritual civilization, and who give it its color and peculiar quality.

To create a rough proportionality between performance and remuneration—and it is clear that it is impossible to reach anything like mathematical equivalence—is a task of sizeable dimensions. A combination of the methods of free bargaining—individual and collective—adherence to standards prevailing in the community, and some degree of official supervision may promise the most satisfactory results. The postulates of justice also demand that, as far as possible, equal work should be recompensed by equal pay.[23] This ideal, again, cannot be easily carried into effect. Local variations, due to the economic state of certain enterprises and other special conditions, may become inevitable, and a rigid and tariff-like setting of wage norms for certain occupations may often do more harm than good. However, as a general guideline in devising wage policies the principle is entitled to recognition as a fundamental axiom of distributive justice.

In this as well as other areas of wage policy, the law of supply and demand often cannot be ignored without detrimental consequences. Unless the undesirable alternative of a "command" economy [24] is chosen, in which every member of society is assigned his occupation by the government, fluctuations on the labor market, attractiveness and unpopularity of certain jobs, the occurrence of regional shortages of labor, etc., are factors which may have to be taken into account in the determination of wage rates. While the principle of supply and demand should not function as the exclusive or dominant yardstick of regulation, it is entitled to recognition as an auxiliary principle of great importance. Here again, we are confronted with a situation where social necessity may erect barriers to the realization of untarnished justice.

The payment of excessively high salaries even for superior performance would not appear useful from an individualistic or social standpoint and should therefore be avoided. Psychological experience seems to show that extremely wealthy persons seldom enjoy a full measure of happiness. They tend to be worried about a possible loss of their fortunes, and they are often unable to establish genuine human relationships because of a nagging suspicion that persons seeking their company or friendship are actuated by ulterior motives. It is also not desirable for a man to transmit assets of tremendous size to his children. Since accomplishment in life is usually due to the overcoming of challenges and obstacles, the early beckoning of a life of ease and abundance, coupled with the absence of a stimulus for work, may create a condition which is unfavorable to the development of a useful and productive personality. From a social point of view, the payment of emoluments which far exceed the financial means required to lead a very comfortable life affording the enjoyment of many luxuries is inadvisable because of the dissipation of assets which could be put to a more needful and constructive use.[25]

The principle of compensation according to work should form the primary but not exclusive rationale of distributive justice in society. As was suggested earlier,[26] there ought to be a rock bottom layer of remuneration based on the consideration of essential needs. Justice requires that "workers receive a wage sufficient to lead a life worthy of man and to fulfill family responsibilities properly." [27] In a civilized society, each person who serves society according to his capacities should be deemed entitled, not to a bare subsistence minimum, but to a fair measure of security and comfort for himself and his family.[28] This postulate is grounded on that aspect of justice which concerns itself with the elimination of social conditions incompatible with human dignity.

160

Sec. 21. *Private and Public Property.*

Property is another important social institution which has been in the forefront of the discussion about justice. In some form or other, this institution is recognized in all legal systems, because good order and social peace can hardly exist until the power to utilize and dispose of consumptive goods and to control the productive instrumentalities is located in some persons, groups, or collective units. One of the chief problems which in our era has caused an ideological division of mankind into two camps is the extent to which ownership rights should be vested in private individuals or public bodies. This problem has assumed immense significance in our time and discussions of it are often charged with strong emotional overtones.

Some legal philosophers have glorified the institution of private property and have pronounced it to be the mainstay of a healthy social order. John Locke declared that "the great and chief end . . . of men uniting into commonwealths, and putting themselves under government, is the preservation of their property." [1] He also insisted that "the supreme power cannot take from any man any part of his property without his own consent." [2] Jeremy Bentham was convinced that interference with private property rights in the system of production would lead to a "deadening of industry" and loss of creative initiative.[3] The French nineteenth-century economist Frederick Bastiat denounced socialism as a system of "plunder" and demanded that "all the measures of the law should protect property and punish plunder." [4] The Encyclical *Rerum Novarum* of Pope Leo XIII advanced the thesis that "private ownership is in accordance with the law of nature," [5] and some modern neo-scholastic authors have likewise stressed the supreme importance of private property for the effective organization of the social order.[6]

While Bastiat had argued that the abolition of private property would constitute a legal endorsement of plunder and robbery, Pierre-Joseph Proudhon in the same century advocated exactly the opposite theory, viz., that private property and robbery are "synonymous terms." [7] Karl Marx, contrary to a widely-held belief, took a less radical approach to the problem. "The distinguishing feature of Communism," he said, "is not the abolition of property generally, but the abolition of bourgeois property." [8] This distinction he elaborated by the following explanation: "Communism deprives no man of the power to

161

appropriate the products of society: all that it does is to deprive him of the power to subjugate the labor of others by means of such appropriation." [9] In accordance with this thought of Marx, the private ownership of consumer goods and those productive resources which have a very small potential in the creation of economic power is permitted in the Soviet Union. As John Hazard points out, "accumulation of wealth in the form of bank balances, State bonds, private residences, motor cars, furnishings, clothing, libraries and musical instruments is a commonplace today." [10] Enjoyment of such property as may be owned privately is protected by the law, and the right to transmit property by will or inheritance is recognized. The situation in other socialist countries, including China, is not essentially different.

The recognition everywhere of private ownership—in consumptive goods and other articles destined for personal use tends to demonstrate, in conjunction with other evidence, that the institution of property is not an arbitrary convention contrived by men, but has some deep roots in the structure of the human personality. Human beings have a possessive urge which can by no means be dismissed simply as a manifestation of greed or predatory instincts. Hegel pointed out quite correctly that a person, in order to develop and preserve his authentic self, needs an external sphere of his freedom.[11] The individuality of a human being expresses itself not only in his character traits and personal qualities, but also in the things with which he surrounds himself. He extends his personality, so-to-speak, into his immediate environment. A lover of natural beauty may find deep satisfaction in a flower garden which he cultivates with care and skill. A person interested in intellectual pursuits may enjoy a private library and greatly profit in his work from the easy availability of the books he owns. A man of mechanical proficiency will cherish his home workshop and tools which enable him to engage in carpentry or similar hobbies and to teach his skills to his children. A connoisseur of art may wish to adorn his residence with paintings, sculptures, and other articles of artistic value. It would be difficult, indeed, to devise a good argument for denying human beings the right to equip or embellish their homes, which are the center of their personal lives, with objects that are congenial to their personality, and whose possession and use give them enjoyment and satisfaction.

It is also generally acknowledged that individuals are entitled to the proceeds of their labor, i.e. the wages or salaries paid to them, although some people would want to put a maximum limit on the amount of remuneration that an individual may receive for his work.

While the urge to own property is founded primarily in the self-seeking side of human nature, it also operates to aid and encourage the expression of altruistic sentiments. It was especially Aristotle who emphasized the relationship of property to the practice of liberality and generosity.[12] A man without property cannot show his love and regard for others by bestowing gifts on them; he cannot assist friends or strangers who are in a condition of need. "Such kindness and help become possible only when property is privately owned." [13]

Aristotle also called attention to the social functions of property in maintaining peace and order in a community and insuring the proper care of things. "When everyone has his own separate sphere of interest, there will not be the same ground for quarrels; and the amount of interest will increase, because each man will feel that he is applying himself to what is his own." [14] Aristotle did not, however, believe that *all* property in a commonwealth should necessarily be private; he spoke of a system which "would combine the merits of a system of community of property with those of the system of private property." [15] But since he was convinced that men are prone to take better care of objects which they own personally than of things which they own in common with others, he advocated the recognition of private property rights on a wide scale.

The state cannot, of course, be indifferent to the uses which owners make of their property. All legal orders impose restrictions on such use in the interest of health, safety, morals, and the general welfare. In the language of American constitutional law, the right of property finds its limitation in the legitimate exercise of the state's police power. A person may not use his property in a manner which endangers the lives and possessions of others. He may not create a nuisance which interferes with the convenience or comfort of other members of the community. A man may be prohibited from selling articles which are a menace to public health or morals. He may even be required under the power of eminent domain to yield some property of his to the community, if the state deems it expedient to con-

163

vert it to a proper public use. Furthermore, he must pay taxes to the government as a price for the privilege of living in an ordered and civilized community.

A different frame of reference is presented when we turn from the field of property for personal use to the domains of industry, agriculture, commerce, and transportation. Here we are concerned with the instrumentalities which produce and distribute the goods needed by society to sustain its members and to build a flourishing civilization. At stake here are not so much the comforts and personal satisfactions of individuals, but the wellbeing and standard of living of the community as a whole. It is in this sphere of social organization that we encounter today the spectacle of a fundamental and crucial division of mankind into two antagonistic camps which confront each other in an atmosphere of great tension. The adherents of the capitalistic system contend that an economic order based on private ownership of the means of production is the most effective and promising vehicle of social and economic progress. The votaries of the socialist creed, on the other hand, are convinced that the capitalistic system is foreordained to disintegration and defeat, and that mankind can find its salvation only in a transference of the instrumentalities of production and commerce to public ownership. The issue is usually presented by socialists and communists not merely in terms of economic efficiency and expediency. It is also asserted by them that the capitalistic system results in injustice because it entails the exploitation of human labor and leads to the creation of social inequalities which, to the extent in which they exist under this system, are arbitrary and excessive.

Prior to the rise of socialistic states, it was sometimes alleged that a socialist or communist system of production was so much at war with essential features of human nature that soon after its establishment it would break down of its own weight. After fifty years of socialist experimentation, it has become clear that a socialist economy is able to produce goods with a fair degree of efficiency and to maintain a rather constant rate of growth. The controversy has therefore shifted from the question of the *possibility* of a socialist system of production to that of the *relative superiority* of capitalism and socialism. Which of the two systems is more apt to produce a healthy social order, promote human happiness, and achieve a high standard of prosperity?

164

It is obvious that it is impossible at the present time to answer this question with any degree of finality. At this juncture of history, the standard of living in the advanced capitalistic countries far exceeds that prevailing in the socialist orbit, and the gap is not likely to be closed in the near future. But the Soviet Union and other socialist countries have embarked on an ambitious venture to emulate the material achievements of the United States and Western Europe, and it cannot as yet be predicted whether at some time in the future they will succeed in matching or surpassing the economic attainments of these nations.

More definite conclusions can be reached with regard to the question which forms the subject matter of this book, the question whether an economy based on private ownership of the means of production is superior from the point of view of justice to one characterized by public ownership, or whether the opposite of this proposition is true. The answer must be that the dichotomy of private and public ownership provides no clue to the solution of the problem of economic justice. Whether or not an economy is capable of satisfying the just demands of producers, workers, and consumers depends on factors other than the situs of title to the instrumentalities which serve the economic needs of the people. Property is merely a formal legal configuration, a conceptual tool of the law. Its just use depends on how the powers and rights attaching to it are administered in practice.

As far as the free-enterprise economies of the advanced capitalistic countries are concerned, a few considerations will show that the form and location of ownership have little bearing on whether or not this economy can meet the fair claims of all persons and groups participating in the social processes. As Berle and Means have shown, an extensive separation of ownership and control has taken place in the structure of the modern private business corporation.[16] Stockholdings in a corporation may be dispersed among a large number of small investors, each of whom exercises little power in influencing the decisions of management. On the other hand, the officers of the corporation who direct its affairs are, in most instances, not the owners of the enterprise. Even though they may have acquired some stock in their company, their holdings are usually not extensive enough to give them control of the corporation by virtue of majority voting power based on ownership rights. Under these circumstances, "there is no longer any certainty that a corporation will in fact be run primarily in the interests of the stockholders." [17] The chief consequences that have emerged from this separation of ownership and control were described by Robert Heilbroner as follows:

> The uninhibited acquisitive drive of the highly personal corporate leadership of the late nineteenth century began to give way to a much more complex and considered set of business motivations. Making money—maximizing profits—was, of course, still a first rule of business life, since no corporation could long survive without profits. But it was no longer the only, or even always the overriding, rule of business life. More and more managers looked upon themselves as balancing many private "interests" in the general interest of the longevity of the enterprise itself. Their task was now to conduct the *government* of enterprises which had to function in a money-making world, rather than to run those enterprises as vehicles for personal money-making in the nineteenth-century manner. [18]

This state of affairs does not, of course, signify that private ownership of the means of production and the attitudes fostered by this economic system can and will no longer bring about results which the general public tends to regard as disadvantageous. Private economic power, especially in its more concentrated forms, can easily be converted into uses of political influence which may not always be salutary from the vantage point of the common interest. [19] Among other things, the pressures of private power may result in political neglect to develop sufficiently the public sector of the social system. [20] But it is undoubtedly true that the divorce of corporate power from ownership makes it possible for the managers of industry to consider the claims and concerns of groups other than shareholders and thus to avoid a one-sided deference to the interests of one particular class of persons.

Thus, it has become quite common in corporate policy today to foster public relations looking toward the creation of goodwill on the part of the general public. Labor relations are likewise deemed to be of utmost importance. Many enterprises do not consider it feasible or advantageous to keep wages and salaries at the lowest possible level for the purpose of maximizing the profits of shareholders. Regardless of whether the primary motivation for such policies is enlightened self-interest or the pressure of labor unions, it is certain that many business enterprises in the United States today pay wages and salaries which are considered fair by the employees, and the larger corporations often provide other benefits, such as pension funds and recreational facilities, for their working force. Labor contracts and laws in many instances establish safeguards against discriminatory hiring practices and arbitrary dismissals, which were frequent causes of injustice in former times. The power over human beings which ownership of productive facilities used to confer on entrepreneurs and businessmen has been greatly reduced by these developments in modern labor law.[21]

As the existence of a free-enterprise system, as such, throws no light on the question whether or not the actual operation of the system produces just or unjust results, it is likewise certain that ownership of productive facilities by the state or other public agencies does not imply an automatic guarantee of justice for employees or consumers. As Harold Berman has observed,

> Public ownership is a negative formula; it means the absence of private ownership—and no more. What the state owns, nobody owns. Everybody's business is nobody's business. The fundamental economic and legal questions still remain.[22]

Some of the "fundamental economic and legal questions" that remain unsolved by the mere fact of public ownership relate to the treatment of the employees of the enterprise, especially their wages, hours of labor, working conditions, and job security, and to the effectiveness of the enterprise in meeting consumer demands. The experiences with public ownership that have been gained in capitalistic as well as socialistic countries in this century would tend to prove that no generally valid conclusions can be reached concerning the intrinsic superiority of private or public enterprise in the aforesaid respects. In the words of Emil Brunner: "Neither private nor public ownership is in itself just." [23] In some public enterprises the working conditions for employees have been better than in comparable branches of private industry, in other instances they have been less advantageous. The labor policies of the Tennessee Valley Authority in

167

the United States and of many publicly-owned utilities, railroads, and airlines in Europe have given little cause for complaint. As stated earlier, the same has been true for many private companies. The just demands of consumers for quality of goods and efficiency of service can also be met by both types of enterprise. Whether *in the long run* the system of private enterprise will prove superior or inferior on an overall basis to its rival system in guaranteeing economic justice cannot, as we have seen, be forecast at this time.

It has sometimes been argued that the absence or reduced impact of the profit motive in a socialized economy will necessarily destroy any impulse to exploit workers, employees, or consumers, and will thereby eliminate one of the major sources of economic injustice. This argument does not hold its ground in all circumstances. Recent history, especially in the light of developments in Red China, has demonstrated that socialist governments, for the purpose of meeting the powerful competition of the advanced countries of the West, and in order to be ready for any possible military confrontation, have embarked on programs of rapid industrialization in which the labor power of individuals has been exploited to the utmost. Furthermore, the demands of the people for decent housing conditions and better consumer goods have been deferred in the interest of expanding the production of capital goods and armaments. While it may be possible to defend such policies on the ground of "necessity" brought about by existing world conditions, the harshness of the methods used in their implementation does no more satisfy the claims of justice than did the labor policies which were often characteristic of the early stages of capitalist industrial development.

One of the dangers which a complete collectivization of property brings in its train is the absolute dependence of every worker and employee on the benevolent attitude of the public authorities. The threat of exacting conformity of opinion as the price for affording a livelihood always looms in the background as an ominous possibility of the system. One might therefore well agree with the argument made by John Clark against the establishment of exclusive systems of public ownership. "It seems," he said, "that the existence of genuinely independent employers, with some of whom the nonconformist can find employment, is not merely a matter of business liberty, but is one of the indispensable safeguards of true personal liberty." [24]

168

The future will probably see the emergence of productive systems in many countries in which the economy of the market will be complemented or partially superseded by central or regional economic planning. As the German industrialist and statesman Walther Rathenau prophesied, three different types of enterprise are likely to play a major role in such a type of economic order: first, some enterprises undertaken by the state or other public organs, such as municipalities; secondly, a layer of "autonomous" enterprises in some strategic areas of production, to be subject to some supervision by government but unfolding independent initiatives, which will constitute a bridge and intermediate stratum between public and private undertakings; and thirdly, a base of smaller privately-owned business organizations.[25] If this prediction of things to come should turn out to be correct, the question whether such a mixed system of political economy will satisfy the just claims of producers, workers, and consumers from the individual as well as social point of view is unlikely to depend primarily on whether ownership of the instrumentalities of production and distribution is located in a private or public body.

Sec. 22. *Expropriation.*

The dichotomy between private and public property, which was discussed in the preceding section, exists and has existed even in societies characterized by a strongly individualistic philosophy of law, such as the Roman Republic and the American Commonwealth. Besides privately owned real property, the Romans knew publicly owned land *(ager publicus)* from early times, and this form of landholding played an important part in the Roman economic system.[1] In the United States, the public domain comprises very large areas of land, especially in the Western states; much of this land has been leased by the Federal Government to private parties for purposes of grazing or exploitation of natural resources. In all countries, of course, there are considerable amounts of personal property devoted to governmental use, and there are few countries today in which there do not exist at least some productive or transportation facilities which are owned by the state or some other public body.

The original acquisition of lands and other forms of property by the state was in many historical instances due to conquest. The conquering state took land or other goods away from the vanquished peoples and declared it to be the public property of the new sovereign.[2] But appropriation by force of arms has not remained the only instrumentality for the acquisition of public property. All countries have developed certain legal procedures for the transfer of private property into governmental hands. "All the available evidence goes to show that at all stages of history the individual owner was liable to have his property taken from him."[3] The legal devices for such taking of property by the state are variously known as expropriation, eminent domain, confiscation, nationalization, and socialization.

Confiscation of goods by the public authorities has often in the past been used extensively as a mode of punishment for crime,[4] but some trend can be discerned in modern law to limit such forfeitures to the tools and instrumentalities with which an offense has been committed. Today, the chief problems in this field of law relate to expropriation of private property for public use, especially for the purpose of nationalizing industries, branches of trade, and natural resources. Such nationalizations have occurred not only in socialist states, but also in countries with a predominantly non-socialist economy, such as France, England, and Mexico. Serious issues of justice are often presented by such measures in domestic as well as international law.[5]

The right to take property for public use, as such, has seldom been questioned. Grotius remarked that "for the common good the king has a right of property over the possessions of individuals greater than that of the individual owners."[6] Jhering commented on the problem as follows: "Expropriation, far from appearing as an abnormality, or as offending against the idea of property, is on the contrary peremptorily demanded by the latter. Expropriation solves the problem of harmonizing the interests of society with those of the owner."[7] In *Kohl v. United States,* the United States Supreme Court declared that the right of eminent domain is "the offspring of political necessity; and it is inseparable from sovereignty, unless denied to it by its fundamental law."[8] No fundamental law has been discovered which contains a flat denial of the governmental power to expropriate. But a large number of modern constitutions make it clear that private property cannot be taken by the state except for public purposes, and that an adequate compensation must be paid to the owner.[9]

These two typical limitations on the power of eminent domain pinpoint the two principal problems of justice that arise in connection with expropriations. If an absolute ruler were to take real estate away from his subjects for the purpose of enlarging his private landed domain, this would generally be looked upon today as unfair and unjust. It is agreed that property should be condemned by the state only for the performance of programs or tasks which are of general benefit to the public. There may be substantial disagreement as to how far the concept of "public purpose" should be extended, but a compulsory taking of property for the personal uses of government officials clearly violates basic standards of civilized justice. Although exercise of the power to tax for purposes of providing remuneration for governmental employees is also, in a sense, a form of compulsory "taking," this is essentially different from depriving a person of a specific piece of land which is coveted by a public official.

A second major problem emerges when expropriations are undertaken for an indisputable public purpose, but without payment of compensation, or adequate compensation, to the affected owners. Large-scale expropriations of agricultural, industrial, and business properties have occurred in this century in connection with social revolutions, and sometimes (as in the case of the Russian Revolution) such confiscations of property took place without payment of any indemnity. When in the course of such a social transformation rights are granted to the citizens which they did not possess prior to the revolution (for example, a right to remunerative work guaranteed by the government, old age insurance and medical benefits, a right to paid vacations, etc.), the citizens are compensated for the loss of property rights at least to a limited extent. This is a factor which, in appraising the justice of such measures, must be taken into account, especially in the case of poor countries in which the wealth appropriated by the state belonged to a relatively small segment of the population, and where the financial resources available for compensation purposes are seriously restricted. If the social upheaval resulting in acts of nationalization can be characterized as a bona fide revolution undertaken with the aim of improving the social and economic conditions

171

of the people, the overall benefits derived from the change will have to be balanced against the hardships and burdens accompanying the transformation.

The foregoing considerations have no application, however, to foreign property and business interests which were expropriated without compensation, because the persons or companies deprived of their properties would not obtain any benefits from the revolutionary changes which have occurred and could not, in most cases, avail themselves of the new rights which were granted to the citizens as a result of the institution of a new order. It is not surprising, therefore, that much of the discussion relating to the expropriation problem has centered around the international issues that have arisen out of nationalizations of the property of foreigners.

The Austrian jurist Alfred Verdross, on the basis of extensive studies, has reached the conclusion that a taking of foreign private property without compensation is prohibited by international law. Expropriations of foreign property accompanied by an appropriate indemnification, on the other hand, are generally permitted in his view, provided that such measures are taken in the public interest and do not discriminate between citizens of different states.[10] Verdross bases his conclusions on several international arbitration decrees, a decision of the Permanent Court of International Justice,[11] and a number of treaties. He points out that several nationalization laws passed by socialist countries after World War II have recognized the duty to compensate,[12] and that indemnification of foreign property holders was also stipulated in various international agreements concluded between socialist and nonsocialist countries.[13]

Furthermore, the United Nations General Assembly adopted a resolution in 1962 entitled "Permanent Sovereignty over Natural Resources," which in Art. I, Sec. 4 dealt with the subject discussed here in the following manner:

> Nationalization, expropriation or requisitioning shall be based on grounds or reasons of public utility, security or the national interest which are recognized as overriding purely individual or private interests, both domestic and foreign. In such cases the owner shall be paid appropriate compensation, in accordance with the rules in force in the state taking such measures in the exercise of its sovereignty and in accordance with international law.

The resolution was adopted by a vote of 87 nations in favor, two opposed, and 12 abstentions. It is interesting to note that the Communist bloc (including Cuba) did not cast its ballot against the resolution, but merely abstained from voting.[14]

The heavy vote marshalled in favor of the resolution indicates clearly that the standards of expropriation enunciated in it represent the world majority view, and that active opposition to these principles is restricted to a small fraction of the international community.[15] That the principles are in accord with fundamental notions of justice and fair-dealing can hardly be disputed. If a foreign company has been invited to come into a country to do business there, and has invested money and effort in carrying on an industrial or business enterprise in a bona fide manner, it should not suffer severe losses as a result of social events for whose occurrence it was not responsible.

There are few general rules of law, however, that are entirely without exceptions, and there may be unusual cases in which it would be justifiable to recognize the propriety of a nationalization of foreign property without compensation. Let us assume, for example, that a company operating in a foreign country has employed its workers at wages and working conditions which, taking into account the general social and economic situation in the country, must be regarded as substandard and indefensible, and has derived exorbitant profits from such practices. Or let us take the case where a foreign corporation has used its wealth and economic power in a poor and undeveloped country in order to exercise improper pressures on the government resulting in measures greatly detrimental to the interests of the native population. In such situations, an international application of the "clean hands" doctrine may induce the company's home government to refrain from pressing a compensation claim on its behalf in case of nationalization of its properties, and it may prompt an international tribunal to deny indemnification for the seizures. But inasmuch as we are confronted here with exceptions to a general rule of international law, the burden of proof for the existence of special circumstances justifying denial of the claim is on the government responsible for the taking and should be discharged by it with great specificity.

Troublesome questions have also arisen in cases where the amounts paid for the purpose of indemnifying foreign property owners were claimed to constitute insufficient compensation for the losses suffered by virtue of the taking.[16] That the fair value of the properties seized should be the measure of reimbursement under normal circumstances would appear to be obvious. But if the country undertaking the nationalization is extremely poor and therefore unable to pay prompt and adequate compensation, the problem cannot be disposed of simply by insisting that in that event the measure which would give rise to a compensation claim must be left undone. The government of a developing country may feel that a total or partial socialization of its economy is necessary in order to effect a program of swift industrialization, and international law would overstep its proper bounds if it would attempt to curb the freedom of social and economic experimentation of the members of the international community.[17] Therefore, if a bona fide plea of inability to pay is made by a country, deferment of compensation under appropriate safeguards (such as issuance of securities to mature at a later date), or reduction of the amount to be paid as indemnification, might be deemed acceptable means for solving the problem. Here again it must be emphasized that the postulates of justice call for a consideration of all the various conflicting interests affected by the controversial action, and not merely those of the party making the claim, even though the claim might appear fair and justified on a prima facie appraisal.[18]

CHAPTER V

PENAL JUSTICE

Sec. 23. The Problem of Responsibility.

In the field of criminal law, to which the present chapter is devoted, severe sanctions are often imposed upon individuals who have committed actions involving a breach of the law. Under some circumstances, a person may forfeit his life if he is found guilty of a crime, in other situations long-term imprisonments may be visited upon offenders, which are apt to leave indelible imprints upon their personalities and might even destroy their chances for a further useful life in society. It is not surprising, therefore, that some of the most acute and perplexing problems of human justice have arisen in the field of the criminal law, and that the subject of punishment in particular has agitated the minds of men throughout the centuries; it has aroused the attention not only of lawyers and judges but likewise—and probably with equal vividness—that of philosophers, sociologists, psychologists, and psychiatrists.

As far as the philosophers are concerned, the reason why they have taken an intense interest in the problems of criminal punishment lies in the fact that the justification of punishment depends to a considerable extent upon a determination of the question whether or not human beings are morally responsible for their actions. The relevancy of the connection between moral responsibility and punishment for the practical purposes of criminal justice has sometimes been questioned, but—as will subsequently be argued in greater detail [1]—the objection appears to be without merit. Suffice it to say at this point that blame and punishment must be deemed senseless and cannot be justified under any penological theory unless individuals are accountable for their actions. Consequently, the philosophical issue of freedom of the human will is presented in its full dimensions as a highly material factor in the imputation of criminal responsibility.

At the present time, many psychologists, psychiatrists, and other students of the subject are firmly committed to the doctrine of psychic determinism. According to this doctrine, everything that happens in nature and human life is subject to the operation of inexorable causal laws. In the field of human conduct, this leads to the supposition that every action of a human being, as well as the motivation leading to this action, is necessarily brought about by certain antecedent causes and could not have happened in a manner different from that in which it actually occurred. The decisions and deeds of a human being, it is said, grow out of his individual character, "which is shaped and molded and made what it is by influences—some hereditary, but most of them stemming from early parental environment—that were not of his own making or choosing."[2] According to this theory, every individual is "the product of causes in which his volition took no part."[3] A man's character, fashioned by heredity and environment, is fastened upon him like a strait jacket and prevents him from exercising any genuine freedom of choice.

It would seem to be highly inappropriate from the standpoint of this theory to impute to human beings moral responsibility for their acts. A person can act morally or immorally only if he possesses a certain amount of freedom to decide for or against compliance with ethical standards of value. If such freedom is nonexistent, if men cannot help doing what they do, they should never be blamed or called to account for their doings. This consequence of a strictly deterministic philosophy was stressed in uncompromising language by Fearey:

> There is no more logical justification for ascribing responsibility to an adult man or woman than to a ten-year old car. . . . While no man in his right mind would think of blaming a ten-year old car for bad performance, an adult criminal is everywhere considered responsible for his crime. . . . Man's variegated character and wide capacities have blinded us to the fact that he is in fact as passive to his creation and development, and hence as unaccountable for his actions, as an inanimate machine.[4]

Less radical conclusions concerning the issue of criminal

responsibility have been drawn by other believers in psychic determinism. It has been argued, for example, that even if all of men's actions are the product of a causal nexus in which each step necessitates the next, punishment might still be appropriately administered for utilitarian reasons. The moral fiber of man can be strengthened by the fear of punishment, it is said, and the existence of a criminal prohibition is itself a determining factor in molding or influencing human conduct. The purpose of punishment, according to this conception, is "to control behavior by providing individuals with an additional motive for refraining from criminal conduct—the motive of avoiding punishment." [5]

Viewed from the point of view of justice rather than utility, this rationalization of punishment raises a problem of serious import. It is clear that any person who actually committed a crime was not deterred by the fear of punishment. Hence, he must have been pushed into the commission of the deed by motivating factors of such overpowering strength that they rendered the threat of punishment inefficacious and nugatory. Since, according to deterministic thinking, he could not have helped doing what he did, he was not responsible in any meaningful sense of the term for his dereliction. Thus, society, by inflicting punishment on him, has chosen to sacrifice him for the sake of the common good, in order that he and other members of society might in the future adjust their conduct to the socially required standard. As Justice Holmes, an adherent of this view, sagaciously observed, a man sentenced to death should be deemed to be in the position of a soldier who, although he did not commit a blameworthy act, is forced to die for his country, so that others may live in security.[6]

At the opposite pole from this approach stands the doctrine of indeterminism. It proceeds from the basic assumption that the effect of occurrences and actions does not already preexist in their causes. The events of this world, in their sequence and relatedness, have "a certain amount of loose play on one another," and the future always has "ambiguous possibilities hidden in its womb." [7] In the opinion of Kant, human decisions and actions are free in the sense that they are spontaneous and self-determined, and are not brought about by external determinants in an inexorable process of causal inevitability. "We must understand . . . , by the term freedom, in the cosmological sense, a faculty of the *spontaneous* origination of a state; the causality

177

of which, therefore, is not subordinated to another cause determining it in time." [8] Thus, the freedom of the will "can be efficient independently of foreign causes determining it" and can initiate a series of events.[9] The actions which it originates then enter into the causal nexus and produce new effects in the external world.

Kant realized that, in the case of a criminal offense, there are always present empirical conditions which contribute to its commission. He argued, nevertheless, that for purposes of holding the offender responsible, his act must be deemed self-determined, free, and therefore culpable. This is his thesis:

> We at first proceed to examine the empirical character of the offence, and for this purpose we endeavor to penetrate to the sources of that character, such as defective education, bad company, a shameless and wicked disposition, frivolity, and want of reflection—not forgetting also the occasioning causes which prevailed at the moment of the transgression. In this the procedure is exactly the same as that pursued in the investigation of the series of causes which determine a given physical effect. Now, although we believe the action to have been determined by all these circumstances, we do not the less blame the offender. We do not blame him for his unhappy disposition, nor for the circumstances which influenced him, nay, not even for his former course of life; for we presuppose that all these considerations may be set aside, that the series of preceding conditions may be regarded as having never existed, and that the action may be considered as completely unconditioned in relation to any state preceding, just as if the agent commenced it with an entirely new series of effects. Our blame of the offender is grounded upon a law of reason, which requires us to regard this faculty as a cause, which could have and ought to have otherwise determined the behavior of the culprit, independently of all empirical conditions.[10]

In this view, human reason is a factor of determination which is characterized by its autonomy, i.e. its independence from the course of causality followed in nature. This autonomy of reason is for Kant the basic justification for the attribution of culpability and blame to human beings, regardless of the causal factors rooted in the past of a delinquent which may have influenced his conduct. The human reason in turn is determined by the moral law, and Kant was convinced that a rational being is always capable of realizing the necessity and primacy of this law, and to act in accordance with its promptings.

Kant did not take the position of an extreme indeterminism, which holds that human decisions are in no sense subject to the laws of causation.[11] He was conscious of the fact, as we have seen, that there are empirical factors, such as heredity, environment, and the character of the individual person, which have a bearing on human motivations and actions. Kant believed, however, that man was a citizen of two worlds, the "sensible" and the "intelligible" world, and that as a member of the second world man was endowed with reason, freedom, and moral autonomy. Inasmuch as the intelligible world was to Kant the real and genuine world, while the sensible world of nature was composed of "appearances" only, he considered the normal human being capable of resisting the external forces and irrational impulses pushing him in the direction of unlawful and immoral action.[12]

Kant's approach to the problem of free will is characterized by a profound belief, typical for eighteenth-century rationalist idealism, in the power of human reason to overcome the temptations produced by deeply-seated instinctual drives. The psychological discoveries made in the nineteenth and twentieth century have led us to the insight that even in normal persons the frontal assaults made by irrational urges upon the citadel of reason are often very powerful, and that the empirical character of man sets limits to his capacity to determine himself by rational values and the principles of the moral law. This does not mean, however, that man's actions are shaped exclusively by inborn character traits and environmental factors. There is very little reason to suppose that man, in everything he does, is "the innocent victim of blind forces operating according to mechanical principles." [13] The determination of human actions is not wholly naturalistic and materialistic. We also know the phenomenon of teleological (finalist) determination, i.e. determination by aims and purposes, values, and principles of moral "ought." [14] Determination by causal factors having their origin in a person's past often come into conflict with motivations oriented toward the future, for example, the wish to remain a law-abiding and respected member of the community, or at least

179

to avoid going to prison. Man's place in a world of multiple determinations is described by Nicolai Hartmann as follows:

> His is a dual position; he stands under a two-fold determination. As a natural being, even to his inmost desires and repulsions, he is determined causally, a plaything of the eternal powers of Nature, of powers overwhelmingly superior and operating through him and altogether irrespectively of him. But as a "person" he is the carrier of another sort of determination, which emanates from the ideal realm of values. In his sensing of them he finds himself in part determined by the claim which values make upon him in the form of the Ought. And it is this kind of determinateness which manifests itself in his purposive activity.[15]

Where a battle occurs between causal and teleological determinants, it cannot be assumed that the decision occurs automatically according to the relative strength of the conflicting motivations and without the participation of the conscious ego. Can anyone assert with any degree of persuasiveness that, when there is a choice of alternative courses of conduct, some mechanical, impersonal force entirely alien to the self forces its decision on the helpless individual? Does not all human experience suggest that the self normally plays an active role in the process of decision-making? Alternative solutions are considered, the advantages and drawbacks of various possibilities are weighed, and in close cases the decision may change several times until it becomes final. Is it nothing but illusion to believe that the conscious personality is creatively involved in such an exercise of choice?

There was a time in the past when the inevitability and necessity of human decision-making was deduced from the assumption of universal causality in nature. Sigmund Freud, for example, thought that the scientific approach in the field of psychology firmly demanded an adherence to determinism. If every event in nature is subject to the law of causation, he reasoned, the operations of the human psyche, which in his opinion were rooted in the biological nature of man, must likewise be governed by this law. He said:

> Does he [i.e., his opponent] mean to maintain that

180

there are any occurrences so small that they fail to come within the causal sequence of things, that they might as well be other than they are? Anyone thus breaking away from the determination of natural phenomena, at any single point, has thrown over the whole scientific outlook on the world.[16]

Since these words were written, the philosophy of physics and natural science has gone through a profound metamorphosis. Grave doubts have arisen among natural scientists as to whether or not the external world is governed by principles of universal deterministic causality. Some great physicists, like Einstein and Planck, were unwilling to abandon their belief in strict and unbroken causality, suggesting that the difficulties encountered by modern physics in this area were probably due to our imperfect techniques of observation and measurement.[17] Many other scientists, however, have come to the conclusion that the physical world cannot be a rigidly deterministic system and that indeterminacy and chance also play a role in the processes of nature.[18] Both groups are in agreement that we have no means at the present time to prove the existence of universal deterministic causality.[19]

The theory of psychic determinism, which asserts the unconditional necessity of everything that happens in the realm of human behavior, cannot under these circumstances derive any substantial support from present-day physics. This is an important factor in any up-to-date evaluation of Freud's views, which were based on the philosophical theories dominant in the natural sciences of a bygone epoch. Freud believed, as before him Kant had done, that without the assumption of unbroken causality our scientific picture of the physical world would simply break down.[20] But, as Waismann has pointed out,

the important thing that has emerged is the *possibility* of constructing a theory along different lines, the *legitimacy* of departing from causality, while science has not died or committed suicide on that account. This suffices to disown any claim on the part of Kant to regard causality as an *indispensable* form of our knowledge of the world.[21]

Even more significant for purposes of our discussion is the suggestion put forward by some modern scientists to the effect

181

that a clearcut distinction should be made between causality and determinism. Determinism presupposes the inevitability of an effect produced by an antecedent event, while causality, pursuant to this theory, does not.[22] According to the definition of Born, "determinism postulates that events at different times are connected by laws in such a way that predictions of unknown situations (past or future) can be made." [23] Such predictions are often not possible where an occurrence is causally, but not deterministically, connected with an antecedent event. As the physicist David Bohm points out,

> the behavior of the world is not perfectly determined by any possible purely mechanical or purely quantitative line of causal connection. This does not mean, however, that it is arbitrary. For if we take any given effect, we can always in principle trace it to the causes from which its essential aspects came.[24]

In other words, after a certain effect has taken place, its cause may be clearly traceable, but this does not force us to conclude that the happening of the antecedent event inevitably and with ineluctable necessity brought about the subsequent condition or state. We are no longer convinced that all laws of nature are "iron bonds holding things in an inflexible grip."[25] The term "causation" may be used in a stronger and a weaker sense, and only "the strongest possible causality" should be identified with determinism.[26]

The distinction between causality and determinism has an important bearing on the solution of the problem of human responsibility. It suggests the possibility of holding human beings accountable for decisions and acts which were the terminal point of a discernible causal chain, without at the same time assuming that the causal nexus *compelled* the decision or act and thus rendered them inevitable and unfree. A practical example might serve to illustrate this point. A man, after overcoming his moral scruples and doubts, decides to join an illegal narcotics ring. He is presently out of work and unable to find a suitable job. He has a strong desire to get married and to be able to support his wife. There is nothing in his personal history which points to the existence of compulsive criminal traits. Under these circumstances, his decision can be explained fully in terms of causality, but this does not mean that it was coerced in the sense that he was never confronted with any genuine alternative to the course which he finally chose. After the decision was made, it might be termed "necessary" by virtue of the fact that it was supported by sufficient reasons, and that the act of deciding itself made the final outcome conclusive. This shows that a free, i.e. non-compelled decision may be one of the links in a causal chain that terminates in an act which, viewed from hindsight, is fully and satisfactorily explainable in terms of its antecedent causes.[27]

It has often been claimed in opposition to this view that the hereditary traits of an individual, the environmental influences that have molded him, and his innate character dispositions will determine his actions conclusively and irresistibly. Though this may be true in some cases, as we shall see, the thesis cannot be accepted as a generally valid explanation of human behavior. Inherited traits create predispositions and developmental tendencies which in many instances can be counteracted and modified by education, experience, and other supervening factors. Environmental influences are sometimes assimilated and sometimes resisted, and the fact that an individual in a particular instance succumbed to bad example or irresponsible advice does not mean that he was forced to do so by deterministic necessity. "There is no compulsion either in environment or in heredity," the psychologist Alfred Adler observed. "Children of the same family and the same environment can develop in different ways."[28]

Greater difficulties are presented by the argument that the actions of a person are brought about and necessitated by his character traits. This contention was advanced vigorously by Arthur Schopenhauer. He asserted that the character of a person is innate and indelible; it manifests itself already in early childhood and remains constant throughout his life. "A human being never changes: if he has acted in a certain way in one situation, he will, under fully equal circumstances, act in the same fashion again and again."[29] No individual, he said, has in a given situation a choice between two different courses of conduct: his character compels him to do a certain act, and he can do no other.[30]

Schopenhauer's view would appear to be over-rigid. If we mean by "character" the attitudes usually exhibited by a person and the habits by which his conduct is governed, we shall find that these may change in various ways during an individual's life.[31] For example, we encounter the phenomenon of "conversion" when an individual under the influence of a revered personality or suggestive idea fundamentally changes his patterns of life and his relations with other people. Although it might be true that the most basic traits in the makeup of a personality remain the same, even in the case of such conversion, the human constitution is sufficiently plastic, under ordinary circumstances, as to permit latitude in the making of choices, and sufficiently flexible as to make exact prediction of human actions and reactions impossible. Unless a person is thoroughly pathological, a framework allowing some leeway for adjustment between impulsive tendencies and guidance by reason is built into his personality structure. A normal person can act against an existing set of desires.[32]

Where a confrontation between reason and impulse occurs or, differently expressed, where teleological determination by moral principles and standards of value comes into conflict with causal determination by natural drives, the outcome of the confrontation can seldom be prognosticated with certainty. Schopenhauer cannot be followed when he claims that the same person in the same circumstances will always act in the same way. Some people learn from adverse experience, they gain in maturity and modify their modes of conduct. Man is a malleable creature, although his fundamental constitution and endowments set limits to his viability.[33] In the words of Erich Fromm,

> We are . . . not helpless victims of circumstance; we are, indeed, able to change and to influence forces inside and outside ourselves and to control at least to some extent, the conditions which play upon us.[34]
> Where contradictory inclinations effectively operate within the personality there is freedom of choice.[35]

The view has been advanced by a number of psychoanalysts that a conscious and deliberate weighing of motives is not the road by which most decisions are reached. The factor which, according to this view, turns the scales in most instances is *unconscious motivation*. This theory was formulated by Hospers in the following terms:

> There are many actions—not those of insane persons (however the term "insane" may be defined), nor of a per-

184

son ignorant of the effects of his action, nor ignorant of some relevant fact about the situation, nor in any obvious way mentally deranged—for which human beings in general and the courts in particular are inclined to hold the doer responsible, and for which, I would say, he should not be held responsible. The deed may be planned, it may be carried out in cold calculation, it may spring from the agent's character and be continuous with the rest of his behavior, and it may be perfectly true that he could have done differently *if* he had wanted to; nonetheless his behavior was brought about by unconscious conflicts developed in infancy, over which he had no control and of which (without training in psychiatry) he does not even have knowledge.[36]

Inasmuch as the causes of unconscious motivation are unknown to the actor, it becomes the task of the analyst or psychiatrist to reconstruct the causal background of a deed from circumstantial evidence, especially the childhood recollections of the individual in question. This is, of course, an extremely difficult undertaking, and the conclusions arrived at by the analyst often represent no more than informed guesses. These difficulties were clearly recognized by Freud himself, as the following passage from his writings demonstrates:

> Although the motivation of the parapraxes described in the preceding chapters is something of which from the very nature of the case conscious thought must lack knowledge, it would nevertheless be *desirable* to discover a psychological proof of the existence of that motivation; indeed, for reasons which a closer knowledge of the unconscious reveals, *it is probable that such proofs are somewhere discoverable.*[37]

Freud then proceeded to name two spheres in which he thought that unconscious motivation might possibly be proved: first, with respect to certain aspects of the behavior of paranoiacs (an area in which even the most radical believer in freedom of will would admit psychic determination); and secondly, with respect to the highly specialized and narrowly circumscribed problem of motivation by superstitious beliefs.[38]

Because of the highly speculative character of the theory, it is impossible, as Freud realized, to make broad generalizations concerning the pervasiveness and scope of unconscious determination. On the basis of the available scientific evidence, it would be impermissible to assume that the strength of such motivation is in all or most instances so great that the conscious desire to comply with the law or to suppress irrational urges is certain to be drowned out. That a person can be released from the grip of subconscious motivations, including traumas incurred in childhood, is the avowed basis of all psychotherapy.[39] We have no reason to assume that, although a psychiatrist can sometimes help a person to emancipate himself from unfavorable childhood experiences and irrational impulses, no amount of individual self-liberation is ever within the reach of possibility.

The further assertion has been made that the deterministic conception of man's behavior is empirical and antimetaphysical in character, while indeterminism is based on assumptions of metaphysical provenience. If we use the term "indeterminism" in a broad sense, namely, as a shorthand expression for the conviction that man's volition normally permits him to make choices which, as far as we know, are not predestined, then the reply must be that exactly the converse of the above-stated proposition is true. All the empirical evidence points in the direction of the reality of some measure of free will, while determinism rests on a belief incapable of verification. This fact should not, however, induce us to make a flat denial of the possible truth of the deterministic creed. It is entirely conceivable that there is a supreme power in the universe which directs all human movements according to a purpose and design. Its teleology, if it covers every single human action, has not, however, been revealed to us.

The empirical factors tending to demonstrate free will have been set forth ably and in great detail by Nicolai Hartmann.[40] When men are faced with choices or decisions, they almost inevitably receive the impression: "I can do such and such, but I can also do otherwise; it depends upon me." [41] Such feelings and impressions may be based on illusion or hallucination; but because of their ubiquity and strength, the burden of proof is upon those who allege them to be fictitious and deceptive.

Secondly, the sane individual is willing to assume responsibility for his acts and instinctively rejects the notion that he is a mere marionette of fate without a semblance of autonomy. He feels accountable for what he says and does, although the assumption of responsibility is onerous and in some sense contrary to self-interest. It would be much more comfortable if one could put off the blame for one's derelictions upon an unkind fate.

A radical determinist might reply that the sense of responsibility is merely the result of education and training and need not have any basis in the psychological structure of human beings. This might be true, but in spite of the fact that deterministic teaching is widespread today, most people still seem to believe that they are responsible for their actions. The simplest and most obvious explanation for the pervasiveness and strength of this feeling seems to be that man's sense of responsibility is a concomitant of his freedom and not the result of a fraud perpetrated by nature upon the human race.[42]

Closely related to the existence of a feeling of responsibility is a third facet of human experience: the consciousness of guilt. In the words of Hartmann: "everyone is acquainted with this phenomenon as the voice of conscience and, with its peculiar moral character, as 'remorse.' Ethically these are elemental manifestations, independent of all reflection." [43] The compulsion to confess which, according to modern psychoanalysis, impels many criminals to disclose their deeds to the law-enforcing authorities, is a byproduct of this elemental sense of guilt. "Confession is conscience speaking up," says the psychoanalyst Theodor Reik.[44] Again, it might be contended that the sense of guilt has been inculcated in human beings in the course of many centuries of religious and moral teaching, and that it furnishes no proof for the freedom of the human will. Again, the reply should be that the burden of proving that a common psychological phenomenon is solely the product of unscientific teaching rests upon those who allege that an apparent reality is in fact a sham and a delusion. It would be very difficult to discharge this burden, since this would require the waging of a prolonged campaign with the aim to extirpate the moral sense of man. If the campaign should be successful, it would tend to demonstrate that the sense of guilt was merely the product of cultural conditioning.

Although the empirical evidence strongly points toward the possibility of volitional freedom, there can be no doubt that man's freedom of self-determination is by no means absolute. In the words of Hartmann, "not every will is free, not every man on every occasion is in reality morally responsible." [45] An insane person is deprived of rationality, i.e. of the capacity to have his actions guided by principles of reason, morality, and

187

law, and he is therefore lacking in free volition. But even persons who are not mentally ill in the psychiatric or legal sense may be incapable of offering resistance to causally determined factors anchored in their past, which drive them into anti-social conduct or crime. Adverse childhood experiences, lack of proper education, unfavorable environmental influences, a weakly developed will power may reduce or paralyze the possibility of teleological determination by standards of morality and law, and may cause the offender to abandon himself to his uncontrolled impulses.

Sometimes the inability to resist urges and temptations is the result of the offender's own inertia or of his past failure to work on the improvement of his character and will-power. In that case, he may be incapable of acting responsibly at the time he turns to antisocial conduct or crime, but—like the person who commits a dereliction after having put himself in a state of intoxication—may be blamed for having set the stage for his irresponsibility. But there are also cases where an unfortunate personal history and a whole array of unfelicitous extraneous circumstances have destroyed or seriously diminished the offender's power to act conscientiously and constructively.[46]

It is often very difficult to decide whether a person committing a certain act was completely under the sway of conditions over which he had no control. Many actions are partly free and partly unfree, and we are at a loss to determine conclusively whether or not the person in question could have acted differently.[47] But this difficulty does not force us to abandon the concept of responsibility, although it may induce us to recognize various shadings and degrees of responsibility.[48] As Hartmann suggests, "amidst the various heteronomous determinants of the will one determinant is autonomous, and that suffices as a foundation for self-determination, for imputability, responsibility, and guilt." [49] Only when we have convincing reasons for holding in a particular case that the autonomous determinant, due to factors beyond the control of the acting individual, was rendered wholly inoperative are we justified in denying a person's responsibility for his actions.

Sec. 24. The Justification of Punishment.

The conclusions reached in the preceding section with respect to the subject of responsibility bear a direct and immediate relation to the problem of punishment. Under a deterministic theory of human behavior which denies the moral accountability of men for their actions, it is extremely difficult to defend the institution of punishment. For punishment is a term with moral connotations and, according to the common understanding, presupposes blameworthiness and imputability of guilt. If men cannot help doing what they do, society may still have the right to protect itself against injury inflicted by criminal offenders, but its self-defense should take forms other than the visitation of punishment. If men, on the other hand, possess an amount of free will sufficient to hold them responsible for their actions, punishment becomes a meaningful conception.

The view of punishment which for long periods of history occupied a commanding authority in legal thinking was the retributive theory. Proceeding from the assumption that the human will is free, it holds that a man who has committed a criminal offense has incurred guilt, provided he was sane, and should atone for his deed by pain and suffering. Punishment is inflicted on him, not for the purpose of deterring others from criminal acts or as a measure of rehabilitation and reeducation, but simply because requital for his culpable conduct is due to him. According to Kant, a vigorous protagonist of the retributive theory,

> judicial punishment can never be administered merely as a means for promoting another Good either with regard to the Criminal himself or to Civil Society, but must in all cases be imposed only because the individual on whom it is inflicted *has committed a Crime.* . . . The Penal Law is a Categorical Imperative; and woe to him who creeps through the serpent-windings of Utilitarianism to discover some advantage that may discharge him from the Justice of Punishment, or even from the due measure of it.[1]

The retributive theory also demands that an individual, when he is punished, should receive a penalty commensurate with the severity of his offense. It rejects the idea that for reasons of kindheartedness or forgiveness a serious offense might

189

be met with a mild punishment, or that a crime of relatively slight dimensions might be punished severely and drastically in order to deter others from committing like acts in the future. Punishment should, according to this view, be proportioned to the degree of moral guilt incurred by the offender.

The retributive theory probably stood at the threshold of the history of criminal law and still reflects the feeling of justice of the average man today. In the words of Bradley:

> If there is any opinion to which the man of uncultivated morals is attached, it is the belief in the necessary connexion of punishment and guilt. Punishment is punishment, only where it is deserved. We pay the penalty, because we owe it, and for no other reason, and if punishment is inflicted for any other reason whatever than because it is merited by wrong, it is a gross immorality, a crying injustice, an abominable crime, and not what it pretends to be.[2]

Some psychoanalysts and lawyers have argued that the instinctive belief of the common man in the rightness of retributive justice is so pervasive that those charged with the administration of the criminal law cannot afford to disregard it. "The people demand atonement; the psychological understanding of the offender, generally speaking, does not remove this demand. . . . Scientific insight will sooner be thrown overboard than the gratification of an emotional drive."[3] Because of the strength of this popular sentiment, even though it may be irrational and based on misconceptions, the principle of proportionality between crime and punishment cannot, according to this view, be altogether abandoned in the administration of the criminal law.

Other authors have argued that the retributive concept of punishment is vindictive and primitive, and that an educative campaign should be conducted to eradicate it from the minds of the people. The urge to punish is considered by these writers the chief obstacle to the adoption of a rational penal code.[4]

There can be no quarrel with the contention that a modern system of penology cannot be based on the idea of vengeance. The impulse of vengeance is largely irrational and likely to lead to excessive manifestations of the retributive urge. Since the notion of retribution is often identified in popular understanding with vindictiveness, there is some merit in the proposal to abandon its use in the theory of criminal punishment.[5] But the fact that the term retribution has acquired this undesirable connotation should not blind us to the fact that the doctrine of punishment connected with it contains some valuable ingredients, which will have to be preserved in our thinking on criminal justice.

First, the retributive notion hammers home to us the truth that punishment is imposed for a past offense, and that the nature and seriousness of this offense cannot be lost sight of in fixing the penalty. The purely utilitarian theories of punishment are oriented toward the future; they seek to deter people from committing crimes or to accomplish the rehabilitation of convicted offenders. But punishment should also convey to the wrongdoer the community's disapprobation of his conduct and remind him that he has disrupted the public peace and order. This public expression of moral disapproval implicit in punishment not only may have prospective educational value for the lawbreaker, but it also contains a condemnation of his past action.[6] This is a necessary and constructive step in the maintenance of the moral and social order. Goodhart has wisely observed that

> without a sense of retribution we may lose our sense of wrong. Retribution in punishment is an expression of the community's disapproval of crime, and if this retribution is not given recognition then the disapproval may also disappear. A community which is too ready to forgive the wrongdoer may end by condoning the crime.[7]

This is a refined and civilized conception of retributive justice which has severed all connection with vindictiveness and vengeance.

The retributive theory has the further merit of emphasizing the relationship which exists between punishment and guilt. From the vantage point of a utilitarian theory placing the entire weight on the aim of protecting society from harm, the conviction of innocent persons might be considered justifiable if an overwhelming advantage to society could be secured from taking such a step.[8] If usefulness to society or the state becomes the sole touchstone of penal policy, legitimation can be found for measures such as imposition of the death penalty on speeding automobile drivers, the shooting of hostages, and the execution of insane criminals. A view of punishment which attaches one-

191

sided importance to the prospective social effects of its use accords insufficient recognition to the moral sensibilities of men, which demand that men in general should be punished only for having broken the law in a setting of blameworthy conduct.

Even a utilitarian theory which is oriented primarily towards reformation and reeducation of individual offenders does not take adequate account of this deep-seated conviction. Ewing addressed himself to this point as follows:

> Suppose that in a particular case it is impossible to find the real criminal, but suppose also that we got hold of a person generally believed guilty so that the deterrent effects of punishing him would be the same as if he were really guilty. Suppose, further, that psychological experts would assure us that his character would benefit by a spell of imprisonment. (Even a very good man's character often benefits by suffering: very possibly it is more likely than a bad man's to do so). That surely would not make the punishment right, yet it ought to on the utilitarian theory.[9]

Ewing concludes that "in general, the utilitarian theory as usually stated at least, seems to overlook the point that punishment has an essential reference to the past and that justice does not consist merely in producing good consequences."[10] This statement merits wholehearted approval.

Thirdly and lastly, a retributive theory divorced from the idea of vengeance will insist that the kind and size of the penalty should be adapted to the nature and severity of the offense and should also take into consideration the degree of moral guilt incurred by the offender. This aspect of the theory embodies an important requirement of justice. The sense of justice demands that, just as there should be a proper relation between accomplishment and reward, there should be at least a rough proportionality between crime and punishment.[11]

It has been argued that it is impossible to establish a meaningful correlation between a violation of law and a penalty fixed for its commission. What intrinsic logical connection exists, for example, between an assault and a fine of $100, or between an act of embezzlement and a six-months prison sentence?

This argument points up certain difficulties facing a judge who is engaged in determining an appropriate form of punish-

192

ment, but it does not demonstrate the impossibility of arriving at a reasonable measure of correspondence between offense and sanction. It is possible to grade derelictions in an ordered scale according to the degree of their social dangerousness.[12] Even if the criminal code does not provide such a scale, the judge, at least under a system of definite sentencing, will almost invariably take the seriousness of the offense into account in setting the punishment. To impose life imprisonment for the stealing of a loaf of bread by a hungry man, or to decree a $50 fine for the commission of a murder would be an obvious violation of elementary justice.[13] In less extreme situations, too, there often exists a widespread popular feeling that a certain sentence was either too harsh or too lenient in relation to the deed that had been committed.

In view of the strength and persistence of the sense of proportionality, which appears to be firmly anchored in the human psyche, it is desirable that the legislator should make a deliberate effort to assess the gravity of various types of crimes and to fix maximum and minimum limits of punishment.[14] In some rare instances it might even be deemed proper to provide a definite amount of fine or a determinate period of imprisonment. On the other hand, for the purpose of avoiding undue rigidity in the administration of criminal justice, the sentencing authority may have to be authorized to impose a sentence below the statutory minimum where mitigating circumstances are present, and perhaps a punishment above the statutory maximum where aggravating factors can be shown to exist. The advantage of such statutory guidelines for the sentencing process lies in the fact that such a system apprises the organs charged with this function as to how the community evaluates and ranks an offense in the light of its effects upon the public order. The system will also have the beneficial feature of helping to reduce arbitrariness in sentencing practices.

In many states of the United States today, the determination of the actual length of a prison term is withdrawn from judicial cognizance and vested in an administrative agency, such as a parole board or other correctional authority. Although there are advantages connected with such a system, it is open to certain objections from the point of view of justice. Sentencing forms such a vital part of a criminal proceeding that much can be said in favor of leaving at least the initial determination of a sentence to the chief organ for the administration of criminal justice, the judge. He is in the position of resting his decision upon all factors brought out into the open at a formal public hearing, plus any additional information (such as a presentence report) that might be obtained after conviction. It would also seem highly desirable to have the considerations relevant to the character and scope of punishment stated in a judicial opinion accompanying the judgment.

Contrary to the practice presently prevailing in the United States (which contrasts with the policy followed in most other countries), the sentence imposed by the court should be made subject to appellate review. It is likely that the observance of two important postulates of justice would be strengthened by allowing such recourse. First, the maintenance of a fair proportion between offense and penalty is of such importance in upholding respect for the criminal law that disregard of the requirement by the trial judge should be made a proper ground for challenge. Secondly, the possibility of reviewing a sentence would be helpful in implementing another basic constituent of justice, namely, the principle that equal situations should be treated equally.[15] A certain uniformity of disposition at the sentencing level would appear to be a worthwhile objective of penal policy.[16] The morale of prisoners is adversely affected by wide disparities in sentences for offenses committed under similar conditions and circumstances. If a convict feels that a grave injustice has been done in his own case, or in cases of fellow-prisoners, his chances of rehabilitation are thereby reduced. Furthermore, public confidence in the administration of criminal justice tends to become undermined by prevalence of arbitrary practices. The extension of appellate review to the sentencing process would result in some unification of sentencing policies for relatively large geographical regions. Where several appellate courts exist (as for example, in the federal system), additional progress in attaining a reasonable degree of consistency can be made through the adoption of common guidelines for these courts.

There is, on the other hand, considerable merit in maintaining a certain degree of flexibility in the processes of sentencing. Even where a definite sentence is initially imposed by judicial action, a subsequent reduction of this sentence by parole or pardon should always remain within the range of possibility. In administering the system of release from imprisonment prior to the expiration of the sentence, especially the parole system, the decisions should be based on individualized factors, such as

194

the personality of the convict, his prior history and record, and his chances of becoming readjusted to a normal life in society. For the purpose of avoiding caprice it is, however, advisable to promulgate a set of general instructions or regulations setting criteria for the granting of parole.[17]

The foregoing considerations were designed to show that the ancient doctrine of retribution, although it started out from crude notions of retaliation and vengeance, embodies certain postulates of justice which still retain significance and weight today. The demand that the punishment should fit the crime, and that it should be neither too severe nor too lenient in relation to the character of the offense, accentuates the principle of proportionality which forms an important ingredient in the notion of justice. It has also been pointed out that insistence on a type of punishment commensurate with the seriousness of the offense tends to facilitate (although not to guarantee) some measure of equality in the treatment of offenders who have committed like offenses under like circumstances.

Notwithstanding these positive contributions to a fair administration of criminal justice, the retributive principle has a number of weaknesses and drawbacks which render it unfit to serve as the exclusive or even predominant rationale of penal justice. As Ewing has correctly stated, "the retributive theory cannot stand as a complete account of the function of punishment."[18] First, the proportionality to be established between crime and penalty can only be a rough and approximate one, because no reliable gauges are available to ensure exactness of measurement. Secondly, the proportionality notion presupposes that it is always possible to assess the degree of moral guilt incurred by the offender and to fix the penalty accordingly. For reasons that were discussed in the preceding section, this is sometimes an extremely difficult undertaking. The scope of free agency present in the commission of a crime is often hidden from the judge's eye. There are many cases in which an accused person, although not legally insane, was reduced in his freedom of self-determination to such an extent that his action must be viewed as predominantly unfree. An unfortunate life history and a faulty psychological development may have substantially lessened the ability of the offender to adjust himself to the demands of proper social behavior, but the scope of diminution of his free volition cannot always be reliably estimated.[19] Where the perpetrator of a criminal deed is impulse-ridden and predisposed toward antisocial conduct, so that the odds are strongly stacked against his chances to resist criminal temptation, moral blameworthiness might be slight, but the need for protecting society might be great. It is also true that the retributive theory, because of a certain rigidity inherent in it, is not well adapted to an appraisal of personality factors which may have to condition and qualify the application of generalized standards of punishment. In these situations, the doctrine of proportionality between guilt and punishment does not provide us with the tools for finding a satisfactory solution, because it does not take into account all factors that should be considered in the disposition of the case.

Because of these deficiencies of the retributive theory, utilitarian considerations cannot be excluded from the administration of criminal justice. There are three main policies of a pragmatic nature which occupy a legitimate place in a system of penology: prevention of crime, protection of society, and rehabilitation of convicted offenders. These rationales of punishment will be discussed in turn in the remaining part of this section.

It is a widely accepted axiom today that punishment, by exercising a deterrent effect on potential wrongdoers, serves as a useful instrumentality for the prevention of crime. This axiom has not remained unchallenged, however. Some authors have doubted that deterrence of future offenders should be made an objective of penal policy. These authors are convinced that the hereditary traits of a criminal and the social environment in which he has grown up drive him into crime with inescapable necessity, and that the threat of punishment will therefore remain wholly inefficacious. The psychiatrist Zilboorg, for example, has said: "No realistic results can be brought forward to support the claims of the principle of the 'deterrent effect' . . . We must bear in mind that punishment, despite the traditional belief to the contrary, has apparently no deterrent effects on crime."[20] The same position has been taken by Barnes and Teeters: "The claim for deterrence is belied by both history and logic. History shows that severe punishments have never reduced criminality to any marked degree." [21]

To such assertions Ewing has replied that "only an unreasonable fanatic could say that punishment by the State has no effect in deterring possible criminals and that crime would not enormously increase without it." [22] It is, of course, true that some criminals are unaffected by the threat of punishment; their

196

inability to resist their criminal predisposition is so strong that they would commit unlawful acts even if they were sure of capture and punishment.[23] Many others—perhaps the majority of lawbreakers—perpetrate their acts in the distinct hope that they will be able to avoid detection. They are potentially deterred by the fear of punishment, but this fear is overcome by the conviction that they will be resourceful enough to escape the meshes of the law. There is little doubt that the number of offenders in this category can be reduced by a tightening of the enforcement system. This is well attested by the fact that the number of common crimes declines dramatically when an authoritarian regime comes into power which substantially increases the strength of the police force.

> In the authoritarian countries there is a sharp diminution in the totals for each of the common law felonies, once we eliminate politically oriented crimes. In the specific categories of homicide, robbery, burglary, sex crimes, larcenies, and felonious assaults the totalitarian states . . . exhibit a law-abiding profile, when compared to the United States, England, France, and other democratic countries. . . . It is evident that democracies must pay a price for freedom—that price must be a somewhat higher crime rate than might be found in a totalitarian state.[24]

It should not be inferred from this statement, however, that only a totalitarian government is in a position to combat crime effectively. The experience was made in a number of American cities that even improvements in the system of street lighting may result in a substantial decrease in the incidence of certain crimes.

Some interesting material concerning the effectiveness of criminal sanctions was furnished by the experience of countries which suffered a temporary breakdown in law enforcement. In 1944, the German occupation authorities arrested the entire Danish police force. During the remainder of the occupation, police duties were performed by an improvised and unarmed watch corps whose activities were for the most part ineffectual. The consequences of this state of affairs were described by Andenaes as follows:

> The crime rate rose immediately, but there was a wide

197

discrepancy here between the various types of crimes. While in the whole of 1939 only ten cases of robbery were reported in Copenhagen, the figure by 1943 had risen to ten a month, as a result of the wartime conditions. After the action against the police the figure quickly rose to over 100 a month and continued to rise.[25]

Andenaes added that the amount of rape and other sex offenses did not increase materially during the policeless period in Copenhagen. He raised the question, however, what the effect of slackness in enforcement would have been in the long run:

> That rape is a crime not alien to the normal human personality (unlike incest) can be verified in times of war and occupation. In an occupation army where discipline in this matter is lax, the incidence of rape is commonly high. If discipline is strict, on the other hand, as with the German army of occupation in Norway during the war, the crime hardly ever occurs.[26]

A similar laboratory test of the efficacy of deterrence was provided by the experience of East Pakistan after that country had gained its independence in 1947. Because of ineptness and venality of the police force, large numbers of offenses were not prosecuted at all for a certain period of time. As reported by a university professor from Pakistan, "in the same degree as the enforcement of the laws was neglected, the number of offenders increased." [27] Violence as well as crimes against property became widespread, and the prevalence of disorder and lawlessness subverted the foundations of democracy.

The most fundamental mistake made by those who deny the deterrent effect of the criminal law is their failure to realize that "to justify punishment it is not necessary to prove that it *always* prevents crime by its deterrent quality. It is enough to indicate that there would be more crime if all punishment were abolished." [28] In other words, the proper question to be asked is: How many people would have committed crimes if there had been no threat of punishment? Since aggressive and destructive tendencies are hidden in the psychological makeup even of normal persons, a control of human behavior by providing motives for abstention from criminal conduct is an indispensable prerequisite of effective social organization.[29]

The most satisfactory way of maximizing the preventive

effect of the criminal law is, as Ewing correctly observes, "not by severity but by making conviction almost certain." [30] In former centuries, it was often thought that harshness or cruelty of punishment were necessary to achieve its deterrent objectives. This view was erroneous for several reasons. First, experience has shown that a barbaric system of punishment makes the common people unwilling to cooperate in the enforcement of the criminal law; they tend to shield the wrongdoer rather than to deliver him up to his torturers. Secondly, such a system fosters perjured testimony on the part of the witnesses to prevent conviction; and thirdly, it contributes strongly to the reluctance of juries to arrive at a verdict of guilty.[31] Cruel methods of punishment have often been instituted in order to compensate for weaknesses in the machinery for apprehending criminals, but they have usually failed to accomplish the objectives for which they were conceived. When discovery of crime and prompt conviction are fairly certain, society can afford a rational and humane system of criminal law.

Although policies designed to prevent crime are usually advocated on utilitarian grounds, it should not be overlooked that they are also required in the interest of justice. A state that does not make an utmost effort to protect the life, limb, and property of its citizens does not live up to the basic postulates of just ordering.[32] Justice in criminal law is concerned not only with the fair treatment of persons accused of crime, but also with the security of the general public against violence and other forms of wrongful conduct. It might be repeated at this point that, in order to accomplish this goal, the administration of the criminal law must be accompanied by educative measures designed to sharpen the community's sense of right and wrong.[33] It is society's duty "to build up each individual's sense of responsibility as a guide and stimulus to the constructive development of his capacity for effectual and fruitful decision." [34]

The deterrence principle is designed not only to erect fences against criminal conduct by members of the community at large, but also to discourage future unlawful acts by the convicted offender himself. There are instances, however, where success in attaining the last-mentioned objective is impossible or improbable because the lawbreaker belongs to the class of undeterrable criminals. Where this situation exists, it is of particular importance to protect society against future wrongdoing by such individuals.

In the case of insane offenders who cannot be held criminally responsible, it is generally agreed that they should be committed to an institution for the mentally ill until they are cured, or for lifetime if their condition is irremediable and they present a continuing danger to other citizens. But there are also offenders who are not legally insane but so strongly habituated to criminal activity that neither deterrence nor reformation can be expected in their case. They can be punished for their acts, but the fact must be recognized that the degree of their social dangerousness exceeds the measure of their moral guilt.

There would seem to be no good reason for abandoning in these cases the principle of justice that punishment should be commensurate with the scope of culpability. On the other hand, a detention beyond the term of punishment would appear to be called for on grounds of public safety, if strong proof can be furnished that release of the prisoner would pose a serious menace to the community.[35] Social utility alone would not be sufficient to sanction such far-reaching measures. Since an individual should not be used as a mere means to further the aims of the collectivity,[36] it must also be asked whether a policy of detention beyond the term of imprisonment will stand scrutiny before the bar of justice. It is relevant to observe in this connection that an incorrigible criminal is liable to fall back into crime each time he is released from prison and thus does not face an existence worthy of a human being. Because of the serious nature of prolonged detention it is essential, however, to prove convincingly that recidivism is practically certain, and such a finding should not be made unless the person in question has been sentenced more than twice to prison terms for a serious offense. Termination of the detention should be ordered as soon as good ground exists for assuming that the danger incident to release has ceased or substantially diminished.

In the United States, a system of detention largely detached from criminal guilt has been established in a number of states for sexual psychopaths. Such persons upon conviction or (in some states) accusation may be referred to a state hospital or similar institution, where they are held in custody for an indeterminate period and treated (provided that appropriate facilities are available) until they no longer constitute a danger to the community. These laws are based on the consideration that society must be protected against sex offenders by detaining them as long as necessary.[37]

The laws in question have often been criticized on the ground that they indiscriminately throw together serious crimes and offenses of a slight character.[38] Thus they may lead to a prolonged detention of persons who have committed derelictions of small danger to the public. It has also been found difficult in many instances to reach an informed decision as to whether or not a person in custody has recovered sufficiently from his psychopathic condition to be eligible for release.[39] This, according to Tappan, "has resulted in a situation in which individuals whose conduct is no more than a nuisance in the community may be incarcerated for long periods of time, because hospital authorities are disinclined to affirm that the patient is cured." [40] In his opinion, curable sex offenders of the dangerous type can usually be treated fully within the criminal sentences which they will receive in regular criminal proceedings when a major crime has been committed. Predictions as to when dangerous sex crimes are apt to be committed by a person seem to be beyond the present capacity of the experts, according to Tappan.[41] For clearly dangerous offenders a custodial detention beyond the term of imprisonment would appear justifiable under some circumstances.

The fourth major objective of criminal punishment is rehabilitation. It aims at the reeducation and reformation of convicted offenders in order to enable them to return to freedom at the earliest possible time and to prepare them psychologically for the resumption of a normal life. Programs of correctional treatment are in their nature concerned with the welfare of the individual convict and may therefore come into conflict with other objectives of the criminal law, such as deterrence and public protection. For example, since prison life often has a demoralizing and debilitating effect on the inmates, rehabilitory considerations may call for short sentences or early release on parole, whereas a policy of minimum confinement may interfere with the accomplishment of deterrence. In a multiple-goal system of punishment, such as is advocated here, the problem can be solved only by the maintenance of a proper balance between the various aims of the criminal law. The wrongdoer should be prepared for readmission into the fold of the community at the earliest time consistent with the safety of society. The correctional system must be so organized that, with all due consideration for enlightened methods of individual treatment, the need for general prevention of crime and public protection is not lost sight of.

It is again the principle of proportionality that must be observed here as the proper standard of justice. In administering a fair and effective system of punishment, regard must be had for a reasonable measure of proportionality, not only between crime and penalty but also between the interests of the individual offender and those of the general public. Neither exclusive emphasis on the need for protecting society nor exclusive solicitude for the individual lawbreaker are desirable objectives of correctional policy. Here as in other branches of the law, justice requires consideration of the interests of all who are or may be significantly affected by a legally relevant measure or action.

Sec. 25. *Strict Liability.*

In his work on the Common Law, Justice Holmes advanced the thesis that "the purpose of the criminal law is only to induce external conformity to rule." [1] In order to accomplish this purpose, he maintained, the law is ready to sacrifice the individual to the general good. Holmes did not deny that the criminal law, in general, is founded on blameworthiness. "Such a denial would shock the moral sense of any civilized community; or, to put it another way, a law which punished conduct which would not be blameworthy in the average member of the community would be too severe for that community to bear." [2] He insisted, however, that the tests for determining culpability should be largely external, and "independent of the degree of evil in the particular person's motives or intentions." [3] Blameworthiness under his theory only means non-observance of that standard of care and foresight which an average prudent member of the community would adhere to; it does not refer to the degree of personal guilt incurred by the individual offender.[4] "So far from its being true, as is often assumed, that the condition of a man's heart or conscience ought to be more considered in determining criminal than civil liability, it might almost be said that it is the very opposite of truth." [5] The standards of the criminal law require every man at his own peril to come up to a certain height. "They take no account of incapacities, unless the weakness is so marked as to fall into well-known exceptions, such as infancy or madness." [6]

Although the Holmesian theory does not go so far as to suggest that mental states, intentions, and motives are wholly irrelevant elements in determining criminal liability, the general tenor of his arguments spells out his conviction that "the criminal law is non-moral, that expediency is its *ultima ratio*." [7] Theory and fact agree, Holmes declared, in permitting the punishment of those "who have been guilty of no moral wrong, and who could not be condemned by any standard that did not avowedly disregard the personal peculiarities of the individuals concerned." [8]

Holmes' approach to penal liability is strongly influenced by the positivistic philosophy which dominated nineteenth century and early twentieth century thinking. This philosophy concentrates its attention on external, physical phenomena amenable to verification by sensory data. It takes a sceptical attitude toward judgments dependent on the ascertainment of inner states of mind, holding these to be largely inaccessible to direct observation.[9]

Holmes' positivism was accompanied by a strong belief in psychic determinism which strengthened his conviction that personal culpability should not be made the foundation of criminal liability.[10] As was pointed out earlier,[11] Holmes felt that an accused criminal, after having been driven into his crime by forces beyond his control, could be compared to a soldier marched into battle and sacrificed, if necessary, to the interests of the state. "The law does undoubtedly treat the individual as a means to an end, and uses him as a tool to increase the general welfare at his own expense," and Holmes considered this course of action perfectly proper.[12]

Although Justice Holmes' ideas on non-moral responsibility did not purport to serve as a justification of strict liability in criminal law, they did in fact facilitate and encourage the recognition and development of such a theory.[13] Absolute liability without fault is a progeny of nineteenth century positivism and comports well with the Holmesian notion that the external standards prescribed by the criminal law often require men to act at their peril.

The original rule of Anglo-American law, which was maintained for many centuries, was to the effect that an act cannot be punished unless it had been committed intentionally, recklessly, or (in some cases) negligently.[14] For the large majority of common law offenses, presence of a guilty state of mind *(mens rea)* was insisted on. An American court declared: "It is a sacred principle of criminal jurisprudence that the intention to commit the crime is of the essence of the crime, and to hold that a man shall be criminally responsible for an offense of the commission of which he was ignorant at the time would be intolerable tyranny." [15] There were instances, however, where a negligent failure to use due diligence and care was made the basis of criminal liability; although in cases of inadvertent negligence *mens rea* in the strict, technical sense is absent, punishment was still grounded on the imputation of blameworthiness and fault.

A departure from the principle of culpability occurred in England in 1846. In *Regina v. Woodrow*,[16] a dealer was held liable to pay a statutory penalty for the possession of adulterated tobacco, although he had purchased it as genuine and had no knowledge or cause to suspect that it was adulterated. In 1849, an American court subjected an individual to a criminal penalty for the doing of an act without regard to what his intent may have been.[17] But it was not until about twenty years later that the number of decisions dispensing with blameworthiness as an essential element of criminal responsibility began to increase rapidly in England and the United States. Many of the early decisions imposing absolute liability were under statutes prohibiting the sale of impure or adulterated food, but the principle soon spread to other fields, such as traffic offenses, illegal sales of intoxicating liquors, sales of misbranded articles, violations of anti-narcotic acts.[18]

The United States Supreme Court approved the doctrine of strict liability in *U.S. v. Balint*.[19] The indictment charged a violation of the Narcotics Act for which a prison sentence up to five years could be imposed. The question was whether the indictment was demurrable for want of an allegation that the defendants sold the prescribed drugs with knowledge of their character. The court held that the statute did not make such knowledge an element of the offense. The defendants were held liable to conviction even if their mistake as to the nature of the drugs had been non-negligent. In *U.S. v. Dotterweich*,[20] the *Balint* doctrine was applied to the president of a pharmaceutical company who was charged with introducing into interstate commerce a drug that had been mislabeled in violation of the federal Food, Drug, and Cosmetic Act. Although there was no proof that Dotterweich knew or should have known of any misbranding, his conviction to a fine and sixty days probation was affirmed. In *Morissette v. U.S.*,[21] however, the Supreme Court insisted that the doctrine of strict liability was to be restricted to what is usually called "public welfare offenses" (i.e. violations of modern regulatory laws) and was not to be extended to the traditional common law crimes.

Under the doctrine of strict liability, a person may be convicted of certain offenses even though through no fault of his he lacked the knowledge necessary to avoid transgression of the law. Such a doctrine, even if a limited scope is assigned to it, violates elementary postulates of justice and should for this reason be abandoned.[22] No act for which absolute liability is imposed should remain a crime or criminal violation; "if it is found that the legislative wish is to impose absolute liability, the act must be removed from the list of crimes, and a non-criminal sanction imposed." [23]

Some important objections to criminal liability without fault were summarized by Packer as follows:

> To punish conduct without reference to the actor's state of mind is both inefficacious and unjust. It is inefficacious because conduct unaccompanied by an awareness of the factors making it criminal does not mark the actor as one who needs to be subjected to punishment in order to deter him or others from behaving similarly in the future, nor does it single him out as a socially dangerous individual who needs to be incapacitated or reformed. It is unjust because the actor is subjected to the stigma of a criminal conviction without being morally blameworthy. Consequently, on either a preventive or a retributive theory of criminal punishment, the criminal sanction is inappropriate in the absence of *mens rea*.[24]

It has sometimes been asserted that a regulatory penal law dispensing with the requirement of fault is necessary in the public interest to protect the community from hazards connected with the operation of certain businesses. The purpose of such a law is, in the words of Friedmann, "to apply stricter standards of inquiry and control to transactions which may endanger public security." [25] Such a view is based on a pure theory of utilitarianism, according to which "the purpose of the criminal law is only to induce external conformity to rule," and which is ready "to sacrifice the individual so far as necessary in order to accomplish that purpose." [26] It is true that requiring men

205

under certain circumstances to act at their peril may have the effect of making them more careful and diligent in the performance of their duties.[27] But if justice, as contended in this treatise, is a higher value in social life than mere expediency,[28] then it is improper to ride roughshod over the legitimate expectation of men that they will not be punished for innocent acts.

Even from the standpoint of utilitarian expediency, punishment of public welfare offenses without regard to culpability is not required. As Hall has pointed out, administrative procedures and remedies for protecting the general public against certain dangers resulting from modern technological developments are widely available today, so that reliance on absolute criminal sanctions has become unnecessary.[29] Inspections of manufactured articles, removal of deleterious goods from the market, embargoes on shipments, revocations of licenses to do business, refusals to grant permits to automobile drivers suffering from certain handicaps are among the administrative devices which can be utilized to enhance public safety.[30] Administrative fines imposed on a business enterprise as such for violation of a regulatory law may in some instances serve as appropriate vehicles of enforcement. All these measures are preferable to individual penal liability without fault, because they do not carry with them the stigma of criminal conviction.

The argument has also been propounded that the presence of strict liability offenses may have the effect of keeping certain classes of people from engaging in certain kinds of activity. As suggested by Wasserstrom, "a person who did not regard himself as capable of conducting an enterprise in such a way as not to produce the deleterious consequences proscribed by the statute might well refuse to engage in that activity at all." [31] As Wasserstrom observes, however, unscrupulous persons will not be deterred from engaging in activities which create hazards for the public if the statutory penalties are small.[32] This effect of strict liability can be achieved only if the penalties imposed for violation are substantial. The consequence would then be that severe punishments may be visited upon persons who are wholly ignorant of having broken the law and are not even guilty of negligence. This position is wholly indefensible upon considerations of justice. The policy of deterring undesirable or careless persons from undertaking business operations carrying risks for the public can be accomplished in a fairer way by the imposition of proper statutory standards and their enforcement by adequate administrative machinery. In the light of this possibility, the statement that "strict liability could be supported on the theory that the need to prevent certain kinds of occurrences is sufficiently great so as to override the undesirable effect of punishing those who might in some other sense be 'innocent'," [33] carries no conviction whatsoever.

A further reason that has been advanced in favor of strict liability relates to the difficulty of proving culpability. Since the burden of demonstrating intent or negligence in the commission of public welfare offenses is sometimes substantial, it is proposed to alleviate it by excluding evidence of ignorance or observance of proper care. But the desire to relieve the public prosecutor of an onerous duty can never furnish a justification for the commission of an injustice. With respect to the common crimes, the argument would certainly be rejected out of hand, since it overthrows a cornerstone of civilized jurisprudence, namely, the requirement that the guilt of the defendant must be established beyond a reasonable doubt. It is hard to see any compelling reason why fundamental axioms of fairness and justice should be sacrificed in the case of public welfare offenses.

It is true that proof of intent or negligence in violating modern regulatory laws often presents a more troublesome problem than establishment of *mens rea* in the prosecution of ordinary offenses. For example, where defects in the manufacture or preparation of mass-produced goods have occurred, it is often difficult to pin the blame for having departed from legally imposed standards or prohibitions on a particular person in a business enterprise. This is not a sufficient reason for abandoning the test of culpability. It might be proper in this area of the law to permit the judge or jury to infer the presence of intent or carelessness from the whole set of circumstances surrounding the alleged violation, without the necessity of probing deeply into the state of consciousness of the accused person. This might also be recognized as legitimate procedure in the case of certain traffic offenses. For example, where a person drives through a red light, a detailed proof of intent or negligence by the prosecution should usually not be insisted on, unless the defendant asserts facts (such as sudden and unforeseeable loss of consciousness) which militate against a finding of blameworthiness. Speeding normally also suggests culpable conduct, unless the defendant is perhaps able to show that his speedometer was inaccurate and he was not negligent in failing to discover the defect.

English and American courts have sometimes taken the position that the absence in statutory enactments of words such as "intentionally," "wilfully," or "negligently" indicates a legislative intent to dispense with the mental element in the commission of the offense.[34] Under the view here advocated, legislative elimination of culpability would, under the American system of law, deprive the statute of constitutionality, on the ground that imposition of absolute criminal liability is inconsistent with fundamental standards of due process. The courts would, however, be justified in reading the requirement of blameworthiness into the statute for the purpose of salvaging its validity under the Constitution. If this is done, a negligent commission of the public welfare offense would ordinarily be sufficient to justify the imposition of the statutory sanction.[35]

The American Model Penal Code has adopted an intermediate position between those who reject absolute liability altogether and those who are willing to recognize it without limit in the area of regulatory offenses. The Model Code prohibits the imprisonment of innocent wrongdoers, but allows the infliction of fines for violation of regulatory penal laws.[36] This solution represents a substantial improvement over the previous state of the law, which did not consider the nature and severity of punishment a relevant factor in sanctioning or condemning absolute liability.[37] The fines sanctioned by the Model Code are administrative or quasi-civil rather than criminal, and conviction for a "violation," as the offense is called, shall not give rise to any disability or legal disadvantage based on conviction for a criminal offense.[38]

A form of strict liability not justifiable by principles of justice was also created by the felony-murder rule. According to this rule, a person who kills another in the course of the commission of another felony (such as robbery, burglary, or arson) is guilty of murder, even though the killing was unintentional or even accidental.[39] The rule has been abolished in England and mitigated by the American Model Penal Code.[40] Other vestiges of absolute liability in the general law of crimes (as distinguished from public welfare offenses) can be found in the area of sexual offenses. In some bigamy cases, even a reasonable mistake regarding the death of the first spouse was held to constitute no defense.[41] In *Regina v. Prince,*[42] the defendant was convicted of taking an unmarried girl below the age of sixteen from the possession of her father against his will.

208

According to the findings of fact, the girl had told the defendant that she was eighteen, he had believed her, and the jury had concluded that his belief was reasonable. Such decisions are relics from an age in which civilized conceptions of justice had not as yet fully matured, and these forms of strict liability are gradually being removed from the legal system.[43]

Objections must also be raised against the imposition of vicarious responsibility in criminal law.[44] To hold one person liable for the criminal transgressions of another person was, as far as we know, not offensive to the sensibilities of primitive people, but it is repugnant to the moral sentiments of a civilized community. "To make a practice of branding people as criminals who are without moral fault tends to weaken respect for the law and the social condemnation of those who break it." [45] To make a blameless person responsible for the dereliction of his agents or employees may be justifiable in the civil law of torts, but it cannot be defended as a form of criminal liability.[46]

The common law did not recognize vicarious liability, except in a few minor and highly limited instances,[47] but the notion was accepted in some modern English and American statutes and municipal ordinances. For example, where the employees of a tavern serve or sell liquor to minors or drunkards, the owner is often made criminally responsible. Where negligence in supervision or failure to give proper directions can be established, liability of the owner is unobjectionable. But where the offense was committed in the absence of the owner and without his express or implied authorization, or perhaps even contrary to his orders, only the employee guilty of violation of the prohibition should be punished.[48]

Justice Holmes attempted to support his non-moral theory of criminal liability by a historical argument to the effect that legal history discloses a movement from emphasis on culpable wrongdoing in the early period toward an ever-increasing devaluation of the mental and moral element in criminal conduct.[49] The soundness of this view has been questioned by eminent scholars. It has been shown that in primitive Anglo-Saxon law, a wrongdoer was frequently punished for having done a certain act, without any reference to the state of mind which accompanied its commission. Even a purely accidental deed was in many instances punishable.[50] This crude law was later modified in accordance with subtler ideas of moral guilt introduced into English law by the medieval Church.[51] Throughout the Middle

Ages and the first four centuries of the modern era, emphasis on *mens rea* was strong and almost universal. It was not until the advent of positivism in the nineteenth century that a trend toward recognition of certain forms of absolute liability set in.[52] But coincident with the criticism which was leveled against the positivistic philosophy in the second half of the twentieth century, the doctrine of criminal liability without fault was subjected to vigorous attacks, as we have seen. There is good reason to believe that these attacks will bear fruit in due course of time and bring about an abandonment of a theory which cannot be reconciled with the most elementary demands of fairness.

Sec. 26. Ignorance and Mistake.

In his *Nicomachean Ethics,* Aristotle offers the following theory concerning the elements of blameworthy conduct:

> Whether . . . an act is or is not an act of injustice, or of justice, depends on its voluntary or involuntary character. When it is voluntary, the agent is blamed, and only in that case is the action an act of injustice. . . . By a voluntary action . . . I mean any action within the agent's own control which he performs knowingly, that is, without being in ignorance of the person affected, the instrument employed, and the result.[1]

Aristotle also makes the suggestion that "the ignorance that makes an act blameworthy is not ignorance displayed in moral choice (that sort of ignorance constitutes vice) . . . but particular ignorance, ignorance of the circumstances of the act and of the things affected by it; for in this case the act is pitied and forgiven, because he who acts in ignorance of any of these circumstances is an involuntary agent." [2] Among his examples of errors which tend to render an action involuntary are the following: (1) a man mistakes his son for an enemy; (2) a man mistakes a sharp spear for one with a button on it; (3) a man fatally poisons another by giving him medicine with the intention of saving his life. In these instances, Aristotle declares, the doer is ignorant of the nature of his act and the effect it will produce.[3] Some-

210

what surprisingly, he adds the qualification that the act should be spoken of as involuntary only under the further condition that "the agent feels sorrow and regret for having committed it." [4]

Aristotle thus takes the position that, as a general rule, a man should not be blamed for an act unless he is aware of the particular circumstances in which he is acting. Even though he develops his theory in connection with his discussion of justice, the purpose of his remarks is not to state the elements of criminal liability. Aristotle is talking about moral blameworthiness, not about legal punishment. This explains his notion that only a repentant doer of an involuntary act should be absolved from blame. A refusal to feel regret for an unintentional wrong amounts in his opinion to subsequent acquiescence or approval. If A on a hunting trip shoots B and kills him, believing him to be a deer, Aristotle would hold A morally accountable if later he expresses his satisfaction at having caused B's death. But this does not mean that he would want to see him punished for murder. He might not have objected to A's punishment for negligent homicide if A had been careless; but since he did not discuss the problem of negligent wrongdoing, his views on this subject are unknown to us.

Aristotle's distinction between voluntary and involuntary offenses, even though it was not offered by him as a contribution to the theory of legal responsibility, has an important bearing on a problem of criminal law which has a number of complicated and puzzling aspects: the legal relevance of ignorance and mistake with respect to the factual circumstances attending the commission of a crime. Let us first consider the examples recited by Aristotle himself as illustrations of involuntary wrongdoing.

He suggests, first, that a man who hurts his son believing him to be his enemy is acting involuntarily. Does this mean that Aristotle would exculpate A from blame if, intending to hit his enemy B, he kills his own son with a deadly weapon? In a cryptic passage Aristotle, with his remarkable circumspection, intimates that in this particular instance of involuntary acting he would affirm the culpability of A's conduct:

> Of involuntary actions some are pardonable and some are not. Errors not merely committed in ignorance but caused by ignorance are pardonable; those committed in ignorance, but caused not by that ignorance but by unnatural or inhuman passion, are unpardonable.[5]

Thus if A in a fit of hatred seeks to kill his enemy but by an error as to the identity of his victim strikes his own son, Aristotle would not consider such action excusable.

Anglo-American law in this situation applies the doctrine of "transferred intent." The defendant is treated as though he had intended to hit the person whom he did strike, even though he acted under a mistake of identity.[6] This solution is perfectly in accord with the requirements of justice. The law prohibits the deliberate killing of a human being, and this prohibition is clearly violated in the case of an *error in objecto*. Even though the act, as Aristotle points out, was involuntary as to the particular person killed, the actor may justly be punished for the voluntary killing of a human being.

The problem becomes more complicated if A, intending to shoot B, misfires and kills C. In this case, too, Anglo-American law employs the doctrine of transferred intent. If the killing of B, had it succeeded, would have been murder, the *mens rea* requisite for the commission of this crime is transferred to C, so that A is held responsible for the intentional killing of C. "The defendant is . . . treated for legal purposes as though he had intended to hit the object that he did hit, though in fact he did not have the intent, nor even was reckless as to it." [7]

Aristotle would probably have disagreed with this conclusion, since the killing of C was involuntary and, although it might have been blameworthy if "unnatural or inhuman passion" was in the last analysis responsible for it, it should not be punished as an intentional crime. From the standpoint of justice, the Anglo-American solution is indeed questionable on this very ground, namely, that the actual crime committed—the killing of C—was not an intentional one.[8] Under German law, which is preferable in this regard, A could be punished only for the *attempted* murder of B. If he was negligent with respect to the shooting of C, he could in addition be sentenced for negligent homicide.[9]

Aristotle's second example deals with an error concerning the instruments used to accomplish an unlawful act. Let us suppose that A throws his spear at B, believing the spear to be covered by a button, while in fact its sharp point is exposed. A's intention is to frighten B and perhaps to hurt him slightly, but as a consequence of the throw B suffers serious injuries.

Aristotle holds that in this case the harm suffered by B

212

was involuntarily inflicted, and this view appears to be well taken. If we assume, for example, that injuring a person by throwing a sharp spear at him constitutes aggravated assault, A because of his error should not be convicted for this crime unless, under the legal system in question, this form of assault can be committed through recklessness, and A was in fact reckless. If he was merely negligent,[10] he should be held criminally responsible only if the commission of a negligent battery is a punishable offense.

The error committed in Aristotle's third example was one that related primarily to the effects expected to follow from a person's action. A gave B a medicine intended to save his life, but the effect of the medicine was to kill the patient. In this case A should not be punished in the absence of recklessness or negligence. If the medicine was, for instance, a new drug that had been thoroughly tested with every conceivable precaution, but which produced fatal consequences in its first application to a human being, the physician should be absolved from liability, unless he made a negligent error with respect to the suitability of the drug in curing the particular disease involved.

American courts have sometimes restricted the scope of excusable errors of fact by the requirement that the mistake must be a "reasonable" one.[11] It would seem, however, that there can be no justification for insisting on reasonableness of the mistake if the crime in question is punishable only in the presence of intent. For example, where a defendant charged with larceny proves to the satisfaction of the court that due to a mistake of identity he believed the article to be his, the fact that a man of average prudence would probably have realized the mistake cannot be regarded as a substitute for the required intention to steal.[12] Only where a crime can be committed recklessly or negligently should the reasonableness of the mistake be viewed as a material factor.[13]

When a wrongdoer is cognizant of the factual elements of the offense he is committing, but does not know that his acts are punishable as a crime, his lack of legal knowledge ordinarily cannot be pleaded as a defense. The maxim that ignorance of the law is no excuse was already recognized in ancient Roman law,[14] and it has been adopted as a general principle of criminal jurisprudence (subject perhaps to certain exceptions) in the civil law and common law jurisdictions of the modern world.[15]

Several theories have been propounded to justify the axiom. Austin thought it was necessary because an effective administration of the law would be impossible in its absence:

> If ignorance of law were admitted as a ground of exemption, the Courts would be involved in questions which it were scarcely possible to solve, and which would render the administration of justice next to impracticable. If ignorance of law were admitted as a ground of exemption, ignorance of law would always be alleged by the party, and the Court, in every case, would be bound to decide the point. . . . And, for the purpose of determining the *reality* and ascertaining the *cause* of the ignorance, the Court were compelled to enter upon questions of fact, insoluble and interminable.[16]

The administration of the criminal law would indeed be seriously obstructed if ignorance of law were generally admitted as a defense. The adoption of the opposite principle, according to which no punishment could be inflicted "unless the crime was committed with knowledge of the legal prohibition" [17] would lead to absurd consequences. In every criminal case the prosecution would have to prove that the accused had read the criminal provision on which the indictment was based, or that someone had apprised him of its contents. Knowledge that the action was in violation of the most fundamental canons of right conduct would, according to this view, not be sufficient for the imposition of criminal responsibility.

The reason adduced by Austin in favor of *ignorantia legis non excusat* is, however, purely utilitarian. It does not address itself to the question as to whether the maxim comports with the requirements of justice. Furthermore, the Austinian argument, even if it is considered persuasive, would militate only against recognition of a *universal* immunity created by ignorance of the law. It does not serve to prove that the administration of justice would also be arrested if the defense were allowed in some limited instances.

Justice Holmes defended the maxim by a somewhat different line of reasoning. He disagreed with Austin's suggestion that the difficulty of proving knowledge of the law was a sufficient justification for rejecting the plea of *ignorantia juris*. "If justice requires the fact to be ascertained, the difficulty of doing so is

214

no ground for refusing to try." [18] The true explanation of the rule, he felt, was "the same as that which accounts for the law's indifference to man's particular temperament, faculties, and so forth." [19] Public policy and considerations of social utility compel us to disallow mistake of law as an excuse. "It is no doubt true that there are many cases in which the criminal could not have known that he was breaking the law, but to admit the excuse at all would be to encourage ignorance when the law-maker has determined to make men know and obey, and justice to the individual is rightly outweighed by the larger interests on the other side of the scales." [20]

The shortcomings of a view which elevates the public welfare to the rank of an almost exclusive criterion of criminal liability have been discussed in the preceding section. By sacrificing the individual to the accomplishment of a collective purpose, society treats him as a means rather than an end.[21] This attitude toward the individual has been repudiated here as incompatible with the notion of justice.[22]

Another defense of the *ignorantia juris* maxim was put forth by Hall. To admit ignorance of the law as an excuse would be, according to the interpretation placed upon his theory by Morris, "to contradict a postulate of the legal order which requires that the law be determined not by what private persons believe it to be but rather by what authoritative organs declare it to be." [23] Hall rests his defense of the maxim primarily on the principle of legality. The rules of the criminal law represent objective ethical prescriptions which an individual cannot render inoperative by professing ignorance of them.[24] It is not easy to reconcile this approach of Hall with his general theory of criminal liability, which insists strongly on the *mens rea* element and even seeks to eliminate negligence as a form of criminal guilt.[25] The principle of legality on which he relies in substantiating his view means primarily that there should be no punishment in the absence of a well-defined rule of criminal law; the principle appears to have little relation to the question as to whether misconceptions entertained with regard to such rules should be deemed relevant or irrelevant.

When the problem is looked at in the light of the postulates of justice, it becomes necessary to separate the common crimes, such as murder, robbery, theft, rape etc. (often called *mala in se)* from the technical offenses which without a specific prohibition would not be regarded as meriting punishment *(mala prohibita).*

215

With respect to the first category, a plea of ignorance of the law cannot, in the absence of circumstances of a most unusual character, be countenanced.[26] The common law of crimes embodies the basic rules of right conduct recognized in society and indispensable to the maintenance of a durable social organization. It can be assumed that these rules are known by everybody who lives in society and does not suffer from a severe mental defect.[27] In making such knowledge mandatory we do not, as Holmes suggested, sacrifice the individual to the interests of society. We merely recognize that man is, at least with part of his being, a social creature who can be expected to be cognizant of the most essential requirements of social intercourse. No injustice is done to the individual in holding him, in his capacity as a social being, to a knowledge of the elementary principles of right and wrong.[28]

Problems arise, however, in instances where a person who was generally familiar with the norms of the criminal law embarked on an illegal undertaking because he was ignorant of the *scope* of a particular criminal prohibition. Let us assume, for example, that an individual is engaged in a transaction on the borderline between embezzlement and lawful conduct after having received the advice of counsel that his actions would not expose him to criminal prosecution. If the advice was erroneous, should his plea of error be accepted by a court?

It is generally held that advice of counsel, even though given and followed in good faith, furnishes no excuse to a person for violating the law and therefore cannot be relied upon as a defense in a criminal action. This rule has been justified by the consideration that "if an accused could be exempted from punishment for crime by reason of the advice of counsel, such advice would become paramount to the law." [29] This argument is not wholly convincing, since the complexity of modern law is so great that consultation with an attorney is often the only practical expedient for a layman to bring himself into conformity with the law; it is somewhat tenuous to argue that the advice of counsel, if lay reliance on it is protected in some situations, thereby becomes "paramount to the law." It would seem that fairness to the accused demands recognition of the defense in cases lying on the borderline of a common crime, provided that the defendant acted with due diligence and procured the services of a competent attorney.[30]

When we turn to the area of *mala prohibita,* the problem

assumes a different complexion. There has taken place in recent decades a tremendous proliferation of administrative regulations carrying criminal sanctions, business offenses, and traffic laws. Nobody can be expected or required to familiarize himself with all of these enactments. The clue to the solution of the problem is indicated by Andenaes in the following statement:

> Nobody needs to know the rules applicable to all spheres of human activity. What is required is knowledge of two things: first, the general rules of society, which apply to everybody; secondly, the special rules governing the business or activity in which the individual is engaged. A person who wants to build a house, drive a car or engage in commerce must acquaint himself with the rules applying to the activity in question. But a fisherman need not study the legislation on industry; a farmer may live happily in ignorance of the laws of navigation.[31]

As a general rule, as Andenaes suggests, a man should be required to acquaint himself with the rules and regulations applicable to his trade, business, or profession. He should also keep himself informed of changes in the law by reading trade journals or professional periodicals.[32] Any negligent failure to do so will deprive him of the defense of ignorance in a criminal proceeding.

The defense of ignorance should be available, on the other hand, if a violation of a new rule or regulation occurred before it had been published or otherwise been made available to the violator.[33] The same result should, of course, obtain if a rule had never been published. Also, a stranger in a country who was caught breaking a technical criminal prohibition should be permitted a valid defense if he can show that he had entered the country recently and had had no chance to familiarize himself with legislation of this type.

The United States Supreme Court dealt with a similar problem in *Lambert v. California*.[34] A municipal ordinance of Los Angeles provided that it shall be unlawful for any convicted person to remain in the city for more than five days without registering with the police. Mrs. Lambert, an ex-convict and resident of Los Angeles who apparently was ignorant of the ordinance, did not report to the police. The Supreme Court in this instance upheld the plea of ignorance of law. It might be

217

surmised that, if the registration requirement had been posted in her lodging house, she would not have been heard with the defense that she had failed to read the notice. The case might also have been decided differently if registration requirements of this kind had been common throughout the United States, so that a person in the absence of special circumstances would be presumed to be acquainted with such legislation.

We thus reach the conclusion that an unqualified application of the maxim *ignorantia legis non excusat* does not comport with the demands of justice. The maxim holds good, with almost no exceptions, for the traditional crimes which everybody living in an organized community is expected to recognize as proscribed forms of behavior. The principle should not, on the other hand, be applied to technical and administrative offenses when the defendant is able to offer a strong and persuasive excuse for his ignorance of the prohibition.

Sec. 27. Necessity as a Criminal Defense.

In the *Case of the Speluncean Explorers,*[1] Lon Fuller presented a fictitious set of facts which serves well to illustrate the problem of justice to be discussed in this section. The four defendants were trapped in a cave due to a landslide of rocks blocking the entrance. By means of a portable wireless machine they were able to communicate with the rescue party which, under the most difficult conditions, attempted to remove the obstruction. Upon their question how long it would take to release them, the engineers in charge of the project answered that at least ten days would be required. The imprisoned men described their conditions and the rations they had taken with them and asked for a medical opinion whether they would be able to live without food for ten days longer. A physician informed them that there was little possibility of this. When the imprisoned men were finally released, it was learned that on the twenty-third day after their entrance into the cave one of them had been killed and eaten by his companions. The victim had been selected by the method of drawing lots.

The facts of the case are modeled upon an actual occurrence which became the subject of a criminal proceeding before an English court. In *Regina v. Dudley and Stephens,*[2] the crew of the yacht "Mignonette," consisting of three adult seamen and a boy of seventeen or eighteen, were compelled to abandon ship and take to an open boat. For a number of days they subsisted on pitiably small rations. On the eighteenth day in the boat, one-thousand miles way from land, without any food for seven days and without water for five, the sacrifice of the boy was suggested by two of the men to the third one, who refused to assent. Two days later the boy, who was then in a very weak condition, was killed, and all of the three men fed on his body for four days until they were rescued by a passing ship. The two men responsible for the killing of the boy were indicted for murder and sentenced to death, but the Crown commuted the sentence to six months' imprisonment.

The *Case of the Speluncean Explorers* poses the problem which is the subject of this section more clearly and directly than the *Dudley* case. In his comment on *Dudley* Justice Cardozo, asking the question "Who shall know when masts and sails of rescue may emerge out of the fog?", seemed to feel that where even the slightest possibility of rescue exists, the sacrifice of a human life would never be warranted.[3] But in the *Speluncean* case, the possibility of saving the lives of the men was practically nil. Furthermore in the *Dudley* case, even if the court had deemed the killing justifiable in principle, the propriety of the method of selection might have been questioned. In the *Speluncean* case, the choice of the victim by drawing lots could not, as such, be deemed unreasonable.[4]

A feature common to *Dudley* and the *Speluncean Explorers* was the absence of a statute or well-recognized rule of law dealing with the situation at hand. The law in these two cases penalized the premeditated killing of a human being by the mandatory imposition of the death penalty, and all of the elements of the crime of murder were fulfilled. The question then was whether the extreme emergency in which the defendants found themselves should be held to constitute an excuse absolving the defendants from criminal liability. The court in *Dudley* denied that necessity or self-preservation could furnish such excuse. "Who is to be the judge of this sort of necessity? By what measure is the comparative value of lives to be measured?"[5] More recently, Edmond Cahn gave his endorsement to the position of the English court. In the case of men in a lifeboat, he argued, even though their predicament might be extreme, "if none sacrifice themselves of free will to spare the others—they must all wait and die together."[6]

It is submitted that this position, in spite of the revolting circumstances presented in the *Dudley* case, is not justified. An act which results in the net saving of lives under conditions where there is no reasonable hope of preserving all of the lives at stake should not be adjudged to constitute punishable homicide. As Williams correctly observes, a rule "allowing necessity as a defence to homicide where the minority are killed to preserve the majority is on the whole more satisfactory than the opposite." [7]

It is not only the fact that several lives will be rescued in such situations at the expense of one that should be taken into account. It is also relevant that many other persons (such as spouses, children, and other dependents) may be deprived of loved ones and their support if a sacrifice of all the lives exposed to the emergency is insisted on by the law. In view of this broader aspect of the situation, a determination of the victim by lot may not in all cases be the least unsatisfactory method of selection. For example, if two of three persons trapped in an emergency have large families dependent on their support, while the third one is an unmarried man of no unusual attainments, a decision to sacrifice the latter ought not to be deemed capricious.

The chief problem involved in this type of case is one of comparing and balancing values. The English court in *Dudley* asked the question, "By what measure is the comparative value of lives to be measured?" The answer must be that, as a general proposition, the value of several lives exceeds that of one life. Even a person who takes the view that the worth of one genius overbalances the value of many ordinary persons would not have to quarrel with the solution here suggested as long as it is conceded to him that, if there is a genius among the periled group, he should be among those who are saved.

Taking the position that the visitation of punishment is inappropriate in such situations does not imply that the acts done by men in desperation for the purpose of saving their lives can be called "just" acts. Killing an innocent person can under no circumstances be deemed to be in accordance with justice. But, as has been shown earlier, unjust actions sometimes become unavoidable because of an extreme pressure of circumstances.[8] In such instances, the injustice that was committed should not be imputable to the doer, whether it be an individual or a public organ, provided that the emergency was a most serious one and no reasonable alternatives for avoiding the action were available.

Modern codifications of the law of necessity tend toward accepting the position here advocated. The American Model Penal Code recognizes the defense of necessity, in the absence of statutory provisions denying it in particular circumstances, where conduct otherwise punishable is engaged in for the purpose of avoiding harm or evil "greater than that sought to be prevented by the law defining the offense charged." [9] The draft of a new German Penal Code provides: "Where someone in a present, not otherwise preventable danger to life, limb, freedom, honor, property, or other legal good commits an act for the purpose of averting the danger from himself or another person, and where a balancing of the conflicting interests, especially the legal rights at stake and the degree of danger by which they are threatened, yields the result that the interest sought to be protected outweighs the interest which is violated, the action is not unlawful insofar as it is an appropriate means for warding off the danger." [10] A similar position is taken by the new Russian Principles of Criminal Law.[11]

A different problem is presented when one person, in an emergency which poses a mortal peril to him, saves himself from destruction by taking the life of another person. A famous example is the case of the "plank of Carneades," which was discussed by an ancient Greek philosopher. Two shipwrecked men in the deep sea struggle for possession of a plank which will float only one, and one of them succeeds in throwing off the other, knowing that this will result in his being drowned. In this case we are not, as in our earlier examples, faced with a disproportion between the values at stake and a preservation, by the commission of an otherwise unlawful act, of a greater value at the expense of a lesser one. In Carneades' case, one human life stands against another human life, and the question arises whether or not a privilege should be given to anyone to sacrifice the life of another person in order to save his own.

The question was answered in the affirmative by Thomas Hobbes in the following passage:

> If a man by the terrour of present death, be compelled to doe a fact against the Law, he is totally Excused; because no Law can oblige a man to abandon his own preservation. And supposing such a Law were obligatory;

221

yet a man would reason thus, *If I doe it not I die presently; if I doe it, I die afterwards; therefore by doing it, there is time of life gained;* Nature therefore compells him to the fact.[12]

This position of Hobbes was prompted by the extremely high value which he assigned to the principle of self-preservation in his philosophy of man and society: to him it was the foremost natural right of human beings.[13] But if we approach the problem on the basis of the doctrine of natural law, we shall have to take into account the fact that the command not to harm other human beings has also been pronounced by many philosophers, including Hobbes himself, to be a principle of natural justice.[14] At best, therefore, we are confronted with a conflict between two general principles, and there exists no obvious or self-evident criterion for determining which of these two should prevail. It is also necessary to realize that self-preservation is usually not considered an absolute right which must be protected under all circumstances: in case of war, for example, self-preservation will have to give way to other values considered paramount to it.

It must be conceded to Hobbes, on the other hand, that in instances like the plank case the threat of punishment, because of the elementary strength with which the instinct of self-preservation manifests itself in such a predicament, could hardly operate as a deterrent. Furthermore, if the act should be punishable as murder (or even only as manslaughter), everybody would expect utmost leniency on the part of the court and, if the penalty was inflexibly fixed, would hope for commutation of the sentence by an act of executive clemency. This shows that the ordinary rules of the law of homicide are felt not to be suitable for a satisfactory disposition of the problem.

It might be said that in cases of this description the outer limits of effective legal action have been reached. But it would probably not be proper to conclude that for this reason a person who takes another's life for the purpose of saving his own should always be immune from punishment. For example, if we vary the facts of the plank case by assuming that the plank was first occupied by a young girl who was later pushed off by an old man determined to gain possession of it, some doubts may arise in our minds whether the rigid principle advocated by Hobbes

222

might not have to be made subject to some limitations and qualifications.

The draft of a new German criminal code has adopted a flexible maxim to deal with such cases. In situations not involving the sacrifice of a lesser good for the sake of a greater good, an otherwise punishable act committed by someone for the purpose of averting a serious danger threatening himself or someone close to him is excusable if under the particular circumstances he cannot be expected to endure the danger.[15] The action is deemed excusable, but not justifiable, which entails the consequence that the exercise of self-defense in resistance to it would be legal. Since we are moving here along the outer boundaries of the legal system close to the no-man's land of the state of nature, the broad measure of discretion afforded to the judge by this provision would seem to be eminently desirable.

When duress is exercised by one person to compel another to commit a criminal act, the resulting problems of legal policy are similar to those posed in the case of extreme emergencies caused by natural events. The chief question to be determined is whether a person should be absolved from criminal liability if he is forced, at the point of a gun or other coercive method, to perpetrate a crime. In the United States, duress has generally been held to be a defense to a charge of any crime except murder. Thus, if A tells B that he faces immediate death unless he kills C, and B complies with the command, B is usually considered guilty of homicide.[16]

This solution, for the reasons discussed in connection with the plank case, is not satisfactory as an invariable principle to be applied indiscriminately in all cases involving killing under duress. The Model Penal Code has adopted a much more elastic and satisfactory standard for dealing with this problem:

(1) It is an affirmative defense that the actor engaged in the conduct charged to constitute an offense because he was coerced to do so by the use of, or a threat to use, unlawful force against his person or the person of another, which a person of reasonable firmness in his situation would have been unable to resist.

(2) The defense provided by this Section is unavailable if the actor recklessly placed himself in a situation in which it was probable that he would be subjected to duress. The defense is also unavailable if he was negli-

gent in placing himself in such a situation, whenever negligence suffices to establish culpability for the offense charged.[17]

This formulation permits the courts to adjudicate each situation in the light of its attendant circumstances. For example, a prisoner of war confronted with the peril of immediate death or severe torture unless he divulges a military secret or otherwise collaborates with the enemy may be granted exculpation, whereas he is obligated to endure lesser forms of mistreatment.[18] It would not be unreasonable to hold, however, that where the secret to be extracted is of sufficient magnitude, the prisoner ought to withstand even a threat of death or serious bodily injury. A member of a gang of criminals who is compelled by his associates to commit a murder may not have an excuse while an ordinary citizen forced by death threats to kill should, at least in some cases, be permitted to avail himself of the defense of duress.

A factor which may be material in dealing with the problem of homicide under coercion is whether or not the victim of the homicide would have died even in case of resistance to the duress. Thus, if a prison guard, at the threat of execution, is commanded to shoot a number of prisoners of war in violation of the rules of international law, his defense that numerous other men were available to perform the act had he refused would appear to be deserving of consideration.[19] As a general rule, men should not be required to make a wholly futile sacrifice of their lives. It might be argued, however, that resistance to illegal commands should be encouraged by all means, and that a general denial of the defense might induce persons subjected to such commands to resist compliance. The argument is not without force; but Hobbes' psychological observation that men faced with immediate death are not likely to be deterred in any event by the fear of future punishment would appear to hold true in such cases. Furthermore, a person placed in an extreme moral conflict of this character would hardly expect to suffer the ultimate penalty should he be later indicted for carrying out the order. Again, the proper disposition of the case, if it should arise, would depend on the circumstances. Refusal to execute orders of utmost cruelty, for example, should normally be demanded of a man of reasonable fortitude.

The examples discussed in this section were designed to show

224

that problems of justice must sometimes be solved by the adoption of broad, flexible standards which leave a great deal of leeway for the judicial authorities to handle the situation in the light of all relevant circumstances. This is particularly true in borderline cases where strong arguments can be advanced on both sides of the question, and where one specific and perhaps unusual fact may furnish the lever which turns the scales of decision.

CHAPTER VI

INTERNATIONAL JUSTICE

Sec. 28. The Protection of Human Rights.

The areas of significant problems of justice traversed thus far in this book were confined chiefly to matters within the domestic jurisdiction of individual states. These problems involved the mutual relations of individuals and groups within an organized political community, and also the relations of these individuals and groups to their government. It can be stated as a general proposition that some progress toward the realization of justice—however modest this progress may appear if judged from an ideal viewpoint—has been made during the last few centuries in the advanced countries of the world. True enough, substantial enclaves of injustice continue to exist in the legal systems of these countries. In some of them, the most serious gaps and deficiencies are found in the sphere of race relations. In others, the image of justice is tarnished by onerous restrictions on political freedom, especially the freedom to express unorthodox opinions. Again in others, shortcomings in the administration of justice caused by undue delays in adjudication or incompetent personnel cast a cloud over the adequacy of the legal system. In spite of these defects, the large majority of the citizens of these countries would hardly have the feeling that the legal order was totally permeated with injustice, and there would be widespread concurrence that the legal prescriptions governing the everyday life and relations of men were, on the whole, fairly reasonable and satisfactory. Such progress as has been made does not, of course, warrant the optimistic conclusion that wholesale relapses into unjust conditions are beyond the pale of possibility.

An entirely different situation prevails when we leave the domain of domestic law of the civilized countries and enter the realm of international relations between states. It would appear safe to state that little progress has been made to this day in securing a fair measure of order and justice in the domain of international affairs. Although the norms of international law have been successful in curtailing the reign of international anarchy in some important respects, this branch of the law thus far has not been able to provide safe principles for dealing with the most momentous problem of the atomic age: the prevention of international disorder and war. As far as the most crucial and portentous aspects of international relations are concerned, the following words of Emil Brunner would still seem to hold true today:

> The sphere of international relations is dominated, apart from rare exceptions, by a purely egoistic principle of power, veiled more or less by diplomatic courtesy, but mitigated only by the calculation that wars are expensive and their issue often or generally uncertain. Up to the present, in any case, national egoism, the intention of every state to take as much as possible and to give only what cannot be withheld has been, practically speaking, the dominating motive in the relations of states to each other.[1]

One of the chief obstacles lying in the path of achieving justice in international relations is the determination of the leading nations to insist on the preservation of a more or less unlimited quantum of national sovereignty. This problem constitutes the crux of present-day difficulties in creating a world order governed by reason and law.

According to Jean Bodin, an author who presented the first elaboration of the doctrine of sovereignty in the sixteenth century, the concept denotes "the most high, absolute, and perpetuall power over the citisens and subjects in a Commonweale." [2] Although during the early period of its development the theory of sovereignty was still mitigated by traditional notions of divine and natural law,[3] such limitations tended to evaporate with the growth of a legal positivism which refused to recognize any higher-law restrictions on governmental authority. Yet only the most radical positivists carried the idea of national sovereignty to the ultimate bounds of its logic.[4] Most writers on the subject were willing to acknowledge that the internal authority of the

227

state may be made subject to constitutional restraints placing fetters on the exercise of legislative, executive, and judicial power. It was also widely conceded that the external power of the state may be curbed not only by treaty obligations freely assented to by national governments, but also by rules of customary international law and the general principles of law recognized by civilized nations.[5] As Kelsen has said:

> There is not and there cannot be, a fundamental right of sovereignty of the states, if this term is taken in its original sense—of supreme authority. As subjects of international rights the states are subjected to international law, even if international law is considered to be a part of national law. Hence, the states as subjects of rights are as little "sovereign" as the individual is "sovereign" under national law.[6]

This statement contains a great deal of truth. It must be taken into account, however, that international law is an incomplete system replete with lacunae, and that the most substantial gaps will be found precisely in those areas where the clashing interests of national states provide ample opportunities for the creation of serious threats to world peace.[7] International law has thus superimposed only a thin and brittle layer of restrictions on national power, and state sovereignty, although not absolute, is fully preserved in many fields of international activity.[8] Because of the highly fragmentary character of international controls, Kelsen's assertion that states have no more sovereignty than the individual possesses under domestic law lacks persuasive force.

One of the areas in which international law guarantees a wide measure of regulatory latitude to the authority of individual states is the exercise of jurisdiction over persons and groups within their territory. According to the traditional doctrine of international law, "the norms of international law can impose obligations and responsibilities and confer rights only upon states, and not upon individuals." [9] The modern law of nations has recognized some exceptions to this rule.[10] But these exceptions do not detract greatly from the summary powers possessed by national states to fix the status of individuals and determine the scope of their rights and duties. If a state deals with its nationals in a cruel and inhuman fashion, or if it denies them the fundamental rights and freedoms essential to the healthy development of the human personality, no issue cognizable by international law is ordinarily presented by such treatment.

The exercise of power by states over a certain class of persons within its territory is sought to be limited by a doctrine which, although it has not as yet found general acceptance by the community of nations, appears to be gaining increasing stature in international law. This is the doctrine of the international minimum standard of justice as applied to aliens.[11] This standard requires that aliens under the jurisdiction of a state must be treated in accordance with elementary principles of civilized and humane justice. More specifically, the state in which the alien resides must protect his life, bodily integrity, honor and personal property.[12] It must safe-guard the exercise of his religion, as long as his religious practices do not come into conflict with basic principles of morality and public order.[13] He must be permitted to enter into transactions necessary to secure the basic needs of his existence.[14] He must be accorded access to the courts, the benefits of an impartial adjudication of controversies to which he may become a party, and freedom from arbitrary arrest and cruel and inhuman treatment and punishment.[15]

The foundation for the minimum standard of justice as applied to aliens was laid in the works of the early writers on international law, such as Vitoria, Pufendorf, and Vattel.[16] It is still held, however, that the rights flowing from the recognition of the minimum standard are not original rights of the alien which he can enforce directly; the power to vindicate these rights rests with the state of which he is a national or subject and may be exercised in the discretion of that state.[17] It must also be stressed that the doctrine of the minimum standard is still being opposed by a number of states, especially in the Latin-American orbit.[18] However, the opposition seems to be gradually waning, and a Draft Convention on International Responsibility of States for Injury to Aliens, which is presently under consideration by the International Law Commission of the United Nations, has given full sanction to the international minimum standard.[19]

It is to be hoped that the international standard of justice protecting aliens will serve as a stepping stone toward a more general recognition of international human rights. There is some arbitrariness in the assumption that, although aliens are entitled to civilized treatment as human beings and will be protected by international law in their fundamental interests, the decent treatment of their own citizens by states and governments is of no concern to the community of nations. As Lauterpacht has observed, it is the somewhat paradoxical result of the minimum standard doctrine that "the individual in his capacity as an alien enjoys a larger measure of protection by international law than in his character as the citizen of his own State." [20] It adds to the anomaly that the home state of the alien may invoke the doctrine of the minimum standard against another state although it falls short of that standard in treating its own citizens.

One motivation in establishing an international minimum standard of justice for aliens has been the desire to uplift social, cultural, and legal conditions in the less advanced areas of the world. Insistence on fairness to aliens has sometimes tended to inure to the benefit of nationals, since a government can ill afford to mete out a better treatment to foreigners than it accords to its own nationals. Yet recognition of the minimum standard has been slow and spotty, and even where fear of reprisals or damage claims has resulted in compliance with its mandates, this has not necessarily prevented outrageous conduct of states toward their own subjects.

Advocacy of a widened international protection of human rights might call forth the objection that solicitude of international law for such rights transcends the boundaries of its jurisdiction and constitutes an undue interference with the domestic sovereignty of states.[21] Various recent developments in international law demonstrate quite clearly, however, that the treatment of individuals by their own governments is no longer deemed to be wholly within the sphere of internal jurisdiction of states.[22] The Charter of the United Nations, for example, lists the promotion of universal respect for human rights and fundamental freedoms as one of the aims of United Nations Organization. It also contains a pledge by members of the organization to take joint and separate action for the achievement of this objective.[23] Although it has been doubted that these provisions embody binding precepts of law rather than hortatory declarations of principle,[24] the inclusion of such statements in the Charter militates against the assumption that the treatment of nationals by their governments continues to be a matter reserved to the unlimited discretion of individual states.

In the practice of the United Nations, too, concern for a fair treatment of individuals and minority groups has been evinced by a number of actions taken by its organs. Thus, the treatment of Indian immigrants and the *apartheid* policy of the Government of the Union of South Africa have on several occasions been condemned by the Security Council and the General Assembly of the United Nations.[25] The refusal of the Soviet Government to permit Russian wives of foreign nationals to leave the Soviet Union was denounced by the General Assembly in 1949.[26] The peace treaties concluded in 1947 with Hungary, Bulgaria, and Rumania obligated these countries to secure to all persons under their jurisdiction "without distinction as to race, sex, language or religion, the enjoyment of human rights and of the fundamental freedoms, including freedom of expression, of press and publication, of religious worship, of political opinion and of public meeting." Charges that these provisions had been violated by the obligated governments led to proceedings in the General Assembly, which expressed its concern at the accusations and requested the International Court of Justice to render an advisory opinion on certain procedural aspects of the controversy.[27] A Convention on Genocide, outlawing the destruction of national, ethnic, racial, or religious groups, was adopted by the General Assembly in 1948 and submitted to the members of the United Nations for their ratification.[28]

Furthermore, in 1948 the United Nations General Assembly adopted an International Declaration of Human Rights, which was approved by forty-eight nations and disapproved by none; eight nations abstained from voting.[29] The Declaration is essentially a political and ethical document, a charter of ideals of justice and common standards of achievement for the nations of the world. But it may also have an indirect legal effect as an indication of worldwide trends and in this way influence future legal decisions in the international field.

The Declaration seeks to promote the recognition of three different categories of rights. The first category consists of the traditional freedoms from restraint which have been espoused in the Western World during the last few centuries. Included in this group are the right to life, liberty, and privacy, freedom of movement and protection against arbitrary arrest, the right

231

to own property, freedom of speech, freedom of assembly, and freedom of religious expression.[30] These rights, which are to be enjoyed on a nondiscriminatory basis, may be termed *individual* rights, since they are designed to protect the power and initiative of individuals from undue interference by the state.

The second category includes the right to social security, the right to work, the right to rest, the right to a fair wage, and the right to education.[31] These rights may be denominated social rights, since they depend for their realization on organized community actions. The main objective underlying the recognition of these rights is to guarantee to each member of society a standard of living adequate for the health and wellbeing of himself and his family.

The Declaration also seeks to promote certain other rights whose realization presupposes a certain type of political organization. The Declaration mentions the right of democratic participation in government, equal access to public office, equality of suffrage and secrecy of the ballot.[32] It also names the right to a nationality and the privilege to change one's nationality.[33]

Among the political rights in a wider sense must be counted the procedural rights set out in the Declaration. They comprise the right to a fair and public trial, presumption of innocence, and prohibition of retroactive as well as cruel punishment.[34]

The rights espoused by the Declaration are not recognized as absolutes; they are deemed subject to reasonable limitations. Thus, the propriety of restrictions imposed in order to meet the requirements of morality, public order, and the general welfare is expressly acknowledged.[35] Furthermore, legislation against subversive activities aimed at the destruction of a free society is upheld as permissible.[36]

It is contemplated that the Declaration of Human Rights be followed by a Covenant on Human Rights, or a series of such covenants. In contrast to the Declaration, such covenant or covenants would contain legally binding provisions for the recognition and protection of human rights.

The latest drafts prepared by the United Nations Committee on Human Rights comprise two covenants, one of which is designed to secure economic, social, and cultural rights, while the other one deals with civil and political rights.[37] The guarantees forming the subject matter of these covenants are essentially the same as those found in the Declaration of Human Rights, but some additions and detractions were made.[38] Some sweeping generalizations found in the Declaration gave way to provisions characterized by greater precision, concreteness, and differentiation. Restrictions of certain rights adopted for the purpose of protecting the public interest and general welfare were sanctioned by the covenants.[39] Furthermore, the Draft Covenant on Civil and Political Rights provides that "in time of public emergency which threatens the life of the nation and the existence of which is officially proclaimed, the States Parties hereto may take measures derogating from their obligations under this Covenant to the extent strictly required by the exigencies of the situation." [40] No derogations may, however, be made from the rights relating to protection from arbitrary deprivation of life, freedom from torture and inhuman punishment, and a few others.[41] It is also provided that any propaganda for war and any advocacy of national, racial, or religious hatred that constitutes incitement to discrimination, hostility, or violence shall be prohibited by law.[42]

Is there any chance that these covenants will be adopted and put into effect by the nations of the world, or at least a large number of them? The following opinion is voiced by McDougal and Bebr: "As grand as is the vision which inspires the United Nations human rights program and as indispensable as such vision may be to the achievement of a free, peaceful, and abundant world society, it is improbable in the present world context of bipolarized and other bloc power and of imminent expectations of violence, that startling new progress can be quickly effected on a global scale either in the acceptance of new authoritative prescriptions about human rights or in the establishment of workable enforcement measures." [43] In the United States, opposition to an international covenant of rights has sometimes been expressed on the ground that such a covenant regulates matters which under the federal system belong primarily to the jurisdiction of the several states, and which should therefore not be touched by the federal government in the exercise of its treaty power. Assuming, however, the correctness of the conclusion reached here that the protection of basic individual rights has become a subject of proper concern to the international community, the objection can be overcome by pointing out that the federal government does in that event possess the competence to deal with this matter by international agreements binding upon the states.[44]

Greater difficulties are posed by the question whether public opinion in those countries in which its force is strong enough to influence the decision-making processes will be ready to accept an international regulation of human rights. Hans Morgenthau has asserted that the nation-state is today the recipient of man's highest secular loyalties, and that people therefore look to their own nations rather than to a world organization for the protection of their personal rights and interests.[45] There is indeed serious doubt whether sufficient support could be marshalled in democratic countries for the ratification of an international agreement which tells national governments how to go about safeguarding the rights of their own citizens. In nondemocratic countries, on the other hand, in which popular opinion carries little weight in the formation of official policies, governments may be unsympathetic to the objectives sought to be effectuated by agreements of this type.

In assessing the chances for an international protection of rights, we can dismiss at the outset the argument that we are confronted here with a recent and revolutionary idea without a basis in past experience. There are precedents in international theory and practice older than those already adverted to which defend and sanction international action for purposes of protecting basic human rights. To be sure, when such views were first voiced in international legal doctrine, such action was advocated only in extreme instances of outrageous conduct by states. Grotius, for example, said in the seventeenth century: "Regarding . . . barbarians, wild beasts rather than men, one may rightly say what Aristotle wrongly said of the Persians, who were in no way worse than the Greeks, that war against them was sanctioned by nature." [46] The author of the celebrated *Vindicae Contra Tyrannos,* published in 1579 at the time of the religious wars in France, justified interference "in behalf of neighboring peoples who are oppressed on account of adherence to the true religion or by any obvious tyranny." [47] In the course of time, the radius to be allowed for foreign interposition became somewhat enlarged in the opinion of some authors. Thus, Professor Borchard wrote in 1915:

When a state under exceptional circumstances disregards certain rights of its own citizens, over whom presumably it has absolute sovereignty, the other states of the family of nations are authorized by international law to intervene on the grounds of humanity. When these "human" rights are habitually violated, one or more states may intervene in the name of the society of nations and may take such measures as to substitute at least temporarily, if not permanently, its own sovereignty for that of the state thus controlled.[48]

Lauterpacht appears to subscribe to the view that "when a State renders itself guilty of cruelties against and prosecution of its nationals in such a way as to deny their fundamental human rights and to shock the conscience of mankind intervention in the interest of humanity is legally permissible." [49]

The doctrine of humanitarian intervention was put into practice by governments on several occasions, although usually in a mild form. In the nineteenth century, the major world powers interposed with the Turkish government on behalf of Christian minorities suffering from persecution. In 1863, the treatment of Polish insurgents by Russia brought about strong protests by other powers. Great Britain and the United States intervened in the early twentieth century on account of inhumanities perpetrated in the Congo. The United States on several occasions lodged strong diplomatic representations because of outrages committed against Jews in Czarist Russia and Rumania.[50]

In the twentieth century the idea tended to gain ground that a protection of human rights could be accomplished more effectively by international agreements than by isolated instances of diplomatic intervention. Thus, a number of treaties guaranteeing the rights of minorities were concluded after World War I, and the peace treaties entered into after World War II contained provisions designed to grant protection to minorities and other groups.[51] Perhaps the most noteworthy example of an international agreement creating binding governmental obligations with respect to the fair treatment of individuals is presented by the European Convention for the Protection of Human Rights and Fundamental Freedoms, which was signed in Rome in 1950 and went into effect in 1953; it entrusts the enforcement of these rights to a European Commission of Human Rights and a European Court of Human Rights.[52]

The history of the doctrine of humanitarian intervention shows that human beings in one national unit are by no means disinterested in, or impassive to, the treatment of human beings subject to another sovereignty. Men are by nature disinclined to consider sovereign state power as a supreme, ultimate fact of international life which eclipses or eliminates the need for concern with individual human values and wellbeing. As civilization advances, men come to feel to an increasing extent that "fundamental human rights are rights superior to the law of sovereign states." [53] Strong emotions are often engendered in human beings endowed with any degree of sensitivity when the government of a country embarks on a course of persecution and oppression toward its own people, regardless of whether or not legal theory regards such a course of action to be fully within the range of sovereign powers of that government.

It is obvious, however, that humanitarian intervention is, under the conditions of the modern world, an inept means of exhibiting concern for universal human rights. If such intervention is limited to minor actions evincing disapproval of certain governmental policies, it is likely to remain ineffective. If, on the other hand, the intervention assumes major proportions, it may produce a threat to world peace. Furthermore, it is clear that any kind of intervention would have to be restricted to extreme instances of outrageous governmental conduct, while the development of international solicitude for a fair treatment of human beings and decent living conditions would proceed beyond the demand for a bare minimum standard.

Under these circumstances, an attempt to solve the problem of human rights by means of international agreements imposing specified obligations upon the participating nations is superior to the other vehicles of international policy discussed above, provided that adequate procedures for the enforcement of such agreements can be devised. It is likely, however, that an almost worldwide campaign designed to strengthen the conscience of mankind would be necessary to make the political atmosphere in the various national states ripe for the adoption of such measures. Under present world conditions, progress toward the attainment of this goal is apt to be slow. There are many countries whose accomplishments in the sphere of human rights fall as yet grievously short of the standards proclaimed in the International Declaration of Human Rights and the draft covenants. And even in those countries which are well on their way toward the realization of these standards, the people as well as the politicians, without a great deal of prodding and spurring, might easily succumb to the social law of inertia.

Sec. 29. *The Preservation of Peace.*

The close tie that binds together the idea of justice and the protection of human rights can easily be discerned by the observer of the social scene. The great historical struggles for justice have in most instances had their causes of origin in the denial of fundamental rights, such as freedom, equality, or security, to whole peoples or to certain classes within a nation. The relation that exists between justice and peace, on the other hand, is not quite as clear and obvious to the inquiring mind. The wars of the past have not always had a decisive impact on the systems of justice of the countries involved in them. Moreover, some wars have in their ultimate effects aided the cause of justice by removing an unenlightened or despotic regime from power, or by replacing an inferior or obsolete social structure by a more civilized and advanced one.

It is the advent of the atomic age that has brought the problems of justice and peace into close connection. The likelihood that a future war would wreak unprecedented destruction and misery on large parts of the world casts a deep shadow over the chances to reconstruct the social order of devastated countries on a basis of justice after such a cataclysmic event. Justice could hardly thrive in the rubble of pulverized cities where men, women, and children, in the face of a lack of adequate food and shelter and often disabled by the effects of radioactive contamination of the air, would try to eke out a submarginal existence. A primitive war of survival would in all likelihood be waged by men against men under such conditions until a modicum of order was finally restored. The hope of rebuilding a social order in which men can live together in freedom, equality, and security, achieve economic prosperity, and build a rich cultural life probably would have to be postponed for centuries in the countries most grievously affected by a future war.

If a major war should occur, there is a remote possibility that fear of total destruction would restrain the participating nations from resorting to the most extreme potentialities inherent in the use of modern atomic weapons. In that event the amount of devastation caused by the war might possibly remain within bounds which, as the experience of the last war shows, would allow reconstruction within a fairly short period of time. But this chance, apart from offering little cause for comfort, cannot be deemed to be very large. Even if some restraint were shown in the initial stages of a future war, it is likely that the party fearing to be the loser would finally resort to measures of desperation that would unloose the total horrors of modern warfare, with all its frightful consequences for humanity.

There can also be little hope that the values for which a future war might—genuinely or ostensibly—be waged, such as defense of freedom and human dignity, could survive a nuclear holocaust. It is more likely, as Fromm predicts, that "the traumatic effects of such a catastrophe would lead to a new form of primitive barbarism" and to a "dehumanized, dictatorial regime for the survivors".[1] As Morgenthau portrays the predicament in which nations find themselves in our age:

> If a great nation does not go to war in the face of a challenge to its national existence, it will lose it through the creeping dissolution of appeasement and subversion. If it goes to war in the face of such a challenge, it may at best preserve its freedom from foreign domination, but is likely to lose the substance of what made its national life worth living.[2]

It is clear that, in view of such prospects, no one concerned with salvaging for humanity the values of civilization and justice can ignore or bypass the problem of peace.[3]

Peace today is jeopardized by a power struggle among nations which is greatly sharpened and intensified by a clash of conflicting ideologies. The chief participants in the struggle wish to remake the world in the image of their own political, economic, and social ideas, and they are convinced that the opposing ideology is a symbol and representation of the forces of evil with which permanent coexistence or genuine compromise cannot be achieved. Contests accompanied by deep ideological convictions are likely to be fought with the fanatical determination and cruelty which was characteristic of the religious wars of the past.

Some men of good will and humanitarian intentions who are deeply perturbed at the prospect of a large-scale destruction of civilization in many parts of the world have made a strong plea that nations, instead of moving toward the brink of national suicide, should stop assuming the posture of gladiators and make every effort to replace the anarchical rule of power by a rule of world law designed to preserve universal peace. Clark and Sohn, for example, in addition to advocating general disarmament and the creation of a world police force, have outlined a plan for a global system of conciliation and adjudication. Those disputes, they propose, which are capable of adjudication through the application of legal principles, should be referred to the International Court of Justice whenever the United Nations General Assembly finds that the continuance of the dispute is likely to endanger international peace. In case of such submission, the court would have compulsory jurisdiction to decide the case, even if one of the parties should refuse to come before the court.[4] To make possible the solution of controversies which are not of an exclusively legal nature, the authors propose the establishment of a new international tribunal, to be known as the World Equity Tribunal and to be composed of fifteen judges elected by the General Assembly. The jurisdictional powers to be exercised by this tribunal are described as follows:

> In ordinary circumstances this World Equity Tribunal could not make binding decisions, as distinguished from recommendations, except with the consent of the parties. But provision is made that if the General Assembly votes by a large special majority, i.e., by a three-fourths majority of all the Representatives then in office (including two thirds of all the Representatives from the twelve largest nations), that the carrying out of the Tribunal's recommendations is essential for the preservation of peace, the recommendations of the Tribunal shall become enforceable by the same means as a judgment of the International Court of Justice.[5]

Inauguration of a world rule of law through compulsory adjudication of international disputes was also advocated by Sir Hersh Lauterpacht, a former British judge on the International Court of Justice. Lauterpacht maintained that "while it is not difficult to establish the proposition that all disputes between States are of a political nature, inasmuch as they involve more or less important interests of States, it is equally easy to show that all international disputes are, irrespective of their gravity, disputes of a legal character in the sense that, so long as the rule of law is recognized, they are capable of an answer by the application of legal rules".[6] Thus, he felt that all international controversies are justiciable and can be settled by the International Court of Justice, provided that the nations of the world,

239

in the interest of preserving peace, are willing to recognize its compulsory jurisdiction.[7]

The position that every international conflict is capable of being solved by legal means does not appear to be tenable. Although one need not agree with Morgenthau that international law, like any other system of law, is "of necessity an ally of the status quo",[8] there are situations involving vital interests of states or the effectuation of policy objectives considered essential by them which under the present state of world affairs do not lend themselves to determination by a court of law.

One group of situations falling in this category are those where legal norms or standards of adjudication permitting judicial settlement of the problem are lacking. For example, there are no legal standards which have any bearing on the question whether a certain nation in Asia should have a free or a planned economy, a liberal-democratic or an authoritarian-communist political regime. When other nations, for ideological or balance-of-power reasons, intervene in a civil war fought in that country to decide its political and economic future, no international court could decide the issues underlying the struggle in a manner that would be accepted by the contestants as a verdict of impartial justice. Yet in an era in which "wars of liberation" waged in smaller nations are often supported or opposed by the big powers, the gravest dangers to world peace are posed by conflicts of this character.

The deeper reason for the inability of the law to cope with many matters of high international policy dividing the nations is not, as Morgenthau believes, that law can do nothing except preserve the status quo. Although the International Court of Justice as well as its predecessor, the Permanent Court of International Justice, have exhibited a rather conservative attitude toward the problems of the international order,[9] there is no intrinsic necessity for an international tribunal to rely exclusively on those sources of decision which tie the law to the past, such as international custom or international agreements. No basic principle of legal adjudication prohibits the use of considerations of justice and reason, as well as reliance on strong trends of thought and opinion prevailing in the international community, to counteract the inertial forces which often prevent the law from adjusting itself to the needs of a new day. The real difficulty confronting judicial settlement of the most dangerous international disputes is created by the absence, in

240

the present stage of international development, of standards of reason and justice in the most fundamental areas of conflict which would be accepted by nations regardless of ideological commitment. To return to the example used earlier, wars of "national liberation" waged by insurgent groups against non-communist governments are considered by the Soviet Union and China as just wars deserving the support of the socialist nations, while the United States views them as intolerable disturbances of the international order.[10]

A rational person might ask the question whether the principle of preserving peace in a world facing the obliteration of civilized existence through war could not be regarded by nations as a sufficiently persuasive "standard of justice and reason" to be employed by an international court in determining international disputes. This appears to be the position of Lauterpacht when he propounds the following argument:

> The first function of the legal organization of the community is the preservation of peace. Its fundamental precept is, 'there shall be no violence'. But this primordial duty of the law is abandoned and the reign of force is sanctioned as soon as it is admitted that the law may decline to function by refusing to adjudicate upon a particular claim, at least to the extent of pronouncing that violence must not be used for the purpose of enforcing it.[11]

Lauterpacht concludes that it is inconceivable for a court to pronounce a *non liquet* (refusal to decide) because of absence of a legal norm.[12] The court would ordinarily be in a position to use its "creative discretion" in finding a suitable disposition for the case, although Lauterpacht is aware that there are some limits to the lawmaking powers of international tribunals.[13]

Recourse to considerations of justice and reasonableness appears to be sanctioned by Article 38 of the Statute of the International Court of Justice, which lists the "general principles of law recognized by civilized nations" among the sources of international adjudication. Since courts in national systems of law often fill the inevitable gaps in the law by using arguments based on general principles, such as equity, justice, reason, convenience, and the nature of things,[14] international courts are authorized to utilize the same technique. The scope of this type of argumentation is, however, more narrowly confined in international law than in domestic jurisprudence. When a national court uses standards of justice as a rationale of decision, it is usually referring to well-established juristic ideals and value patterns of the societal order of which the court is an organ. Some of these ideals and valuations may transcend national boundaries, but this is not a condition of their application by a national court. The situation is materially different in the international domain. Unless an international court can make a bona fide determination to the effect that a principle of reason and justice has gained supranational validity and represents a consensus of opinion among nations, or at least among the nations involved in the dispute before it,[15] the court is barred from enforcing the general principle. This follows necessarily from the fact that an international court is an instrumentality of the international community, and not of any particular nation or group of nations.

In our time the most acrimonious controversies take place among nations with widely differing social and economic systems. This reduces the chance of finding a common denominator which, in the absence of a positive precept, could serve as a legal foundation for the solution of such conflicts.

Let us suppose, for example, that the International Court of Justice, in the interest of preserving peace, should be called upon to settle the controversy over the status of Berlin. There can be no doubt that there are a number of questions connected with this controversy that lend themselves to judicial determination. However, a decision based simply on an interpretation of existing treaties and agreements could not remove the causes of friction, since these very treaties and agreements form the ground of dissatisfaction with the existing situation. Thus, for all practical purposes the court would have to change the status quo and write a new treaty which would redefine the status of the city. But what legal rules or general principles of justice would be available to the court in discharging this task? What standards of adjudication could it use to determine whether Berlin should be internationalized or become part of the Federal Republic of Germany, whether it should be protected by soldiers of the nations which occupied the city in 1945 or by a United Nations police force, whether East and West Berlin should be jointly or separately administered? Fundamental changes in political structure do not, as a rule, lend themselves

242

to cognition by the law. Where a question can be settled by alternative courses of action and the answer is wholly or primarily within the discretion of the decision-maker, involving no issue of intrinsic justice which imperatively demands one particular solution, the matter is political in character. Thus the International Court, in the unlikely event that its regular judicial powers should be invoked to dispose of the Berlin problem, would probably have to disaffirm its jurisdiction on the ground that the dispute was political and therefore non-justiciable.[16]

A different situation would be presented if the International Court were asked to decide the case *ex aequo et bono*,[17] or if the case were submitted to a World Equity Tribunal (such as the one proposed by Clark and Sohn). In those events, the judges on the tribunals in question would not have to search for specific norms or general principles of law determinative of the question, but could presumably rely on their own resourcefulness and sense of justice to find an equitable solution. But it is most unlikely that the parties to the dispute, if it involves their vital interests or chief policy goals, would be willing, either by special agreement or general consent, to abdicate their powers of decision to a judicial body. Even if the contestants were animated by a genuine desire to preserve world peace, they would still prefer to attain this objective by policies of strength or accommodation, as the case may be, which would leave them a degree of decisional initiative and choice which they would have to renounce in case of judicial determination. It is the possibility of an adverse decision in a matter considered fundamental by the parties that militates most strongly against the chance of instituting a world rule of law under present conditions. As a former judge on the International Court of Justice has said:

> The States concerned rarely have an equal interest in requesting a settlement *ex aequo et bono*. Advantageous for the party conscious of the weakness of his claims from the point of view of the existing law, it usually offers few attractions to his opponent.[18]

We must thus reluctantly come to the conclusion that, although the idea of world peace through law possesses a much greater potentiality for avoiding war than a diplomacy of threats and compromise, dominant opinion in the leading countries today is not yet ready to entrust peacemaking and the resolution of disputes involving major power positions to judicial tribunals. As Morgenthau points out:

> To accept beforehand the authoritative decision of such a dispute by an international court, whatever it might be, is tantamount to surrendering control over the outcome of the power contest itself. No nation has been willing to go so far.[19]

Even when an international conflict is susceptible of decision according to clearcut principles of law, nations are often reluctant to submit it to a court, because they are fearful that the decision might go against them and convinced that their national interest cannot tolerate an adverse decision. The following remarks by De Visscher illustrate the difficulty:

> In the eyes of the politician, a dispute appears justiciable or not according as its more or less intimate connection with State interest permits or forbids the State to surrender its personal and discretionary decision in regard to it. From a political point of view, a government may refuse to submit a dispute to judicial settlement without disputing the existence of legal rules binding on the judge.
>
> International practice demonstrates the reluctance of governments to submit to compulsory decision conflicts of high political significance, not because it would be impossible for the judge to decide them, but because his decision would not satisfy the grievance out of which such conflicts spring. They hold a conflict to be politically non-justiciable when they know that satisfaction of their claims can be found only in a change in the legal position protected by the law in force.[20]

Another obstacle to compulsory settlement of international disputes is lack of confidence by national governments in the impartiality and detachment of international judges. The Soviet bloc, for example, would not entrust the disposition of the Berlin problem to a court consisting of a majority of judges from non-communist countries. The United States would show extreme reluctance in having an international court determine questions vital to its national interest if the judges from communist and non-aligned countries would together compose the majority of the court.

Absence of trust in judicial neutrality, even though it may sometimes impugn the integrity of a judicial body unjustly, is not entirely without warrant where clashes between fundamentally different world views are at issue.[21] It would be extremely difficult for an American or British judge to sponsor a settlement of the Berlin dispute which would strengthen the position of the Soviet bloc. And the difficulty confronting the judges on the other side would be even greater. The most controversial problems in public domestic law as well as public international law often cannot be divorced from value commitments of a fundamental nature. In a bipolar or tripolar world, a judge's integrity and sense of moral duty cannot always save him from taking sides, consciously or unconsciously, in the ideological struggle which dominates international affairs today.

The foregoing comments should not be interpreted as a resigned admission that the dominating role played by power politics in the twentieth century must for an indefinite future eclipse the hope for a more rational conduct of international affairs. This author does not subscribe to the pessimistic conclusions reached by the partisans of the "neo-realistic" school of international politics. Hans Morgenthau, an influential American political scientist and protagonist of this creed, states his basic thesis as follows:

> Domestic and international politics are but two different manifestations of the same phenomenon: the struggle for power. . . . A political policy seeks either to keep power, to increase power, or to demonstrate power.[22]

Morgenthau does not go to the extreme of contending that political action can never have any aims other than the maintenance or enhancement of power. He concedes that realization of ethical principles—such as freedom and the good life of the community—may be the ultimate objective of political action. The immediate goal of such action, however, always and invariably in his opinion, is power, and a political or social ideology often serves merely as a pretext and rationalization for the exercise or expansion of power.[23] Statesmen think and act "in

245

terms of interest defined as power," [24] and international politics in particular is nothing but "a continuing effort to maintain and to increase the power of one's nation and to keep in check or reduce the power of other nations." [25] This dominating role of power in international politics is not a temporary phenomenon but exists "of necessity." [26] The concept of power itself is defined by Morgenthau as comprising "anything that establishes and maintains the control of man over man." [27]

A similar notion of the reality of international politics is entertained by the British jurist Georg Schwarzenberger. Thus far, he states, power has been the overriding consideration in international relations; international law and morality have been relegated to relatively subordinate positions.[28] International law in the world of today serves above all the purpose of reinforcing power relations. "In a society in which power is the overriding consideration, the primary function of law is to assist in maintaining the supremacy of force and the hierarchies established on the basis of power, and to give to this overriding system the respectability and sanctity law confers." [29] International morality, too, serves in the first place the purpose of sanctifying state policy. Yet even in the sphere of power politics, "statesmen must take for granted a minimum of international morality; for their own understandings with allies ultimately rest on the moral principle that the pledged word ought to be honored." [30] Furthermore, there is also in international society some scope for action based on concern for justice and respect for law, generosity, and any of the other values in the catalogue of international morality.[31] Schwarzenberger expresses some hope that the contemporary game of power politics played by sovereign nations will not forever remain the lot of mankind.[32] "The alternative to anarchy is government, and the alternative to an international society is an international community." [33]

Schwarzenberger, after painting a dark picture with Hobbesian overtones of the contemporary international scene, does not dismiss the prospect of a better future. The neo-realistic philosophy of Morgenthau, on the other hand, holds out less hope for improvement in the foreseeable future. Morgenthau is convinced that the power impulse is so deeply ingrained in statesmen and politicians that the appeal to moral principles can have only a limited effect. It cannot do much more than mitigate the rigors of the power struggle.[34] He also suggests that, in any event, moral standards must be subordinated to those of power politics, and he decries the "legalistic-moralistic approach" to international relations.[35]

Morgenthau finds the roots of this state of affairs in human nature itself. He asserts that "all human beings seek power," and that "the desire to attain a maximum of power is universal."[36] He recognizes, however, that a counterpoise to this impulse exists "in the desire of the prospective victim of the power of others to defend his freedom against this threat." [37] He also observes that it has always been the function of morality, especially within the confines of a particular social order, "to keep aspirations for power within socially tolerable bounds." [38]

The theory of Morgenthau, notwithstanding the caveats and qualifications with which he surrounds it, assigns an exaggerated weight to the power motive, conceived in terms of an impulse to control the bodies and minds of men. Erich Fromm has convincingly shown that the term "power" denotes two contradictory concepts: power as capacity to produce, and power as domination over others. Power in the second sense, he argues, is a perversion of power in the first sense.[39] Where the power to produce, to create, and to relate oneself in sympathy and love to other human beings is lacking, the desire to exert power over others "as though they were things" becomes substituted for it. Such an attitude toward human beings is not compatible with a humanistic philosophy of man and life.

The chief objection to Morgenthau's view is that he seems to use the term power exclusively in its objectionable second sense, and that he hypostatizes his concept of power almost into an absolute natural law of political life. This is a doctrine fraught with danger, and the danger is increased because of the fact that a supposedly "realistic" descriptive theory, if men accept it and act upon it, almost invariably (and often against the wishes of its author) becomes transformed into a normative principle of action. As the Austrian jurist and sociologist Wurzel sagaciously observed:

> If an opinion (thesis) is believed in with sufficient strength, and if the belief is, numerically and timewise, sufficiently well established, it will in some fashion transform the object, i.e. the social structure, usually in the direction of an adaptation of reality to the—possibly false—thesis. The discrepancies are gradually removed, the false thesis becomes true.[40]

247

Thus, if men are told that they are irrational beings, that an order based on reason is a myth and an illusion, and if this belief takes a firm hold in the human mind, irrational behavior will increase and become widespread, potentially assuming the dimensions of a social menace. This is apt to happen even though normal human beings are by nature perfectly capable of controlling their irrational impulses in many life situations. If statesmen and politicians are advised that "international politics, like all politics, is a struggle for power," [41] and that "statesmen think and act in terms of interest defined as power," [42] they will tend to adjust their political philosophy and conduct to what has been presented to them as an indisputable law of nature or true proposition of science.

It is true that the will to power often operates as a strong force in individual as well as social life. It is also true that "in any generation there are the strong and aggressive types who long for power or adventure." [43] But it cannot be conceded that the drive to dominate, like the drive to live and to propagate, is "common to all men," [44] and that it constitutes the necessary primary force in shaping the history of mankind. Such a statement does not correctly reflect the attitude of the average healthy individual toward life,[45] nor does it account for the actions of those political leaders who have set an example of what we call "statesman-like action" in domestic and foreign affairs.

Great statesmen like Pericles, Marcus Aurelius, Jefferson, and Lincoln were not primarily or exclusively motivated in their political actions by the desire to dominate men or exercise power over them. Their chief intention was to improve social conditions in their countries and take leadership in building a good society. Morgenthau would probably not dispute this statement, because he believes that achievement of ethical objectives may form the more remote and ultimate purposes of political action.[46] But he interprets all short-range and immediate goals of domestic and international politics solely in terms of maintenance or increase of power and holds that other standards must be subordinated to considerations of power.[47]

It is not the purpose of this analysis to deprecate the importance of the power concept in explaining the facts of political life. As was pointed out earlier,[48] the exercise of power frequently constitutes an indispensable means for the attainment of political aims. Lincoln in the American Civil War sought to accomplish a great humanitarian objective, but he needed a powerful army willing to obey his command in order to win this war. Franklin D. Roosevelt sought to reform the American economy, but he could not have accomplished his purpose without securing a powerful hold over the minds of Congressmen and Senators, without whose cooperation his program could not have been carried out. A revolutionary leader inspired by social ideals may wish to change the social system of his country, but he would be unlikely to succeed without gaining power over large masses of people. Similar considerations apply to the non-political sphere. A powerful mind is needed to produce great works of science, a powerful body to perform arduous physical tasks.

Thus power constitutes an important instrumental value, and its possession is needed to accomplish many worthwhile tasks. It should never be viewed as a goal value, however, regardless of whether the goal is an immediate or remote one. If power is looked upon as an end in itself, it becomes in Fromm's words, "perverted." That a political figure like Hitler, who was driven by an insatiable and demonic drive to exercise power over men, exhibited severe psychopathological symptoms is generally acknowledged today. As Fromm rightly observes, people in whom power is the all-consuming motive are the exception rather than the rule.[49]

It is true, as the German historian Meinecke states, that an individual needs a minimum of power to assert himself in the world. He should use this power to perfect himself mentally and morally. It is also true, as Meinecke adds, that "the servant rarely remains a pure servant, he wants to participate in ruling and thus taints action according to normative standards with an earthly-naturalistic color." [50] The power impulse is probably impervious to complete rational control. But the fact that the accomplishment of ideal objectives is always hampered by the operation of irrational forces does not support the conclusion of some "realists" that all higher effort is more or less futile.[51]

The same thoughts are applicable to the sphere of political and international action. States, too, need a minimum of power to keep their place in the international community. They may also have to protect their security by alliances. As the example of Holland, Sweden, Switzerland, and other small countries shows, however, a nation can be a highly respected member of the international community without attempting to maximize its political influence or military strength. It might also be pointed out that the weak and fragmented Germany in which Goethe, Schiller, and Beethoven lived was admired by the world as a citadel of civilization, while the powerful Germany of Adolf Hitler constituted a menace to the safety and happiness of every woman, man and child throughout the world.

The main purpose of a political commonwealth is to build a rich material and cultural life for its citizens and to compete peacefully with other nations in pursuing this objective. Hard necessity may under some circumstances force a nation to engage in a policy of strength and to deviate, at least for a time, from the chief objective of organized political life, but this does not justify a generalized assertion that "whenever [nations] strive to realize their goal by means of international politics, they do so by striving for power." [52] This statement could be accepted only if employment of the power of reason and persuasion in the councils of nations is included in the notion of power politics and elevated to the rank of one of its major instrumentalities. But this is not the sense in which the concept is generally understood by the statesman and the common man.

It thus becomes necessary to reverse the priorities stated by Morgenthau. Primacy in political science and practice must be given to social ideals and the notion of the common good, on a national as well as supranational level. The presence and strength of the power impulse must, however, always be reckoned with and given due consideration in the calculations of statesmen. That it is not unrealistic to assign priority to political morality over political power is well attested by the fact that men have always fought more valiantly for political ideals, such as freedom, equality, or self-determination, than for the purpose of preserving or expanding the power of their rulers. [53]

Men are born to cooperate (sometimes by competitive methods) in the endeavor of civilization-building. [54] They are not born to dominate or oppress other men. The same principle applies to nation-states. They were created to cooperate (sometimes by competitive methods) in the endeavor of civilization-building on a world-wide basis. They were not formed for the purpose of dominating or oppressing other nations. [55]

Cooperation among nations requires some concern for the interests of other states and an application of the Golden Rule in international affairs. [56] The common laws of morals and justice which should be followed by individuals in their mutual relations must also, as a general rule, govern the relations between nations. If a state practices the opposite of what it preaches, it will enjoy no more respect in the community of nations than an individual who follows such a course will earn in a community of men. Although we have seen that the wars of the past, by creating larger political units or eliminating obsolete political and social systems, have sometimes—although their result was imposition of the rule of one nation over another —indirectly furthered the cause of civilization,[57] it is unlikely, for the reasons pointed out earlier in this section, that any wars of the future could accomplish objectives beneficial to mankind. The avoidance of such wars must therefore become the foremost concern of modern statecraft in international affairs.[58]

Sec. 30. *World Government.*

The historical experience accumulated by mankind in the field of international politics seems to suggest that in a world of sovereign nation-states the goal of universal peace is incapable of being attained. Emery Reves, for example, has reached the conclusion, based on an analysis of basic political forces operative in history, that "war takes place whenever and wherever nonintegrated social units of equal sovereignty come into contact."[1] He maintains, on the other hand, that "wars always ceased when a higher unit established its own sovereignty, absorbing the sovereignties of the conflicting smaller groups."[2] In other words, unless and until some sovereign power is set up over and above the clashing political entities, international war cannot be banished from this globe.

This theory, in its logical consequences, leads to the conviction that nothing short of world government can preserve universal peace. Such a government, according to Reves, would be in a position to eliminate the frictions likely to escalate into war by the promulgation of laws passed by a world parliament.[3] He expresses the view, which can be supported by good reasons, that in the future disagreements threatening peace between states must be solved, not or at least not primarily by the conclusion of treaties or by resort to international tribunals, but by the use of regularized legislative procedures.[4]

The adoption of this solution would, of course, entail a renunciation of the right to national sovereignty. The power to pass laws and enact other measures deemed necessary to remove tensions conducive to violence would have to be yielded to a government of the world. The right to national self-determination would have to be abandoned or at least seriously curtailed. Self-determination, according to Reves, is an anachronism. "It asserts the sacred right of every nation to do as it pleases within its own frontiers, no matter how monstrous or how harmful to the rest of the world." [5]

The thesis of Reves that world peace cannot be secured until this planet is brought under unified political control cannot be proved to be logically unassailable. There is at least a theoretical possibility that rational thinking and wisdom in action might be combined to make nations and their leaders refrain from the supreme folly of nuclear war. But the odds are not favorable to a prediction that reason will become universal and by its own strength inhibit the disintegrative forces operative in the world today.

Two major attempts at enhancing international collaboration to prevent war have been made in this century. The first of these attempts resulted in the founding of the League of Nations after the termination of the First World War. The League was, however, unable to ward off a second and much more destructive Armageddon. It has sometimes been asserted that the chief reason for the failure of the League to accomplish its objectives was the requirement of unanimous consent, which was a prerequisite for collective action directed against a disturber of the peace. It has also been pointed out that the League of Nations Covenant did not contain a general prohibition of war as an instrument of national policy, and that the League exhibited a number of other structural weaknesses.[6] But the principal cause for the League's inability to prevent the Second World War was probably the unwillingness of Britain and France, its leading members, to stop the aggressive designs of Nazi Germany at a time when this would still have been possible.

The generalized unanimity rule of the League Covenant was abandoned in the United Nations Charter of 1945 in favor of a unanimity requirement limited to the big powers. The five permanent members of the Security Council must concur in all enforcement measures designed to maintain or restore international peace and security. Recommendations by the General Assembly, on the other hand, may be adopted by simple or qualified majorities. No powers of resolving international con-

252

troversies by the enactment of legislation binding on all nations were conferred on any organ of the United Nations.

Because of the antagonistic policies of the two main world powers, the United States and the Soviet Union, the United Nations Organization has been able to put a halt to international violence only in those rare instances where the interests of the United States and the Soviet Union happened to coincide (as for instance in the Suez crisis of 1956). Since there can be no effective government of the United Nations if one permanent member of the Security Council dissents from a proposed measure of collective action, the organization rests on a highly insecure basis. The only hope for the preservation of peace, as Morgenthau has stated, is "international government of the United States and the Soviet Union acting in unison." [7]

The rise of China as a world power which has thrown down the gauntlet both to the United States and the Soviet Union has added new complications to the international situation. And yet, if the latter two countries would stand firmly together in their determination to contain Chinese power within its present borders, the chances for maintaining world peace would still be quite substantial. No strong hope for achieving this objective can, however, be expressed. The conflict of interests between the United States and the Soviet Union in other areas of international concern is probably too pronounced to render an undeviating common effort to stem the tide of war possible.

It is even less to be expected that the demonstrated shortcomings of the United Nations will result in the early creation of a world government. The Soviet Union as well as China are at present strongly opposed to any schemes of this character.[8] In the United States, although there are groups advocating a worldwide federation of nations, enthusiasm for such a project is generally weak. The political and moral sentiments necessary to support supranational rule are as yet insufficiently developed in human consciousness. Nationalism, demanding an unquestioned loyalty to the nation-state, still retains an immensely potent hold over the minds of men.[9] The time for supplementing or supplanting the national public interest by the recognition of a supranational common good is not as yet at hand.

If world peace (not counting perhaps the incidence of smaller localized wars) can be preserved under the present organization of the international community, it is unlikely that a world state will ever become a reality. If mankind, on the other hand, should experience another great trauma through the occurrence of a major war, the pressures in favor of establishing a unified political control for the entire globe are apt to become very strong at the end of such a war. Whether world government would then be created by mutual agreement or imposed by one nation or a small group of nations on the others must, of course, remain an open question today. What can be predicted with a fair degree of certainty is that such a world government would be federative rather than unitary. A confederation or federation of states would be set up in which certain enumerated functions would be delegated to a federal government, while substantial powers of regulation would continue to reside in the individual states composing the union.

The chief power that would have to be delegated to a government of the world is, of course, the power to secure and enforce peace among the constituent political units. To that end, a military force of sufficient size would have to be maintained by that government. But, as was pointed out before, the preservation of peace within a political organization is possible only when the chief causes of discord and friction between the members of that organization have been eliminated or at least substantially reduced. The creation of a judicial system capable of adjudging and settling conflicts among the component units, with prohibition of recourse to violence, would be an indispensable but not a sufficient condition for the functioning of the organization. If the federation should include states with an abundance of natural resources and others with a deficiency of such resources, and if the favored states refuse to share their resources with the disfavored ones, such economic disparity could easily produce a condition of dangerous dissatisfaction which could threaten the existence of the world state. The setting up of onerous barriers to commerce and trade among the constituent units might also jeopardize the success of the venture. The federal government therefore would have to be granted legislative power to regulate economic relations and commerce among the individual states. A further source of dissension and strife among the member states might be produced by the ill-treatment of national minorities or religious groups within the borders of a particular political unit. For this reason, authority to protect human rights against oppressive policies and discriminatory practices would have to be vested in the world government.

It also bears emphasis that some degree of consensus among

254

men throughout the globe concerning the fundamental values and postulates of just social ordering would be necessary to ensure the success of an experiment in worldwide political control. If the members of one constituent unit should look upon the political or economic system of another unit as an outrage or monstrosity, a harmonious cooperation of states would thereby become seriously impeded. This should not, however, be construed as a suggestion that all of the member states of a world union should operate under the same political, economic, and social institutions. On the contrary, healthful diversity and the possibility of social experimentation on a local or regional level should be deemed a highly desirable feature of a federated world state. The need for pluralism and diversified richness would be particularly great in the area of cultural life.[10] But general tolerance and acceptance of such diversity, within the limits imposed by the necessity of pursuing certain common aims, would be an indispensable precondition for the proper functioning of a *civitas maxima*.

The chances are propitious that the present sharp divergences in the economic and political philosophy of the world's nations are going to be narrowed down in the course of time. Extreme forms of individualism and collectivism in social and economic life are likely to give way to less one-sided approaches to the problems of societal organizations. Such a convergence of social systems, although it will not—it is hoped—result in a drab global uniformity, will reduce the obstacles which presently stand in the way of creating a world community dedicated to the aim of advancing the cause of the human race as a whole.

It has sometimes been asserted that in a peaceful and organized world mankind would become debilitated from lack of provocative challenges and invigorating risks, such as are provided by the steelbath of struggle and war. The argument has lost its force under the conditions of our age, in which wars are waged to a considerable extent without actual fighting and through the mechanical extermination of large numbers of non-combatants. "In such a war," says John Strachey, "there would be little room for courage, endurance, comradeship—for those military virtues, the flickering light of which has at least relieved the blood and filth of traditional warfare." [11] Furthermore, if the alternative to a world governed by reason and law is a huge "radio-active poison desert," [12] the flourishing of vigorous daring and hardihood in an enfeebled and probably dehu-

255

manized mankind could not be expected if the latter alternative should eventuate.

William James has shown in an illuminating essay that it is possible to produce moral equivalents for the institution of war. Risk, intrepidity, contempt of softness, he said, must remain the rock upon which political societies are built.[13] But these virtues, in his view, can be fostered by means other than the waging of destructive wars. Conscription for the conquest of nature should take the place of military conscription.[14]

There can be little doubt that the idea underlying the founding of the Peace Corps by President Kennedy would have appealed strongly to William James. Strenuous work performed for constructive and humanitarian purposes in unfamiliar climates, in teeming jungles or arctic wastes, under primitive and hazardous conditions, would supply much of the opportunity for vigorous self-discipline which the wars of the past afforded to some extent. Other chances for testing personal courage, determination, and endurance are offered by mountain climbing, skiing, and other healthful sports. Unforeseen by James, the programs in progress for the exploration and conquest of space also constitute inexhaustible sources for the activation and preservation of the manly virtues.

"War becomes absurd and impossible from its own monstrosity," said William James in the pre-nuclear age, adding that "I look forward to a future when acts of war shall be formally outlawed as between civilized peoples." [15] We do not know how close the day for the advent of universal peace is at hand, and, as shown before, it is unlikely to arrive without a careful and prudent planning of justice on a supranational scale.[16] Since even the possibility of a total extinction of mankind through nuclear war cannot be wholly discounted, any undue optimism with respect to the future of the human race is equivalent to shutting one's eyes before the grimness of present-day realities. It is preferable to reconcile oneself to the probability that mankind will have to go through the most severe trials and tribulations before a firm foundation can be laid for the reign of peace and justice throughout the world.

Epilogue: Justice and the Theory of Values.

At the beginning of this treatise, various conflicting theories were set forth which attempted to explain the nature of values in general, but the insights which an analysis of the specific value of justice might yield with respect to this controversy were reserved for discussion at the end of this study. It is the purpose of this Epilogue to take up the thread which was laid aside in the introductory section and to examine the question as to what gains, if any, might be derived from our inquiry into the phenomenon of justice for a better understanding of the generic character of human values.

It was pointed out in the first section that a theory which today enjoys great popularity in England, the United States, and some other countries deems values to be rooted in the subjective and emotional side of human nature and for this reason denies cognitive significance to human judgments regarding values. According to this view, which is often referred to as the doctrine of logical positivism, a philosopher or social scientist may investigate sentiments of value from a genetic point of view, by trying to show the causal factors responsible for their origination, growth, and prevalence in a certain society. On the other hand, any assertion by him of a proposition concerning the intrinsic rightness or wrongness of a value judgment would constitute nothing but an "ejaculation" of a personal feeling and therefore lack meaning in any scientific or philosophical sense.

An attempt has been made in this treatise to show that this approach delimits the proper scope of scholarly and philosophical endeavor in too narrow a fashion. The position has been taken that the permissible range of rational inquiry concerning the value of justice is not restricted to probing into the causal factors giving rise to various attitudes toward justice, but may be extended to the goals of just ordering as well as the means conducive to the adequate realization of these goals.[1] The argument was advanced that a demonstration of the goals of justice is possible if we assume that men wish to live in a societal order which renders human existence tolerable and worthwhile. This is a presupposition which cannot be shown to be true by any mathematically exact method of proof but which is, in the words of Victor Kraft, "rooted in the general conditions of human life."[2]

We are faced here with objective factors and not merely with subjective reactions, and it might be well to summarize some of the facets of reality which condition or influence a general determination of the goals of just ordering. Men are dominated by the life instinct which, although it can become stunted and perverted, impels them to enhance their existence and unfold their productive powers and special aptitudes.[3] Unless pathological conditions causing regression intervene, men are actuated by their constitution and native endowments to transcend their animal nature and use their specifically human powers of reason and creative imagination in the building of civilizations.[4] Although the contributions which individual men will make to the endeavor of civilization-building are necessarily different, as well as unequal in quantity and quality, no convincing argument can be devised to show that some men, groups, classes, or nations should not be permitted to "share with others in the same basic experience of living." [5] Contrary to a widespread belief held in antiquity, there also exists no general justification or need, in view of the strength of the human desire for liberty, for denying the status of freedom to some men on the ground that a class of slaves or serfs is indispensable to the growth of any form of culture.[6] In addition to freedom and equality, justice must also guarantee a certain measure of order and security to men, since "as long as most of man's energy is taken up by the defense of his life against attacks, or to ward off starvation, love of life must be stunted." [7] Justice must also respond to another facet of the human sense of justice, viz., the strong feeling that fairness and proportionality should prevail in transactions of exchange, in the distribution of honors and rewards, and in the administration of punishment.[8]

It is logically possible to deny the validity of these ontologically-founded aims of justice, but it is difficult, in the light of the knowledge and experience accumulated by mankind in the course of many centuries, to make out a convincing and rational argument which repudiates the value of civilization, pleads for nullification rather than enhancement of existence, advocates oppression and exploitation, and glorifies the bestial qualities in men. As Kraft has pointed out, observance of the law of the jungle and general unconcern for the feelings, interests, and claims of one's fellowmen cause disintegration and ultimate destruction of society, and that this is a result which sane human beings cannot wish for.[9] The fact that the large majority of men, if in possession of the information required to make an intelli-

258

gent judgment, would concur in preferring the life-affirming values to a denial of existence, is an additional argument in favor of accepting the ultimate goals summarized above, but the chief instrumentality for establishing their prima facie validity is the strength of the supporting reasons as weighed against the weakness of the opposing considerations. It would appear to be impossible to prove that men should *not* use their powers and talents to enrich civilization and promote the finer and higher values of life, but instead employ their energies in a primitive and brutal struggle for daily survival.

If the desirability of the final goals is recognized, a detached and objective discussion of the means necessary for their attainment is not rendered nugatory by the possibility and likelihood of disagreement. A considerable volume of subjectivity with respect to judgments of good social policy is inevitable, but there are also situations where such a judgment is so plausible, and so superior to potential counterarguments, that reasonable men will accept it and will reject the opposing position as objectively untenable.[10] Who, for example, would be willing to defend the thesis that the protection of life, limb, and property against crime should be left to the individual rather than entrusted to government, or that in the administration of the legal system integrity and honesty on the part of judges should be discouraged rather than fostered? These examples, which could be supplemented by many others, offer sufficient disproof for the proposition that normative judgments are necessarily subjective and idiosyncratic. We must therefore reach the conclusion that an analysis of the goals of justice and of the means appropriate to their realization tends to disestablish the correctness of the position supported by the logical positivists.

Turning next to the theory of Ralph Barton Perry, we found that he proposed to use the term value as a synonym for the object of an interest.[11] This conception of value is broader than that of logical positivism because it includes in its scope social purposes and rational objectives. This breadth of the concept is partly a strength and partly a weakness of Perry's approach. Viewing the problem through the prism of the theory of justice, the deficiency of Perry's concept of value stems from the fact that there are interests which are disvaluable and therefore cannot be legitimately promoted by the agencies of justice. There are persons with morbid or psychopathic traits who desire to pursue interests and aims which an adequately organized system of law cannot countenance. Such are, for example, sadistic activities, sexual aggression, destructive practices directed against persons or property, excessive greed and craving for power at any cost. It is not only contrary to common linguistic usage but also ethically questionable to assert that "value in the generic sense attaches promiscuously to all objects of all interests." [12] The dichotomy between values and disvalues must be preserved, unless we wish to drain the notion of value of its positive connotations and reduce it to a meaningless neutrality.

We shall turn now to the position of Scheler and Hartmann, according to which values are ideal, timeless objects which exist independently of subjective human acts of valuation and are experienced through intuitive perception. [13] This view, like the Platonic theory of ideas, divorces values from human consciousness and ascribes to them an absolute and objective character. The value of justice, for example, must be clearly distinguished under this view from personal manifestations of the sense of justice, which may be misguided or lacking in intuitive clairvoyance.

The element of truth contained in this theory is the realization that the notion of justice is not devoid of absolute and objective components. Justice is an absolute value in the limited sense that its opposite cannot legitimately form the chosen goal of social action. [14] Only a willfully irrational man could contend that we should love and promote injustice. "In the constitution of the rational animal I see no virtue which is opposed to justice," said the Emperor Marcus Aurelius, [15] and Aristotle declared that justice, in its nature, can never be ruinous to a state. [16] There are situations where deficiencies of insight or inescapable necessities may prevent men from achieving a full measure of justice, [17] but this does not mean that any government or group of individuals has the moral or legal right to make the perpetration of injustice a deliberate aim of its activities. [18]

There are also certain concrete principles of justice that may claim validity. Thus, it can never be just for a man to torture an innocent child, or to kill his neighbor because he has expressed disagreement with his views. It can never be just for a judge to convict a man on the basis of evidence known to him to be perjured. It can never be just for a nation to wage war on a sister nation because its ruler derives pleasurable feelings of self-aggrandizement from such action. If a suggestion by Arthur Pap

260

is followed, it is also arguable that a standard of justice may be absolute within a certain system of evaluation.[19] Thus, the due process and equal protection principles might be said to constitute absolutes in the American system of public law because all legislative and administrative action, without exception, must move within the confines of these constitutional mandates.

Justice also has certain objective components in the sense that it must strive to realize certain social goals and avoid realizing others. To give men that degree of freedom and equality conducive to maximum development of their productive powers is an imperative of justice which can be validated by objective considerations; the same is true for the demand that a just order should guarantee that degree of security and order which permits men to live a worthwhile and dignified life free from fear of aggression and depredation.[20] These goals are not, however, absolute in the sense that they are unconditioned by, and unrelated to, any external and contingent factors. There may be stages of civilization in which a realization of freedom and equality is not as yet a practical possibility, and there may be temporary conditions in which the effectuation of order and security must yield to the overriding compulsion to allow for dynamic change accompanied by temporary disorder.[21] The technological, psychological, social and economic realities of the time and place often set limits to the execution of the objectives of just social ordering.

The dynamic and contingent elements in the notion of justice make it difficult to visualize justice as an a priori structure, an ideal essence, or an eternal and immutable image (in the Platonic sense) of which human beings may have obtained a glimpse prior to their earthly lives. The fact that the sense of justice often manifests itself in an essentially similar form in human beings merely points to uniformities in the psychic and mental makeup of human beings; it does not corroborate the presuppositions of value-realism. We must conclude, therefore, that the theory of justice does not supply general philosophy with a sufficient amount of tangible evidence to support the conception of values as ideally subsisting entities.

Objection may also be made to the view of Scheler and Hartmann on the ground that it elevates intuitive perception to the rank of an exclusive faculty for the discernment of values. It need not be denied that intuition may sometimes provide significant flashes of insight into the nature and essential elements of

261

values. It has been shown, however, that at least with respect to the value of justice rational argumentation and comparison of the weight of opposing arguments play an exceedingly important role in the validation of propositions pertaining to this area of discourse. These methods of value-cognition are, of course, non-intuitive in character.

In order to understand and explain the notion of justice, a metaphysical hypostatization of the concept into an ideal object is not required. Although we must recognize a general concept of justice apart from individual just actions, this general concept need not be thought of as having an existence independent of human consciousness. Concepts are constructions of the human mind which, by way of generalization, abstraction, or classification, reflect the realities of the material, psychological and spiritual modes of being. This is the position of conceptualism, which can be conveniently employed in the analysis of justice.[22]

The notion of justice relates to a multitude of normative phenomena which are held together by certain common characteristics. These common features cannot be easily defined but, generally speaking, they have their nucleus of reference in the proper coordination of the relations or regulation of the activities of the members of a group and the proper allocation of rights, powers, and duties among them with a view to satisfying the reasonable needs and aspirations of individuals and at the same time promoting maximum productive effort and social cohesion. An attempt was made in this treatise to show that a completely just order would be one in which each individual, as a free and equal partner in a joint enterprise, is enabled to contribute to the best of his ability to the common good, conceived in terms of the highest possible development of civilization, and in turn receives the satisfaction of his basic needs and, over and above this, rewards proportional to his achievements. It was emphasized throughout the book, however, that all human endeavors to achieve justice are necessarily impeded by various contingencies and the limitations of human wisdom. No society can therefore be expected to do more than draw its inspiration from an image of justice which, considering the state of its material, intellectual, and moral development, reflects the highest potentialities of achievement of which it is for the time being capable.

NOTES

SEC. 1.

1. Edmond Cahn describes the sense of justice as "an indissociable blend of reason and empathy." *The Sense of Injustice* (New York, 1949), p. 26. But instances also occur where the response to an injustice is wholly emotional, or where a purely rational evaluation takes place. See the more detailed discussion of the problem *infra* Sec. 6.
2. John Dewey, *Theory of Valuation* (Chicago, 1939), p. 1.
3. A. J. Ayer, *Language, Truth and Logic* (London, 1950), pp. 107-108; Rudolf Carnap, "Philosophy and Logical Syntax," in M. White, *The Age of Analysis* (Boston, 1955), pp. 216-220. Cf. also Victor Kraft, *The Vienna Circle*, transl. A. Pap (New York, 1953), pp. 182-183. The theory carries a great deal of authority today in England, the United States, and the Scandinavian countries.
4. Hans Kelsen, *General Theory of Law and State*, transl. A. Wedberg (Cambridge, Mass., 1949), p. 13; Kelsen, *What is Justice* (Berkeley, 1957), p. 21.
5. R. B. Perry, *General Theory of Value* (New York, 1926), pp. 115-131; Perry, *Realms of Value* (Cambridge, Mass., 1954), pp. 2-3.
6. Perry, *General Theory of Value*, p. 116.
7. Victor Kraft, *Rationale Moralbegründung* (Vienna, 1963), p. 26; S. L. Hart, *Treatise on Values* (New York, 1949), pp. 56, 65, and "The Nature and Objectivity of Ethical Judgments," 15 *Philosophy and Phenomenological Research* 360, at 366 (1955).
8. Max Scheler, *Der Formalismus in der Ethik und die Materiale Wertethik* (Halle, 1927), pp. 8, 14, 20, 47.
9. Nicolai Hartmann, *Ethics*, transl. S. Coit (London, 1932), Vol. I, pp. 183-189, 206-212, 217-226. A similar position with respect to the values of the legal order was taken by Luis Recaséns Siches, "Human Life, Society, and Law," in *Latin-American Legal Philosophy* (Cambridge, Mass., 1948), pp. 18-22.
10. See Epilogue: Justice and the Theory of Values.

SEC. 2.

1. Hans Kelsen, *General Theory of Law and State*, transl. A. Wedberg (Cambridge, Mass., 1949), p. 4.
2. *Ibid.*

3. It would seem that there is at least one semantic law which every scientist and scholar should observe, viz., that phenomena exhibiting essentially dissimilar characteristics should be denoted by different terms.
4. This point was validly made by E. N. Cahn, *The Sense of Injustice* (New York, 1949), p. 13. See also C. J. Friedrich, "Justice: The Just Political Act," in *Justice*, ed. C. J. Friedrich and J. W. Chapman (*Nomos*, Vol. VI, New York, 1963), p. 30: "It is a remarkable fact that men's feelings are more sharply aroused by an act of injustice than by one of justice."
5. On the doctrine of just war see Arthur Nussbaum, *A Concise History of the Law of Nations*, rev. ed. (New York, 1954), pp. 10-11, 36-38 and passim.
6. On the difference between a decision according to justice and a decision according to law see *infra* Sec. 3.
7. *Maclean v. The Workers' Union*, 24 Q. B. D. 166 (1889).
8. On the manner in which the sense of justice manifests itself in the nursery see F. R. Bienenfeld, *Rediscovery of Justice* (London, 1947), Part I.
9. The word "good," for example, embraces so many meanings and instances of application that one might easily despair of assigning a definable sense to it. For this reason the English philosopher George Moore considered "good" a simple, primitive, undefinable term. *Principia Ethica* (Cambridge, Eng., 1954), pp. 6-17. But Moore took the position that "good," although incapable of definition, was a meaningful term.
10. Giorgio Del Vecchio says in *Justice*, ed. A. H. Campbell (New York, 1953), p. 85, that "justice . . . culminates in the requirement that *every subject shall be recognized (by others) for* what he is worth, that to everyone shall be assigned (by others) what belongs to him."
11. The term "legal justice" has been used by some authors to denote the obligations owed by the citizens to the organized community. For example, the man who does not pay his taxes, thereby depriving the government of funds necessary to promote the common good, commits a violation of legal justice. See Jean Dabin, "General Theory of Law," in *The Legal Philosophies of Lask, Radbruch and Dabin*, transl. K. Wilk (Cambridge, Mass., 1950), p. 463; Viktor Cathrein, *Recht, Naturrecht und Positives Recht* (Darmstadt, 1964), p. 54.
12. H. L. A. Hart, *The Concept of Law* (Oxford, 1961), p. 155. See also Gerhart Husserl, "Justice," 47 *International Journal of Ethics* 271, at 274 (1937).
13. On the relation between justice and equality see *infra* Sec. 10.
14. Hart, *op. cit. supra* n. 12, p. 153.
15. Arthur Schopenhauer, "Die Grundlage der Moral," in *Sämtliche Werke* (Leipzig, 1891), Vol. III, pp. 595, 598; John Stuart Mill, *Utilitarianism*, ed. O. Piest (New York, 1957), p. 65.

SEC. 3.

1. "Personal authority can have its source in . . . the surrender to the extraordinary, the belief in *charisma*, i.e. actual revelation or grace resting in such a person as a savior, a prophet, or a hero." Max Weber, *Law*

in Economy and Society, ed. M. Rheinstein (Cambridge, Mass., 1954), p. 336.

2. Philip Selznick, "Natural Law and Sociology," in *Natural Law and Modern Society* (Cleveland, 1962), p. 171.

3. See Edgar Bodenheimer, "Reflections on the Rule of Law," 8 *Utah Law Review* 1, 8-10 (1962).

4. Thus, returning to an example used earlier, if a law prescribes that persons who have criticized government officials should be confined to a concentration camp for lifetime, a particular confinement satisfies the principle of legality if the statutory criteria have been met.

5. S. A. Golunskii and M. S. Strogovitch, "The Theory of the State and Law," in *Soviet Legal Philosophy*, transl. H. W. Babb (Cambridge, Mass., 1951), p. 392; O. S. Ioffe and M. D. Shargorodskii, "The Significance of General Definitions in the Study of Problems of Law and Socialist Legality," 2 *Soviet Law and Government* 3 (1963).

6. Ioffe and Shargorodskii, *op. cit. supra* n. 5, p. 8.

7. "The wreckers understood clearly that it was precisely in an atmosphere of arbitrary lawlessness that they could most readily carry on their black work, whereas a firmly established system of legality—order and discipline—removes the possibility of their doing harm, and means that they will unflinchingly be exposed and rendered harmless." Golunskii and Strogovitch, *op. cit supra* n. 5, p. 393.

8. This was the position of Aristotle. See *Politics*, ed. E. Barker (Oxford, 1946), Bk. III, Ch. xv. 1286a and Ch. xvi 1287a.

9. See, for example, Plato, *The Statesman*, transl. J. B. Skemp (New York, 1957), 294a and 294b: "Law can never issue an injunction binding on all which really embodies what is best for each; it cannot prescribe with accuracy what is best and just for each member of the community at any one time."

10. Frederick Engels, *Anti-Dühring*, ed. C. P. Dutt (New York, 1934), p. 309. It is interesting to note that present-day Soviet legal theory seems to be on the verge of abandoning this "withering away of law" doctrine of Marxian philosophy. See P. S. Romashkin, "Problems of the Development of the State and Law in the Draft Program of the CPSU," 1 *Soviet Law and Government* 3, at 9 (1961): "Under communism rights and duties will organically blend into uniform norms of communist intercourse, the observance of which will become a need and habit for all people." It is maintained, however, that in the fully matured communist society a special coercive state apparatus for enforcing the rules of community life will become unnecessary. *Ibid.*

11. John Austin, *The Province of Jurisprudence Determined*, ed. H. L. A. Hart (London, 1954), p. 262. See also *id.*, p. 190: "Law itself is the standard of justice. What deviates from any law is unjust with reference to that law. . . ."

12. Hans Kelsen, *General Theory of Law and State*, transl. A. Wedberg (Cambridge, Mass., 1949), p. 14.

13. Alf Ross, *On Law and Justice* (Berkeley, 1959), p. 280. See also Frederick Pollock, *A First Book of Jurisprudence*, 6th ed. (London, 1929), p. 32: "Law being once established, *just*, in matters of the law, denotes what is done in express fulfillment of the rules of law, or is approved and allowed by law." But Pollock admits that justice also has an ethical meaning which is not identical with its legal signification. *Id.*, p. 33.

265

14. David Granfield, "The Scholastic Dispute on Justice," in *Justice*, ed. C. J. Friedrich and J. W. Chapman (*Nomos*, Vol. VI, New York, 1963), p. 238.
15. Iredell Jenkins, "Justice as Ideal and Ideology," in *op. cit. supra* n. 14, p. 203.
16. *Ibid.*
17. Giorgio Del Vecchio, *Justice*, ed. A. H. Campbell (New York, 1953), pp. 156-158. The thought that there can be no just order if everybody acts lawlessly will be developed further *infra* Sec. 12.
18. Max Rümelin, *Die Gerechtigkeit* (Tübingen, 1920), p. 6.
19. F. L. Windolph, *Leviathan and the Natural Law* (Princeton, 1951), p. 30.
20. Emil Brunner, *Justice and the Social Order*, transl. M. Hottinger (New York, 1945), p. 18.
21. This author has stated his general views on the question in *Jurisprudence: The Philosophy and Method of the Law* (Cambridge, Mass., 1962), pp. 223-227, 302-303.

SEC. 4.

1. Aristotle, *Nicomachean Ethics*, transl. H. Rackham (Loeb Class. Lib. ed., Cambridge, Mass., 1947), Bk. V. i. 15.
2. Felix Cohen, *Ethical Systems and Legal Ideals* (Reissue, New York, 1959), p. 7.
3. F. S. C. Northrop says in "Law, Language and Morals," 71 *Yale Law Journal* 1017, at 1025 (1962): "To be a properly trained lawyer or a judge of integrity is to be concerned with the intrinsically good and just as well as the instrumental."
4. Adam Smith, "The Theory of Moral Sentiments," in *Adam Smith's Moral and Political Philosophy*, ed. H. W. Schneider (New York, 1948), p. 117.
5. Immanuel Kant, *Fundamental Principles of the Metaphysics of Morals*, transl. T. K. Abbott (New York, 1949), p. 11. Arthur Pap has termed this approach "the ethics of motives," as contrasted to the utilitarian "ethics of consequences." *Elements of Analytic Philosophy* (New York, 1949), p. 47.
6. Karl Mannheim, *Diagnosis of Our Time* (New York, 1944), p. 122.
7. *Ibid.*
8. Kant, *The Philosophy of Law*, transl. W. Hastie (Edinburgh, 1887), p. 32.
9. H. L. A. Hart, *The Concept of Law* (Oxford, 1961), p. 169, is in agreement with the position taken here.
10. S. L. Hart, *Ethics* (New York, 1963), p. 26. A good exemplification of this proposition is the case of a dictator who believes honestly that he is acting in accordance with the highest interests of his country, but who by his political actions brings suffering, war, and devastation upon his country and the world.
11. Not only it is incorrect to say that morality is only interested in good intentions, but it must also be stressed that the law concerns itself with actions producing effects in the external world as well as states of mind accompanying such actions. Examples are given in this author's *Jurisprudence: The Philosophy and Method of the Law* (Cambridge, Mass., 1962), pp. 248-249.

266

12. S. E. Toulmin, *An Examination of the Place of Reason in Ethics* (Cambridge, Eng., 1950), p. 132. See also Melvin Rader, *Ethics and Society* (New York, 1950), p. 118: "Morality enjoins men to live with that degree of wisdom and justice and kindliness without which life, in any age or in any society, is intolerable."
13. Tobit 4:15; Matth. 7:12; Confucius, *Analecta* 15:23; Mahabharata 13, 113, 9; Dhammapada 129-139.
14. Thomas Hobbes, *Leviathan*, ed. A. D. Lindsay (Everyman's Lib. ed., London, 1914), Ch. 26.
15. John Stuart Mill, *Utilitarianism*, ed. O. Piest (New York, 1957), p. 22.
16. Kant, *op. cit. supra* n. 5, p. 38: "Act only on that maxim whereby thou canst at the same time will that it should become a universal law."
17. T. V. Smith, "Ethics," 5 *Encyclopedia of the Social Sciences* 603 (New York, 1931).
18. Robert Maciver, "The Deep Beauty of the Golden Rule," in *Moral Principles of Action*, ed. R. N. Anshen (New York, 1952), p. 41. See also *id.*, p. 43: "The golden rule is the *only* ethical principle . . . that can have a clear right of way everywhere in the kind of world we have inherited."
19. See further discussions of the Golden Rule *infra* Secs. 6, 10 and 29.
20. See *infra* Ch. II.
21. L. L. Fuller, *The Morality of Law* (New Haven, 1964), pp. 5-9.
22. *Id.*, p. 9.
23. Leo Tolstoy, *Resurrection*, transl. L. Maude (London, 1916), Bk. II, Ch. 40.
24. This is also the position of Alfred Verdross, *Abendländische Rechtsphilosophie*, 2d ed. (Vienna, 1963), p. 289.
25. W. D. Lamont, *The Principles of Moral Judgment* (Oxford, 1946), p. 170.
26. See on this problem H. L. A. Hart, *The Concept of Law* (Oxford, 1961), p. 175.

SEC. 5.

1. John Stuart Mill, *Utilitarianism*, ed. O. Piest (New York, 1957), p. 10.
2. *Id.*, pp. 10-11.
3. *Id.*, pp. 11-12.
4. "*Good* means pleasure, or the cause of pleasure." Jeremy Bentham, *Theory of Legislation*, transl. from the French of E. Dumont by C. M. Atkinson (London, 1914), p. 3. See also his definition of utility in *An Introduction to the Principles of Morals and Legislation* (Oxford, 1823), Ch. I. ii.
5. Bentham, *Theory of Legislation*, p. 42.
6. Bentham, *Principles of Morals and Legislation*, Ch. X. xxxviii n. 2.
7. See Mill, *op. cit. supra* n. 1, Ch. V.
8. This analysis of justice is found *id.*, pp. 54-58.
9. *Id.*, p. 63.
10. *Id.*, pp. 64-65.
11. *Id.*, p. 78.
12. A similar position was taken *supra* Sec. 4.
13. That this assumption is basic to an understanding of hedonism was

shown by G. E. Moore, *Principia Ethica* (Cambridge, Eng., 1934), pp. 62-63. See also Mill, *op. cit. supra* n. 1, p. 10.

14. Mill, *op. cit. supra* n. 1, Ch. IV. Arthur Pap argues that "the utilitarian (in contrast to the egoistic hedonist) . . . defines the right act as the one which will bestow a balance of pleasure upon society as a whole, not just upon the agent." *Elements of Analytic Philosophy* (New York, 1949), p. 47. A thorough reading of Bentham and Mill will reveal, however, that in their opinion the pursuit of pleasure by each individual will, as a general rule, be conducive to the greatest happiness of the greatest number. But see *infra* n. 26.

15. Erich Fromm, *Man for Himself* (New York, 1947), pp. 175-180. See also John Dewey, *Theory of the Moral Life*, ed. A. Isenberg (New York, 1960), p. 39: "Pleasures are so externally and accidentally connected with the performance of a deed, that attempting to foresee them is probably the stupidest course which could be taken in order to secure guidance for action." Dewey points out that a clearcut distinction must be made between pleasure and happiness. *Id.*, pp. 38, 44-47.

16. Fromm, *op. cit supra* n. 15, p. 179.

17. Kurt Goldstein, *Human Nature in the Light of Psychopathology* (Cambridge, Mass., 1951), pp. 140, 227-228. See also Fromm, *The Sane Society* (New York, 1955), p. 202: "Happiness results from the experience of productive living, and the use of the powers of love and reason which unite us with the world."

18. S. L. Hart, *Treatise on Values* (New York, 1949), p. 44.

19. See Fromm, *op. cit. supra* n. 17, pp. 200-204.

20. Bentham, *Principles of Morals and Legislation,* Ch. IV. v. 5.

21. See Fromm, *op. cit. supra* n. 17, pp. 201-202.

22. Moritz Schlick, *Problems of Ethics,* transl. D. Rynin (New York, 1939), p. 127.

23. Nicolai Hartmann, *Ethics,* transl. S. Coit (London, 1932), Vol. I, pp. 149-151. Bernard Shaw says in a similar vein: "The pursuit of happiness is the nearest way to frustration and suicide, happiness being a by-product of beneficial activity and comfortable circumstances." G. B. Shaw, *Everybody's Political What's What* (New York, 1945), p. 284.

24. Hartmann, *op. cit supra* n. 23, p. 149.

25. Max Scheler, *Der Formalismus in der Ethik und die Materiale Wertethik* (Halle, 1927), p. 95.

26. Mill, *Autobiography* (The World's Classics, London, 1924), p. 120.

27. Fromm, *op. cit. supra* n. 15, pp. 189-190.

28. L. L. Fuller, *The Morality of Law* (New Haven, 1964), p. 18.

29. See *infra* Ch. II.

SEC. 6.

1. Piero Calamandrei, *Procedure and Democracy*, transl. J. C. and H. Adams (New York, 1956), p. 8.

2. Hans Kelsen, "The Pure Theory of Law," 50 *Law Quarterly Review* 474, at 482 (1934); Kelsen, *What is Justice* (Berkeley, 1957), p. 21.

3. Kelsen, *What is Justice,* p. 228. Examples of varying concepts of justice are found on pp. 5-8, 227-228.

4. Kelsen, "The Pure Theory of Law," p. 482.

5. Kelsen, *What is Justice*, p. 200. See also *id.*, p. 355: "Judgments about ultimate ends or supreme values are, in spite of their claim to an objective validity highly subjective."

6. See the criticism of pure empiricism by Max Planck, *Where is Science Going* (New York, 1932), pp. 70-94. On the general problems of method in the natural sciences see also F. S. C. Northrop, *The Logic of the Sciences and the Humanities* (New York, 1947), Chs. IV, VI, VII; Victor Kraft, *Erkenntnislehre* (Vienna, 1960), pp. 106-107, 120-122.

7. Morris Cohen, *Reason and Nature* (Glencoe, Ill., 1931), p. 17. See also *id.*, p. 108: "Scientific system is not attained by merely adding facts. . . . We need some guiding principle to explore and take account of all possibilities and to introduce order into the chaos of unconnected facts."

8. Albert Einstein, "On the Generalized Theory of Gravitation," 182 *Scientific American* 13, at 15 (1950). The necessity for the formation of speculative hypotheses in science is also emphasized by John Dewey, *The Quest for Certainty* (Capricorn ed., New York, 1960), p. 310.

9. Kurt Goldstein, *Human Nature in the Light of Psychopathology* (Cambridge, Mass., 1951), Chs. II and III. The cognitive part of reason, as a special and distinct function, is often called "intellect."

10. A. N. Whitehead, *The Function of Reason* (Boston, 1929), pp. 28-29.

11. *Id.*, p. 34.

12. *Id.*, p. 20.

13. *Id.*, pp. 10-17. Whitehead rejects in strong language the view held by some psychologists that purpose is irrelevant to the explanation of behavior. He says, among other things: "Scientists animated by the purpose of proving that they are purposeless constitute an interesting subject for study." *Id.*, p. 16.

14. Cohen, *op. cit. supra* n. 7, p. 21.

15. The principle is stated in *Supreme Malt Products Co. v. Alcoholic Beverages Control Commission*, 133 N. E. 2d 775, at 778 (Mass., 1956); *Massachusetts Commission Against Discrimination v. Colangelo*, 182 N. E. 2d 595, at 600 (Mass., 1962). Today legislation is rarely invalidated by the courts on this ground.

16. Morris Ginsberg, *Essays in Sociology and Social Philosophy* (New York, 1960), Vol. II, p. 245.

17. Cohen, *op. cit. supra* n. 7, p. 9.

18. See A. C. Ewing, *Ethics* (London, 1953), p. 127: "The majority of ethical differences are due to differences of belief as to matters of fact." See also Victor Kraft, *Die Grundlagen einer Wissenschaftlichen Wertlehre*, 2d ed. (Vienna, 1951), pp. 190-191.

SEC. 7.

1. Arnold Brecht, *Political Theory* (Princeton, 1959), pp. 124-125.

2. *Id.*, pp. 125, 130-131. See also Max Rheinstein "What Should Be the Relation of Morals to Law," 1 *Journal of Public Law* 287, at 300 (1952).

3. Max Weber, *On the Methodology of the Social Sciences*, transl. E. A. Shils and H. A. Finch (Glencoe, Ill., 1949), pp. 54-57.

4. *Id.*, p. 52.

5 Max Weber, *Gesammelte Aufsätze zur Wissenschaftslehre* (Tübingen, 1922), p. 546 (Translation mine).

6. Weber, *op. cit. supra* n. 3, p. 53. See also the summary of Weber's thought on this subject in Brecht, *op. cit. supra* n. 1, pp. 221-231.
7. Weber, *op. cit. supra* n. 5, p. 551.
8. *Id.*, p. 544.
9. Morris Ginsberg, *Essays in Sociology and Social Philosophy* (Melbourne, 1956), Vol. I, p. 138.
10. J. Bronowski, *The Common Sense of Science* (London, 1951), p. 127.
11. Nicolai Hartmann, *Das Problem des Geistigen Seins*, 3rd ed. (Berlin, 1962), pp. 296-300. See also F. S. C. Northrop, *The Complexity of Legal and Ethical Experience* (Boston, 1959), pp. 108-112, discussing the evidence of neurology and introspective psychology tending to show that behavior is a response not only to stimuli, but also to ideas.
12. Northrop, *op. cit. supra* n. 11, pp. 57, 192, 255.
13. *Id.*, p. 78. See also the instructive example discussed on pp. 265-266.
14. *Id.*, p. 244.
15. Frederick Vinding Kruse, *The Foundation of Human Thought* (London, 1949), p. 201.
16. *Id.*, pp. 203-204.
17. *Id.*, pp. 233, 251. See also Vinding Kruse, *The Community of the Future* (New York, 1952), pp. 94-99.
18. Vinding Kruse, *Erkenntnis und Wertung* (Berlin, 1960), pp. 212-213.
19. Vinding Kruse, *op. cit. supra* n. 15, p. 250.
20. In a television interview held on May 18, 1964, Prime Minister Nehru of India stated that few people among the Buddhists today believe in renunciation of life, and that the large majority wish to improve the material and other conditions of life. Some further comments on this subject are found in Edgar Bodenheimer, "The Province of Jurisprudence," 46 *Cornell Law Quarterly* 1, at 4-5 (1960).
21. See Victor Kraft, *Erkenntnislehre* (Vienna, 1960), p. 178. William James was in agreement with this conception of truth. *The Meaning of Truth* (New York, 1909), pp. 217-220.
22. Kraft, *op. cit. supra* n. 21, suggests that the designations "true" and "false" may have to be extended to analytical sentences whose truth is due to the laws of logic.
23. See in this connection the valuable comments of Victor Kraft, *Rationale Moralbegründung* (Vienna, 1963), pp. 30-36, 45-46.
24. *Id.*, pp. 33-34. The tie between justice and truth is strongly emphasized by C. J. Friedrich, "Justice: The Just Political Act," in *Justice*, ed. C. J. Friedrich and J. W. Chapman, *Nomos*, Vol. VI (New York, 1963), pp. 38-39.
25. See Erich Fromm, *Man for Himself* (New York, 1947), pp. 210-218; Bronislaw Malinowski, *Freedom and Civilization* (Bloomington, Ind., 1960), pp. 276-280; William James, "The Moral Equivalent of War," in *Essays on Faith and Morals* (New York, 1943), pp. 311-328.
26. In accord: Brecht, *op. cit. supra* n. 1, pp. 404-416.
27. See *supra* Sec. 6.
28. Ginsberg, *op. cit. supra* n. 9, p. 21.
29. Hartmann, *op. cit supra* n. 11, p. 16.
30. According to Martin Buber, *Two Types of Faith* (New York, 1961), p. 7, faith "by its nature does not rest upon 'reasons,' just as it does not grow from such; reasons of course can be urged for it, but they are never sufficient to account for my faith." This definition, which one

can fully approve, excludes social philosophy from the branches of thinking based on faith.

31. This writer, however, is strongly inclined to distinguish between the original writings in normative philosophy on the one hand and the teaching activities of social philosophers on the other. The aims to be pursued in these two areas are different. Nothing should prevent a scholar or university professor from publishing his views on public affairs and his proposals for social change, and one need not object if a tone of passionateness and partisanship occasionally creeps into the argument. But in the classroom it is the duty of the teacher to promote and encourage original and independent thinking on the part of the students, and this task is easily frustrated if the teacher allows an attitude of indoctrination and proselyting zeal to prevail in his classroom performance. This does not mean that the teacher should be discouraged from stating his personal opinions in academic lectures or discussions, but he should always acquaint his listeners with opposing viewpoints, invite and welcome debate and dissent, and avoid dogmatic rigidity and even the slightest touch of doctrinaire intolerance.

SEC. 8

1. On the concept of natural law, which will not be investigated in this treatise, see Edgar Bodenheimer, *Jurisprudence: The Philosophy and Method of the Law* (Cambridge, Mass., 1962), Ch. 46, and "The Case Against Natural Law Reassessed," 17 *Stanford Law Review* 39 (1964).
2. See the literature cited by Bodenheimer, *Jurisprudence,* p. 189.
3. Albert Schweitzer, *Civilization and Ethics,* 3rd ed. (London, 1949), p. 242. It should be noted, however, that there is a nonethical denotation of "good" which refers to the utilitarian value of an object and does not exclude implements of destruction. Thus a well-constructed machine gun is sometimes called a "good" machine gun.
4. See *infra* Sec. 29.
5. See Leon Radzinowicz, *History of English Criminal Law* (New York, 1948), Vol. I, pp. 1-40. The death penalty was, for example, applied to persons found in the company of gypsies.
6. *Id.,* pp. 91-97. On the problem of disproportionality between crime and punishment see *infra* Sec. 24.
7. See the summary of the arguments for and against capital punishment in Thorsten Sellin, *The Death Penalty* (Philadelphia, 1959), pp. 15 ff; see also H. A. Bedeau, *The Death Penalty in America* (Garden City, N. Y., 1964).
8. See the statistics collected by Sellin, *op. cit. supra* n. 7, pp. 34-50. See also United Nations, *Capital Punishment* (New York, 1962), pp. 53-56.
9. See the discussion of this question *infra* Sec. 24.
10. An entirely different problem is presented, of course, when a political society decrees the death penalty as punishment for minor offenses. It would be extremely difficult to advance any plausible arguments in favor of such a policy, and the English experience discussed earlier would presage serious difficulties of enforcement.
11. This is also the position of Glanville Williams, *The Sanctity of Life and the Criminal Law* (New York, 1957), pp. 315-316, whose cautious

271

proposals for legalizing euthanasia under appropriate safeguards are fully endorsed by this writer. See also H. Wechsler and J. Michael, "A Rationale of the Law of Homicide," 37 *Columbia Law Review* 701, at 739-740 (1937).

12. Williams, *op. cit. supra* n. 11, pp. 321-324.

13. *Id.*, pp. 327-328; Helen Silving, "Euthanasia," 103 *University of Pennsylvania Law Review* 350, at 353-354 (1954). The reluctance of juries to convict shows that punishment of euthanasia has no anchorage in public sentiment.

14. Williams, *op. cit. supra* n. 11, p. 312.

15. *Id.*, pp. 249-254, 273-283, 288-290; Silving, *op. cit. supra* n. 13, pp. 369-378. In England, a parliamentary act of 1961 abolished the crimes of suicide and attempted suicide.

16. Robert Gordis, *The Root and the Branch* (Chicago, 1662), p. 230. Gordis does not personally advocate the use of criminal sanctions but shows that the Judaeo-Christian tradition, as contrasted with the Greco-Roman, has always regarded suicide as a cardinal sin.

17. Captain Oates, for example, took his life during an Antarctic expedition because his illness made him a hindrance to the continuation of the venture. See Williams, *op. cit. supra* n. 11, p. 269. Cf. Sidney Hook, "The Ethics of Suicide," 37 *International Journal of Ethics*, 173, at 178 (1927).

18. The great strength of the reasons speaking against punishment of attempted suicide has no bearing on the question whether incitement to suicide should be made a criminal offense. Weighty arguments exist here in favor of punishment as a separate crime (not as murder), subject perhaps to a few limited exceptions. See Hermann Mannheim, *Criminal Justice and Social Reconstruction* (New York, 1946), pp. 12-13; Silving, *op. cit. supra* n. 13, pp. 376-378.

19. 331 Fed. 2d 1000 (1964); rehearsing denied, 331 Fed. 2d 1010 (1964).

20. She based her refusal on a passage in the Scriptures to the effect that one should not drink blood.

21. See Arnold Brecht, *Political Theory* (Princeton, 1959), pp. 154, 268-269.

22. In war, for example, a warning that an art treasure may have to be destroyed in order to save lives may lead to the abandonment of a particular enemy position.

23. See Schweitzer, *op. cit. supra* n. 3, pp. 45, 222-223; Gordis *op. cit. supra* n. 16, pp. 153-154, 159.

SEC. 9.

1. Aristotle, *Politics*, transl. E. Barker (Oxford, 1946), Bk. I. Ch. II. 1252b; Bk. III, Ch. IX. 1280a and b.

2. Gustav Radbruch, "Legal Philosophy," in *The Legal Philosophies of Lask, Radbruch, and Dabin*, transl. K. Wilk (Cambridge, Mass., 1950), p. 97.

3. Albert Schweitzer, *The Decay and Restoration of Civilization*, transl. C. T. Campion (London, 1923), p. 35.

4. *Id.*, p. 36. See also Roscoe Pound, *A World Legal Order* (Tufts University, 1959), p. 3: "Civilization, as fact or as idea, may be taken as the starting point for the social sciences. Defining it as the develop-

ment of human powers to constantly greater completeness, it has two sides: The maximum of human control over physical nature and over internal or human nature of which men are for the time being capable."

5. Arnold Toynbee is inclined to define civilization in ethical terms. He says: "Perhaps it might be defined as an endeavour to create a state of society in which the whole of mankind will be able to live together in harmony, as members of a single all-inclusive society. This is, I believe, the goal at which all civilizations so far known have been aiming unconsciously, if not consciously." *A Study of History*, Vol. XII (Oxford, 1961), p. 279.

6. Schweitzer, *op. cit. supra* n. 3, pp. 36-37, 61. It might be pointed out that Schweitzer rejects the attempt made by some ultra-conservative German philosophers, such as Oswald Spengler, to contrast "culture" and "civilization" and to deprecate the latter as mere material progress. To Schweitzer, the meaning of the two terms is essentially the same. The same position is taken in this book.

7. Admiration of cultural attainments should not be limited to the civilization in which one lives. A Buddhist philosopher like Radhakrishnan is just as affirmative in his judgment of the achievements of Greek civilization as any Western interpreter. See S. Radhakrishnan, *Eastern Religions and Western Thought* 2d ed. (London, 1940), pp. 3-7.

8. Albert Schweitzer, *Civilization and Ethics*, transl. C. T. Campion, 3rd ed. (London, 1946), p. 11: "For us Westerners civilization consists in this: that we work simultaneously for the perfecting of ourselves and of the world."

9. This is the deeper meaning of the statement made by President John F. Kennedy in his inaugural address on January 20, 1961 to the effect that Americans should ask, not what society can do for them, but what they can do for society. See also Erich Fromm, *Beyond the Chains of Illusion* (New York, 1962), p. 178: "Man's task in life is precisely the paradoxical one of realizing his individuality and at the same time transcending it in arriving at the experience of universality." Similar thoughts have been expressed by Nicolai Hartmann, "Das Ethos der Persönlichkeit," in *Kleinere Schriften* (Berlin, 1955), Vol. I, p. 315.

10. Erich Frank, *Philosophical Understanding and Religious Truth* (London, 1945), p. 116.

11. Schweitzer, *op. cit. supra* n. 8, p. 213. (Some changes were made in the translation).

12. S. L. Hart, *Ethics* (New York, 1963), p. 81. See also Stephen Pepper, *Ethics* (New York, 1960), p. 68. "Many of the great heroes of political history are the successful social reformers—Pericles, Marc Antony, Cromwell, Washington—or the martyrs to causes which come to be approved—Buddha, Socrates, Jesus, Thomas More. These men were nonconformists, and by the theory of the cultural relativists were all bad men."

13. Sigmund Freud, *Civilization and Its Discontents*, transl. J. Riviere (London, 1930), pp. 63, 73.

14. *Id.*, p. 90.

15. *Id.*, p. 91. See also the account of Freud's theory of civilization in Herbert Marcuse, *Eros and Civilization* (New York, 1962), Ch. 4.

16. Max Scheler, *The Nature of Sympathy*, transl. P. Heath (London, 1954), pp. 207-208. This concept of psychic energy not identical with

273

the energy of the sexual drive was accepted by Erich Fromm, *The Heart of Man* (New York, 1964), p. 64.

17. Scheler, *op. cit. supra* n. 16, pp. 208-209. See also Scheler, *Die Stellung des Menschen im Kosmos* (Darmstadt, 1930), pp. 70-71.

18. Erich Fromm, *The Sane Society* (New York, 1955), p. 28. A similar position is taken by the Austrian psychiatrist Viktor Frankl in his *Theorie und Therapie der Neurosen* (Vienna, 1956). To Frankl, loss of meaning in life is the most frequent cause of neurosis and mental disturbance.

19. Fromm, *op. cit. supra* n. 18, pp. 37-38. See also Fromm, *op. cit. supra* n. 16, pp. 37-61.

20. Fromm, *op. cit. supra* n. 18, pp. 7-8.

21. See Nicolai Hartmann, *Das Problem des Geistigen Seins,* 3rd ed., (Berlin, 1962), pp. 105-106.

SEC. 10.

1. See *supra* Sec. 9.

2. Friedrich Nietzsche, *The Will to Power,* transl. A. M. Ludovici, Vol. I, p. 297 (*Complete Works,* ed. O. Levy, Vol. 14, London, 1909).

3. Nietzsche, *The Twilight of the Idols,* transl. A. M. Ludovici, p. 54 (*Complete Works,* Vol. 16, London, 1911).

4. Nietzsche, *Human, All-Too Human,* trans. H. Zimmern, p. 342 *(Complete Works,* Vol. 6, London, 1909).

5. Nietzsche, *Gesammelte Werke* (Musarion ed., Munich, 1920-1926), Vol. 7, p. 31.

6. Nietzsche, *op. cit. supra* n. 3, pp. 108-109.

7. Nietzsche, *op. cit. supra* n. 2, Vol. I, p. 383; Vol. II, p. 310.

8. *Id.,* Vol. II, p. 297.

9. *Id.,* p. 370. See also *op. cit. supra* n. 5, Vol. 14, p. 50: "To give everyone his due—that means to will justice and accomplish chaos." (Translation mine).

10. Nietzsche, *Beyond Good and Evil,* transl. H. Zimmern, pp. 176-177 (*Complete Works,* Vol. 12, London, 1923).

11. *Id.,* p. 226. See also *op. cit. supra* n. 5, Vol. 3, p. 281: "Slavery is essential to culture." (Translation mine).

12. Nietzsche, *op. cit. supra* n. 2, Vol. II, p. 134. Nietzsche thought that the abolition of slavery meant the annihilation of the higher species and the destruction of its happiness. *Id.,* Vol. I, p. 255. See also *op cit. supra* n. 5, Vol. 11, p. 218.

13. Nietzsche, *op. cit. supra* n. 5, Vol. 17, p. 249.

14. The following passage demonstrates, among others, that in Nietzsche's view the rulers of society were not bound to promote the common interest and general welfare of the citizens: "A great man: who feels that he has the right to sacrifice human beings like a military commander—not in the service of an idea, but because he wants to rule." *Op. cit. supra* n. 5, Vol. 14, p. 209.

15. Adolf Hitler, *Mein Kampf* (English ed., New York, 1939), p. 99.

16. *Id.,* pp. 102-103.

17. Hermann Rauschning, *Gespräche mit Hitler* (New York, 1940), pp. 231-233.

18. On the "magnificent" blonde beast, "avidly rampant for spoil and victory," see Nietzsche, *The Genealogy of Morals*, transl. H. B. Samuel, p. 40 (*Complete Works*, Vol. 3, Edinburgh, 1910). See also *op. cit. supra* n. 2, Vol. I, p. 255: "The insistence upon spreading 'humaneness' . . . is all humbug."
   Compassion was termed a "sin" by Nietzsche (*op. cit. supra* n. 5, Vol. 12, p. 29), Christian morality a "capital crime" (*op. cit. supra* n. 2, Vol. I, p. 206).
19. Mussolini, like Hitler, often emphasized his indebtedness to Nietzsche's philosophy.
20. Further comments on this problem will be found *infra* Sec. 14.
21. According to Nietzsche, master morality is "self-glorification"; the antithesis "good" and "bad" means practically the same as "noble" and "despicable"; the noble man determines his morality himself: "What is injurious to me is injurious in itself." Nietzsche also argued that "a radical enmity toward selflessness belongs to a noble morality"; that the noble man has duties only toward equals and "may act towards beings of a lower rank . . . just as it seems good to one, or 'as the heart desires' "; that every aristocratic morality "counts intolerance itself among the virtues, under the name of 'justice'." Nietzsche, *op. cit. supra* n. 10, pp. 227-230, 235.
22. This is correctly emphasized by S. A. Lakoff, *Equality in Political Philosophy* (Cambridge, Mass., 1964), p. 239, and Viktor Kraft, *Rationale Moralbegründung* (Vienna, 1963), p. 57. See also S. L. Hart, *Treatise on Values* (New York, 1949), p. 14: "If masters confer higher values upon themselves, this does not mean that they possess them."
23. See *supra* Secs. 4 and 6.
24. Immanuel Kant, *Fundamental Principles of the Metaphysics of Morals*, transl. T. K. Abbott (New York, 1949), p. 50.
25. Rudolph von Jhering expresses the opinion in his *Geist des Römischen Rechts*, 8th ed. (Basel, 1953), Pt. II, p. 180, that in general the position of slaves in antiquity was not essentially different from that of household servants today. A similar position was taken by Bronislaw Malinowski, *Freedom and Civilization* (Bloomington, Ind., 1960), p. 298.
26. See M. I. Rostovtzeff, *History of the Ancient World*, 2d ed. (Oxford, 1930), Vol. II, pp. 105-106, 118; C. E. Van Sickle, *Political and Cultural History of the Ancient World* (New York, 1948), Vol. II, p. 243. Erich Fromm says: "Man is not meant to be a thing; he is destroyed if he becomes a thing; and before this is accomplished he becomes desperate and wants to kill all life." *The Heart of Man* (New York, 1964), p. 57.
27. Acceptance of the Kantian principle does not imply that men cannot be subjected to social duties aiming at the promotion of the common good. Thus, if there are many small towns in a country which are without medical services, enactment of a law requiring young doctors to practice for three years after graduation in such a town does not degrade human beings into instrumentalities of the state. Such a law can be justified on the theory that men derive many benefits from organized community life and must reciprocate by making beneficial contributions to the general welfare. Drafting doctors into the army presents a similar problem.
28. R. H. Tawney, *Equality*, 3rd ed. (London, 1938), p. 208.
29. *Id.*, p. 23. See also S. Radhakrishnan, *Eastern Religions and Western*

Thought, 2d ed. (Oxford, 1940), p. 368: "Equality refers to opportunity and not to capacity. While it recognizes that men are unequal in scale and quality, it insists that every human being shall have the right and the opportunity to contribute to human achievement, as far as his capacity goes."

30. The fellow students of St. Thomas Aquinas thought him slow-witted and called him "the dumb ox." A Platonic philosopher-king charged with the function of placing men into their proper social class probably would have been unable to discover the qualities of intellectual leadership possessed by St. Thomas.

31. A summary of the social philosophy of Josef Popper-Lynkeus, who was a strong advocate of a guaranteed subsistence program for all is found in H. I. Wachtel, *Security for All and Free Enterprise* (New York, 1955), pp. 85-114. If such a system is adopted, safeguards against its misuse, for example by irresponsible types of idlers, would have to be provided.

32. J. K. Galbraith, *The Affluent Society* (Boston, 1958), p. 329. See the further discussion of the problem *infra* Sec. 20.

33. See H. L. A. Hart, *The Concept of Law* (Oxford, 1961), pp. 153-163; F. R. Bienenfeld, *Rediscovery of Justice* (London, 1947), pp. 19-27; E. N. Cahn, *The Sense of Injustice* (New York, 1949), pp. 14-15.

34. Morris Ginsberg, *Essays in Sociology and Social Philosophy* (Melbourne, 1960), Vol. I, p. 67. See also *supra* Sec. 2.

35. Arnold Brecht, *Political Theory* (Princeton, 1959), pp. 305-312, generally leans toward this position. He believes that ordinarily no scientific standard is available to determine the justness of equal and unequal treatment.

36. See *supra* Secs. 6 and 7.

37. See the further discussion of this question *infra* Sec. 14.

38. Alf Ross, *On Law and Justice* (Berkeley, 1959), p. 280.

39. *Id.*, p. 284.

40. See the comments on this question by A. M. Honoré, "Social Justice," 8 *McGill Law Journal* 77, at 85-86 (1962).

41. See, for example, Heinrich Henkel, *Einführung in die Rechtsphilosophie* (Munich, 1964), p. 308.

42. See in this connection Martin Kriele, *Kriterien der Gerechtigkeit* (Berlin, 1963), pp. 91-94.

43. Aristotle, *Nicomachean Ethics*, transl. H. Rackham (Loeb Class. Lib. ed., Cambridge, Mass., 1947), Bk. V. x. 4.

44. The problem is discussed in greater detail by Edgar Bodenheimer, *Jurisprudence: The Philosophy and Method of the Law* (Cambridge, Mass., 1962), pp. 194-195, 215-217, 309-313. See also the monographic study of the subject by Heinrich Henkel, *Recht und Individualität* (Berlin, 1958). On the need for some degree of individualization in sentencing practices see *infra* Sec. 24.

45. This is rightly emphasized by Henkel, *op. cit. supra* n. 41, pp. 320-321. The problem will be dealt with by this writer in a separate study.

276

1. John Stuart Mill, *On Liberty*, ed. C. V. Shields (New York, 1956), p. 117. Very similar is the definition of Bertrand Russell: "Freedom in general may be defined as the absence of obstacles to the realization of desires." "Freedom and Government," in *Freedom: Its Meaning*, ed. R. N. Anshen (New York, 1940), p. 251.

2. For a detailed analysis of different conceptions of freedom see M. J. Adler, *The Idea of Freedom*, 2 vols. (Garden City, N. Y., 1958-1961).

3. J. B. S. Haldane, "A Comparative Study of Freedom," in *Freedom: Its Meaning*, p. 450.

4. Immanuel Kant, "Preface to the Metaphysical Elements of Ethics," in *Critique of Practical Reason and Other Works*, transl. T. K. Abbott, 6th ed. (London, 1927), p. 317. See also *id.*, p. 318: "Two things are required for internal freedom: to be *master* of oneself in a given case . . . and to have *command* over oneself . . . , that is to *subdue* his his emotions and *govern* his passions."

5. G. W. F. Hegel, *The Philosophy of Right*, transl. T. M. Knox (Oxford, 1942), p. 27 (par. 15).

6. *Id.*, pp. 107 (par. 149) and 231 (addition to par. 18).

7. Friedrich Engels, *Anti-Dühring*, transl. E. Burns ((New York, 1934), p. 128: "Freedom . . . consists in the control over ourselves and over external nature which is founded on the knowledge of natural necessity."

8. *Id.*, p. 307.

9. Haldane, *op. cit. supra* n. 3, p. 451.

10. This point is well made by E. S. Brightman, "Freedom, Purpose, and Value," in *Freedom: Its Meaning, supra* n. 1, pp. 496-497.

11. Engels, *op. cit. supra* n. 7, pp. 310-312; Auguste Comte, *System of Positive Polity*, transl. J. H. Bridges (London, 1875), Vol. I, p. 296.

12. On causality and its interplay with chance in the natural processes see David Bohm, *Causality and Chance in Modern Physics* (New York, 1957).

13. Cf. L. T. Hobhouse, *The Elements of Social Justice* (New York, 1922), p. 75: "The ultimate foundation of liberty . . . is that it is a condition of spiritual growth." On freedom of the will see *infra* Sec. 23.

14. A good example is Montesquieu's doctrine of separation of powers. He believed that it was a description of the English system of government, but his proposals were original and differed widely from the British pattern. His ideas made a strong impact on the founders of the American commonwealth, and it was in the United States that his recommendations—often in exact compliance with their formulation— were put into effect.

15. Hegel, *op. cit. supra* n. 5, p. 40 (par. 41). A more detailed discussion of the right to property will be found *infra* Sec. 21.

16. H. D. Aiken, "The Justification of Social Freedom," in *Liberty*, ed. C. J. Friedrich (*Nomos*, Vol. IV, New York, 1962), pp. 135-136.

17. *Id.*, pp. 132-133, 138-139.

18. This is correctly emphasized by John Somerville, "Toward a Consistent Definition of Freedom and Its Relation to Value," in *Liberty, supra* n. 16, pp. 289-290.

19. This is convincingly demonstrated in the article by R. M. McIver, "The Meaning of Liberty and Its Perversion," in *Freedom: Its Meaning, supra* n. 1, pp. 278-287.
20. That the claims of freedom and opportunity are sometimes in conflict is shown by Harry W. Jones, "Freedom and Opportunity as Competing Social Values," in *Liberty, supra* n. 16, pp. 227-242.
21. Paul Tillich, "Freedom in the Period of Transformation," in *Freedom: Its Meaning, supra* n. 1, pp. 133-134. See also Melvin Rader, *Ethics and Society* (New York, 1950), p. 296.
22. Helmut Coing, *Grundzüge der Rechtsphilosophie* (Berlin, 1950), pp. 197-198.
23. Erich Fromm has shown in *Escape from Freedom* (New York, 1941) that man, if his urge to engage in meaningful activities and to relate himself to the world becomes frustrated in a social order based on abstract conceptions of freedom, he may turn away from freedom and identify himself with a totalitarian political movement.
24. On these three elements of civilization see *supra* Sec. 9.
25. A. N. Whitehead, "Aspects of Freedom," in *Freedom: Its Meaning, supra* n. 1, p. 56: "A doctrine as to the social mingling of liberty and compulsion is required. A mere unqualified demand for liberty is the issue of shallow philosophy, equally noxious with the antithetical cry for mere confrontation to a standard pattern."
26. Thomas Mann, "Freedom and Equality," in *Freedom: Its Meaning, supra* n. 1, p. 76.

SEC. 12.

1. David Bohm, *Causality and Chance in Modern Physics* (New York, 1957), pp. 149-150.
2. J. M. Clark says in "Forms of Economic Liberty and What Makes Them Important," in *Freedom: Its Meaning,* ed. R. N. Anshen (New York, 1940), p. 313: "Liberty . . . requires some degree of underlying security if it is to have much effective meaning and content." The importance of security as a value of the legal order is also stressed by Jeremy Bentham, *The Theory of Legislation,* ed. C. K. Ogden (London, 1931), pp. 96-99.
3. Roscoe Pound, "A Survey of Social Interests," 57 *Harvard Law Review* 1, at 9-10, 17 (1943). See also F. E. Dessauer, *Stability* (New York, 1949), pp. 154-155: "Civilizaton and its advance can be understood as a sequence of attempts to push back the jungle, to replace unpredictable and unsettling caprice and wilfullness by order, to create expanding spheres of legitimate control, and to transform men into citizens."
4. Rudolph von Jhering, *Law as a Means to an End,* transl. I. Husik (New York, 124), pp. 330-331, 380. It might be observed that in the relations between individuals, too, security in the sense of non-disappointment of expectations raised by one's conduct, is a significant aspect of justice. See *supra* Sec. 2.
5. See Nicolai Hartmann, *Ethics,* transl. S. Coit (London, 1932), Vol. II, p. 231.
6. The problems connected with external security and the preservation of peace are discussed *infra* Sec. 29.

7. On the social philosophy underlying workmen's compensation see Arthur Larson, "The Nature and Origins of Workmen's Compensation," 37 *Cornell Law Quarterly* 206, at 209-211 (1952).
8. See I. S. Falk, "An Introduction to National Problems in Medical Care," 6 *Law and Contemporary Problems* 497 (1939); Note, "The Essentials of an Adequate Health Program," 59 *Yale Law Journal* 292 (1950).
9. When the Job Corps was established under the Economic Opportunities Act of 1964, it was reported that over 100,000 applications for employment were received on the first day open for registration.
10. The case in favor of a guaranteed minimum income essential to a decent human existence was argued *supra* Sec. 10. See also the further comments *infra* Sec. 20.
11. See *International Survey of Social Security* (Geneva, 1950).
12. See *International Declaration of Human Rights*, Arts, 22-25.

SEC. 13.

1. Aristotle, *Nichomachean Ethics*, transl. H. Rackham (Loeb Class. Lib. ed., Cambridge, Mass., 1947), Bk. V. v. 1; *Metaphysics*, Bk. I, Ch. 5, in *The Basic Works of Aristotle*, ed. R. McKeon (New York, 1941), p. 698.
2. Ex. 21:24.
3. Henri Bergson, *The Two Sources of Morality and Religion*, transl. R. A. Audra and C. Brereton (London, 1935), p. 55. (The translation has been slightly changed).
4. Aristotle, *Nichomachean Ethics*, Bk. V. v. 4.
5. *Id.*, Bk. V. iii. 8.
6. *Id.*, Bk. V. iii. 6.
7. *Id.*, Bk. V. iv.
8. Giorgio Del Vecchio, *Justice*, ed. A. H. Campbell (New York, 1953), p. 1. See also Emil Brunner, *Justice and the Social Order*, transl. M. Hottinger (New York, 1945), p. 224.
9. Bergson, *op. cit. supra* n. 3, p. 54. Cf. also Jean Piaget, *The Moral Judgment of the Child*, transl. M. Gabain (London, 1932), p. 197.
10. Bernhard Rehfeldt, *Die Wurzeln des Rechts* (Berlin, 1951). Rehfeldt shows that even in illegal transactions adequate compensation is insisted upon, citing as an example the barter system which developed in Germany after the collapse in 1945 in contravention of the statutory law and which produced its own rules of fair exchange.
11. John Rawls, somewhat one-sidedly perhaps, identifies justice with fairness. "Justice as Fairness," 67 *Philosophical Review* 164 (1958) and "Constitutional Liberty and the Concept of Justice," in *Justice*, ed. C. J. Friedrich and W. Chapman *(Nomos*, Vol. VI, New York, 1963), p. 98. For a criticism see W. Chapman, "Justice as Fairness," in *Justice*, p. 147.
12. This problem will be discussed in greater detail *infra* Sec. 24.
13. Bergson, *op. cit. supra* n. 3, p. 64.
14. C. J. Friedrich emphasizes that the need for "a *balanced* evaluation of the persons it affects" is a precondition of a just political act. "Justice: The Just Political Act" in *Justice, supra* n. 11, p. 43 (Underscoring supplied).

1. See *supra* Sec. 8.

2. Aristotle, *Politics,* transl. E. Barker (Oxford, 1946), Bk. I. 1255a. See in this connection René Marcic "Sklaverei als 'Beweis' gegen Naturrecht und Naturrechtslehre," 34 *Oesterreichische Zeitschrift für Oeffentliches Recht* 181 (1964).

3. *Id.,* Bk. I. 1253b. In the passages that follow Aristotle seems to intimate, however, that even under such conditions slaves would still be needed for household purposes.

4. Josef Kohler, *Philosophy of Law,* transl. A. Albrecht (New York, 1921), p. 93.

5. Bronislaw Malinowski, *Freedom and Civilization* (Bloomington, Ind., 1960), pp. 299-300, 302.

6. In the Hellenistic period of Greek history, preceding the Roman conquest, women received a limited amount of elementary education. See U. Wilamowitz, J. Kromayer, and A. Heisenberg, *Staat und Gesellschaft der Griechen und Römer,* 2d ed. (Berlin, 1923), p. 203.

7. See C. J. Herrick, *The Evolution of Human Nature* (Austin, 1956), pp. 241, 399.

8. St. Thomas Aquinas, *Summa Theologica,* transl. Fathers of the English Dominican Province (London, 1913-1925), Part II (First Part), Qu. 96, Art. 6.

9. See J. ten Broek, E. N. Barnhart, and F. W. Matson, *Prejudice, War and the Constitution* (Berkeley, 1954), pp. 207-208, 325-327; E. V. Rostow, "The Japanese-American Cases—A Disaster," 54 *Yale Law Journal* 489 (1954); cf. also *Korematsu v. United States,* 323 U.S. 214 (1944).

10. See *supra* Sec. 12.

11. John Locke, in discussing the problem of executive prerogative, said: "It is fit that the laws themselves should in some cases give way to the executive power, or rather to this fundamental law of Nature and government—viz., that as much as may be all members of the society are to be preserved." *Two Treatises of Civil Government* (Everyman's Lib. ed., London, 1924), Bk. II, Ch. 14. The same position was taken by Thomas Jefferson. See *The Political Writings of Thomas Jefferson,* ed. E. Dumbauld (New York, 1955), p. 145. On necessity as a defense to a criminal charge see *infra* Sec. 27.

12. "In our day we have seen the claims of expediency grossly prostituted; for it is under that name—or some other like 'the healthy consciousness of the people,' or the Good of the Nation or even the Will of the Fuehrer—that Justice has been degraded into Policy, which is the same thing as degrading it into Power." C. K. Allen, "Justice and Expediency," in *Interpretation of Modern Legal Philosophies,* ed. P. Sayre (New York, 1947), p. 23.

13. "Law is that which is useful to the German nation" is an often-quoted statement by a jurist of Hitler's Third Reich. See 3 *Zeitschrift der Akademie für Deutsches Recht* 321 (1936).

14. See *supra* Sec. 5.

1. The concept is used in a comprehensive sense in the article by Alan Gewirth, "Political Justice," in *Social Justice*, ed. R. B. Brandt (Englewood Cliffs, N. J., 1962), p. 119.

2. This narrower concept underlies the work by Otto Kirchheimer, *Political Justice: The Use of Legal Procedures for Political Ends* (Princeton, 1961).

3. F. W. Jerusalem, *Der Staat* (Jena, 1935), p. 83 (Translation mine).

4. The necessity for maintaining the contrast between the political and the social principle is stressed by Martin Buber, *Zwischen Gesellschaft und Staat* (Heidelberg, 1952). This book was written to refute the basic thesis propagated by Bertrand Russell in his work *Power: A New Social Analysis* (New York, 1938).

5. One particular manifestation of social justice, namely, justice in economic life, will be treated separately in Chapter IV.

6. Emil Brunner, *Justice and the Social Order*, transl. M. Hottinger (New York, 1945), p. 196.

7. *Ibid.*

8. Aristotle, *Politics*, transl. E. Barker (Oxford, 1946), Bk. I, Ch. ii. 1253a: "All things derive their essential character from their function and their capacity; and it follows that if they are no longer fit to discharge their function, we ought not to say that they are still the same things, but only that by an ambiguity they still have the same names."

9. Destruction is, of course, always incidental to a war initiated by a government. As was pointed out *supra* Sec. 14, the wars of the past have sometimes indirectly furthered the development of civilization. The destruction referred to in the text is destructiveness for its own sake, not for the aim of national growth, as understood in the preatomic era. Further thoughts on this problem will be found *infra* Sec. 29.

10. Thomas Hobbes, *Leviathan*, ed. M. Oakeshott (Oxford, 1946), Ch. XXI.

11. Ernst Cassirer, *The Myth of the State* (New Haven, 1946), p. 173.

12. Giorgio Del Vecchio, *Grundlagen und Grundfragen des Rechts* (Göttingen, 1963), p. 271.

13. The following pertinent observation by Friedrich Schiller may be quoted here: "The state is not an end in itself. It is important only as a means to the realization of an end which is no other than the development of all the faculties of man and cultural progress. If a constitution hinders this development, if it hinders intellectual progress, it is harmful and worthless, no matter how ingeniously it is conceived and how perfectly it may function in its own way." "The Legislation of Lycurgus and Solon," in *Friedrich Schiller: An Anthology for Our Time*, ed. F. Ungar (New York, 1959), p. 213.

14. These thoughts will be elaborated *infra* Sec. 19.

15. See *supra* Sec. 10 and *infra* Sec. 29.

16. See *infra* Sec. 18 for a discussion of this problem.

SEC. 16.

1. See *supra* Secs. 10 and 15.
2. Plato, *The Republic,* transl. A. D. Lindsay (Everyman's Lib. ed., New York, 1950), Bk. I. 338.
3. This weakness of the democratic selection process is emphasized by F. Vinding Kruse, *The Community of the Future* (New York, 1952), pp. 658-665.
4. Alexis de Tocqueville, *Democracy in America,* transl. H. Reeve (New York, 1899), Vol. I, pp. 202-203. Cf. also George Bernard Shaw's sarcastic overstatement in "The Revolutionist's Handbook" from *Man and Superman:* "Democracy substitutes election by the incompetent many for appointment by the corrupt few."
5. Vinding Kruse, *op. cit. supra* n. 3, p. 650.
6. Aristotle, *Politics,* transl. E. Barker (Oxford, 1946), Bk. IV. Ch. xi. 1295b. and 1296a.
7. *Id.,* Bk. III. Ch. xiii. 1284a and b.
8. *Id.,* Bk. III. Ch. xi. 1282b; Ch. xv. 1286a.
9. Emil Brunner, *Justice and the Social Order,* transl. M. Hottinger (New York, 1945), p. 200.
10. On this danger see Plato, *op. cit. supra* n. 2, Bk. VII. 560-564.
11. Edward Gibbon, *The Decline and Fall of the Roman Empire* (New York, 1931), p. 70: "If a man were called to fix the period in history of the world, during which the condition of the human race was most happy and prosperous, he would, without hesitation, name that which elapsed from the death of Domitian to the accession of Commodus."
12. Polybius, *The Histories,* transl. E. S. Shuckburgh (Bloomington, Ind., 1962), Bk. VI. 7-9.
13. *Id.,* Bk. VI. 3.
14. Kurt von Fritz, *The Theory of the Mixed Constitution in Antiquity* (New York, 1954), p. 306.
15. *Id.,* p. 307.

SEC. 17.

1. W. A. R. Leys and C. M. Perry, *Philosophy and the Public Interest* (Chicago, 1959), p. 44.
2. Edgar Bodenheimer, "Prolegomena to a Theory of the Public Interest," in *The Public Interest,* ed. C. J. Friedrich (*Nomos,* Vol. V, New York, 1962), p. 209. Certain points discussed above in the text are elaborated in greater detail in this essay.
3. Jeremy Bentham, *An Introduction to the Principles of Morals and Legislation* (Oxford, 1823), p. 3.
4. Bertrand Russell, "Freedom and Government," in *Freedom: Its Meaning,* ed. R. N. Anshen (New York, 1940), pp. 260-261.
5. The opposite position is taken by Glendon Shubert, *The Public Interest* (Glencoe, Ill., 1960), pp. 223-224, and F. J. Sorauf, "The Conceptual Muddle," in *op. cit. supra* n. 2, p. 190. Both of these authors believe that the notion of public interest serves no useful function.
6. That the claims of justice sometimes find their limits in compelling considerations of necessity was shown *supra* Sec. 14.

282

7. E. S. Griffith says in "The Ethical Foundations of the Public Interest," in *op. cit. supra* n. 2, p. 21: "What helps one person or group may hurt another. Just as the late Isaiah Bowman well stated, 'No one principle ever exhausts the meaning of a situation,' so in a more mundane fashion a full illumination of the short- and long-range consequences of a given decision usually shows effects varying from person to person and group to group in a complex and contradictory fashion."

8. *Roth v. United States,* 354 U.S. 476, at 484 (1957), dealing with laws against obscene publications.

9. In *Beauharnais v. Illinois,* 343 U.S. 250 (1952), the United States Supreme Court upheld the group libel law of the state of Illinois against constitutional objections.

10. Walter Lippmann, *Essays in the Public Philosophy* (Boston, 1955), p. 126.

11. Alexander Holtzoff, "The Relation between the Right to a Fair Trial and the Right to Freedom of the Press", 1 *Syracuse Law Review* 369, at 371 (1950). See also G. O. W. Mueller, "Problems Posed by Publicity to Crime and Criminal Proceedings", 110 *University of Pennsylvania Law Review* 1 (1961).

12. See *Free Press—Fair Trial,* ed. F. E. Inbau (Northwestern University, 1962), pp. 10-11, 138. See also Letter from seven Harvard Law School Professors to the *New York Times,* Dec. 1, 1963, reprinted in W. B. Lockhart, Y. Kamisar, and J. H. Choper, *Constitutional Law* (St. Paul, 1964), p. 810: "The fact is that justice is incompatible with the notion that police, prosecutors, attorneys, reporters and cameramen should have an unlimited right to conduct *ex parte* public trials in the press and on television".

13. 205 U.S. 454, at 462 (1906).

14. Instances have occurred where the accused's failure to pass a lie-detector test was reported in the newspapers, although lie-detector evidence is at present inadmissible in the courts. See *Free Press—Fair Trial, supra* n. 12, p. 9.

15. In *Craig v. Harney,* 331 U.S. 367 (1947), the United States Supreme Court sanctioned an intemperate press criticism of an elective judge, made for the purpose of inducing him to grant a new trial to the defendant. The criticism of the decision by E. N. Griswold, "Absolute is in the Dark", 8 *Utah Law Review* 167, at 180 (1963), appears to be well taken.

16. See the Model Statute proposed in Note, "The Case against Trial by Newspaper", 57 *Northwestern University Law Review* 217, at 251-253 (1962).

17. See B. S. Meyer, "Free Press v. Fair Trial: The Judge's View", 41 *North Dakota Law Review* 14, at 22 (1964).

18. See *Escobedo v. Illinois,* 378 U.S. 478 (1964), marking a step in that direction. Serious curbs on the admissibility of confessions were also established in *Massiah v. United States,* 377 U.S. 201 (1964); *People v. Modesto,* 398 Pac. 2d 753 (Cal., 1965); *Mallory v. United States,* 354 U.S. 499 (1957).

19. 338 U.S. 49, at 59 (1949).

20. See Canon 15 of the *Canons of Professional Ethics of the American Bar Association:* "Nothing operates more certainly to create or to foster popular prejudice against lawyers as a class, and to deprive the profession of that full measure of public esteem and confidence which belongs

to the proper discharge of its duties than does the false claim, often set up by the unscrupulous in defense of questionable transactions, that it is the duty of the lawyer to do whatever may enable him to succeed in winning his client's cause . . . He must obey his own conscience and not that of his client".

21. *United States v. Lefkowitz*, 285 U.S. 452, at 464-466 (1932); *Harris v. United States*, 331 U.S. 145, at 154 (1947), where Chief Justice Vinson stated: "This Court has frequently recognized the distinction between merely evidentiary materials, on the one hand, which may not be seized either under the authority of a search warrant or during the course of a search incident to arrest, and on the other hand, those objects which may validly be seized including the instrumentalities and means by which a crime is committed, the fruits of crime such as stolen property, weapons by which escape of the person arrested might be effected, and property the possession of which is a crime".

22. See *Henry v. United States*, 361 U.S. 98 (1959); *Wong Sun v. United States*, 371 U.S. 471 (1963).

23. The definition of the public welfare (a term which largely coincides in scope with the public interest) by Vera Bolgár, "The Concept of Public Welfare", 8 *American Journal of Comparative Law* 44, at 47 (1959), places emphasis both on the protection of individual rights and the potential need for restricting the scope of these rights: "The legal definition of public welfare is therefore the extent to which a given society accepts regulation by law in the sphere of individual rights and, conversely, the extent to which these rights, if violated, are given protection by the law".

24. Examples are laws prohibiting bigamy and polygamy, outlawing or limiting the distribution of obscene materials, or regulating the sale of narcotic drugs.

SEC. 18.

1. See L. B. Boudin, *Government by Judiciary* (New York, 1932), Vol. II, pp. 548-549. See also J. B. Thayer, "The Origin and Scope of the American Doctrine of Constitutional Law", 7 *Harvard Law Review* 129, at 149 (1893), who for reasons indicated in the text would restrict judicial review to the narrowest possible bounds.

2. See C. L. Black, *The People and the Court* (New York, 1960), pp. 178-181.

3. See E. V. Rostow, "The Democratic Character of Judicial Review", 66 *Harvard Law Review* 193 (1952).

4. U.S. Constitution, 14th Amendment: "Nor shall any state deprive any person of life, liberty, or property, without due process of law; nor deny to any person within its jurisdiction the equal protection of the laws". Basic Law of the Federal Republic of Germany, Art. I (1): "The dignity of man is inviolable. To respect and protect it is the duty of all state authority".

5. 3 *Entscheidungen des Bundesverfassungsgerichts* 230-234 (1953); Ernst Friesenhahn, "Die Verfassungsgerichtsbarkeit in der Bundesrepublik Deutschland", in *Verfassungsgerichtsbarkeit in der Gegenwart* (Cologne, 1962), pp. 151-152. In the United States, national security, although not specificially mentioned in the operative provisions of the Constitution,

is considered a constitutional value entitled to judicial protection.

6. G. D. Braden, "The Search for Objectivity in Constitutional Law", 57 *Yale Law Journal* 571, at 594 (1948).
7. Herbert Wechsler, "Toward Neutral Principles of Constitutional Law", 73 *Harvard Law Review* 1, at 15 (1959). See also *id.*, p. 19: "A principled decision in the sense I have in mind, is one that rests on reasons with respect to all the issues in the case, reasons that in their generality and their neutrality transcend any immediate result that is involved".
8. A. S. Miller and R. F. Howell, "The Myth of Neutrality in Constitutional Adjudication", 27 *University of Chicago Law Review* 661, at 667, 671, 189 (1960).
9. *Id.*, p. 689.
10. No judge would take the position that shouting fire in a crowded theater or the disclosure of military secrets to an enemy are sanctioned by the principle of free speech.
11. Louis Henkin, "Some Reflections on Current Constitutional Controversy", 109 *University of Pennsylvania Law Review* 637, at 655 (1961).
12. The notion of "objective spirit", originally devised by Hegel, has been thoroughly analyzed by Nicolai Hartmann, *Das Problem des Geistigen Seins,* 3rd ed. (Berlin, 1962), pp. 175-375.
13. Justice Robert H. Jackson, in a posthumous work, criticized his colleagues on the United States Supreme Court for their unwillingness to yield ground on matters of personal conviction: "The fact is that the Court functions less as one deliberative body than as nine, each Justice working largely in isolation except as he chooses to seek consultation with others. These working methods tend to cultivate a highly individualistic rather than a group viewpoint". *The Supreme Court in the American System of Government* (Cambridge, Mass., 1955), p. 16.
14. Erwin Griswold states in a comment in 74 *Harvard Law Review* 94 (1960) that "when decisions are too much result-oriented, the law and the public are not well served". A constant overthrowing of established principles in the interest of an individualized administration of justice is clearly incompatible with the rule of law. But when a case arises in which the application of a broadly formulated principle causes an obvious injustice, a reformulation or restriction of the principle may become necessary, especially when the principle was not really designed to cover this particular case.

SEC. 19.

1. Adam Smith, *An Inquiry into the Nature and Causes of the Wealth of Nations,* ed. E. Cannon (Mod. Lib. ed., New York, 1937), Bk. IV, Ch. IX (p. 651).
2. *Id.*, Bk. V, Ch. I, pt. III (p. 681).
3. *Ibid.*, art. 1 (p. 682).
4. *Ibid.*, art. 1 (p. 689).
5. *Ibid.*, art. 1 (pp. 690-716).
6. *Id.*, Bk. II, Ch. IV (p. 339).
7. *Id.*, Bk. II, Ch. I, pt. III, art. 2 (pp. 716-740).
8. Herbert Spencer, *The Man versus the State* (Caldwell, Idaho, 1944), p.

138. See also *id.*, p. 79: "Government is begotten of aggression and by aggression".

9. *Id.*, p. 143.

10. Spencer, *Social Statics* (New York, 1873), p. 138; Sidney Fine, *Laissez Faire and the General Welfare State* (Ann Arbor, 1964), pp. 32-46; Richard Hofstadter, *Social Darwinism in American Thought* (Boston, 1955), pp. 31-50.

11. W. G. Sumner, *What Social Classes Owe to Each Other* (New Haven, 1925), p. 101. On Sumner's philosophy see C. A. Beard and M. R. Beard, *The American Spirit* (New York, 1942), pp. 339-347; Hofstadter, *op. cit. supra* n. 10, pp. 51-66.

12. Sumner, *op. cit. supra* n. 11, p. 119.

13. Sumner, *Essays*, ed. A. G. Keller and M. R. Davie (New Haven, 1934), Vol. I, p. 422: "The assertion that all men are equal is perhaps the purest falsehood in dogma that was ever put in human language".

14. *Id.*, p. 476.

15. *Id.*, p. 478.

16. *Id.*, p. 481.

17. *Id.*, p. 485.

18. *Id.*, p. 106.

19. Sumner, *op. cit. supra* n. 13, Vol. II, p. 107.

20. *Id.*, p. 159: "The Christian Church of the fourth and fifth centuries, by its indiscriminate almsgiving on a large scale, helped in the degeneration of the Roman state".

21. Smith, *op. cit. supra* n. 1, Bk. IV, Ch. VII, pt. III (pp. 594-595); see also *id.*, Bk. IV, Ch. II (p. 423). Here again, Smith states his views in a cautious form, using words like "frequently" or "in most instances" in order to indicate that the principle does not hold good in all cases.

22. Smith, "The Theory of Moral Sentiments", in *Adam Smith's Moral and Political Philosophy*, ed. H. W. Schneider (New York, 1948), p. 215.

23. Spencer, *op. cit. supra* n. 10, p. 74. See also Spencer, *Principles of Ethics* (New York, 1898), Vol. I, pp. 204-205, 215-218.

24. Spencer, *op. cit. supra* n. 10, p. 80.

25. *Id.*, p. 475.

26. See *supra* Sec. 17. See also E. V. Rostow, *Planning for Freedom* (New Haven, 1959), pp. 366-367.

27. Descriptions of some of the undesirable practices which were the result of laissez-faire in the United States are found in H. D. Lloyd, *Wealth against Commonwealth* (New York, 1894); C. C Regier, *The Era of the Muckrakers* (Chapel Hill, 1932); Upton Sinclair, *The Jungle* (New York, 1906).

28. Sumner, *op. cit. supra* n. 13, Vol. II, p. 228; Vol. I, p. 95.

29. For an able discussion of this problem see J. K. Galbraith, *The Affluent Society* (Boston, 1958), pp. 251-269.

30. Smith, *op. cit. supra* n. 1, Bk. V, Ch. IX (p. 651).

31. See *supra* n. 22.

32. Galbraith, *op. cit. supra* n. 29, p. 259.

33. *Id.*, p. 253. First steps toward the elimination of such conditions were taken in various legislative enactments passed by the 89th Congress in 1965.

34. Sumner, *op. cit. supra* n. 13, Vol. I, p. 106.

35. This sentence was written on the day when Senator Goldwater was

decisively defeated in the American Presidential election of 1964. A substantial part of his defeat must be attributed to his advocacy of laissez-faire and his antipathy to modern social legislation.

36. Emil Brunner, *Justice and the Social Order*, transl. M. Hottinger (New York, 1945), p. 176.
37. Henry Ford, *My Life and Work* (London, 1922), p. 270.
38. See *supra* Sec. 6. Cf. also A. N. Whitehead, *Adventures of Ideas* (New York, 1933), p. 42: "No one now holds that, apart from some further directive agency, mere individualistic competition, of itself and by its own self-righting character, will produce a satisfactory society".

SEC. 20.

1. See *supra* Sec. 19, n. 37.
2. David Ricardo, *Principles of Political Economy and Taxation* (London, 1891), p. 70: "The natural price of labour is that price which is necessary to enable the labourers, one with another, to subsist and perpetuate their race, without either increase or diminution".
3. On the iron law of wages see K. W. Rothschild, *The Theory of Wages* (New York, 1954), pp. 6-10, 36-37.
4. *Id.*, pp. 4-5.
5. Karl Marx, *Capital*, transl. S. Moore and E. Aveling (Chicago, 1906), Vol. I, Chs. IX, XII, and XIX.
6. See Anton Menger, *The Right to the Whole Produce of Labor*, transl. M. E. Tanner (New York, 1962), pp. 101-116.
7. Some economists have contended that labor union policies cannot prevail against the automatic, unalterable laws of the market. Convincing arguments against this position are furnished by Rothschild, *op. cit. supra* n. 3, pp. 106-115.
8. Other limitations of a purely economic theory of wages, such as sociological factors, ideological pressures, moral ideas, etc., are discussed by Rothschild, *id.*, pp. 171-174.
9. See *supra* Sec. 10.
10. On the Golden Rule see *supra* Secs. 4 and 6.
11. L. A. Leontiev *et al.*, "Political Economy in the Soviet Union", 8 *Science and Society* 115, at 125 (1944).
12. The term "surplus product" is preferred by Soviet economists to "surplus value" to avoid the implication of exploitation. See Alec Nove, *The Soviet Economy* (New York, 1961), p. 273.
13. H. J. Berman, *Justice in the U.S.S.R.*, rev. ed. (New York, 1963), p. 111. See also *id.*, pp. 405-407 and Nove, *op. cit. supra* n. 12, pp. 30-39, 165-166. Recently, there has been a growing official emphasis on the obligation to make profits in the sense indicated.
14. Karl Marx, *Critique of the Gotha Programme*, ed. C. P. Dutt (New York, 1938), p. 10.
15. Hans Kelsen, *Reine Rechtslehre*, 2d ed. (Vienna, 1961), p. 384.
16. *Id.*, pp. 384-385.
17. This is also Kelsen's interpretation of Marxian ideology. See *id.*, p. 385.
18. There are persons who will do creative work out of an inner, compelling urge, without requiring stimulation by external inducements. But the number of such persons (who include some of mankind's great-

est geniuses) has never been large. Many gifted persons depend on motivation stimulated by the expectation of material reward.

19. In the Soviet Union, incentives for work such as differentiated wages, payment for piece work, and bonuses have been found necessary to increase production. See E. C. Brown, "The Soviet Labor Market", in *The Soviet Economy: A Book of Readings,* ed. M. Bornstein and D. R. Fusfeld (Homewood, Ill., 1962), pp. 203, 218; Nove, *op. cit supra* n. 12, pp. 116-117; R. L. Heilbroner, *The Making of Economic Society* (Englewood Cliffs, N. J., 1962), p. 228.

20. Chaim Perelman, *The Idea of Justice and the Problem of Argument,* transl. J. Petrie (London, 1963), p. 20.

21. Brown, *op. cit. supra* n. 19, pp. 200-202.

22. See F. Vinding Kruse, *The Community of the Future* (New York, 1952), p. 609.

23. See in this connection Art. 23, sec. 2 of the International Declaration of Human Rights: "Everyone, without any discrimination, has the right to equal pay for equal work".

24. Heilbroner, *op. cit. supra* n. 19, pp. 12-14.

25. President Franklin D. Roosevelt on several occasions made the proposal that a top limit of $25,000 be placed upon an individual's net income, after taxes. See S. I. Rosenman, *Working with Roosevelt* (New York, 1952), pp. 340, 358. I should imagine that at the present day he might have suggested a limit of $40,000 or $50,000.

26. See *supra* Sec. 10.

27. Encyclical "Mater et Magistra" of Pope John XXIII (May 15, 1961), in *The Papal Encyclicals,* ed. A. Fremantle (New York, 1963), p. 346.

28. See the discussion of the concept of "fair wage" by A. C. Pigou, *The Economics of Welfare,* 4th ed., (London, 1932), pp. 593-606.

SEC. 21.

1. John Locke, *Two Treatises of Civil Government* (Everyman's Lib. ed., London, 1924), Bk. II, ch. ix, sec. 124.

2. *Id.,* Bk. II, ch. ix, sec. 138.

3. Jeremy Bentham, *The Theory of Legislation,* ed. C. K. Ogden (London, 1931), ch. x.

4. Frederic Bastiat, *The Law,* transl. D. Russell (Irvington-on-Hudson, 1950), pp. 10, 22-28.

5. *The Papal Encyclicals,* ed. A. Fremantle (New York, 1963), p. 170. See also *id.,* p. 354.

6. J. Messner, *Social Ethics,* transl., J. J. Doherty (St. Louis, 1949), p. 175: "The fundamental institution for the organization of social economy is private ownership"; T. E. Davitt, *The Elements of Law* (Boston, 1959), p. 253: "The main assurance of liberty is property".

7. P. J. Proudhon, *What Is Property?,* transl. B. R. Tucker (New York, undated), p. 15. While the charge that property is robbery or theft is reiterated frequently in this work, a thorough reading will disclose that Proudhon did not intend to repudiate all forms of private property but only those that are not the direct fruits of labor, as for example rent, interest, and profit.

8. Karl Marx, *The Communist Manifesto*, transl. S. Moore (Chicago, 1954), p. 41.
9. *Id.*, p. 46.
10. J. H. Hazard, *Law and Social Change in the U.S.S.R.* (Toronto, 1953), p. 19.
11. G. W. F. Hegel, *The Philosophy of Right*, transl. T. M. Knox (Oxford, 1942), p. 40 (par. 41). On Hegel's philosophy of property see Roscoe Pound, *An Introduction to the Philosophy of Law*, rev. ed. (New Haven, 1954), p. 120. Cf. also Luis Recaséns Siches, *Tratado General de Filosofía del Derecho*, 2d ed. (Mexico City, 1961), pp. 582-587.
12. Aristotle, *Politics*, transl. E. Barker (Oxford, 1946), Bk. II, ch. v. 1263b.
13. *Ibid.* See also Messner, *op. cit. supra* n. 6, p. 787.
14. Aristotle, *op. cit. supra* n. 12, Bk. II, ch. v. 1263a.
15. *Ibid.*
16. A. A. Berle and G. C. Means, *The Modern Corporation and Private Property* (New York, 1933), particularly Bk. IV. See also Berle, "Property, Production, and Revolution", 65 *Columbia Law Review* 1 (1965).
17. Berle and Means, *op. cit. supra* n. 16, p. 333.
18. R. L. Heilbroner, *The Making of Economic Society* (Englewood Cliffs, N. J., 1962), p. 131.
19. *Id.*, p. 139: "Unquestionably, the political and social influence of the great corporations poses problems with which capitalism will have to contend for many years to come".
20. J. K. Galbraith, *The Affluent Society* (Boston, 1958), pp. 251-269, and *supra* Sec. 19.
21. The way in which property, in the course of modern industrial development, became a source of power over men was described by Karl Renner, *The Institutions of Private Law and Their Social Functions*, ed. O. Kahn-Freund (London, 1949), pp. 105-122. A summary of Renner's views is found in Wolfgang Friedmann, *Law in a Changing Society* (Berkeley, 1959), pp. 69-74.
22. H. J. Berman, *Justice in the U.S.S.R.*, rev. ed. (New York, 1963), p. 98.
23. Emil Brunner, *Justice and the Social Order*, transl. M. Hottinger (New York, 1945), p. 178.
24. J. M. Clark, "Forms of Economic Liberty and What Makes Them Important", in R. N. Anshen, ed., *Freedom: Its Meaning* (New York, York, 1940), p. 327.
25. Walther Rathenau, *Von Kommenden Dingen* (Berlin, 1917), pp. 141-151.

SEC. 22.

1. It was common practice for the state to permit private occupation and cultivation of the public lands against payment of a tribute (vectigal). The state could reclaim the land but seldom made use of this right. In the course of development the tribute became merely nominal. The size of the public domain was very large, since most of the land in the provinces fell in this category. See B. Kübler, *Geschichte des Römischen Rechts* (Leipzig, 1925), pp. 121-124; L. Zancan, *Ager Publicus* (Padua, 1935).
2. With respect to Rome see Theodore Mommsen, *Römisches Staatsrecht*

(Leipzig, 1887), Vol. III, p. 731; Zancan, *op. cit. supra* n. 1, p. 6. When England was conquered by the Normans, all the land in the realm became the king's land. W. F. Walsh, *A History of Anglo-American Law*, 2d ed. (Indianapolis, 1932), p. 33. Much of the land in the Western part of the United States was taken from the Indians.

3. F. A. Mann, "Outlines of a History of Expropriation", 75 *Law Quarterly Review* 188, at 189 (1959). This statement is corroborated by comparative anthropological research. See Ralph Linton, "Universal Ethical Principles", in *Moral Principles of Action*, ed. R. N. Anshen (New York, 1952), p. 655.

   Although in ancient Rome expropriations occurred only in exceptional circumstances, the device of ordinary purchases of private land by the state, sometimes under political pressure, was well known. See Max Kaser, *Das Römische Privatrecht* (Munich, 1955), Vol. I, p. 343; Fritz Schulz, *Principles of Roman Law* (Oxford, 1936), p. 161.

4. See T. F. T. Plucknett, *A Concise History of the Common Law*, 5th ed. (Boston, 1956), pp. 431, 443; Note, "Forfeiture of Property Used in Illegal Acts", 38 *Notre Dame Lawyer* 727 (1963).

5. Although a subsequent chapter of this book deals with problems of international justice, it seems inadvisable to separate the municipal law issues concerning expropriations from those arising in the international field. They are therefore considered together in this section.

6. Hugo Grotius, *De Jure Belli ac Pacis*, transl. F. W. Kelsey (Oxford, 1925), Bk. I, Ch. I. vi.

7. Rudolph von Jhering, *Law as a Means to an End*, transl. I. Husik (New York, 1924) pp. 391-392.

8. 91 U.S. 367, at 371-372 (1875).

9. See Mann, *op. cit. supra* n. 3, pp. 208-210.

10. Alfred Verdross, *Völkerrecht*, 5th ed. (Vienna, 1964), pp. 366-367; see also J. G. Starke, *An Introduction to International Law*, 5th ed. (London, 1963), p. 248; S. J. Rubin, "Nationalization and Compensation", 17 *University of Chicago Law Review* 458, at 460 (1950); B. A. Wortley, *Expropriation in Public International Law* (Cambridge, Eng., 1959), Ch. VII; Georg Dahm, *Völkerrecht* (Stuttgart, 1958), Vol. I, pp. 512-517.

11. *Case concerning Certain German Interests in Polish Upper Silesia*, P. C. I. J., Ser. A, No. 7, p. 22 (1926).

12. See, for example, the Yugoslav laws regarding nationalization and expropriation, *Collection of Yugoslav Laws* (Belgrade, 1963), Vol. III; A. R. Rado, "Czechoslovak Nationalization Decrees," 47 *American Journal of International Law* 795 (1947); Isi Foighel, *Nationalization* (Copenhagen, 1957), pp. 56-69.

13. See the treaties listed in A. Verdross, "Die Nationalisierung Niederländischer Unternehmungen in Indonesien," 6 *Nederlands Tijdschrift voor Internationaal Recht* 278, at 282-283 (1959).

14. See S. M. Schwebel, "The Story of the U.N.'s Declaration on Permanent Sovereignty over Natural Resources", 49 *American Bar Association Journal* 463 (1963).

15. The two countries which voted against the resolution were France and the Union of South Africa.

16. See the discussion of the problem, with case citations, by Starke, *op. cit. supra* n. 10, p. 249.

17. In accord: Wolfgang Friedmann, *Law in a Changing Society* (Berkeley, 1959), p. 454; Dahm, *op. cit. supra* n. 10, Vol. I, pp. 516-517.
18. This postulate of justice is recognized in the Basic Law of the Federal Republic of Germany, Art. 14, Sec. 3, which reads as follows: "Expropriation shall be admissible only for the wellbeing of the general public. . . . The compensation shall be determined after just consideration of the interests of the general public and the participants."

SEC. 23.

1. See *infra* Sec. 24.
2. John Hospers, "What Means This Freedom," in *Determinism and Freedom in the Age of Modern Science,* ed. S. Hook (New York, 1958), p. 119.
3. *Id.,* p. 124. For an older statement of this viewpoint, see Enrico Ferri, *Criminal Sociology,* transl. J. I. Kelly and J. Lisle (Boston, 1917), pp. 293, 308.
4. R. A. Fearey, "Concept of Responsibility," 45 *Journal of Criminal Law, Criminology, and Police Science* 21, at 24 (1954); see also Hospers, *op. cit. supra* n. 2, pp. 119-129.
5. J. Michael and H. Wechsler, *Criminal Law and Its Administration* (Chicago, 1940), p. 8. Cf. also P. H. Nowell-Smith, *Ethics* (Melbourne, 1954), pp. 303-304; Moritz Schlick, *Problems of Ethics,* transl. D. Rynin (New York, 1939), p. 152.
6. *Holmes-Laski Letters,* ed. M. de Wolfe Howe (Cambridge, Mass., 1953), p. 806. The problem will be discussed further in Sec. 24.
7. William James, "The Dilemma of Determinism," in *Essays on Faith and Morals* (New York, 1943), p. 150.
8. Immanuel Kant, *Critique of Pure Reason,* transl. J. M. D. Meiklejohn, rev. ed. (New York, 1900), p. 300.
9. Kant, *Fundamental Principles of the Metaphysic of Morals,* transl. T. K. Abbott (New York, 1949), p. 63. For a summary of Kant's view see M. J. Adler, *The Idea of Freedom* (Garden City, 1958), Vol. I, pp. 480-483. Cf. also Nicolai Hartmann, *Ethics,* transl. S. Coit (London, 1932), Vol. III, pp. 33-36, 53-61.
10. Kant, *op. cit., supra* n. 8, pp. 311-312.
11. This view, which has never been advocated by any thinker of rank, will be disregarded in the following discussion. It will be assumed throughout that decisions are brought about by motivations, and that a causal connection exists between motivation and decision.
12. Kant realized, however, that it was not known to us "how much [in our decisions] is the result of the action of free-will, how much is to be ascribed to nature and blameless error," and that it was difficult therefore to judge human conduct with perfect justice. *Op. cit. supra* n. 8, p. 310 (footnote.)
13. A. C. Benjamin, *An Introduction to the Philosophy of Science* (New York, 1937), p. 420.
14. See Hartmann, *op. cit. supra* n. 9, Vol. III, pp. 59, 63-64, 73-85, 210-211. Not only philosophers, but also biologists and neurologists are turning again to the concept of teleology to explain human behavior. See E. W. Sinnott, *The Biology of the Spirit* (New York, 1955), pp. 75-100; A. Rosenblueth, N. Weiner, and J. Bigelow, "Behavior, Purpose and

Teleology," 10 *Philosophy of Science* 18 (1943); C. J. Herrick, *The Evolution of Human Nature* (Austin, 1956), pp. 132-135.

15. *Id.*, p. 80.

16. Sigmund Freud, "A General Introduction to Psycho-Analysis," in *The Major Works of Sigmund Freud* (Great Books of the Western World, Chicago, 1952), p. 454.

17. See letter from Einstein to Born, reproduced in Max Born, *Natural Philosophy of Cause and Chance* (Oxford, 1949), p. 122; Max Planck, *Where Is Science Going* (New York, 1932), pp. 99-100.

18. See David Bohm, *Causality and Chance in Modern Physics* (New York, 1957), pp. 2, 20-25; Born, *op. cit. supra* n. 17, pp. 47, 101, 109, 121; Niels Bohr, *Atomic Theory and the Description of Nature* (New York, 1934), p. 4; Hermann Weyl, *The Open World* (New Haven, 1932), pp. 45-51.

19. See James Murphy, Introduction to Planck, *op. cit. supra* n. 17; Erwin Schroedinger, *Science and the Human Temperament*, transl. J. Murphy and W. H. Johnston (New York, 1935), pp. 50, 147.

20. Freud differed from Kant in that he deemed human psychic and mental phenomena subject to exactly the same laws of causality which govern physical nature.

21. Friedrich Waismann, "Verifiability," in *Essays on Logic and Language*, ed. A. Flew (Oxford, 1955), pp. 132-133.

22. If this theory is correct, the statement by F. Alexander and H. Staub, *The Criminal, the Judge, and the Public*, rev. ed. (Glencoe, Ill., 1956), p. 126, that "if we accept the principle of causality in the field of human behavior, it follows that whatever a person does is determined by certain natural laws" contains a *non sequitur*.

23. Born, *op. cit. supra* n. 17, p. 9.

24. Bohm, *op. cit. supra* n. 18, p. 159. See also *id.*, p. 141: "The determinations of any purely causal theory are always subject to random disturbances, arising from chance fluctuations in entities, existing outside the context treated by the theory in question."

25. Paul Weiss, *Nature and Man* (New York, 1947), p. 17. According to Weiss, there are in nature and human life "free occurrences by which indeterminate possibilities are made into deterministic actualities." *Id.*, p. 18.

26. F. S. C. Northrop, Introduction to Werner Heisenberg, *Physics and Philosophy* (New York, 1958), pp. 11-16; Northrop, "Causation, Determinism, and 'the Good,'" in *Determinism and Freedom in the Age of Science*, ed. S. Hook (New York, 1958), pp. 188-189. See also Erich Fromm, *The Heart of Man* (New York, 1964), p. 143: "Nothing is uncaused, but not everything is determined."

27. See Weiss, *Nature and Man*, pp. 18-19. Cf. also *id.*, p. 10: "The effect is necessarily what it is. In terms of what has gone before, it is inevitable. Yet it need not have been." Hartmann says in *op. cit. supra* n. 9, Vol. III, p. 49: "When the will has chosen, it presents itself unmistakably as determined. The choice itself consists in the introduction of a decisive determinant." Cf. Raphael Demos, "Human Freedom—Positive and Negative," in *Freedom—Its Meaning*, ed. R. N. Anshen (New York, 1940), p. 605: "There are causes from which the effect does not follow necessarily."

28. *The Individual Psychology of Alfred Adler*, ed. H. L. and R. R. Ansbacher (New York, 1956), p. 417.

29. Arthur Schopenhauer, "Preisschrift über die Freiheit des Willens," in *Sämtliche Werke* (Leipzig, 1891), Vol. III, pp. 429-432 (Translation mine).
30. *Id.*, p. 439. See also Fearey, *op. cit. supra* n. 4, p. 23.
31. In accord: A. C. Ewing, *Ethics* (London, 1953), p. 155; Henri Bergson, *Time and Free Will*, transl. F. L. Pogson (London, 1912), p. 172; C. A. Campbell, "Is 'Freewill' a Pseudo-Problem?", 60 *Mind* 441, at 463-464 (1951).
32. Campbell, *op. cit. supra* n. 31, pp. 463-464; Ewing, *op. cit. supra* n. 31, p. 157.
33. Bergson, *Time and Free Will*, p. 172, says: "Our character is altering imperceptibly every day." See also Raphael Demos, *op. cit. supra* n. 27, p. 607, who speaks of "the ability of the self to modify its nature." Cf. also H. J. Berman, "Law as an Instrument of Mental Health in the United States and Soviet Russia," 109 *University of Pennsylvania Law Review* 361, at 368-369 (1961).
34. Erich Fromm, *Man for Himself* (New York, 1947), p. 233. See also D. E. Trueblood, "Contemporary Psychiatry and the Concept of Responsibility," in *Psychiatry and Responsibility*, ed. H. Schoeck and J. W. Wiggins (Princeton, 1962), pp. 30-31.
35. Fromm, *op. cit. supra* n. 26, p. 143. See also *id.*, pp. 130-131: "When ruled by passions, man is in bondage; when by reason, he is free. . . . Freedom is nothing other than the capacity to follow the voice of reason, of health, of well-being, of conscience, against the voices of irrational passions."
36. Hospers, *op. cit. supra* n. 2, p. 114.
37. Freud, "The Psychopathology of Everyday Life," in *The Complete Psychological Works*, ed. J. Strachey (London, 1960), Vol. VI, p. 254 (Underscoring supplied).
38. *Id.*, pp. 255-256.
39. See R. P. Knight, "Determinism, 'Freedom', and Psychotherapy," 9 *Psychiatry* 251 (1946); Morris Ginsberg, "The Nature of Responsibility," in *Essays in Sociology and Social Philosophy* (Melbourne, 1956), Vol. I., p. 82. See also Fromm, *op. cit. supra* n. 26, pp. 146-147: "Freud also recognized that the compulsion to act in certain irrational and thus destructive ways can be changed—by self-awareness and by effort. Hence his work is the attempt to devise a method of curing neurosis by self-awareness, and the motto of his therapy is: 'The truth shall make you free'." Fromm points out that Freud, in spite of what he said about himself, was not a determinist in the strict sense of the term.
40. Hartmann, *op. cit. supra* n. 9, Vol. III, pp. 143-181.
41. *Id.*, p. 145.
42. *Id.*, pp. 154-171.
43. *Id.*, p. 173.
44. Theodor Reik, *The Compulsion to Confess* (New York, 1959), p. 205. See also *id.*, p. 201: "Something of a need for punishment finds its partial gratification in the compulsion to confess."
45. Hartmann, *op. cit. supra* n. 9. Vol. III, p. 252. See also Bergson, *op. cit. supra* n. 31, p. 166: "Freedom . . . is not absolute, as a radically libertarian philosophy would have it; it admits of degrees."
46. "Some people have no freedom to choose the good because their character structure has lost the capacity to act in accordance with the good. . . . In the majority of men, however, we deal with contradictory in-

clinations which are so balanced that a choice *can* be made." Fromm, *op. cit. supra* n. 26, pp. 131-132.

47. Fromm, *op. cit. supra* n. 34, p. 234. See also Gordon Hawkins, "Freewill, Responsibility, and Punishment," 1963 *Archiv für Rechts- und Sozialphilosophie,* Beiheft No. 39, p. 117.
48. See *infra* Sec. 24.
49. Hartmann, *op. cit. supra* n. 9, Vol. III, p. 252.

SEC. 24.

1. Immanuel Kant, *The Philosophy of Law,* transl. W. Hastie (Edinburgh, 1887), p. 195. Whether Hegel was likewise a defender of retributive punishment, as has often been asserted, is a matter of dispute. See A. C. Ewing, *The Morality of Punishment* (London, 1929), pp. 22-25.
2. F. H. Bradley, *Ethical Studies,* 2d ed. (Oxford, 1927), p. 26.
3. F. Alexander and H. Staub, *The Criminal, the Judge, and the Public,* rev. ed. (Glencoe, Ill., 1956), pp. 211, 212. See also J. C. Flugel, *Man, Morals, and Society* (New York, 1945), pp. 169-170; M. R. Cohen, "Moral Aspects of the Criminal Law," 49 *Yale Law Journal* 987, at 1011 (1940).
4. See, for example, Henry Weihofen, *The Urge to Punish* (New York, 1956), p. 13; Weihofen, "Retribution is Obsolete," in *Responsibility,* ed. C. J. Friedrich (*Nomos* Vol. III, New York, 1960), pp. 116-127; H. E. Barnes and N. K. Teeters, *New Horizons in Criminology,* 2d ed. (New York, 1951), pp. 817-818.
5. This has been suggested, for example, by Lord Longford, *The Idea of Punishment* (London, 1961), p. 62.
6. See Ewing, *op. cit. supra* n. 1, p. 84: "The infliction of pain is society's way of impressing on him that he has done wrong." See also Henry Hart, "The Aims of the Criminal Law," 23 *Law and Contemporary Problems* 401, at 436-438 (1958); F. W. Foerster, *Schuld and Sühne* (Trier, 1961), pp. 24-25, 31-32.
7. A. L. Goodhart, *English Law and the Moral Law* (London, 1953), pp. 92-93.
8. H. L. A. Hart, "Murder and the Principles of Punishment," 52 *Northwestern University Law Review* 433, at 454 (1957). Hart himself takes the position that the individual "has a valid claim not to be made the instrument of society's welfare unless he has broken its laws" (*Id.,* p. 455), but this qualification embodies a principle of justice which is anchored more securely in a refined form of the retributive theory than in a utilitarian justification of punishment.
9. A. C. Ewing, *Ethics* (London, 1953), pp. 173-174.
10. *Id.,* p. 174.
11. On proportionality as a component of justice see *supra* Sec. 13. Cf. also H. L. Packer, "Making the Punishment Fit the Crime," 77 *Harvard Law Review* 1071 (1964).
12. "There is, I think, a vital need that legislation should distinguish between major and minor offenses and should reasonably differentiate among the major crimes for purposes of sentence possibilities." Herbert Wechsler, "Sentencing, Correction, and the Model Penal Code," 109 *University of Pennsylvania Law Review* 465, at 474 (1961).

13. In 1958, great indignation was aroused in the United States by a death sentence imposed by a state court for a robbery involving $1.95.

14. Art. 6 of the Model Penal Code, Official Draft, May 4, 1962, pp. 91-101, divides offenses into various categories and fixes, in the case of felonies, flexible minimum and definite maximum terms of imprisonment.

On the problem in general see Helen Silving, "The 'Rule of Law' in Criminal Justice," in *Essays in Criminal Science,* ed. G. O. W. Mueller (South Hackensack, N. J., 1961), p. 77.

15. See *supra* Sec. 10.

16. "Inequality and disparity between sentences imposed in different districts for similar offenses involving like circumstances is a troublesome and vexatious problem that has been receiving considerable attention for the past few years. It is obviously repugnant to one's sense of justice that the judgment meted out to an offender should be dependent in large part on a purely fortuitous circumstance; namely, the personality of the particular judge before whom the case happens to come for disposition. While absolute equality is neither desirable nor attainable, a greater approach to similarity of treatment than now prevails appears to be desirable, if not essential." Robert H. Jackson, *Annual Report of the Attorney General of the United States for 1940,* pp. 5-6. See also F. L. Van Dusen, "Trends in Sentencing since 1957," 35 *Federal Rules Decision* 381 (1964).

17. See Model Penal Code, Art. 305, Official Draft, May 4, 1962, pp. 284-302, specifying such criteria. Complaints have been voiced in the United States that parole boards are sometimes governed by extraneous considerations (overcrowding of prisons, saving public funds, pressures by attorneys) in discharging their functions.

18. Ewing, *op. cit. supra* n. 9, p. 167.

19. In cases where a substantial reduction of self-determination can be proved, the introduction of a concept of diminished responsibility, resulting in a mitigation of punishment, may prove helpful. See Barbara Wooton, "Diminished Responsibility," 76 *Law Quarterly Review* 224 (1960).

20. Gregory Zilboorg, *The Psychology of the Criminal Act and Punishment* (New York, 1954), p. 27.

21. Barnes and Teeters, *op. cit. supra* n. 4, pp. 1015-1016.

22. Ewing, *op. cit. supra* n. 9, p. 173. See also Cohen, *op. cit. supra* n. 3, pp. 1015-1016.

23. Hans von Hentig, "The Limits of Deterrence," 29 *Journal of Criminal Law, Criminology, and Police Science* 555, at 560 (1938): "The principle of deterrence has its limits, because human nature is not under all circumstances and at all events responsive to the menace of punishment." See also Gerald Gardiner, "The Purposes of Criminal Punishment," 21 *Modern Law Review* 117, at 124 (1958).

24. D. E. J. Macnamara, "Crime Patterns in Democratic and Totalitarian Societies," 1 *Journal of the Association for Psychiatric Treatment of Offenders* 1, at 4 (1957).

25. Johs. Andenaes, "General Prevention—Illusion or Reality," 43 *Journal of Criminal Law, Criminology, and Police Science* 176, at 187 (1952).

26. *Id.,* p. 189.

27. K. J. Newman, "Punishment and the Breakdown of the Legal Order:

The Experience in East Pakistan," in *Responsibility*, ed. C. J. Friedrich (*Nomos*, Vol. III, New York, 1960), p. 133.

28. Cohen, *op. cit. supra* n. 3, pp. 1015-1016.
29. Henry Hart, *op. cit. supra* n. 6, p. 408: "The desire of the ordinary man to avoid the moral condemnation of his community, as well as the physical pains and inconveniences of punishment, . . . [is] a powerful factor in influencing human behavior which can scarcely with safety be dispensed with." See also J. Michael and H. Wechsler, *Criminal Law and its Administration* (Chicago, 1940), p. 8.
30. Ewing, *op. cit. supra* n. 1, p. 58.
31. *Id.*, p. 59. See also Andenaes, *op. cit. supra* n. 25, p. 192, and *supra* Sec. 8.
32. See *supra* Sec. 12.
33. See Ewing, *op. cit. supra* n. 1, pp. 83-84.
34. Hart, *op. cit. supra* n. 6, p. 410. Cf. Foerster, *op. cit. supra* n. 6, pp. 31-32.
35. The Draft of a new Penal Code for the Federal Republic of Germany, in Sec. 85, allows custodial detention of dangerous recidivists as a non-punitive security measure. Reference should also be made to Model Penal Code Sec. 7.03, Official Draft, May 4, 1962, p. 109, authorizing extended sentences for criminals of a particularly dangerous type.
36. See *supra* Sec. 10.
37. For a review of laws of this kind see A. H. Swanson, "Sexual Psychopath Statutes: Summary and Analysis," 51 *Journal of Criminal Law, Criminology, and Police Science* 215 (1960).
38. See, for example, F. J. Hacker and M. Frym, "The Sexual Psychopath Act in Practice," 43 *California Law Review* 766 (1955). These authors point out that under some of the laws in this field no distinction is made between a rapist of children and a "peeping Tom." Cf. also M. Guttmacher and H. Weihofen, "Sex Offenses," 43 *Journal of Criminal Law, Criminology, and Police Science* 153, at 154 (1952).
39. See P. W. Tappan, "Some Myths about the Sex Offender," 19 *Federal Probation* 7, at 9-10 (June, 1955).
40. Tappan, *Crime, Justice, and Correction* (New York, 1960), p. 416.
41. *Id.*, p. 417.

SEC. 25.

1. O. W. Holmes, *The Common Law* (Boston, 1938), p. 49.
2. *Id.*, p. 50.
3. *Ibid.*
4. *Id.*, p. 51, 76.
5. *Id.*, pp. 49-50.
6. *Id.*, p. 50.
7. This, according to Jerome Hall, is the nub of Holmes's penal philosophy. Hall, *General Principles of Criminal Law*, 2d ed. (Indianapolis, 1960), p. 153. For a criticism of Holmes's theory see also Peter Brett, *An Inquiry into Criminal Guilt* (Sydney, 1963), pp. 137-144.
8. Holmes, *op. cit. supra* n. 1, pp. 44-45.
9. Jerome Hall, "Interrelations of Criminal Law and Torts," 43 *Columbia Law Review* 753, at 769 (1943).

10. Holmes, *op. cit. supra* n. 1, p. 49.
11. See *supra* Sec. 23.
12. Holmes, *op. cit. supra* n. 1, pp. 46-47. See also *id.*, p. 48: "Public policy sacrifices the individual to the general good . . . and justice to the individual is rightly outweighed by the larger interests on the other side of the scales."
13. E. S. Binavince, "The Ethical Foundation of Criminal Liability," 33 *Fordham Law Review* 1, at 28-29 (1964).
14. F. B. Sayre, "Mens Rea," 45 *Harvard Law Review* 974 (1932); A. J. Harno, "Some Significant Developments in Criminal Law and Procedure," 42 *Journal of Criminal Law, Criminology, and Police Science* 427, at 431 (1951).
15. *Duncan v. State,* 7 Humphr. 148, at 150 (Tenn., 1846).
16. 15 M. and W. 404, 153 Eng. Rep. 907 (Exch., 1846).
17. *Barnes v. State,* 19 Conn. 397 (1849). The case involved the sale of liquor to a common drunkard. There was no proof that the convicted tavern owner knew that the buyer was a common drunkard. The opinion suggests the possibility of negligence, without making it clear whether negligence would be insisted on as a prerequisite of punishment. In *Commonwealth v. Boynton,* 2 Allen 160 (Mass., 1861), involving the sale of intoxicating liquor, the court held that the seller was bound to ascertain the nature of the article at his peril.
18. See F. B. Sayre, "Public Welfare Offenses," 33 *Columbia Law Review* 55, at 73, 84-88 (1933).
19. 258 U.S. 250 (1922). For an analysis of the case see H. L. Packer, "Mens Rea and the Supreme Court," 1962 *Supreme Court Review* 107, at 113-116.
20. 320 U.S. 277 (1943).
21. 342 U.S. 246 (1952). See also *Dennis v. United States,* 341 U.S. 494, at 500: "The existence of a *mens rea* is the rule of, rather than the exception to, the principles of Anglo-American criminal jurisprudence."
22. The same conclusion is reached by Hall, *op. cit. supra* n. 7, pp. 342-359; Glanville Williams, *Criminal Law: The General Part,* 2d ed. (London, 1961), pp. 258-261; Henry Hart, "The Aims of the Criminal Law," 23 *Law and Contemporary Problems* 401, at 422-425 (1958); G. O. W. Mueller, "Mens Rea and the Law Without It," 58 *West Virginia Law Review* 34 (1955).
23. A. L. Gausewitz, Note, 12 *Wisconsin Law Review* 365, at 366 (1937). See also Jerome Hall, "Prolegomena to a Science of Criminal Law," 89 *University of Pennsylvania Law Review* 549, at 566-567 (1941).
24. H. L. Packer, *op. cit. supra* n. 19, p. 109.
25. Wolfgang Friedmann, *Law in a Changing Society* (Berkeley, 1959), p. 199. See also Justice Frankfurter in *United States v. Dotterweich, supra* n. 20, at 284-285.
26. Holmes, *op. cit. supra* n. 1, p. 49.
27. R. A. Wasserstrom, "Strict Liability in the Criminal Law," 12 *Stanford Law Review* 731, at 736: "It might be the case that a person engaged in a certain kind of activity would be more careful precisely because he knew that this kind of activity was governed by a strict liability statute."
28. See *supra* Sec. 14. The doctrine of strict liability also violates the principle that no man should be used as a mere means for the accomplishment of collective objectives. See *supra* Sec. 10.

29. Hall, *op. cit. supra* n. 7, pp. 351-352.
30. See in this connection the instructive article by F. P. Lee, "The Enforcement Provisions of the Food, Drug, and Cosmetic Act," 6 *Law and Contemporary Problems* 70 (1939).
31. Wasserstrom, *op. cit. supra* n. 27, p. 737.
32. *Ibid.*
33. *Id.*, p. 739.
34. See, for example, the cases cited by Williams, *op. cit. supra* n. 22, pp. 219-227; *United States v. Balint, supra* n. 19; *Groff v. State,* 85 N. E. 769 (Ind., 1908); R. M. Perkins, *Criminal Law* (Brooklyn, 1957), pp. 692-712.
35. I cannot go along with the suggestion by Jerome Hall indicated by the title of his article "Negligent Behavior Should Be Excluded From Criminal Liability," 63 *Columbia Law Review* 632 (1963). There is moral fault in not paying sufficient attention to the safety and other interests of one's fellowmen, and it is appropriate for the criminal law to stimulate the requisite degree of foresight and care.
36. Model Penal Code Sec. 2.05, Official Draft, May 4, 1962, pp. 31-32.
37. See, for example, the cases cited *supra* n. 19 and 20, where the statutes in question authorized substantial prison sentences.
38. See Model Penal Code Sec. 1.04(5), Official Draft, May 4, 1962, pp. 6-7.
39. See, for example, *State v. Thorne,* 117 Pac. 58 (Utah, 1911); *People v. Cabaltero,* 87 Pac. 2d 364 (Cal., 1939).
40. See English Homicide Act, 5 & 6 Eliz. II, Ch. 11, Sec. 1 (1957); Model Penal Code, Sec. 210.2, Official Draft, May 4, 1962, p. 125.
41. *Commonwealth v. Mash,* 48 Mass. 472 (1844); *Commonwealth v. Hayden,* 40 N.E. 846 (Mass., 1895). See Hall, *op. cit. supra* n. 7, pp. 395-397.
42. 13 Cox Crim. Cas. 138 (1875). See also the statutory rape cases listed by Sayre, *op. cit. supra* n. 18, p. 73.
43. See, for example, *People v. Vogel,* 299 Pac. 2d 850 (Cal., 1956); *People v. Hernandez,* 393 Pac. 2d 673 (Cal., 1964); Model Penal Code Sec. 213.6(1), Official Draft, May 4, 1962, pp. 149-150.
44. See the discussion of this problem by F. B. Sayre, "Criminal Responsibility for the Acts of Another," 43 *Harvard Law Review* 689 (1930); Williams, *op. cit. supra* n. 22, pp. 266-286; J. L. J. Edwards, *Mens Rea in Statutory Offenses* (London, 1955), pp. 217-243.
45. Williams, *op. cit. supra* n. 22, p. 259.
46. The general principle at stake is well illustrated by the following passage from the Old Testament: "The fathers shall not be put to death for the children, neither shall the children be put to death for the fathers: every man shall be put to death for his own sin." *Deuter.* XXIV:16.
47. Williams, *op. cit. supra* n. 22, pp. 267-269.
48. The opposite position is taken by *Commissioners of Police v. Cartman,* 1 Q.B. 655 (1896); *State v. Lundgren,* 144 N.W. 752 (Minn., 1913); *Commonwealth v. Koczwara,* 155 A 2d 825 (Pa., 1959).
49. See Holmes, *op. cit. supra* n. 1, pp. 3-4, 41-50.
50. See W. S. Holdsworth, *A History of English Law,* 3rd ed. (London, 1923), Vol. II, pp. 51-53; F. Pollock and F. W. Maitland, *History of English Law,* 2d ed. (Cambridge, Eng., 1909), p. 470; H. Potter, *Historical Introduction to English Law,* 4th ed., (London, 1958), p. 357; Sayre, *op. cit. supra* n. 14, pp. 977-981.
51. Holdsworth, *op. cit. supra* n. 50, Vol. II, pp. 53-54; T. F. T. Plucknett,

"The Relations between Roman Law and English Law," 3 *University of Toronto Law Journal* 24, at 43 (1939); Sayre, *op. cit. supra* n. 14, pp. 982-984.

52. See the sketch of the historical development by Sayre, *op. cit. supra* n. 18, pp. 56-67.

SEC. 26.

1. Aristotle, *Nicomachean Ethics*, transl. H. Rackham (Loeb Class. Lib. ed., Cambridge, Mass., 1947), Bk. V. viii. 2-3.
2. *Id.*, Bk. III. i. 15.
3. *Id.*, Bk. III. i. 17.
4. *Id.*, Bk. III. i. 19.
5. *Id.*, Bk. V. viii. 12.
6. Glanville Williams, *Criminal Law: The General Part*, 2d ed. (London, 1961), p. 138. The same position is taken in German law. E. Kohlrausch, *Strafgesetzbuch*, 30th ed. (Berlin, 1932), p. 88.
7. Williams, *op. cit., supra* n. 6, p. 126.
8. See the criticism of the principle by Williams, *id.*, p. 135. Since under Anglo-American law murder can be committed recklessly, A may be held responsible for murdering C if he knew that he was a bad shot and might kill a third person, but did not care whether or not this result would occur. But in that instance the punishment should be less severe than in the case of intentional killing.
9. See Kohlrausch, *op. cit. supra* n. 6, p. 86; E. Mezger, *Strafrecht* (Munich, 1931), p. 314.
10. For example, he had checked the spear a few minutes before using it and found it covered by the button, but someone subsequently removed the button and he failed to check again before throwing the spear.
11. See, for example, *United States v. Short*, 4 U.S.C.M.A. 437, at 445 (1954); *State v. Town*, 160 N.W. 10, at 12 (Iowa, 1916). Cf. Jerome Hall, *General Principles of Criminal Law*, 2d ed. (Indianapolis, 1960), p. 366.
12. This appears to be the position of the American Model Penal Code. Ignorance or mistake as to a matter of fact is a defense if "the ignorance or mistake negatives the purpose, knowledge, belief, recklessness or negligence required to establish a material element of the offense." Sec. 2.04(1), Official Draft, May 4, 1962, p. 30. See also Williams, *op. cit. supra* n. 6, pp. 201-205.
13. See Swiss Federal Penal Code, Art. 19: "If the offender had been able to avoid the error by acting with due caution, he shall be punished for negligence, provided that the negligent commission of the act is punishable." (Translation mine.)
14. Dig. 22. 6. 9: Ignorance of law is ordinarily prejudicial, ignorance of fact non-prejudicial. The extent to which the maxim was applied in criminal law is controversial.
15. See Williams, *op. cit. supra* n. 6, pp. 287-345; E. R. Keedy, "Ignorance and Mistake in the Criminal Law," 22 *Harvard Law Review* 75 (1908); R. M. Perkins, "Ignorance and Mistake in Criminal Law," 88 *University of Pennsylvania Law Review* 35 (1939).
16. John Austin, *Lectures on Jurisprudence*, 5th ed. by R. Campbell (London, 1885), Vol. I, pp. 482, 483.

17. P. K. Ryu and H. Silving, "Error Juris: A Comparative Study," 24 *University of Chicago Law Review* 421, at 469 (1957).
18. O. W. Holmes, *The Common Law* (Boston, 1938), p. 48.
19. *Ibid.* See also *supra* Sec. 25.
20. *Ibid.*
21. This is admitted by Holmes, *id.*, pp. 46-47: "The law does undoubtedly treat the individual as a means to an end, and uses him as a tool to increase the general welfare at his own expense."
22. See *supra* Secs. 10 and 15.
23. Herbert Morris, *Freedom and Responsibility* (Stanford, Cal., 1961), p. 344.
24. Hall, *op. cit. supra* n. 11, pp. 382-383.
25. See *supra* Sec. 25, n. 35.
26. This was recognized by Aristotle. See *supra* n. 2.
27. For this reason, the plea of ignorance of law is hardly ever encountered in prosecutions for serious crimes. See Hall, *op. cit. supra* n. 11, p. 384.
28. It is difficult to conceive of exceptions to the principle. One will have to think of highly unusual circumstances, such as the case of a human being nursed by wolves in the woods who suddenly enters human society. Stories of this kind have been reported, but their authenticity has been questioned. See Ashley Montagu, "Wolf Children," in *Man in Process* (New York, 1961), pp. 60-65.
29. *Hopkins v. State,* 69 A 2d 456 (Md., 1950). See also Hall, *op. cit. supra* n. 11, p. 387; Williams, *op. cit. supra* n. 6, p. 304.
30. See *Long v. State,* 65 A 2d 489 (Del., 1949), where a similar position was taken.
31. Johs. Andenaes, "Ignorantia Juris in Scandinavian Criminal Law," in *Essays in Criminal Science,* ed. G. O. W. Mueller (South Hackensack, N. J., 1961), p. 223.
32. Williams, *op. cit. supra* n. 6, p. 292.
33. See Model Penal Code Sec. 2.04(3)(a), Official Draft, May 4, 1962, p. 31; Andenaes, *op. cit. supra* n. 31, p. 224.
34. 355 U.S. 225 (1957).

SEC. 27.

1. 62 *Harvard Law Review* 616 (1949).
2. 14 Q.B.D. 273 (1884).
3. B. N. Cardozo, "Law and Literature," in *Selected Writings,* ed. M. E. Hall (New York, 1947), p. 390.
4. In *United States v. Holmes,* 26 Fed. Cas. 360, No. 15,383 (1842), sixteen passengers were thrown out of a life boat on orders of the mate. The court held that the action was unlawful for two reasons: (1) sailors not necessary for navigation should have been sacrificed before the passengers; and (2) the choice of the victims should have been made by lot.
5. 14 Q.B.D. 273, at 287 (1884).
6. E. N. Cahn, *The Moral Decision* (Bloomington, Ind., 1955), p. 71.
7. Glanville Williams, *Criminal Law: The General Part,* 2d ed. (London, 1961), p. 740. There are situations, however, where particular classes of persons are subjected to a legal duty to suffer hardship and danger by reason of vocational commitments. In *United States v. Holmes, supra*

n. 4, the court held that in case of a shipwreck the lives of passengers must be favored over those of the sailors. Soldiers, policemen, firemen, and mountain guides will rarely be permitted to avail themselves of the defense of necessity.

8. See *supra* Sec. 14.

9. Model Penal Code Sec. 3.02, Official Draft, May 4, 1962, p. 45. The comments to this section list the following illustrations: "Property may be destroyed to prevent the spread of a fire. A speed limit may be violated in pursuing a suspected criminal. An ambulance may pass a traffic light. Mountain climbers lost in a storm may take refuge in a house or may appropriate provisions. A cargo may be jettisoned or an embargo violated to preserve a vessel. . . . A druggist may dispense a drug without the requisite prescription to alleviate distress in an emergency."

10. Draft of a Penal Code (Bonn, 1960), Sec. 39 (Translation mine).

11. Art. 14, transl. in 6 *Review of Contemporary Law* 171 (1959).

12. Thomas Hobbes, *Leviathan* (Everyman's Lib. ed., London, 1914), Ch. 27. Other writers subscribing to this position are listed by Williams, *op. cit. supra* n. 7, p. 738.

13. "The Right of Nature . . . is the Liberty each man hath, to use his own power, as he will himself, for the preservation of his own Nature; that is to say, of his own life; and consequently, of doing any thing, which in his own Judgement, and Reason, he shall conceive the aptest means thereunto." *Id.*, Ch. 14.

14. St. Thomas Aquinas included both self-preservation and avoidance of harm to others in his catalogue of natural law principles. *Summa Theologica*, transl. Fathers of the English Dominican Province (London, 1913-1925), Pt. II, 1st pt., qu. 94,, art. 2. See also Hobbes, *De Cive*, ed. S. P. Lamprecht (New York, 1949), Ch. III. 4; Samuel Pufendorf, *Elementa Jurisprudentiae*, transl. W. A. Oldfather (Oxford, 1931), Bk. II, observ. iv. 4.

15. *Op. cit. supra* n. 10, Sec. 40.

16. See Jerome Hall, *General Principles of Criminal Law*, 2d ed. (Indianapolis, 1960), pp. 437-439; Williams, *op. cit.* supra n. 7, p. 754; L. Newman and L. Weitzer, "Duress, Free Will and the Criminal Law," 30, *University of Southern California Law Review* 313, at 316-317 (1957), pointing out that some American courts have permitted the defense in homicide cases.

17. Model Penal Code Sec. 2.09, Official Draft, May 4, 1962, p. 40.

18. See *United States v. Fleming*, 7 U.S.C.M.A. 543 (1957); *Iva Ikuko Toguri D'Aquino v. United States*, 192 Fed. 2d 338 (1951); Note, "Misconduct in the Prison Camp," 56 *Columbia Law Review* 709 (1956).

19. It is assumed that the defense of superior orders would not lie in such cases.

SEC. 28.

1. Emil Brunner, *Justice and the Social Order*, transl. M. Hottinger (New York, 1945), p. 230.

2. Jean Bodin, *The Six Bookes of a Commonweale*, ed. K. D. McRae (Cambridge, Mass., 1962), p. 84.

3. **Bodin himself** said: "As for the lawes of God and nature, all princes and people of the world are unto them subject. . . . Wherefore in that wee said that soveraigne power in a Commonweale to be free from all lawes, concerneth nothing the lawes of God and nature." *Id.,* p. 92.

4. John Austin, for example, maintained that "supreme power limited by positive law, is a flat contradiction in terms" and drew from this supposition the conclusion, among others, that international law could not be considered a system of law. *The Province of Jurisprudence Determined,* ed. H. L. A. Hart (London, 1954), pp. 142, 201, 254.

5. See Art. 38 of the Statute of the International Court of Justice. Cf. also Georg Schwarzenberger, *Power Politics* (New York, 1951), p. 89. There is a strong tendency in the Soviet literature on international law today to recognize only such restraints on national sovereignty to which a state has given its assent. This position reduces the efficacy of customary rules and general principles of law as sources of international law. See G. I. Tunkin, "Remarks on the Juridical Nature of Customary Norms of International Law," 49 *California Law Review* 419 (1961) and *Völkerrecht der Gegenwart* (Berlin, 1963), pp. 77-78, 120-129; Wolfgang Friedmann, *The Changing Structure of International Law* (New York, 1964), p. 329.

6. Hans Kelsen, *Principles of International Law* (New York, 1952), p. 156.

7. This observation will be developed more fully *infra* Sec. 29.

8. The use of a concept of *relative* sovereignty is advocated by Alfred Verdross, *Völkerrecht,* 5th ed. (Vienna, 1964), pp. 8-9. See also M. S. Korowicz, "Present Aspects of Sovereignty," 102 *Recueil des Cours* 1, at 108 (1961).

9. Kelsen, *op. cit. supra* n. 6, p. 114. Kelsen rejects this doctrine as "incorrect." *Ibid.*

10. Thus, pirates and war criminals may be tried under the rules of international law. Rights of individuals may be created by treaties which, if the treaty so provides, may be enforced directly by such individuals. See H. Lauterpacht, *International Law and Human Rights* (London, 1950), pp. 27-47, 122; M. S. McDougal and G. C. K. Leighton, "The Rights of Man in the World Community," 59 *Yale Law Journal* 60, 82-90 (1949); Friedmann, *op. cit. supra* n. 5, pp. 232-242.

11. See A. H. Roth, *The Minimum Standard of International Law Applied to Aliens* (Leiden, 1949); Edwin Borchard, "The 'Minimum Standard' of the Treatment of Aliens," 38 *Michigan Law Review* 445 (1940); Alfred Verdross, "Les Règles Internationales concernant le Traitement des Etrangers," 37 *Recueil des Cours* 325 (1931); Georg Dahm, *Völkerrecht* (Stuttgart, 1958), Vol. I, pp. 503-511.

12. The problems connected with expropriation have been discussed elsewhere. See *supra* Sec. 22.

13. Roth, *op. cit. supra* n. 11, p. 148.

14. Such as contracts designed to procure food and shelter. A duty to grant aliens a right to gainful employment is not, however, included in the requirements of the minimum standard. See Roth, *id.,* p. 157; Verdross, *op. cit. supra* n. 8, p. 371. For the United States see *Truax v. Raich,* 239 U.S. 33 (1915).

15. See Roth, *id.,* pp. 141, 144-145, 181; Clyde Eagleton, *The Responsibility of States in International Law* (New York, 1928), pp. 118-121; United

States (Chattin) v. Mexico, in W. W. Bishop, *International Law*, 2d ed. (Boston, 1962), pp. 636-641.

16. See *Francisco de Vitoria and his Law of Nations*, ed. J. B. Scott (Oxford, 1934), Appendix A, p. xxxvi: "It is reckoned among all nations inhumane to treat visitors and foreigners badly without some special cause." See also Samuel Pufendorf, *De Jure Naturae et Gentium*, transl. C. H. and W. A. Oldfather (Oxford, 1934), p. 403; Emmerich de Vattel, *The Law of Nations*, ed. J. Chitty (Philadelphia, 1863), p. 173.

17. Roth, *op. cit. supra* n. 11, pp. 22, 51; Lauterpacht, *op. cit. supra* n. 10, p. 7; M. S. McDougal and G. Bebr, "Human Rights in the United Nations," 58 *American Journal of International Law* 603, at 609-610 (1964).

18. The theory opposed to the minimum standard is often referred to as the "equality doctrine" or "doctrine of national treatment." According to this view, a state has discharged its obligations toward aliens as soon as it has placed them on a footing of equality with its own nationals. See Roth, *id.*, pp. 62-80; Borchard, *op. cit. supra* n. 11, pp. 450-454.

19. For the text of the Draft Convention see 55 *American Journal of International Law* 548 (1961).

20. Lauterpacht, *op. cit. supra* n. 10, p. 121.

21. See United Nations Charter Art. 1, Sec. 7: "Nothing contained in the present Charter shall authorize the United Nations to intervene in matters which are essentially within the domestic jurisdiction of any state or shall require the Members to submit such matters to settlement under the present Charter."

22. See P. C. Jessup, *A Modern Law of Nations* (New York, 1950), pp. 87-93; McDougal and Leighton, *op. cit. supra* n. 10, pp. 77-82.

23. See United Nations Charter Arts. 55 and 56.

24. See *Sei Fujii v. State*, 242 Pac. 2d 617, at 620-622 (1952); M. O. Hudson, "Integrity of International Instruments," 42 *American Journal of International Law* 105, at 106-107 (1948); Kelsen, *op. cit. supra* n. 6, p. 144. The position that Arts. 55 and 56 of the United Nations Charter subject the members to binding legal obligations was taken by Lauterpacht, *op. cit. supra* n. 10, p. 34; Heinz Guradze, *Der Stand der Menschenrechte im Völkerrecht* (Göttingen, 1956), p. 110; Georg Dahm, *op. cit. supra* n. 11, Vol. I, pp. 423-424.

25. See L. B. Sohn, *Cases on United Nations Law* (Brooklyn, 1956), pp. 592-670; McDougal and Bebr, *op. cit. supra* n. 17, pp. 635-636.

26. Sohn, *id.*, pp. 670-692.

27. See Bishop, *op. cit. supra* n. 15, pp. 66-68; McDougal and Bebr, *op. cit. supra* n. 17, p. 636.

28. McDougal and Bebr, *id.*, p. 615; Bishop. *id.*, pp. 475-476.

29. The abstainers were the countries of the Soviet bloc, Saudi Arabia, and the Union of South Africa.

30. See International Declaration of Human Rights Arts. 1-4, 12-13.

31. *Id.*, Arts. 22-26.

32. *Id.*, Art. 21.

33. *Id.*, Art. 15. A right to seek political asylum is proclaimed in Art. 14.

34. *Id.*, Arts. 5, 8-11.

35. *Id.*, Art. 29, Sec. 2.

36. *Id.*, Art. 30.
37. For the text of these two drafts see 58 *American Journal of International Law* 857-872 (1964). For comments on the covenants see McDougal and Bebr, *op. cit. supra* n. 17, pp. 619-628.
38. The most important omissions are the right to own property and the right to change one's nationality. Among the rights added is freedom from imprisonment for debt.
39. The Draft Covenant on Economic, Social and Cultural Rights permits limitations in the interest of the general welfare. Art. 4. The Draft Covenant on Civil and Political Rights authorizes restrictions on certain freedoms in the interests of national security, public safety, order, health, morals, or the protection of the rights and freedoms of others. Arts. 18-21.
40. Draft Covenant on Civil and Political Rights Art. 4, Sec. 1. This provision accords with the suggestion made *supra* Sec. 14 that a temporary suspension of principles of justice may be inevitable under conditions of imperative necessity.
41. Draft Covenant on Civil and Political Rights Art. 4, Sec. 2.
42. *Id.*, Art. 26. On the desirability of prohibiting incitement to group hatred see *supra* Sec. 17.
43. McDougal and Bebr, *op. cit. supra* n. 17, p. 640. Certain positive proposals for an international protection of human rights and goal values are found in McDougal, "Perspectives for an International Law of Human Dignity," in McDougal and Associates, *Studies in World Public Order* (New Haven, 1960), pp. 987-1019.
44. See McDougal and Leighton, *op. cit. supra* n. 10, pp. 94-106.
45. H. J. Morgenthau, *Politics Among Nations*, 3rd ed. (New York, 1963), p. 511.
46. Hugo Grotius, *De Jure Belli ac Pacis*, transl. F. W. Kelsey (Oxford, 1925), Bk. II, Ch. XX. 40.
47. See E. C. Stowell, *Intervention in International Law* (New York, 1921), p. 55.
48. E. M. Borchard, *The Diplomatic Protection of Citizens Abroad* (New York, 1915), p. 14. A number of other writers have opposed the right of humanitarian intervention. See citations in Stowell, *op. cit. supra* n. 46, p. 58.
49. L. Oppenheim and H. Lauterpacht, *International Law*, 8th ed. (New York, 1955), Vol. I, p. 312.
50. For a history of diplomatic intercession on humanitarian grounds see Stowell, *op. cit. supra* n. 46, pp. 63-125. See also Dahm, *op. cit. supra* n. 11, Vol. I, pp. 420-421.
51. Examples are listed in McDougal and Bebr, *op. cit. supra* n. 17, p. 609.
52. For the text of the Convention see *European Commission of Human Rights: Documents and Decisions* (The Hague, 1959), pp. 4-36. For comments on the Convention and its implementation see H. Mosler, "The Protection of Human Rights by International Legal Procedures," 52 *Georgetown Law Journal* 800 (1964); J. Greenberg and A. R. Shalit, "New Horizons for Human Rights," 63 *Columbia Law Review* 1384 (1963); Oppenheim and Lauterpacht, *op. cit. supra* n. 49, pp. 746-749. Adherence to the Convention by the countries of Western Europe is not, however, complete. See Georg Schwarzenberger, *Power Politics*, 3rd ed. (New York, 1964), p. 466.
53. Lauterpacht, *op. cit. supra* n. 10, p. 70.

1. Erich Fromm, *May Man Prevail?* (Garden City, N. Y., 1961), pp. 195, 8.
2. H. J. Morgenthau, *In Defense of the National Interest* (New York, 1952), p. 58.
3. Albert Schweitzer says in *Friede oder Atomkrieg* (Munich, 1958), p. 47: "The goal upon which, from now on for an indefinite future, our attention must be fixed is to make sure that international controversies will be settled not by war but by peaceful means." (Translation mine).
4. G. Clark and L. B. Sohn, *World Peace through World Law*, 2d ed. (Cambridge, Mass., 1960), p. xxxiii.
5. *Id.*, p. xxxv. With respect to the enforcement of the judgments of the International Court of Justice, the authors propose that the General Assembly may direct economic sanctions or, in the last resort, action by a United Nations Peace Force to ensure compliance. *Id.*, p. xxxiv.
6. H. Lauterpacht, *The Function of Law in the International Community* (Oxford, 1933), pp. 157-158.
7. Positions similar to Lauterpacht's have been taken by Hans Kelsen, *Principles of International Law* (New York, 1952), pp. 380-384 and Georg Dahm, *Völkerrecht* (Stuttgart, 1958), Vol. II, pp. 492-494. The traditional distinction between political and legal disputes is maintained by W. W. Bishop, "The International Rule of Law," 59 *Michigan Law Review* 553, at 564 (1961); Julius Stone, *Legal Controls of International Conflicts* (New York, 1954) pp. 146-152; Charles De Visscher, *Theory and Reality in Public International Law* (Princeton, 1957), pp. 331-339.
8. Morgenthau, *Politics Among Nations*, 3rd ed., (New York, 1963), p. 427. As a consequence of his position, Morgenthau maintains that "whenever the issue is one of preservation or fundamental change of the status quo, the answer of the courts is ready before a question is even asked: they must decide in favor of the existing status quo and refuse the demand for change."
9. Lauterpacht admits that present international law "is more static than any other law." *Op. cit. supra* n. 6, p. 249.
10. See George Ginsburgs, " 'Wars of National Liberation' and the Modern Law of Nations," 29 *Law and Contemporary Problems* 910 (1964).
11. Lauterpacht, *op. cit. supra* n. 6, p. 64.
12. *Ibid.*
13. *Id.*, pp. 255, 80, 103.
14. See Edgar Bodenheimer, *Jurisprudence: The Philosophy and Method of the Law* (Cambridge, Mass., 1962), Ch. XVI.
15. In *United States v. La Jeune Eugenie*, 26 Fed. Cas. 832, No. 15, 551 (1822), involving seizure by Americans of a French ship engaged in the slave trade, Judge Story held that the countries affected by the litigation (the United States and France) both considered the slave trade to be repugnant to "the obligations of good faith and morality, and the eternal maxims of social justice." Although no positive rule of international law prohibited the slave trade, Judge Story in this case enforced a general principle of justice and humanity recognized by the two nations concerned.
16. The United States Supreme Court in a number of cases has drawn a distinction between legal and political questions, and has declared the

305

latter to be non-justiciable. See *Luther v. Borden,* 7 How. 1 (1849); *Coleman v. Miller,* 307 U.S. 433 (1939).

17. According to Art. 38, Sec. 2 of the Statute of the International Court of Justice, the court may decide a case *ex aequo et bono* if the parties agree thereto.
18. De Visscher, *op. cit. supra* n. 7, p. 338.
19. Morgenthau, *op. cit. supra* n. 8, p. 429. Cf. also Julius Stone, *Quest for Survival* (Cambridge, Mass., 1961), p. 21.
20. De Visscher, *op. cit. supra* n. 7, pp. 331-332.
21. The discussion of the problem of judicial impartiality in international controversies by Lauterpacht, *op. cit. supra* n. 6, pp. 215-216, would seem to be guided by a spirit of overoptimism.
22. Morgenthau, *op. cit. supra* n. 8, pp. 38-39. For my own appraisal of the potentialities of the future see *infra* Sec. 30.
23. Morgenthau, *id.,* pp. 88-94.
24. *Id.,* p. 5.
25. *Id.,* p. 234.
26. *Id.,* pp. 31, 35.
27. *Id.,* p. 9. The control achieved by power extends to the minds as well as actions of men. *Id.,* p. 28.
28. Georg Schwarzenberger, *Power Politics,* 3rd ed. (New York, 1964), p. 14.
29. *Id.,* p. 199. Yet Schwarzenberger concedes that "international law is not only a law of power but also a law of reciprocity, and even traces of the law of co-ordination can be detected." *Id.,* p. 203.
30. *Id.,* p. 220.
31. *Id.,* pp. 149-150.
32. *Id.,* pp. 531, 533.
33. *Id.,* p. 531.
34. Morgenthau, *op. cit. supra* n. 2, p. 35; *op. cit. supra* n. 8, p. 231.
35. Morgenthau, *op. cit. supra* n. 8, p. 12. The legalistic-moralistic approach to international problems is also criticized by G. F. Kennan, *American Diplomacy,* 1900-1950 (Chicago, 1951), pp. 95, 100.
36. Morgenthau, *op. cit., supra* n. 8, pp. 262, 210.
37. *Id.,* p. 102.
38. *Id.,* p. 228.
39. Erich Fromm, *Man for Himself* (New York, 1947), pp. 87-88.
40. K. G. Wurzel, *Die Sozialdynamik des Rechts* (Vienna, 1924), p. 5.
41. Morgenthau, *op. cit. supra* n. 8, p. 27.
42. *Id.,* p. 5.
43. Schwarzenberger, *op. cit. supra* n. 28, p. 61.
44. *Id.* p. 33.
45. The mentally healthy individual does not wish to dominate his wife, children and friends. He also will try to get along on an amicable basis with his business associates or co-employees. If he occupies a position of supervision he will, if he is well adjusted to life, treat those over whom he exercises authority as human beings and with proper consideration of their interests. As Fromm observes, "domination springs from impotence and in turn reinforces it, for if an individual can force somebody else to serve him, his own need to be productive is increasingly paralyzed." *Op. cit. supra* n. 39, p. 88.
46. Morgenthau, *op. cit. supra* n. 8, pp. 27, 88.
47. *Id.,* p. 12.

48. See *supra* Sec. 15.
49. Erich Fromm, *Beyond the Chains of Illusion* (New York, 1962), p. 108.
50. Friedrich Meinecke, *Die Idee der Staatsräson* (Munich, 1925), p. 534. (Translation mine).
51. "A person may be able to recognize things as they are (or as his culture maintains them to be), but he is unable to enliven his perception from within. Such a person is the perfect 'realist,' who sees all there is to be seen of the surface features of phenomena but who is quite incapable of penetrating below the surface to the essential, and of visualizing what is not yet apparent." Fromm, *op. cit. supra* n. 39, p. 89.
52. Morgenthau, *op. cit. supra* n. 8, p. 27.
53. This is admitted by Morgenthau in the following passage: "To rally a people behind the government's foreign policy and to marshall all the national energies and resources to its support, the spokesman of the nation must appeal to biological necessities, such as national existence, and to moral principles, such as justice, rather than to power. This is the only way a nation can attain the enthusiasm and willingness to sacrifice without which no foreign policy can pass the ultimate test of strength." *Id.*, p. 89.
54. Marcus Aurelius wrote in his *Meditations:* "For we are made for co-operation." *The Stoic and Epicurean Philosophers,* ed. W. J. Oates (New York, 1940), p. 497.
55. President Franklin D. Roosevelt stated in his Inaugural Address on March 4, 1933: "In the field of world policy I would dedicate this nation to the policy of the good neighbor—the neighbor who resolutely respects himself and, because he does so, respects the rights of others—the neighbor who respects the sanctity of his agreements in and with a world of neighbors." Roosevelt, *Looking Forward* (New York, 1933), p. 266.
56. Edmund Burke said: "Nothing is so fatal to a nation as an extreme of self-partiality, and the total want of consideration of what others will naturally hope or fear." "Remarks on the Policy of the Allies with respect to France," in *Works* (Boston, 1889), Vol. IV, p. 447.
57. See *supra* Sec. 14.
58. This is not denied by Morgenthau, who holds that "all-out nuclear war becomes a self-defeating absurdity." *Op. cit. supra* n. 8, p. 23. He appears to believe that the traditional methods of power diplomacy might suffice to cope with the problem. *Id.*, Chs. 31 and 32.

SEC. 30.

1. Emery Reves, *The Anatomy of Peace* (New York, 1945), p. 121.
2. *Ibid.* Hans Morgenthau has rightly pointed out, however, that the frequency and destructiveness of civil wars militates against the assumption that the establishment of unified legal control, as such, assures the preservation of peace. *Politics Among Nations,* 3rd ed. (New York, 1963), p. 508.
3. Reves, *op. cit. supra* n. 1, p. 147.
4. Treaties can be abrogated or changed only by consent of all parties and therefore form a less flexible vehicle of international adjustment than

legislation by a representative body. As to the limitations of judicial control see *supra* Sec. 29.

5. Reves, *op. cit. supra* n. 1, p. 192.
6. Morgenthau, *op. cit. supra* n. 2, pp. 472-477.
7. *Id.,* p. 481. "At best—if they are united—they can govern the rest of the world for the purpose of maintaining order and of preventing war. At worst—if they are disunited—there will be no international government at all." *Ibid.*
8. "The explanation is that communists believe exclusively in post-revolutionary internationalism. Only socialist societies, which have finally overcome all capitalist resistance within themselves, can, they are convinced, come together in a world federation (and ultimately in a unitary world society)." John Strachey, *On the Prevention of War* (New York, 1963), p. 220.
9. "The nation . . . is the recipient of man's highest loyalties. Beyond it there are other nations, but no community for which man would be willing to act regardless of what he understands the interests of his own nation to be." Morgenthau, *op. cit. supra* n. 2, p. 511. Erich Fromm points out that this situation could be changed if, among other things, the educational systems of all countries stressed the achievements of the human race instead of the achievements of an individual nation. *The Heart of Man* (New York, 1964), pp. 90-91.
10. Strachey, *op. cit. supra* n. 8, p. 248.
11. *Id.,* p. 74.
12. *Id.,* p. 324.
13. William James, "The Moral Equivalent of War," in *Essays on Faith and Morals* (New York, 1943), p. 323.
14. *Id.,* p. 325.
15. *Id.,* p. 323.
16. The same conclusion is reached by Emil Brunner, *Justice and the Social Order*, transl. M. Hottinger (New York, 1945), p. 246.

EPILOGUE

1. See in particular Secs. 6 and 7 *supra.*
2. Victor Kraft, *Rationale Moralbegründung* (Vienna, 1963), p. 61 (Translation mine).
3. See *supra* Secs. 7 and 8.
4. See Erich Fromm, *The Heart of Man* (New York, 1964), pp. 116-119. It might be reiterated at this point that man's nature contains social as well as antisocial components: Man has the urge to cooperate with others in a common endeavor but is at the same time often ready to assert himself as an authentic self *against* others. See *supra* Sec. 10.
5. *Id.,* p. 52. On the need for reasonable equality and the duty to treat human beings as ends in themselves see *supra* Sec. 10.
6. See *supra* Secs. 10 and 11.
7. Fromm, *op. cit. supra* n. 4, p. 52. See also *supra* Sec. 12.
8. See *supra* Sec. 13.
9. Kraft, *op. cit. supra* n. 2, pp. 45-47.
10. See *supra* Sec. 7.
11. See *supra* Sec. 1.

12. **R. B. Perry**, *General Theory of Value* (New York, 1926), p. 27. Perry argues that the ethical element comes into play only when values are compared and ranked as "higher" and "lower." It would seem, however, that certain strivings are wholly lacking in ethical worth, as commonsense morality has always assumed. For a criticism of Perry see also S. L. Hart, *Treatise on Values* (New York, 1949), p. 42.
13. See *supra* Sec. 1.
14. In this respect justice, like truth and goodness, differs from freedom, equality, and security in that the opposites of these latter values (restraint, inequality, risk) may also, up to a certain limit, receive favorable consideration in the social and legal order. See *supra* Sec. 11.
15. Marcus Aurelius, "Meditations," in *The Stoic and Epicurean Philosophers*, ed. W. J. Oates (New York, 1940), p. 549.
16. Aristotle, *Politics*, transl. E. Barker (Oxford, 1946), Bk. III, Ch. 10. 1281a.
17. See *supra* Sec. 14.
18. See *supra* Sec. 15.
19. Arthur Pap, "The Verifiability of Value Judgments," 56 *Ethics* 178, at 183 (1946). This use of the term involves a certain extension of its customary meaning, since the latter includes timelessness and universality among the attributes of absolutes.
20. The supporting arguments are set forth *supra* Sec. 10-12. It is interesting to note that Aristotle, who cannot by any standard be regarded as an egalitarian thinker, declared that "between people not free and equal political justice cannot exist, but only a sort of justice in a metaphorical sense." *Nicomachean Ethics*, ed. H. Rackham (Loeb Class. Lib. ed., Cambridge, Mass., 1947), Bk. V. vi. 4.
21. See *supra* Secs. 8 and 14.
22. An excellent presentation of this position is found in Victor Kraft, *Erkenntnislehre* (Vienna, 1960), pp. 101-103. Cf. also Hart, *op. cit. supra* n. 12, pp. 56, 65; H. W. B. Joseph, *An Introduction to Logic* (2d. ed., 1916), pp. 25-26, 32.

INDEX OF NAMES

311

312

313